Early Islamic North Africa

DEBATES IN ARCHAEOLOGY
Series editor: Richard Hodges

Early Islamic North Africa

A New Perspective

Corisande Fenwick

BLOOMSBURY ACADEMIC
LONDON • NEW YORK • OXFORD • NEW DELHI • SYDNEY

BLOOMSBURY ACADEMIC
Bloomsbury Publishing Plc
50 Bedford Square, London, WC1B 3DP, UK
1385 Broadway, New York, NY 10018, USA

BLOOMSBURY, BLOOMSBURY ACADEMIC and the Diana logo are trademarks
of Bloomsbury Publishing Plc

First published in Great Britain 2020

Cover design: Terry Woodley
Cover image © Sami Sarkis/Getty

A catalogue record for this book is available from the British Library.

A catalog record for this book is available from the Library of Congress.

ISBN: HB: 978-1-3500-7518-4
       PB: 978-1-3500-7519-1
       ePDF: 978-1-3500-7521-4
       eBook: 978-1-3500-7520-7

Series: Debates in Archaeology

Typeset by RefineCatch Limited, Bungay, Suffolk
Printed and bound in Great Britain

To find out more about our authors and books visit www.bloomsbury.com and
sign up for our newsletters.

For my mother.

Contents

Figures

Acknowledgements

This short book was written because of a profound dissatisfaction with the marginal place that North Africa plays in scholarship of the Islamic world. It has benefited from the support and insights of many people and institutions. It began as the final chapter of a PhD thesis at Stanford University, and became the beginnings of a book at Brown University and the University of Leicester. I completed the manuscript at the Institute of Archaeology, University College London. The research was funded by grants and fellowships from Stanford University, the Social Science Research Council, the Barakat Trust, the Tweedie Foundation and a Geballe Dissertation Prize Fellowship at the Stanford Humanities Center.

One of the great joys of working in North Africa is kind and generous colleagues, and I thank Dirk Booms, Youssef Bokbot, Moheddine Chaouali, Franca Cole, Sam Cox, Andrew Dufton, Dave Edwards, Abdallah Fili, Maria Gatto, Caroline Goodson, Mohamed Hussein, Victoria Leitch, Hassan Limane, Jo Quinn, Andy Merrills, Mariam Rosser-Owen, Martin Sterry, Philipp von Rummel and Andrew Wilson for help at various points, and in many cases too for happy memories of fieldwork or visiting sites in Libya, Algeria, Tunisia and Morocco. I am especially grateful to Andrew Dufton, Andy Merrills, Elizabeth Fentress, and Hugh Kennedy for reading the whole book, and to Lily Mac Mahon and Alice Wright at Bloomsbury for their help throughout the publication process. My greatest debts are to Elizabeth Fentress, Hugh Kennedy, David Mattingly and Lynn Meskell for their encouragement and guidance over the past years, and to my family and friends for their support.

A Note on Arabic and Terminology

I refer to place names and archaeological sites in their most commonly used modern, not ancient or medieval, spellings (e.g., Carthage not Karthago, Volubilis not Walila). This is an imperfect solution to a complex problem, but should enable the reader to more easily find further information about particular sites. In North Africa, Francicized transliterations are most commonly used for Arabic place names and terms (e.g., Maghreb not Maghrib, Kairouan not Qayrawan, ksour not qusur). Italicized Arabic or French words are explained in the Glossary. Dates are given according to the Gregorian rather than Hijri calendar for ease of reference. Throughout, I do not use diacritical marks for Arabic names or terms on the principle that those who read Arabic do not need them, and those who don't are unlikely to find them helpful.

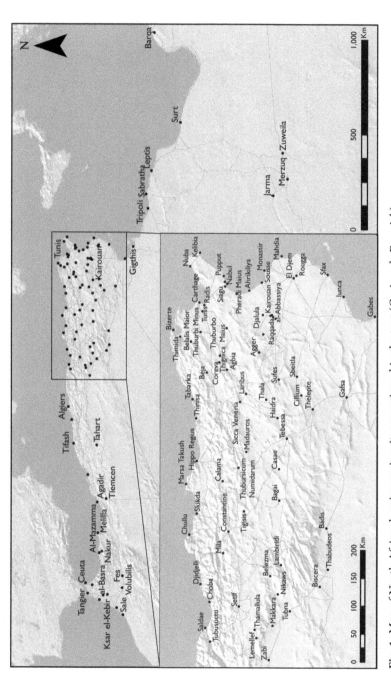

Fig. 1 Map of North Africa showing major sites mentioned in the text (Corisande Fenwick).

Introduction
The Problem of North Africa

Arabian armies first entered Byzantine Africa from Egypt in 642, but unlike the swift conquest of the Middle East, these early raids did not result in conquest and Muslim rule. Instead, the later Arabic accounts describe devastating defeats, widespread revolts and hasty retreats to the safety of Egypt that took place over many decades (Brett 1978; Benabbès 2004; Kaegi 2010). The end, when it finally came, was brutal and short. The Byzantine capital, Carthage, was captured in 697–8, and Africa became Ifriqiya. In a few short years, the Muslim armies reached Morocco and the southern shore of the Mediterranean became part of the Umayyad caliphate. Imperial rule was short-lived. In 739–40, the so-called 'Kharajite revolt' broke out in distant Morocco, and rapidly spread to Tunisia. In its wake, new embryonic Muslim states headed by Arab and Berber elites emerged across North Africa as rivals to the caliphate. The Abbasid caliphate briefly regained control of parts of Ifriqiya in 761–2, but within a few decades, the imperial experiment had failed, and in 800 they abandoned the region to their vassals, the Aghlabids. From this point on, the region was ruled by a constantly changing collection of Muslim states and empires but never again by the Abbasid caliphate.

Islamic North Africa poses a problem for modern scholars. A vast region which made up nearly a third of the caliphate (Fig. 1), it is frequently left out of standard historical and archaeological accounts of the early Islamic world (e.g., Donner 1981; Kennedy 2004). In part, it is this complicated sequence of events that explains the neglect: it does not fit with the tidy narrative of a rapid military conquest followed by Umayyad and Abbasid rule that is told for the central and eastern

Islamic lands. North Africa's distinctive history outside the caliphate has reinforced a second trend – particularly dominant within art history – to depict the region as a provincial backwater with architecture and artistic traditions that were inferior to, or derivative of, developments in the Middle East. So powerful is this outdated core–periphery model that even today, except in passing, Islamic art-history survey books rarely include material from the region.

This marginalization of North Africa is not merely a modern scholarly construction, but is mirrored in the earliest Arabic accounts which provide only limited details on North Africa and its peoples. Those sources that we do possess are often ambivalent about the region and its inhabitants. In a series of apocryphal hadiths (sayings attributed to the Prophet), North Africa is portrayed both as a land of untold riches and the gateway to paradise and as the greatest threat to caliphal power and the gateway to hell (Marçais 1954: 20–2). In the Arabic geographies, North Africa is frequently depicted as one of the wealthiest and most fertile regions of the Islamic world but inhabited by boorish and uncivilized people. Some of its peoples, the Berbers, converted to Islam and joined in the Muslim armies in the conquest of al-Andalus (Iberia), but they famously apostatized twelve times and are often portrayed as unreliable and treacherous (examples in Norris 1982).

North Africa is not only important to study because it fills a 'gap' in scholarly understanding of the Islamic world or because scholars have neglected it. Conquered later and with far more difficulty than Syria or Iraq, it posed different challenges, which the early caliphate ultimately failed to meet. Its late conquest makes it an ideal region to explore larger processes of medieval empire-building, the spread of Islam and the emergence of new urban, economic and cultural forms. North Africa is important precisely because it was a success story for Islam, even where the caliphate failed. Within only a few decades of the conquest, rival states arose in the far west, and by 800 the region was ruled through a succession of states that used Islam to justify their rule over their multi-confessional communities. North Africa therefore provides an ideal opportunity to explore how and why Muslim successor states arose – a phenomenon that has yet to be explored by scholars.

Despite the obvious importance of North Africa in this formative period, our understanding of it remains limited owing to the comparative absence of archaeological and historical research on the period. Although there are a number of monographs treating late antiquity which stretch into the early Islamic period (Pentz 2002; Leone 2007), no book-length study of early Islamic North Africa between the seventh and ninth centuries has previously appeared. There are a handful of important historical analyses of North African dynasties, most of which were written many decades ago (Talbi 1966), as well as some excellent introductory texts which feature archaeological evidence (Djaït 2004; Sénac and Cressier 2012), but there is nothing even close to the number of books and articles that have been dedicated to other regions of the Islamic world, particularly Syria-Palestine and Iraq.

It is, in part, the sheer scale of the region that overwhelms: at its greatest extent, the reach of the caliphate in North Africa stretched from Atlantic Morocco in the west to the western Egyptian desert in the east, and from the shores of the Mediterranean to the oases of the deep Sahara in the south. It encompasses the modern nation-states of Morocco, Algeria, Tunisia and Libya. Each country has its own complex colonial and post-independence history, in which the early Islamic period and archaeology have played different roles. The Arabs called this region the *Maghreb* ('the place where the sun sets') in opposition to the Levant which was known as the *Mashreq* ('the place where the sun rises'), though its precise limits are poorly defined and vary tremendously between period and author. In the period covered by this book, the region is divided into the *Maghreb al-Aqsa* (roughly modern Morocco), the *Maghreb al-awsat* (roughly modern Algeria), *Ifriqiya* (roughly eastern Algeria, Tunisia and part of Tripolitania, Libya) and *Barqa* (Cyrenaica, Libya), which was often ruled from Egypt but will be covered in this book.

But scholarly neglect is also due to a complex historiographical, evidentiary and disciplinary tradition. North Africa's early Islamic history was ignored for much of the nineteenth and twentieth centuries by colonial scholars who dismissed the period as a 'Dark Age'. Thirty years ago, a clear narrative told how the Arab conquest marked the 'end' of Roman Africa, permanently disrupting Mediterranean trade networks and causing a rapid dissolution of urban life and society, a product of a violent and destructive conquest by rapacious Muslim hordes. This view was first popularized in the nineteenth century when Europeans first encountered the spectacular ruins of Roman towns that filled the North African landscape. Various attempts have been made to overturn this narrative for North Africa, most notably by Yvon Thébert and Jean-Louis Biget (1990), who argued in a seminal paper that such assumptions exaggerate both the scale of collapse and the degree of rupture with the classical world. In the last three decades, an explosion of archaeological research has further called into question such neat 'ends' (Pentz 2002; Leone 2007; Fenwick 2013; Stevens and Conant 2016), but the notion of a rupture between the ancient and medieval world has proved a remarkably difficult one to dispel completely.

The second and most often invoked hurdle is the evidence, both written and material. There is not much. As scholars of the Islamic world know well, there are no contemporary Arabic descriptions of the conquests or the first centuries of Muslim rule. Archaeology has not filled in the breach: a complex colonial legacy that privileged Roman archaeology over that of all other historical periods and our poor knowledge of medieval ceramics has until recently made the eighth century invisible to the archaeological eye. In the ninth century, however, there is a surge in the amount and quality of evidence. Historians can draw upon a wealth of conquest accounts, geographies, judicial treatises, religious tracts and biographical dictionaries, while archaeologists can more easily identify ninth-century material culture. Indeed, many of the most remarkable 'firsts' of Islamic art history come from North Africa, including the earliest surviving *minbar* (pulpit), *maqsura* (mosque screen) and *tiraz* (silk textile) and some of the best-preserved ninth-century monumental architecture from anywhere in the Islamic world. This book argues that while there are significant problems with the evidence – most of them created or exacerbated by modern scholarship – there is much more to be said about this pivotal period if we think creatively.

The third hurdle – and perhaps the hardest to overcome – stems from disciplinary divisions. There is an immense gulf between scholars of late antique Africa and Islamic Africa. They inhabit different scholarly worlds, each with a different historiography, journals and conferences, and their own scholarly debates, favoured sites and methodologies. Further widening this gulf is the fact that most scholars working on the late antique period focus on the fourth to sixth centuries, while those working on Islamic Africa work on the ninth century and later. Few are sufficiently familiar with both the classical and medieval periods and their scholarly debates to think constructively across the divide. The formative period of Islam in North Africa thus all too often falls through disciplinary cracks.

Just as damaging are divisions between the different branches and regional traditions of Islamic scholarship. It is not the case that historians, archaeologists and art historians ignore each other's works, but rather that they do not come to terms with the challenges of the evidence, models and historiographic situation each is working within – and sometimes do not even recognize the legitimacy of the approach or research questions. Many historians remain unaware of the potential of material evidence to offer new insights into major debates. Conversely, Islamic archaeologists (still a minority) have focused on single sites or regions rather than attempting synthetic analyses and have yet to show just how archaeological evidence can transform historical debates on, for example, empire, economy and social relations. Greater still is the rift between archaeologists and art historians, who rarely talk to one another despite their shared emphasis on material culture. If it sometimes seems that scholars working in Islamic history, archaeology and art history are from different planets, those working in the Middle East and the Maghreb might as well be from different galaxies. North Africa and the Islamic West is almost completely ignored by the far larger pool of scholars working in the Middle East, an issue that cannot be completely explained away by linguistic barriers or the complexity of North Africa's medieval and modern history.

These hurdles – historiographical, evidential, disciplinary – explain why North Africa has played so little part in broader Islamic histories. But they do not justify its neglect. This short book aims to introduce the Islamic archaeology of this important region to a broader audience, to raise new questions about the key debates between the seventh and ninth centuries, and – above all – to demonstrate why North Africa is relevant to histories of Islam, Europe and Byzantium. It draws on a wealth of recent archaeological research in Morocco, Algeria, Tunisia and Libya, much of it led by my North African colleagues whose work is not sufficiently known outside the region. It demonstrates the need to challenge old, but still powerful, models of early Islamic North Africa, and to place North Africa at the centre of historical debates about the impact of the Arab conquests, the spread of Islam and the transition from the classical to the medieval world. Given the changing nature of the field, this book does not aim to offer a comprehensive history of the period, as there is both too little scholarship and, in what there is, too little consensus. Rather, it offers an archaeological perspective on life in early Islamic North Africa which it is hoped will go some way to filling this lacuna in scholarship as well as acting as a stimulus for future research.

Foundations
Evidence and Interpretation

Historians and archaeologists frequently lament the paucity of sources for the formative period of Islam. This is certainly a challenge for North Africa between the seventh and early ninth centuries, a period that was famously described as *les siècles obscurs* or the 'Dark Ages' by Émile-Félix Gautier (1927). We simply do not possess anything close to the number of written sources for early medieval North Africa that exist for the heartlands of the early Islamic empire or for Roman Africa, while Islamic archaeology is still in its infancy in comparison to the Middle East and al-Andalus. These hurdles have until recently prevented scholars from tackling this pivotal period. Our difficulties in coming to grips with what happened in early Islamic North Africa are not only the result of shortcomings in the evidence. The legacy of European colonialism has had particularly devastating implications for the study and interpretation of Islamic North Africa, perhaps more so than elsewhere in the Islamic world.

If we are to write histories of the early Islamic world that are as rigorous and challenging as they should be, we need to consider carefully the evidence and approaches that we use and why. This chapter outlines some of the specific problems with the North African textual and archaeological evidence, how they relate to the history of the scholarship and their implications for our understanding of the period. One factor that may surprise scholars is the quantity of data available for the seventh to ninth centuries. Of course, there is much that remains unknown or ambiguous – archaeology and archaeologists can do much better – but there is already more that can be done with the evidence that we do possess, if we think creatively.

Texts

The first challenge is the scarcity of the written evidence. It is routine for Islamic historians to complain how few sources are available for the seventh and eighth centuries, and yet they are far better served than their colleagues working on Byzantium. We possess a bewildering amount of information about the conquests and the early caliphate in Arabic; the problem is that it was compiled only several centuries later. In the late ninth and the tenth centuries, Muslim scholars collated and compared oral reports (*khabar*) and traditions (*hadith*) about the Prophet, the conquest and important individuals to try to build up an authoritative picture of the spread of Islam. In the 1970s, 'revisionist' historians claimed that it was impossible to ever develop a satisfying portrait of the early Islamic period, even questioning the existence of the Prophet himself (e.g., Crone and Cook 1977). Their radical views were not widely accepted but prompted many to confront openly the challenges of using the Arabic sources. It is now clear that many of our sources belong to 'an Abbasid vulgate' which in the ninth century created an 'official' history of the seventh and eighth centuries (Borrut 2011: 61–2). Although North Africa has remained largely outside the frenzied scholarly debates that have surrounded the history of the conquest period in the Middle East, an increasingly critical and contextual reading of the Arabic historical tradition has emerged (e.g., Prévost 2008; Picard 2011, 2016).

North Africa poses specific problems of which historians working outside the region may not be fully aware. It is rarely mentioned in the most frequently cited Arabic histories of the early Islamic period, and for good reason. When the earliest surviving accounts of the conquest were compiled in the late ninth century, North Africa had been lost to the caliphate for many decades. It was no success story to be celebrated by historians of the Abbasid court, but an imperial failure to be glossed over. Accordingly, the region is dealt with only cursorily by historians of the Iraqi and Egyptian schools such as Ibn 'Abd al-Hakam (d. 871), al-Baladhuri (d. 892) and al-Tabari (d. 923), writing in Baghdad or

Cairo with the privilege of hindsight about the expensive attempt to rule the Maghreb. Nor are the fragments that they do preserve particularly helpful for scholars looking at social change in this region. Early Arabic historians were far more interested in individuals and their heroic (or cowardly) deeds and speeches than in describing social relations, housing or agriculture. A far fuller picture is given in the detailed, but generally reliable, accounts of much later Western historians such as the Andalusi scholar Ibn ʿIdhari (d. after 1310) and the North African historian Ibn Khaldun (d. 1406) or the large corpus of Ibadi writings (Lewicki 1957). Yet, most modern historians have depended upon the small handful of Iraqi and Egyptian authors to write their accounts of the early Islamic world, rather than the later Western authors, with the result that the gaps and elisions in the early Arabic histories are often taken at face value. Consequently, North Africa and the Islamic West – a third of the early Islamic world – have commonly been relegated to a mere footnote in scholarly accounts.

More can be gleaned from the Arabic geographical descriptions of the region, though these too describe North Africa in much less detail than the central caliphate: vast expanses of North Africa, especially Morocco and western Algeria, are glossed over without comment, sometimes for political reasons and sometimes from ignorance. One of the earliest geographies, the *Kitab al-Buldan* written by al-Yaʿqubi (d. 897–8), is particularly important for archaeologists. Written to serve as a practical guide to the landscape, cities, trade routes and peoples of the Islamic world, al-Yaʿqubi travelled extensively around North Africa in the 870s and 880s before composing his book in Egypt; his description is one of the fullest that we possess. He often includes information on conquest or foundation narratives for individual cities, the goods traded, and the ethnicity and origins of each town's inhabitants, especially if they were of Arabian descent, when their tribal or genealogical affiliation is often given. Later works such as those of Ibn Hawqal (d. *c.* 978), al-Muqaddasi (d. 991), al-Bakri (d. 1094) and al-Idrisi (d. 1165) can also be mined for details on trade routes, towns and their products and inhabitants. These texts are not straightforward 'eye-witness' accounts, however: while some authors such as al-Ya'qubi, Ibn Hawqal and al-Idrisi had travelled extensively around North Africa, others were 'armchair geographers' who had never visited the region and relied on other, now lost, accounts to provide their detail. As a result, the geographies must be read carefully: just as historians had their own agendas, so too did the geographers when selecting the routes, towns and the level of detail to provide.

Further issues arise when we consider *who* wrote our sources. They are rarely written by native North Africans or even those who knew the region, but rather by educated men from the centre with their own prejudices about the peoples of North Africa. For the geographer al-Muqaddasi, a native of Jerusalem writing in the tenth century who had never visited North Africa, Ifriqiya had the most boorish people in the Islamic lands (Al-Muqaddasi 2001: 183). Al-Hamdani (d. 945), his contemporary from Yemen, describes the erotic and war-like nature of the Berbers, pronouncing them 'evil and wicked. . . . liars and cheats, cunning and murderous with a secret hate', though he reserved harsher critique still for sub-Saharan Africans (Norris 1982: 6–7). These derogatory statements reveal more about the ethnocentric biases of their authors than about the habits and practices of North Africans, but they have sometimes misled modern scholars into dismissing medieval North Africa as provincial and undeveloped.

Matters are exacerbated by the lack of a critical historiography of many of the surviving texts by North African authors (see Chapoutot-Remadi 1997). Kairouan was an important centre of intellectual, legal and religious scholarship by the late eighth century, later joined in this role by Fes (Fierro Bello 2017). We can glean some sense of the scale of scholarly production from biographical dictionaries (*tabaqat*) of Ifriqiyan scholars written by Abu l-'Arab al-Tamimi (d. 944) and Ibn Harith (d. early tenth century) which provide us with valuable information about the many local scholars, their lives and their possessions (see Ben Cheneb 1920). Particularly important are the writings of Sahnun (776/7–854/5) the jurist who revised the 'al-Mudawwana', the legal opinions of the school of Medina as stated by the imam Malik b. Anas. Some of this early Maghrebi scholarship still survives today in the library of Kairouan, one of the most important repositories of early Islamic manuscripts in the world.

Those working in the Middle East, particularly in Syria-Palestine, can draw upon contemporary manuscripts and letters in Coptic, Aramaic or Syriac by Christians, Jews and Zoroastrians living under Muslim rule (Hoyland 1997). For North Africa, there is no equivalent corpus of Latin, Greek or Berber writings, though there are monumental inscriptions, tombstones and graffiti in Arabic and less frequently Latin from the early Islamic period (Rossi 1953; Abdeljaouad 2017a, 2017b). In Egypt, the rich Arabic and Coptic papyrological corpus, neglected for many decades, is now providing valuable information on the administrative structure of an early Muslim province, taxation and property rights (Sijpesteijn 2013). Several papyri mention North Africa, including the earliest merchant letter in the early Islamic world (Raghib 1991), and new insights will emerge from this corpus in the future. Finally, Church letters, laws and hagiographies (biographies of saints) from Carolingian Europe and Papal Rome provide tantalizing hints about trade and mobility and Christian communities in North Africa (e.g., Conant 2010; Valérian 2011b).

For archaeologists who are not Arabists, a final obstacle arises from the lack of recent translations of the most important texts. Scholars are reliant on a handful of translations made during the French conquest of Algeria by officials such as Baron William MacGuckin de Slane, an Irishman by birth, who became Principal Interpreter of Arabic of the French Army in Africa. Colonial scholars translated Arabic as well as Latin accounts of North Africa to better understand the native Arab and Berber populations and to define colonial policy (Lorcin 2002). These translations, many over a century old, are riddled with errors and interpretative issues, and often impose colonial assumptions about Arabs or Berbers onto the Arabic sources (Hannoum 2003). There is a pressing need for new translations and critical editions of North African authors like Ibn ʿIdhari, Ibn Khaldun and Sahnun that take on board the recent critical turn in Arabic historiography.

The written sources, however partial and challenging they may be, must certainly be integrated as much as we are able. But for certain questions, Islamic history must depend on Islamic archaeology if we wish to say anything meaningful at all.

Archaeology and material culture

Archaeology's ability to offer a different perspective to the partial and problematic Arabic texts has yet to be fully exploited for the early Islamic period. Archaeology has the potential to offer much bigger bodies of data continuously over time rather than simply small points of light in very dark centuries. It can offer insight into areas of life or geographic regions that do not appear in the written sources. These advantages should not be ignored but nor should the challenges be downplayed. Archaeologists do not impartially reveal the past by digging trenches or counting pot sherds in fields; they actively create their data-set. The decisions that archaeologists make about which sites to study, where to place their trenches, which artefacts to collect and the level of detail provided in publications affect the quality and amount of evidence we can draw upon. In North Africa, despite an early start in the late nineteenth century, Islamic archaeology is far less well developed than the Middle East or al-Andalus, and this raises a series of interpretative dilemmas for scholars. I will outline the key issues: the legacy of colonial clearance, a monumental focus, poor publication, divergent regional coverage and, most importantly, difficulties in dating eighth- and ninth-century activity.

European colonialism had particularly devastating implications for the development of Islamic archaeology in North Africa. France's attack on Algiers in 1830 and the subsequent establishment of the Algerian colony opened vast expanses of uncharted territory to be mapped, recorded and mined for information. Scholars accompanied the French army on the conquest expedition to record the landscape, peoples and architecture of Algeria in the belief that a detailed understanding would lead to better governance. France depicted itself as the heir to Rome, and North Africa's Roman and Christian past became a primary justification for French rule (Lorcin 2002). The European 'discovery' of the spectacular ruins of Roman Africa, the well-preserved towns, temples, and churches, were used to substantiate these claims. Although the colonial narrative first took shape in Algeria, it included the entire Maghreb environment from its inception, and was quickly applied to interpret the archaeology of the subsequently established French protectorates of Tunisia (1881) and Morocco (1912), the Spanish protectorate of Morocco (1912), and the Italian colony of Libya (1911).

Archaeology developed as part of an imperialist discourse that justified European colonization by stressing the 'otherness' of Africa and the barbarity of its inhabitants in contrast to the 'civilizing influence' of Rome and France (Dondin-Payre 1991; Mattingly 1996; Munzi 2001; Oulebsir 2004; Fenwick 2008). The Arabs were regarded as interlopers, whilst the Berbers were viewed as either passive recipients of Roman culture or barbaric savages, incapable of progress without the intervention of Rome or France (e.g., Masqueray 1886; Broughton 1929; Cagnat 1913; Gautier 1927). In the same way, the modern populations – Berber or Arab – were regarded as barbaric and savage, and incapable of self-government (e.g., Picard 1954: 37). These tropes became more significant as the years passed, and were used to claim that the Berbers could be assimilated more easily than the Arabs because of their Roman past. This form of intellectual colonialism had implications for archaeology, resulting in an imbalance of research efforts, with the Roman period prioritized over all other periods, as well as skewing the interpretation of archaeological sites and finds.

Scientific archaeology dates to the 1880s when national antiquities services were established in Algeria and Tunisia. Soon after, in 1898, the explorer Paul Blanchet began excavations at one of the most spectacular abandoned medieval cities of North Africa: the Qala of the Beni Hammad, the 'fortress' of the Hammadid emirs, founded in 1007 as the capital of their Sanhaja Berber dynasty. The ruins of this city overlook the point where the caravan routes from the western Maghreb and Sahara divide to go to either Algiers or Kairouan and Tunis. Apparently built in an astonishing three years, imposing stone-built walls enclose a vast area of 150 hectares filled with numerous richly decorated palaces, carefully laid-out gardens, caravanserai, and what was to be the largest mosque constructed in North Africa before the twentieth century. Excavations continued in 1908 under General Léon de Beylié during the suppression of a revolt in the area (De Beylié 1909), a telling reminder of the close relationship between archaeology and the French army in Algeria. As was typical of archaeology in this period, little attention was paid to the contents of rooms, the landscape setting of the palaces or broader settlement patterns. The result was detailed architectural descriptions, stunning catalogues of stucco, tiles and metalwork, and the first reference corpus of Islamic ceramics (Marçais 1913), but only limited information on the social, economic or political aspects of life in medieval Algeria.

This was one of the earliest excavations at an Islamic site by European archaeologists anywhere in the world (Vernoit 1997). It set a precedent for subsequent Islamic archaeology in North Africa – the excavation of palaces and mosques and the collection of architectural décor and luxury objects – but did not trigger a wider interest in the archaeology of the period. The French and Italian colonial powers continued to closely associate themselves with Rome, as precedent and model for their rule (Lorcin 2002). Archaeology became an important tool in their arsenal. In the following decades, vast expanses of many sites were deliberately cleared down to the spectacular public buildings and elaborate mosaics of the early Roman period, making it very difficult, though not impossible, to reconstruct their later history. Early excavators regarded medieval occupation, especially that of 'Arabs', as an unavoidable nuisance which obscured the more interesting Roman layers. In 1916, the French missionary and archaeologist Père Delattre complained:

> Despite an Arab, Turkish or Spanish building, despite a series of silos, despite the occupation of Arabs on this site, occupation revealed by ceramics, lamps, tiles in glazed faience, we have been able to recognise the plan of this vast Christian building.
>
> Delattre 1916: 252

This derogatory attitude was widespread and resulted until recently in late antique and medieval layers being removed without being recorded in detail. The Islamic heritage was not simply neglected; it was actively destroyed by archaeologists on a scale that seems to me to be unmatched elsewhere in the Mediterranean.

To all intents and purposes, the Arab conquest marked the end-point of archaeological research. This was even codified in early antiquities laws. When, for example, Louis Poinssot wished to strengthen Tunisian antiquities laws in 1921, the Tunisian state became the owner of all antiquities henceforth uncovered, but only those artefacts that pre-dated the Arab conquest (Mahjoubi 1997: 22). Such divisions between antiquity and the medieval period were emphasized even more sharply in a short-lived Franco-Tunisian agreement of 1955 during the negotiations for independence in which the Tunisian Department of Antiquities was to be responsible for all heritage post-dating the Arab conquest, while the French Archaeological Mission in Tunisia continued to be responsible for antiquity (Mahjoubi 1997: 25).

The material culture of medieval North Africa was not neglected, however, by art historians. The publication of Henri Saladin and Gaston Migeon's (1907) *Manuel d'art musulman* marked a major step forward for the study of Islamic architecture and art. Lavishly illustrated, the first volume by Saladin was dedicated to architecture and the second by Migeon was dedicated to decorative arts and painting, a separation that has proved enduring in subsequent scholarship. Saladin had travelled widely throughout French Africa, and much of his volume was dedicated to the 'Moorish' tradition in the Maghreb (North Africa and al-Andalus). Saladin's use of ethno-racial categories such as Moorish or Persian to explain regional diversity and use of dynasties to explain chronological change have been influential in art historical scholarship, as have his arguments that North African art and architecture were derivative of developments in al-Andalus or the Middle East. The tendency to treat regions, dynasties and media as if they were independent has proved enduring in art historical scholarship: it is only recently that scholars have begun to examine internal dynamics or intra-regional connections, and the discipline remains fractured into distinct regional traditions that rarely speak to one another (Flood and Necipoglu 2017).

While archaeology remained a rarity, ground-breaking architectural studies took place in French North Africa. French scholars such as Georges Marçais (1876–1962), Henri Terrasse (1895–1971), Alexandre Lézine (1906–1972) and Lucien Golvin (1905–2002) produced hundreds of important analyses of medieval and early modern cities, palatial complexes, large mosques and fortifications. A handful of excavations also took place at the palatial sites of al-Abbasiyya (Marçais 1925), Sedrata (van Berchem 1954) and Achir (Golvin 1966), but never on the scale of those at Roman sites such as Carthage, Timgad, Volubilis or Lepcis Magna. Much of this work is summarized in Marçais' monumental *L'Architecture musulmane d'Occident* (1954), which remains the fundamental reference work for the architecture of Tunisia, Algeria and Morocco. There was no equivalent Orientalist outpouring of architectural research in Italian Fascist Libya, where, although some Islamic monuments were protected, archaeological research focused almost exclusively upon the Roman period (Munzi 2001); as a result, our knowledge of Islamic architecture in Libya remains limited.

Colonial scholarship has produced a large data-set of well-preserved medieval buildings from the ninth century and later. However, only a handful of monuments – the four congregational mosques of Kairouan, Sousse, Tunis and Sfax, two neighbourhood mosques in Kairouan and Sousse, the al-Qarawiyyin mosque in Fes and the *ribat*s of Sousse and Monastir – have received sustained scholarly attention (e.g., Creswell 1989; Lézine 1966; Marçais 1954). The standard approach was typological; they focused on plan, spatial layouts and decorative features in order to reconstruct different construction phases, which could be then be attributed to different dynasties (e.g., Aghlabid, Fatimid, Zirid, Idrisid, etc.). Such periodizations sit uneasily with archaeological evidence which rarely, if ever, maps neatly onto dynastic history. Architectural studies were sometimes supplemented by small sondages aimed at clarifying construction dates or retrieving luxury objects. This is why archaeologists devoted their energies to the Islamic palatial sites, which contained large assemblages of rich, decorative items that could then be displayed in museums.

Scholarship on glazed ceramics, glass, metalwork, woodwork and textiles – what Islamic art historians term the 'decorative arts' – has focused on a handful of exceptional objects, usually unprovenanced or decorative elements from Raqqada, Sabra al-Mansuriya or the great mosques. The emphasis on museum-quality objects had many unfortunate tendencies: only whole artefacts tended to be recorded (or even kept) and contextual information was rarely recorded. Like the great mosques of Kairouan and Fes, these exceptional pieces continue to feature in every introductory textbook to Islamic art (Ettinghausen et al. 2001: 91–100) but are only approached through aesthetic criteria which privilege the discussion of form over function and context. More troubling still, the handful of rich, luxury items have sometimes been used to paint a picture of North African technological poverty. All too often, North Africans were depicted as passive borrowers rather than innovators in architectural and visual spheres, an attitude that stems both from colonial prejudices about North Africa and from the lack of recent art-historical studies in the region (Anderson 2014; Rosser-Owen 2014).

Interest in Islamic archaeology increased after the Second World War, and accelerated still further under the pioneering leadership of North African scholars after independence and the establishment of the modern nation-states of Libya (1951), Morocco (1956), Tunisia (1956) and Algeria (1962). Islamic archaeology became a recognized department of the Tunisian Antiquities Service in 1948 under Slimane-Mostafa Zbiss who became director after independence. Zbiss began restoration works in the Tunisian medinas and undertook (largely unpublished) excavations at the palace-cities of Raqqada and Sabra Mansouriya as well as in, and around, the Great Mosque of Kairouan (Gutron 2010: 132–6). In Libya, spearheaded by Abdulhamid Abdussaid, Islamic archaeology became a key focus, and important excavations were conducted at the mosques and forts of Ajdabiya, Medinat Sultan

(Barce) and Zuwila in the 1960s and 1970s (Abdussaid 1964; Abdussaid 1971). Finally, Ammar Mahjoubi's (1978) ground-breaking excavations at Belalis Maior (Henchir el-Fouar) between 1959 and 1971 demonstrated the potential of stratigraphic excavations to understand the transition from the late antique to Islamic period.

The colonial legacy proved difficult to shift, however. French, Italian and British scholars did not hand over their intellectual authority after independence, and resources (finances, trained personnel, equipment) were limited for the departments of antiquities in the various Maghrebi countries, particularly for work on the Islamic period (Alaoui et al. 2014: 44–5). Co-operations with foreign institutions continued, particularly with the French in Tunisia, Algeria and Morocco and with the Italians and British in Libya, but as in earlier generations, these focused almost exclusively on Roman archaeology. A seismic shift came in the 1970s and 1980s with the growing maturity of European medieval archaeology and the rise of stratigraphic excavation promoted by the UNESCO Pour Sauver Carthage campaign (Terrasse 1976). Within this milieu, excavations commenced at medieval sites on a larger scale, though still very much less than at Roman sites. This too is changing rapidly, partly because of increased collaboration between medievalists and classical scholars, but also with the growth of diachronic approaches in archaeology which aim to trace their settlement history from prehistory to the medieval period.

Research continues to focus on the mosque and palace, the Islamic city or the late antique/early Islamic transition, but very different trajectories can be seen in the four countries. Islamic archaeology is most developed in Morocco (Fili forthcoming). Influenced by contemporary developments in al-Andalus and European medieval archaeology in the 1980s, scholars such as Andre Bazzana, Patrice Cressier, Charles Redman and Ronald Messier led the way in establishing an Islamic archaeology that combined a close reading of the Arabic sources with field survey, geophysics and targeted excavation. Subsequently, a new generation of Moroccan and foreign archaeologists have established multi-disciplinary projects which employ the latest scientific techniques, including at Volubilis (Walila) (Fentress and Limane 2018), the diachronic excavation at the rural site of Rirha (Callegarin 2016), rescue excavations at Fes and the major open-area excavations at the Almoravid capital Aghmat and the mountain stronghold of Igiliz (Ettahiri et al. 2013). Although much of the archaeological work focusing specifically on the early Islamic period has been small-scale to date, stratigraphic excavation and the strategic use of radiocarbon dating has produced local, site-based ceramic chronologies for the seventh to ninth centuries. As a result, much more is known about the distribution of early medieval towns and the fabric of early medieval towns like Nakur, al-Basra, Volubilis and Sijilmasa, with more data emerging every year (Cressier 2018). Field survey has also proved a successful means of identifying sites of the ninth to fourteenth centuries (Bazzana et al. 1983; Ennahid 2001; Redman 1983), though less so for the fourth to eighth centuries which remain poorly understood. In Morocco, then, we possess information on the eighth and early ninth centuries that is missing for the rest of the Maghreb.

Moving eastwards, very little is known about the archaeology of Islamic Algeria and this remains a problematic gap. Pioneering excavations took place at medieval Sétif and Cherchel in the 1980s (Mohamedi et al. 1991; Potter 1995), but excavations at the Rustamid capital of Tahart (Cadenat 1977) and Achir (Carver and Souidi 1996) are only summarily described. Other Algerian sites, such as the Idrisid mosque at Tlemcen, excavated in the 1970s, have yet to be published (though see Charpentier 2018). The civil war (1990–2002) prompted a hiatus in archaeological research and very little fieldwork has been conducted subsequently.

In Tunisia, research has focused on the palatial sites of Aghlabid Raqqada (Chabbi 1967–1968) and the later Fatimid foundations of Mahdia (Louhichi 1997) and Sabra al-Mansuriya (Cressier and Rammah 2006). Following the model established at Belalis Maior (Mahjoubi 1978), Roman and late antique archaeologists began to consider critically the medieval history of many Roman towns (e.g., Chemtou, Utica, Carthage, Uchi Maius, Althiburos). Importantly, these excavations have begun to produce typologies for early medieval ceramics (Cressier and Fentress 2011), which complements the work conducted on museum collections of medieval ceramics. The countryside is also poorly understood: only the Jerba survey has examined medieval rural settlement and land-use patterns and, though the site gazetteer is published online, the medieval data has yet to be published (Fentress et al. 2009).

In many ways, Libya provides the most comprehensive evidence for the transition from antiquity to the early Islamic period, thanks to a series of multi-period field surveys conducted in coastal, pre-desert and Saharan regions, and targeted excavations of early Islamic phases at the coastal cities of Ptolemais, Lepcis Magna, Sabratha, Tocra and Berenice (see King 1989). The British excavations of the walled Saharan oasis town Jarma have shed light on the medieval Sahara and the nature of trans-Saharan trade (Mattingly 2013). At the time of writing, Libya is in a state of conflict and much of its Islamic heritage – particularly the mosques and marabouts – has been damaged or destroyed.

This history of research creates several challenges for archaeologists. The first and most significant is how we recognize early medieval activity when we see it. The second is the patchiness of the available evidence. Only a small number of sites have been studied satisfactorily, and vast areas of North Africa remain unexplored, including much of Algeria, eastern Morocco and south-west Libya. The bulk of effort has been devoted to palatial sites and monumental architecture rather than housing, industrial complexes, rural settlement and landscape. Nonetheless, there is a large but under-exploited corpus of evidence at our disposal, which can be marshalled to understand the early Islamic period if we remain attentive to the contexts in which archaeological data were produced.

Interpreting the evidence

The French conquest of Algeria in 1830 was followed by the emergence of complex, and often contradictory, narratives about North Africa's past. A great deal of ink was spilled on the question of how Romano-Christian Africa, the home of Cyprian and Augustine, became Arab-Muslim Africa. Before the French conquest of Algeria in 1830, North Africa was typically depicted as a land that had collapsed into decadence under the primitive techniques of the natives. In explaining the collapse, the fifth-century invasion of the Vandals took on great interpretative force, especially for environmental destruction, though the Arabs too were seen as destructive, razing cities and attacking North African Christendom (Davis 2007: 23). This view changed under French rule of the Maghreb, and in less than two decades a narrative emerged that blamed both the inherent savagery of the Berbers and the Arab conquests for destroying the prosperity of Roman Africa. Variants of the catastrophe narrative were used throughout the colonial period to justify and motivate French and Italian colonization across North Africa, though it was never universally accepted.

From the outset, there were distinct differences in how medieval and classical scholars saw this period, in part due to the different evidence they drew upon, and the questions they asked. To simplify only slightly, medieval scholars distinguished between two different Arab conquests: the Arab conquest of the seventh century and the 'invasion' of the Banu Hilal tribes in the eleventh century so vividly described as a 'spreading swarm of locusts' (*jarad muntashir*) by Ibn Khaldun (Camps 1983; Carcopino 1943; Julien 1951). This distinction was popularized by the geographer Émile-Félix Gautier's (1927) highly influential book *Les siècles obscurs du Maghreb: L'islamisation de l'Afrique du Nord* [The Dark Ages of the Maghreb: The Islamization of North Africa]. Gautier explained the collapse of Roman power through the inadequate 'Romanization' of the indigenous populations of North Africa, the Berbers or Moors, and the spread of nomadism at the end of the Roman period. Inassimilable by nature, the Berbers were thought to have ended Roman civilization long before the arrival of the Arabs (e.g., Diehl 1896; Mercier 1895–1896: 194). Crucially, he did not see the seventh-century Arab conquest as devastating for North Africa; he, like other medieval scholars, blamed the migration of the Banu Hilal in the eleventh century for laying waste to the Maghreb: 'The [first] conquest brought the seeds of interesting life. The Bedouin immigration brought only the seeds of death' (Gautier 1927: 386). Like other medieval historians (e.g., Julien 1951: 453–4; Marçais 1954: 60–1), he emphasized continuity in daily life, local craft traditions and urbanism, alongside the spread of Islam in the seventh and eighth centuries.

Yet, the first Arab conquest took on cataclysmic proportions in the writings of classical historians and archaeologists who saw it as an epochal turning point. The Moroccan post-colonial historian Abdallah Laroui (1977) calls this the 'ternary myth', the myth that human history should be divided into antiquity, the middle ages and the modern era. In Europe, the barbarian invasions brought about the end of antiquity; in North Africa, the Arab conquest which brought Islam played the same role. Classical scholars were less familiar with the Arabic sources and drew selectively upon them to underwrite arguments that the Arabs were interlopers and had brought about a rupture with the classical world. The Byzantine historian Charles Diehl painted a particularly bleak picture of the seventh century:

> 'Most cities of Ifrikia (sic), said a historian [the fourteenth-century author Ibn 'Idhari] were abandoned, because of the resistance of the Berbers', the countryside was abandoned, agricultural establishments burnt, water-works destroyed; still today, we find traces of their terrible devastation at every step in the dead cities of Tunisia, most of which remain in the state which the Arab invasion left them.
>
> Diehl 1896: 590

Although early studies relied almost exclusively on textual sources, the ruins of Roman cities became powerful arguments in stone for the 'Dark Age' narrative. The temples, baths and churches of sites such as Carthage, Timgad or Lepcis Magna were taken as physical evidence for the progress of North African history from its florescence in the Roman period to its decay and destruction as a result of Berber resistance and the Arab conquests. Scholars discovered without surprise that Roman monumental buildings were abandoned and repurposed – the construction of huts in their ruins, the use of spolia in mosques, the oileries in the middle of streets – and concluded without hesitation an irremediable decline in urbanism:

> All of the dead cities flourished at the same time: their birth coincides with the establishment of Roman rule in Africa, their apogee with the time of its greatest power, their ruin with its decline. This evolution was accomplished entirely in a few centuries; it had no tomorrow, nothing follows it, nothing precedes it. It is a brilliant episode between two nothingnesses.
>
> Gauckler 1896: 7

This conviction of a profound deurbanization, synonymous with deromanization, discouraged archaeological research on the early Islamic period for many decades.

The 'de-colonization' of history that followed the creation of the modern nation-states of Libya (1951), Morocco (1956), Tunisia (1956) and Algeria (1962) spurred a new interest in the early Islamic period. Colonial narratives were turned on their heads to create histories that supported the nationalist visions of Algeria, Tunisia, Morocco or Libya (see Hannoum 2001: 119–31). The publication in 1970 of Laroui's seminal *L'histoire du Maghreb* (English translation: 1977) marked a turning point in the deconstruction of colonialist paradigms. Laroui had his own 'post-colonial' vision of North Africa, characterized by Maghrebi resistance to Roman occupation and rule just like their twentieth-century counterparts, opposing the occupation of Western colonial power (see also Benabou 1977). A series of important revisionist histories such as Talbi's (1966) authoritative study of the Aghlabid dynasty or Djaït's (1975) critical studies of Umayyad and Abbasid rule were produced but had muted effect on the archaeology of the early Islamic period, which effectively fell between the disciplines of Roman and medieval archaeology.

The disciplinary divisions between classical and medieval scholarship established in the colonial period has created two different streams of research on early Islamic North Africa, each with its own debates, research histories and distinct case studies (Fenwick 2018). The first, led by late antique archaeologists, focuses primarily on 'The End of the

Roman world' and particularly how and when the monuments and public spaces of the classical Roman city were transformed into their medieval form (Leone 2007; Pentz 2002; Thébert and Biget 1990). The second, led by medieval archaeologists, focuses instead on 'Origins' and examines the spread and development of new Islamic modes of life through the lens of new city foundations and urbanization, particularly in Morocco – and to a lesser degree, the spread of new architectural forms such as mosques, *ribats* and town walls (Boone et al. 1990; Cressier 1992; Mahfoudh 2003). In practice, this means that medieval archaeologists start their analyses in the ninth or tenth century when new Muslim cities are founded and new monumental forms appear, whilst late antique specialists are far more interested in tracing the end-point of those Roman towns that are relatively well excavated.

Classical and medieval scholars tend not to engage with each other's work sufficiently, and when they do, rarely unpack the different paradigms and models that the other uses. This has proved particularly problematic for research on the seventh and eighth centuries which is driven by late antique archaeologists who naturally are more comfortable with the debates and agendas of the past thirty years of late antique scholarship (e.g., Leone 2007; Pentz 2002; Thébert and Biget 1990; Panzram and Callegarin 2018) than those of early Islamic scholarship, which is now going through its own revolution. Despite the exemplary work of these scholars, there is an enduring, but decidedly unhelpful, tendency on the part of some other classical scholars to counter an 'Islamic' culture with 'Romano-Byzantine' culture in a way that suggests not only that the Arab conquest of Africa brought about radical cultural and social change, but also that archaeologists can distinguish neatly between the pre- and post-conquest period in the material record. Neither assumption is correct. Just as Roman historians and archaeologists have demonstrated that the Roman conquest of Africa did not instantly create a recognizably 'Roman' package that could be differentiated easily from 'Punic' and 'Numidian' material culture and challenged such essentializing labels (e.g., Mattingly 2011), so too medieval historians and archaeologists see the complex processes of

Islamization and Arabization as distinct and regionally variable phenomena in North Africa that significantly post-date the Arab conquests in the seventh century (Brett 1992; Cressier 1998; Valérian 2011a).

To date, the study of early Islamic Africa has only partly benefited from the enormous expansion in archaeological work on late antiquity that has taken place in the last generation. Yvon Thébert and Jean-Louis Biget (1990) were the first to challenge the rupture model for North Africa in a ground-breaking article on the disappearance of the classical city. Suggesting that North Africa followed the 'polis to madina' pattern outlined by Hugh Kennedy (1985) for Syria, they identified the fourth to early sixth centuries as the point when urban life became 'medieval'. Emphasizing continuity in urban life, trade levels and rural prosperity into the fourteenth century, they argued that the catastrophic rupture caused by the Arab conquest in the seventh century was a myth (Thébert and Biget 1990: 579). Whilst their relocation of urban transformation to the fourth to sixth centuries is now widely accepted, their argument for continuity into the medieval period has only recently been taken up.

North Africa has not seen the same sustained critique of the impact of the Arab conquests as the Islamic Middle East or al-Andalus (e.g., Avni 2014; Magness 2003; Walmsley 2007). The lack of explicit discussion explains the continued influence of the traditional decline and rupture model in North Africa but also makes it difficult to characterize current archaeological thinking on the subject. In the absence of unambiguous statements, one has to turn to the typically brief interpretations of the evidence: scholars argue that rural and urban decline began in most regions by the late sixth century and intensified in the seventh century, whether from weak Byzantine state control, plague, earthquakes, nomadic incursions, or other catastrophes (e.g., Fentress and Wilson 2016; Hitchner 1994; Leone 2007; Leone and Mattingly 2004). After 700, archaeologists find few indicators of urban occupation and almost no rural sites. The seventh and eighth centuries are thus seen as the moment of crisis for North Africa: the prosperous Roman landscape of towns, villas, estates and oil-producing farms replaced by an impoverished and depopulated late Byzantine and early medieval landscape of fortified and quasi-urban settlements (e.g., Gelichi and Milanese 2002). A clutch of recent publications present a different, less prejudiced and more positive view of the transitional period (e.g., Fenwick 2013; Panzram and Callegarin 2018; Stevens and Conant 2016). Yet archaeologists of the early Islamic period, few as they are, still struggle with the weight of the powerfully negative colonial tradition. As a result, though scholars now commonly acknowledge the difficulties in 'seeing' the eighth century, we still have not fully addressed the interpretative issues that prevent the situation from changing.

Accurately dating and identifying early medieval occupation remains the biggest challenge, particularly for the eighth and early ninth century. Durable, mass-produced and ubiquitous, ceramics are the most common means of dating occupation in any period. Unlike the Roman period for which decades of research have produced an exceptionally tight ceramic chronology for African Red Slip (ARS) finewares between the first and seventh centuries (Bonifay 2004; Hayes 1972), our understanding of medieval ceramics is poor. For well over a century, all undecorated medieval pottery was thrown away: only a handful of excavation monographs published descriptions or images of glazed ceramics, never systematically. In the 1980s and 1990s, pioneering work by Adnan Louhichi and Giovanna Vitelli on medieval ceramics assemblages in Tunisian museums established preliminary typologies; however, these collections were often unstratified and lack provenance (Louhichi 2010; Vitelli 1981). New excavations are now refining the typologies for early medieval ceramics (see Cressier and Fentress 2011 for a summary), though the publication of complete assemblages from sites of the eighth century and later is still uncommon.

Our limited understanding of medieval ceramics and the final stages of ARS production has proved disastrous. Put simply, the eighth and much of the ninth century is effectively invisible to archaeologists. North Africa has a 'ceramic gap' between the latest ARS productions in the late seventh or perhaps eighth centuries and the late ninth or tenth centuries when glazed wares begin to be produced (Cressier and Fentress 2011: 3). As we proceed, therefore, it is useful to keep in mind the oft-cited maxim 'absence of evidence is not evidence of absence'. The ninth and tenth centuries are much better understood due to the appearance of monumental architecture (mosques, *ribaṭs*, palaces and so on) and the introduction of glazed ceramics which make it easier to date activity. Coins, in general, are under-used; many excavations report the presence of Islamic coins but rarely publish them or even specify their date. The implications are significant: medieval structures are often dated based on stylistic criteria – typically masonry, architecture or plan. As a result, sites are often dated to a long Islamic, medieval or Arab period, spanning the eighth to nineteenth centuries and rarely broken down into smaller chronological units.

There are further problems with the way in which we read the archaeological evidence in the absence of tight ceramic chronologies. The Arab conquests marked the end of the ancient world; therefore, any buildings or objects that look classical – like ceramics, churches, mosaics, housing plans or certain masonry types – must pre-date 650/700 (depending on whether one takes the battle at Sbeïtla in 647 or the fall of Carthage in 698 as the 'end'). Even when scholars do not try to explain the 'end' of classical Africa, 650/700 is used as a convenient chronological terminus. In turn, the lack of evidence for the eighth century is used as proof that classical Africa had come to an end. Paradoxically, this is often the case even when scholars acknowledge the difficulties in arguing from absence or the 'ceramic gap' between the last ARS productions in the late eighth century and the earliest glazeware productions in the late ninth century. Lack of information does make a period dark for modern scholars, but we must be careful not to confuse this with a darkness serious enough to be apparent to those who lived at the time.

More problematic still are the interpretative issues that arise from the continued focus on a handful of sites that were either famous Roman towns that failed at some point in their history or the spectacular, but short-lived, Islamic dynastic foundations. Archaeologists are drawn to abandoned sites, they are easier to dig, and in North Africa, they are extremely impressive. When it comes to the early Islamic period, however, the emphasis on Roman ruins has exerted a dangerous influence on the scholarly imagination. Our data-set comes from around fifteen atypical towns that prospered in the Roman period but failed at some point in the middle ages and were abandoned (Fenwick forthcoming a). This is why narratives of depopulation, urban ruin and societal collapse in the seventh and eighth centuries have proved so difficult to counter: the evidence from these abandoned Roman towns would seem to support them. Medieval archaeologists, who fully acknowledge this problem of representative bias, have their own corpus of exceptional 'abandoned' sites in the spectacular but short-lived dynastic foundations of the ninth century and later. These are far less well known than the Roman special cases. Excavations have been extremely restricted and largely limited to the palatial sites of Aghlabid Raqqada (Chabbi 1967–1968), the Rustamid capitals of Tahart and Sedrata, and the later Fatimid foundations of Mahdia (Louhichi 1997) and Sabra al-Mansuriya (Cressier and Rammah 2006). We therefore know little about the most successful towns in the early Islamic period, and even less about the countryside where most people would have lived.

In short, the problem is not that we 'cannot' see the eighth century, but that we are not looking in the right places to do so. This is a methodological problem with a methodological solution. The critical evidence lies buried below modern cities: the major centres of early Islamic Africa like Kairouan, Tunis, Tripoli, Tlemcen and Fes have all been occupied continuously. Nonetheless, almost nothing is known about the history of these cities aside from the architecture of monumental buildings, predominantly the *ribats*, mosques and *kasbahs* dating to the ninth century or later. The Moroccan case, and particularly Volubilis, shows that it is possible to identify the eighth and early ninth century if we look for it in the places we might reasonably expect to find it, and use the appropriate tools (local ceramic chronologies, stratigraphic excavation, radiocarbon dating) to identify it.

Conclusion

To write a history of early Islamic North Africa, we must acknowledge that it is far less well served than other parts of the Islamic world. We possess almost no contemporary written sources for the region, and as a result, we are reliant upon sources that were compiled much later, often by outsiders, and are limited in scope and in detail. Islamic archaeology, still an emerging discipline, has not stepped in to fill the breach, so that the period between the late seventh and early ninth centuries often seems invisible. In this sense, early Islamic North Africa is indeed a 'dark age': a period obscured from our view by a lack of textual and archaeological sources. But its darkness is partially a problem of our own making and not so devastating that it should prevent the study of the early Islamic period. The challenge is to avoid replacing the partial tale told by the Arabic literary sources with an even more partial and problematic tale told from exceptional archaeological sites or from supposed silences. This book takes up that challenge. It is a risky and ambitious task that sometimes moves into the realm of speculation. My aim is to propose hypotheses and explanations that will allow the debate to move forward, rather than constructing a definitive history.

2

From Conquest to Muslim Rule

The Arab conquests in the seventh century brought North Africa into the orbit of the Muslim empire for the first time. At its greatest extent, in theory, the rule of the caliphate in Africa stretched from Atlantic Morocco to the Red Sea, and from the shores of the Mediterranean to the oases of the deep Sahara in the south. Understanding such an immense and ecologically varied region poses challenges to the modern archaeologist or historian, but it also presented significant challenges to its Muslim rulers. The new Muslim province encompassed – in theory – over five times the amount of territory of Byzantine Africa and twice that of Rome at its height. Both Mediterranean and Saharan, this immense region was inhabited by a range of different peoples, settled and mobile, some of whom had never been ruled by Rome or Byzantium. On scale alone, Byzantine Africa and the far bigger Muslim Africa are simply incommensurable. The caliphate could not rule Africa as the Romans, Vandals or Byzantines had before them: they had to connect regions and peoples that had never in their history been united under one power – and never would be again.

Surprisingly little has been written about how the first Islamic empire worked in North Africa (Djaït 1967, 1968, 1973). This uncertainty is not only at the level of scholarly discussion about the mechanisms of caliphal rule but extends to basic factual details about the chronology of the conquests. Were the conquests as catastrophic as traditionally imagined, unnoticed, or even welcomed? How was the early province ruled? How much did the incoming Muslims rely upon existing infrastructure, and how much did they import from elsewhere? Scholars have spent more time examining the first question than the second or third. This is, in part, a product of the enduring power of accounts of

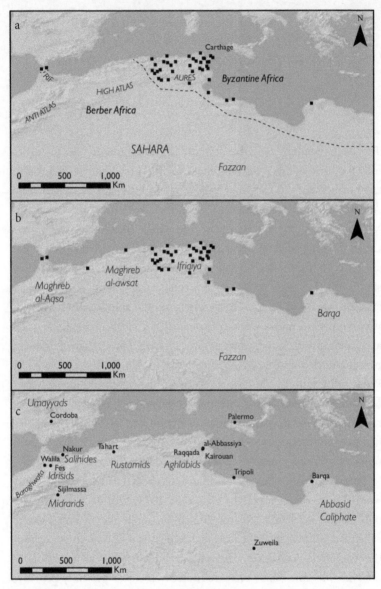

Fig. 2 Map showing North Africa (a) in the seventh century; (b) in the eighth century; (c) in the ninth century (Corisande Fenwick).

the early Islamic world that simultaneously exaggerated the destructive nature of the Muslim conquests whilst downplaying the complexity and strength of the early caliphate and the successor states. These seem to me to be inherently problematic historical perspectives; they also misrepresent what made Muslim rule in North Africa different from what came before under the Byzantines, as well as how North Africa was distinctive from the Islamic heartlands of the caliphate. Far more important as a difference between new and old was the attempt to rule both Byzantine and Berber Africa. This chapter offers a fresh examination of the Arab conquest and early Muslim rule in North Africa from the perspective of recent archaeological discoveries, and also provides a brief introduction to current research on the historical developments of the period.

Byzantine and Berber Africa on the eve of the conquests

When the Muslims entered Africa, they attempted a feat that no state had managed before or since: to rule both Byzantine and Berber Africa (Fig. 2a). On the eve of the conquests, Byzantine rule was limited to the North African coast and the fertile plains of the Tunisian Tell and Sahel, a shadow of Rome's former territories (Diehl 1896; Cameron 2000). The Mauretanias, pre-desert and Saharan regions were peopled by different groups, both settled and mobile. The Arabs called these peoples *al-barbar*, 'the Berbers', distinguishing them from the *Afariq*, the Latin-speaking town-dwellers in the Byzantine territories (Brett 1978: 509–11). These homogenizing labels disguise a great deal of variety, as we shall see, but it is clear that differences between 'Byzantine Africa' and 'Berber Africa' posed substantial challenges to the Umayyads and Abbasids.

Byzantine Africa was one of the most densely urbanized regions of the Mediterranean. It had a majority Christian population, a wealthy Romano-African elite, a public taxation system and a well-integrated road and port network (see Conant 2010). Unlike the Levant or Egypt, North Africa had fallen out of the empire for just under a century (*c.* 439–533), when it was ruled by the Vandal kingdom (Courtois 1955; Merrills and Miles 2010). The eastern Roman empire (known as Byzantium in the scholarly literature) wrested back control of Africa from Vandals in a remarkably short campaign in 533–4. The events of late antiquity affected Africa less than other Mediterranean regions. Archaeology has revealed that the towns and countryside continued to prosper in many regions but underwent significant changes in response to changing patterns of public euergetism and the decline of the classical municipal system (syntheses in Lepelley 1992; Leone and Mattingly 2004; Leone 2007). By the fifth or sixth century, the population had become largely Christian (with small but significant Jewish communities throughout), and there was a period of widespread church-building. Following the Byzantine conquest, many towns were fortified for the first time in their history with either walls or a fort in the sixth century (and to a lesser extent the seventh) (Pringle 1981).

Byzantine Africa's agricultural wealth had long underwritten the region's status as one of the biggest exporters in the Mediterranean. Scholars broadly agree that there was a significant drop in Mediterranean trade and maritime commerce of bulk staple goods (grain, oil and ceramics) during the seventh century (Hodges and Whitehouse 1983). The apparent lack of monumental building projects and the abandonment of many rural sites in the seventh century are further indicators of demographic and economic breakdown. The latest research on rural settlement patterns, numismatics and ceramics supports an image of a region in economic crisis before the first Arab raids and less embedded in Mediterranean networks, though still a significant producer and exporter of goods (Bonifay 2003; Morrisson 2016; Reynolds 2016).

The situation outside the small pocket of Byzantine Africa was very different. Some groups recognized the nominal authority of the Byzantines while others were in small rival 'Moorish' states, semi-autonomous polities that had emerged in late antiquity (Camps 1984; Modéran 2003). We know almost nothing about the form of these states or their rulers, apart from a few tantalizing hints. Some may have been based in Roman cities, such as Altava in western Algeria or Volubilis in Morocco, where funerary inscriptions attest to a Christian community of some kind. Their rulers made powerful statements through the construction of funerary monuments like the impressive *djedar*, monumental tombs in western Algeria, inscribed with Latin texts (Kadra 1983). Their wealth was derived from agriculture and trade, but also from livestock, slaving and raiding. Funerary evidence and linguistic material reveals a great deal of mobility and migration in late antiquity by Berber groups moving in and around the Maghreb (including into Byzantine territory) and the northern Sahara (Fentress and Wilson 2016; Merrills 2018). Limited as our knowledge is of these societies in late antiquity, it is evident that the Muslim governors would have had to deal with very different political structures and systems of rulership in the Far West.

Our archaeological knowledge of 'Berber Africa' is equally poor, and little systematic investigation of the Berber regions has taken place outside the Libyan Sahara. These regions were less densely settled than Byzantine Africa, and the economy was primarily based on subsistence farming and pastoralism. Mobile populations co-existed alongside small-scale settled communities practising oasis agriculture or hill-land farming and the occasional larger settlement such as that of Volubilis, reoccupied in the sixth century after a period of abandonment (Fentress and Limane 2018) but looking very different from the towns in Byzantine Africa that were filled with churches and fortresses. In the Sahara, some oases, such as those in the Libyan Fazzan associated with the Garamantes, were already highly developed by the early Roman period (Mattingly 2003), while the Moroccan oases may only have been brought into cultivation in late antiquity (Mattingly et al. 2017a). There were also religious differences: some groups certainly did practise Christianity and Judaism even though no churches have yet been found, but the majority continued to worship a multitude of gods – ancestor cults and the cult of the ram were extremely important in this region (Benhima 2011).

These crudely drawn regional distinctions between a 'Byzantine' and 'Berber' Africa need to be kept in mind, as they had implications for the reach and efficacy of Umayyad and Abbasid rule. We also need to keep in mind the substantial differences between Africa and the Byzantine regions of the Levant and Egypt that the Arabian armies had already conquered. In Africa, most of the population spoke and inscribed in Latin, not Greek as in Egypt and the Levant, and they looked towards the Papacy in Rome for religious authority rather than to Constantinople. In Africa, there were no Arabian auxiliary troops or mercenaries serving in the Byzantine army or settlements of Arabic-speaking communities in suburbs outside towns and in the countryside, as there were in the Levant in late antiquity (Hoyland 2002: 78–83, 236–42). The far western Maghreb would have seemed more foreign still: the people spoke a variety of Berber dialects (though some would have spoken and written Latin), it was not under Byzantine rule (except perhaps the ports of Ceuta and Tangier); there were very few large settlements, and it did not have a developed monetized economy or taxation system.

The conquests

The later literary sources provide a brief, but clear, outline of the main events in the conquest (Brett 1978; Benabbès 2004; Kaegi 2010; Manzano Moreno 2010). They are, however, often confused about chronology and place names, and must be treated with some caution. Muslim armies first entered Africa from Egypt in 642 on a raiding expedition against the coastal cities of Tripolitania and Cyrenaica and the Saharan oases of the Libyan Fazzan. The most significant of these was an expedition commanded by 'Abd Allah b. Abi Sarh in 647 which defeated the Byzantine army at Sbeïtla in central Tunisia and seized a huge amount of gold as well as thousands of slaves. Gregory, the renegade Byzantine exarch of Africa who had proclaimed himself emperor, was slain. Abi Sarh did not pursue his military advantage with the death of Gregory, but instead agreed to leave Africa in exchange for a huge sum of gold and an annual payment of 330,000 gold *solidi*.

Decades of intermittent raiding against the rich cities of Byzantine Tripolitania and central Tunisia followed. Raiding turned into an attempt to conquer when the Umayyads came to power. In 667–8, the caliph Mu'awiya entrusted the conquest of Ifriqiya to 'Uqba b. Nafi, who founded the *misr* of Kairouan before making his way to the Atlantic. 'Uqba's expedition did not result in victory: Carthage was never captured, and the new city of Kairouan was abandoned in the Umayyad civil war (the Second Fitna) of the 680s when the Arab soldiers retreated to their strongholds in Tripoli and Barca. Once the caliph 'Abd al-Malik had restored Umayyad authority in Syria, a final attempt was made to conquer Africa. The general Hasan b. al-Nu'man was sent with a huge army to Africa; once there, he made agreements with Berber groups and integrated them into his army. Sheer numbers won through in the end. In 697–8, he captured the Byzantine capital, Carthage, and Byzantine Africa became Islamic Ifriqiya.

In a few short years, armies of Arabian and Berber auxiliaries led by the new governor Musa b. Nusayr extended their control over the Berber peoples of the central and western Maghreb. The Berber groups apparently made their *islam*, or submission, as pagans rather than as Christians or Jews (Brett 1992). They converted to Islam and were supposed to pay the alms of believers: many of them were incorporated into Musa's army and participated in the conquest of 711 of al-Andalus, where some subsequently settled. The scale of conversion of Berber tribes and the numbers of Berber soldiers recruited into the conquest armies is unparalleled elsewhere in the Islamic world (Brett 1978: 509–13).

While it is beyond the scope of this book to discuss those North Africans who migrated to al-Andalus (Boone 2009; Manzano Moreno 2006), the important role that North African troops played in the conquests of Iberia is illustrated vividly in the mid-eighth-century Muslim cemetery at Plaza del Castillo (Pamplona, Spain). aDNA analyses revealed that just under two-thirds of the men were of North

African origin in comparison to less than a tenth of the women; a small-scale strontium isotopic study identified a north-eastern Moroccan signature (De Miguel Ibáñez et al. 2016; Prevedorou et al. 2010). Filed teeth of sub-Saharan tradition were identified in twelve individuals, including one female with local genetic markers. The many traumatic injuries in men as well as the frequency of fatal knife wounds show that they were accustomed to combat. This is an Islamized population of North African origin who arrived in the conquest phase, probably as part of the Umayyad army; some men were accompanied by family groups, while others married local females who themselves converted to Islam and assimilated to the cultural norms of this group. As yet, no similar studies of early medieval cemeteries have been conducted in North Africa, but aDNA, isotopic and bioarchaeological analyses offer great potential to assess migration and mobility in this period, and to identify the presence of Arabian and Eastern soldiers and immigrants.

With Byzantine power collapsing and the caliphate in ascendancy, it is small wonder that scholars have taken a particularly dim view of the second half of the seventh century. The lengthy and brutal conquest of North Africa over fifty years was once seen as catastrophic for civic life, urbanism and trade, but this perspective is as exaggerated for North Africa as it is in the Levant (Kennedy 1985; Pentz 1992; Magness 2003; Walmsley 2007; Avni 2014). Archaeology is not good at seeing short-term events, especially the battles, sieges and captures of towns so vividly described in the Byzantine accounts and the conquest chronicles written centuries later (Benabbès 2004; Kaegi 2010). All the same, it is often tempting to associate archaeological layers with historical events, rather than rely upon the evidence of pottery, glass and coins from stratigraphic sequences.

And yet, some tantalizing insights into the conquest phase are visible in the evidence. At the coastal site of Tocra in Cyrenaica (Fig. 3), it seems that in response to the earliest Arab raids, the Byzantines hastily erected a large intra-mural fortress near the eastern gate, probably in 642, to strengthen Tocra's military capabilities (Goodchild 1967: 120–2). In the sixth century, under Justinian, the Hellenistic city

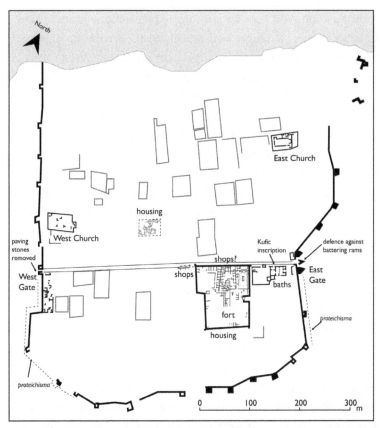

Fig. 3 Plan of Tocra, Libya (adapted from Smith and Crow 1988, with additions from Buzaian 2000).

walls had been remodelled and strengthened; the new fort was constructed in a different technique, and without foundations, using material taken from surrounding buildings, especially the nearby baths, which were reduced and partly demolished to produce a clear line of fire. Perhaps at the same time, the city walls were strengthened by a ditch and outer wall (*proteichisma*) which surrounds much of the most vulnerable parts of the Justinianic curtain wall; this type of double defence is unparalleled at any other North African site and was used to protect cities from siege (Smith and Crow 1998: 67–9). There is evidence at the East and West Gate for last-minute preparations against assault: at the East Gate, a V-shaped structure blocks the *decumanus* to protect the gate from ramming and bombardment; while at the West Gate, the paving stones were lifted from the *decumanus*, making the road impassable (Smith and Crow 1998: 65). The dating of these extra defensive measures is uncertain, but it is tempting to associate them with the description in the Chronicle of John of Nikiu of a Byzantine retreat to Tocra and the strengthening of its fortifications in 642 (Goodchild 1967: 117).

Tocra was captured in 644–5, but it was not destroyed or abandoned at this point. The only possible trace of its capture identified to date is heavy burning on the doors of the fortress; the fortress continued to be occupied, presumably now by a garrison of Arab troops. A second phase of occupation consists of roughly constructed buildings centred on two courtyards, and a bath complex which probably post-dates the Arab capture of the city (Fenwick 2013; Jones 1983). Outside the fortress, life continued much as before. In the centre of the city, excavations have revealed winding streets and alleys that led into houses organized around courtyards occupied between the sixth and eighth centuries, and perhaps later (Buzaian 2000). The houses are relatively humble, built of roughly coursed rubble and mud-brick walls with beaten earth floors, and were used for a mixture of domestic and artisanal activities. Medieval housing was built up against the southern façade of the fortress, as well as a series of later shops that encroached onto the *decumanus* (Jones 1985). The much-reduced bath complex continued to be used, as attested by a Kufic inscription praising Allah on the main doorstep into the atrium (Jones 1984: 111). Tocra, then, is a city where, although there are signs of defensive measures taken to protect it against the Arabs, there is no evidence in the archaeological record for a sudden or violent end to the city.

Carthage, the Byzantine capital of Africa, presents a different picture. The largest city in North Africa, it was protected by the substantial Theodosian wall and could be provisioned by sea in its protected harbour even when under attack. The Umayyad general Hasan b.

al-Nuʿman finally captured the city in 697–8 when he cut the aqueduct and water supply. Carthage's capture had immense symbolic weight, and its second fall, like its first to the Romans, became a *topos* for the collapse of great civilizations in Arabic literature. According to later Arabic sources, its Byzantine inhabitants abandoned Carthage by ship: the city was sacked, its walls destroyed, and its harbour filled in. Ibn ʿIdhari, for example, states that Hasan b. al-Nuʿman 'had Carthage destroyed and dismantled, so that every trace was effaced' (1983 I: 35). Whilst rhetorical exaggeration colours this description of complete abandonment, Carthage is one of the few cases where archaeological evidence seems to match neatly with the written accounts. Destruction or abandonment deposits dating to the late seventh century have been found in various parts of the city, though not everywhere (Fenwick 2019; Stevens 2016). Churches seem to have been particularly affected: the church of Bir el-Knissia was destroyed by fire, and a thick burn layer was found covering the mosaics of the church and its annex (Delattre 1922: 303). Fire also destroyed the north and south transepts of the basilica of Bir Messaouda, and there is a substantial collapse layer elsewhere (Miles 2006). The large martyrial church of Bir Ftouah was also razed between the seventh and ninth century, and quarried for its materials (Stevens et al. 2005). The stones and building material from Carthage were used to build Tunis, and its capitals and columns probably to decorate Great Mosque at Kairouan, a highly symbolic gesture. Carthage did survive (see Chapter 3), but it never regained its former glory or urban splendour.

With the exception of Carthage and perhaps Thuni (later to become Tunis), which were stormed and sacked, almost all of the major towns of Byzantine Africa seem either to have been left undamaged or recovered swiftly. Excavations have found few traces of fire, building collapse or sudden abandonment that can be securely dated to the late seventh century (Fenwick 2019). Of course, the absence of destruction layers reflecting physical events such as fire, demolition or abandonment in much of Tunisia and Libya does not mean that the long conquest phase was not disruptive. As we will see in Chapters 3 and 5, life in towns changed significantly, and there is an increasing regionalization and disruption of long-held commercial networks in the late seventh and eighth centuries that must be in part related to the insecurity of North Africa from the 660s onwards.

Another way to gauge insecurity is by looking at patterns in depositions of coin hoards. The traditional interpretation is that people buried items of worth in response to an external threat of invasion or civil unrest but failed to return later to recover them. It is notoriously difficult to link hoards to particular military events, but a compelling case has been made for the Rougga (anc. Bararus) hoard. Inside a simple house of the Byzantine period in the forum, excavations uncovered a hiding place in the floor that contained a small jug sealed with a ceramic bung and plastered over (Guéry et al. 1982: 12–15, fig. 5). The coins were issued between 592 and 646–7: the terminal date neatly coincides with the first Arab raid into Tunisia in 647. The cache of coins was never retrieved by its owner, but Rougga was not completely abandoned. There is no evidence to suggest that these houses were razed or burned; the area continued to be used for housing with a very similar material assemblage before being given over to a cemetery, and then to artisanal occupation in the tenth to eleventh centuries (Guéry 1981, 1985).

Nonetheless, there is no notable surge in hoarding in Tunisia during the conquest phase: only three of the seventeen known Byzantine hoards of gold coins seem to post-date 642 (see Guéry et al. 1982: 78). The coinage evidence, however, reveals the pressure that Arab raiding placed on the Byzantine empire, and the major financial investment the state made into securing Africa and its food supply in the seventh century. Large numbers of dies for gold coins from Carthage were issued in the early years of Constans II, presumably to pay expenses related to the military defence of the province against Arab raids in the 640s; a similar peak occurs in the mid to late 670s following the foundation of Kairouan and the settlement of Arabs in Byzacena (Morrisson 2016: 189, figs. 9.11 and 9.12). Coins may also have been needed to purchase grain and other foodstuffs from Africa to provision Constantinople after the loss of Alexandria in 642, as is suggested by the seal evidence (Morrisson and Seibt 1982: 293–4). The composition of the Rougga hoard is of special interest in this regard: over 75 per cent of the coins were minted in Constantinople and the rest in Carthage (Guéry et al. 1982). The high proportion of Constantinopolitan coins is exceptional in Africa, where both hoards and stray finds are dominated by local Carthaginian issues. It may be an official payment, or the savings of a local landowner who was paid for providing wheat or other foodstuffs (Morrisson 2016: 194). Despite increasingly harsh Byzantine taxation and the constant threat of Arab raids, this may have been a time of great profit for the largest landowners.

Ruling Africa: The new provincial landscape

If the conquest was not as catastrophic as traditionally thought, within a century or so, the provincial landscape of North Africa had been transformed in ways that had long-term implications for subsequent state-building attempts. Governed from Egypt initially, Ifriqiya was made a separate *wilaya* (province) with its own *wali* (governor) in around 705. The new *wilaya* was divided into Ifriqiya proper (the old Byzantine provinces of Proconsularis and Byzacena), Tripolitania, the Zab (Numsidia), Near Sus and Far Sus. These regions were governed by *'amil* (sub-governors), and further subdivided into districts (*kura*) and cantons (*rustak*), each with their own commander (Djaït 1967, 1968). These regional divisions reveal the limitations of Umayyad control outside the limits of Byzantine control: Ifriqiya was subdivided into many *kura*, each with their own capital, but Near and Far Sus had only district capitals which probably served as bases for slaving expeditions: Tangier and the as-yet unlocated Tarqala (Fig. 2b).

From the outset, the caliphate invested in ensuring a functioning economic system. Taxation and an Islamic monetary system was imposed immediately. North Africa's conquest was completed several years after the caliph 'Abd al-Malik's reform of the currency system in the 690s which introduced a tri-metallic system in three denominations: the gold *dinar*, silver *dirham* and copper *fals*. The new coins were completely different from Byzantine and Sasanian coins in decoration: there were no images of the ruler or religious iconography, only words inscribed in Kufic Arabic. The *shahada* (profession of faith) was included, alongside Quranic verses, the place and date of minting. Although North Africa was conquered after these coinage reforms, the coins minted in Ifriqiya do not follow the same norms as the rest of the empire for several decades (Bates 1995; Jonson 2014). Coins were minted as soon as Carthage was captured in 697–8, presumably to pay the army still on campaign. The first gold *dinars* were minted with the same globular fabric and weight standards as the African Byzantine *solidus*. They also shared the same imagery and were decorated with imperial busts, though the Christian cross on the reverse was usually modified by removing its horizontal bar. Latin translations of the *shahada*, the Muslim profession of faith, start to appear on coins from 707 (a phenomenon unparalleled elsewhere in the Islamic world); the Byzantine dating system was used until 713; bilingual Arabic–Latin inscriptions appear in 716, when images also disappear and silver *dirhams* are minted for the first time, suggesting a shift to the tri-metallic system. In 718–19, Latin inscriptions and dates were finally replaced by Arabic but, as in al-Andalus, the diameter, weight, gold content and legends continued to be slightly different to *dinars* minted elsewhere in the caliphate. North African coinage only became uniform with the currency elsewhere in the empire in 732–3, thirty-seven years after 'Abd al-Malik's coinage reforms (Jonson 2014: 415).

Alongside these changes, it seems likely that within a few decades of the Arab conquests, only Arab coins were legal tender. Only one mixed hoard has been published (Morrisson 1980: 155–6). The hoard is dated to the early eighth century and consists largely of *solidi* of Constantine IV (668–85), as well as two early Arab-Byzantine issues (704–14). The mixture of coins suggests that Byzantine coins continued to circulate in large quantities immediately after the Arab conquest, but the absence of other mixed hoards suggests that Byzantine coins were quickly replaced by the new coins. Byzantine coins were presumably melted down or simply re-struck, as in the example of an early Umayyad copper *fals* from Tocra struck over a Byzantine coin (Buzaian 2000: 95). This pattern occurs earlier in the Levant following the reforms of ʿAbd al-Malik where it seems that the caliphate swiftly instituted and effected a total re-coinage of Byzantine coins, replacing them with their own currency and weight system (Heidemann 1998: 96–7). The slow transformation of the North African coinage reflects the difficulties of imposing new administrative systems in a newly conquered province, but it also reveals the importance that the Umayyad rulers and their governors placed on ensuring a functioning economy and marketplace.

Trade was also quickly standardized according to Arab weight systems. Early glass weights and seals have also been found at several sites (though rarely published or provenanced) (Viré 1956). Many of the weights were used for coinage: it was particularly important to ensure that gold and silver coins had not been shaved or otherwise modified in value, and many of the glass weights include their equivalent weights in specific denominations. Other weights were used to measure grains, olive oil, wine and other goods. One of the earliest securely dated weights is a 20 *ukiya* (ounce) disc with a hole in its centre stamped by ʿAbd al-Rahman (described as *amir*), given to one Masal b. Hammad, the provincial governor (*wali*) of Mila in 745–6 and found near Tébessa (Marçais and Lévi-Provencal 1937). This weight would have been used to measure grain, olive oil or other produce, and shows that commerce was co-ordinated at a provincial level by the amir in Kairouan.

One of the hallmarks of early Muslim expansion was the foundation of new garrison cities, the so-called *miṣr* (pl. *amsar*). These new towns were built to house the soldiers and their families away from local populations and where they could be controlled and paid by the state (Akbar 1989). The sustained attempt to conquer Africa in 670 was marked by the construction of a *miṣr* in the lower Tunisian steppe by the Muslim general ʿUqba b. Nafi (al-Bakri 1913: 84). This new town was fittingly called Kairouan (*al-Qayrawan*, a word of Persian origin meaning 'the camp'). The reasons for locating a new base here were strategic. The site lies in a rich alluvial plain crossed by two of the great *wadis* of Central Tunisia (the Zroud and Merguellil) which feed two large salt lakes (Sidi el-Hani and el-Kelbia) on whose marshes the soldiers' animals could be pastured. Kairouan's location in the lower Tunisian steppe allowed the Umayyads to control the road network between Carthage and south-west Tunisia, as well as the passes to the interior of North Africa, whilst remaining a safe distance from the coast and the threat of the Byzantine fleet. Some thirty years later, after the Byzantine capital of Carthage had finally been captured and sacked in 697–8, a second city, Tunis, was built to be the main harbour and district capital in the north and rapidly became the main launching-pad for Muslim maritime expeditions in the western Mediterranean (Lézine 1971).

The downfall of Carthage is the only example of a provincial capital being abandoned anywhere in the caliphate. For the most part, the Umayyad authorities found the existing administrative and military network adequate for their needs. The old, large Byzantine cities formed the backbone of the provincial and military administration under the Umayyads, Abbasids and their successors, the Aghlabids. The new district capitals had all been military centres in the Byzantine period, including Béja (Vaga) in northern Tunisia, Sousse (Hadrumetum) on the Sahel coast, Gafsa (Capsa) in the pre-desert, Tobna (Thubunae) in the Zab, and Tanja (Tingis) in the far West (Djaït 1973).

Ifriqiya was one of the most densely militarized regions of the caliphate (Fenwick forthcoming a). According to the fourteenth-century historian Ibn 'Idhari, a generally reliable source, the numbers of soldiers were small in the seventh and early eighth centuries, perhaps 50,000 men from different tribes on the Arabian peninsula who had first served in Egypt (Talbi 1966: 21–2). Those who settled in Africa became a small hereditary ruling class composed primarily of the conquerors and their descendants, with very few outsiders (Sato 2007). Land grants were given to some of these soldiers, creating a landed Arab aristocracy with extensive estates, cultivated in some cases by slaves from sub-Saharan Africa (Talbi 1981). Berber soldiers served alongside the Arab soldiers who came and garrisoned the new province, but tensions rapidly arose over how Arabs and Berbers were paid and treated in the army, the continued enslavement of Muslim Berber populations, as well as the oppressive fiscal policies of certain governors against the local populations, even those who had converted to Islam (Fenwick forthcoming b).

Tensions came to a head in 739–40 when the so-called Kharajite revolt broke out in western Morocco and rapidly spread across North Africa and al-Andalus. Large expeditionary forces were sent from Syria to North Africa to deal with the situation, few of whom returned. In the disorder that followed the Kharajite revolt and the slaughter of most of the Arab aristocracy, an Ifriqiyan Arab settler, ʿAbd al-Rahman b. Habib al-Fihri, the great grandson of ʿUqba b. Nafi, seized control. The new Abbasid caliph al-Mansur (r. 754–75) sent a huge army to recover Ifriqiya for the caliphate, but it was now a significantly reduced province confined to Tunisia and eastern Algeria, much the same as Vandal and Byzantine Africa. The Abbasids recaptured Ifriqiya in 761–2 and imported vast numbers of new troops, primarily from Iraq and Iran. By the late eighth century, almost a third of the Abbasid army was concentrated in North Africa (Kennedy 2017). This army, now known as the *jund*, was divided into local garrisons and spread across the towns of Ifriqiya, often replacing earlier Umayyad garrisons (Djait 1973: 111).

The militarization of the North African landscape is a distinctive feature of caliphal rule in Ifriqiya which left a material imprint (Fenwick forthcoming a). The majority of the army would have been housed at Kairouan and Tunis, but unlike other regions of the caliphate, most of the major towns also received a Muslim garrison (of Arab or, less frequently, Berber origin) in the caliphal period (Cambuzat 1982). Long term, the presence of a Muslim garrison seems to have acted as a driver for economic demand and urban growth, but initially at least, they created a sharply divided landscape that separated conqueror from conquered. Garrisons took over the Byzantine forts that most of the towns already possessed at their centres, rather than building anew. Few of these have been excavated, but mosques or prayer rooms have been identified in multiple forts and citadels, including Haïdra, Ain Tuburnuc, Bagaï, Tobna, Laribus, Bordj Hallal and Tigisis, some of which may date to the eighth century (Fenwick 2013: 26). After the recapture of Africa, the Abbasids invested heavily in strengthening the defences at the biggest towns, and towards the end of the eighth century, a new style of fortification – the *ribat* – began to be built along the Tunisian coastline to protect coastal towns and villages from marauding Byzantine fleets in the Mediterranean (Djelloul 1995; Hassen 2001).

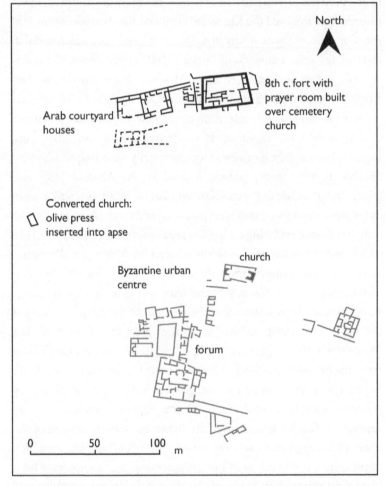

Fig. 4 Plan of Belalis Maior (Henchir el-Fouar), Tunisia (adapted from Mahjoubi 1978, pl. 1 and Google Earth imagery (26 August 2011).

At other towns, new quarters were added outside the walls or in the suburbs to house new communities of soldiers and their families as well as immigrants from the East, as at Volubilis, Pomaria-Agadir and Tangier (Fenwick 2013). Again, few of these extra-mural settlements have been excavated, but many of them contained small mosques and were often laid out on orthogonal plans containing small house plots. A particularly striking feature is the introduction of a new type of courtyard house plan which is not known in North Africa before the Muslim conquests. This segregationist model of Arab-Muslim settlement was already established in the Middle East at sites such as Amman and Ayla (Whitcomb 2007) and seems to be widespread in North Africa.

One such example comes from the small town of Belalis Maior (Henchir el-Faouar) in the Medjerda valley (Fig. 4), ten kilometres east of Béja, the northern district capital which housed garrisons of Arabian and Iranian troops in our period (Bahri 1999: 1–5). Ground-breaking excavations by Ammar Mahjoubi in the 1960s showed that this small town was still thriving in late antiquity, with three small churches and two bath complexes (Mahjoubi 1978). At the end of the sixth or seventh century, the paving of the forum and streets became covered by about 1.3 metres of spoil, which he argues relates to massive destructions across the site. We cannot know whether this is related to the intense fighting between Muslim and Byzantine forces outside nearby Béja in the late seventh century, but it is tempting to connect them.

This small town was prosperous enough to recover after destruction events hit the forum area and some of the churches. A new quarter was established on the edge of the existing town together with a fort and prayer room, presumably to house the new Muslim community of soldiers and their families. The fort was erected on the northern edge of the town over the razed foundations of Christian funerary basilica. This fort is dated tentatively (and controversially) to the late eighth century based on a single coin. It is a simple trapezoidal structure (27.20 x 38.80 m) built of re-used stone with a single protruding entrance on the south side (a simpler version of the *ribat* at Sousse). Inside, a series of rooms were set around a large court; one in the south-east of the fort has a niche interpreted as the *mihrab* of a prayer room. To the west of the fort are at least three courtyard houses with a right-angled entrance leading to a large central courtyard off which modular rooms opened. Elizabeth Fentress has suggested that this type of courtyard plan is Arab in origin, on the basis of its similarity with sixth-century Arab housing from Umm el-Jimal in Jordan (Fentress 2013). A further row of houses to the south of a street is visible on satellite imagery, and perhaps we can see these houses and fort, built on the northern edge of the town, as a new Muslim suburb.

The successor states

The rule of the caliphate lasted barely a hundred years in North Africa. In the wake of the Kharijite revolts, new embryonic Muslim states emerged in the western Maghreb uplands of the Aurés, the pre-desert and the Sahara, and above all in western Morocco (Fig. 2c): the Salihides of Nakur (710), the Barghawata (744), the Rustamids of Tahart (776), the Idrisids of Walila and Fes (788) and the Midrarids of Sijilmasa (758). The forms of these states varied depending on local circumstances. Sometimes, as with the Idrisids of central Morocco or the Rustamids at Tahart (western Algeria), incomers from the Islamic East were involved in these nascent processes of state formation (Aillet 2011). Other cases were very much local initiatives, such as the Barghawata, a group of Berber tribes who established themselves on the Moroccan Atlantic coast and followed their own variant of Islam, producing even a Berber Qur'an (Talbi 1973).

Finally, in 800, even Ifriqiya proper was lost to the caliphate when the Abbasid caliph Harun al-Rashid appointed Ibrahim al-Aghlab, son of an Iranian Arab commander, as hereditary emir of Ifriqiya (see Talbi 1966; Anderson, Fenwick and Rosser-Owen 2017). Ibrahim and his successors quelled the rebellious *jund* and Berber tribesmen and established what was to be the first independent state within the

Abbasid caliphate. Although they continued to acknowledge the sovereignty of Baghdad, they were independent in all but name: they minted gold *dinars*, appointed their own officials and built new palatial towns outside Kairouan to house themselves and their court: al-'Abbasiyya (founded in 800) and Raqqada (founded in 876). Aghlabid rule was not confined to Ifriqiya, but extended across the Mediterranean to parts of Sicily, the Italian mainland, Malta, Sardinia and Corsica (Nef 2017). This was a period of migration and mobility as well as of continued conflict with Byzantium, and North Africans settled in the towns and rural areas of Sicily (Metcalfe 2002: 289–90; Molinari forthcoming).

The end of caliphal rule did not mean the end for North Africa. The long ninth century was famously described as a golden age or renaissance (Marçais 1946a: 55), for it is in this period that archaeologists are able to 'see' again. As we shall see in the following chapters, the cities and countryside were transformed by the construction of new forms of monumental architecture as well as by urban growth, a surge in rural settlement, and investment in infrastructure. Ifriqiya was renowned for its agricultural productivity, raw resources (gold, salt, precious metals) and artisanship. High-prestige items such as ornate glazed ceramics, metalwork and textiles circulated, and trade and commercial networks flourished linking North Africa to sub-Saharan Africa, Europe and Iraq. In the western Maghreb, the establishment of the new Muslim successor states was accompanied by a packet of changes – urbanization, widespread sedentarization, a rise in trade links, the introduction of new types of goods and wares, new forms of social hierarchy and rulership – that were radically different from what had come before.

Cities

Islamic North Africa was a world of cities; this is the image given by Muslim geographers and historians writing several centuries after the conquest. The Egyptian historian Ibn 'Abd al-Hakam (1942) describes the Muslim conquest of Africa through a long list of rich towns falling, often rebelling and having to be recaptured, but rarely being destroyed. His contemporary, the geographer al-Ya'qubi (1892), visited North Africa for himself in the ninth century where he found a world of prosperous cities, towns and villages, a landscape that for those familiar with the classical world seems very like that of early Roman Africa. As we saw in Chapter 1, many classical archaeologists have argued that a rapid dissolution in urban life commenced in most regions by the late sixth century and intensified in the seventh century, resulting in the complete or partial abandonment of many towns, and the fragmentation or 'ruralization' of others into small, scattered zones of habitation within the ruins of the classical towns.

These different visions of the city in North Africa are not simply products of written versus archaeological evidence, patchy as both are. The divisions between late antique and medieval archaeologists outlined in Chapter 1 have adversely affected our understanding of the seventh- and eight-century city which falls between the two disciplines. Late antique archaeologists have naturally been more interested in 'The Fate of the Roman city' and the transformation of classical monuments and public spaces into their medieval form, particularly in a handful of very well-known but atypical towns in Tunisia and Libya that failed during the middle ages (Thébert and Biget 1990; Pentz 2002; Leone 2007; Panzram and Callagarin 2018). This focus on a small number of failed Roman towns explains why the problematic 'dark age' narrative has proved so difficult to shift in North Africa. Medieval archaeologists have rather focused on the 'Origins of the Islamic city' and the spread of new architectural forms such as mosques, *ribats* and town walls, though attention has focused on an even smaller number of new medieval urban foundations (e.g., Boone et al. 1990; Cressier 1992, 2013, 2018). Almost nothing is known archaeologically about the majority of early medieval towns in North Africa, many of which remain occupied until today.

Debate continues upon how one interprets the evidence from several well-excavated towns in Tunisia and Libya that flourished in the Roman period and were abandoned in the middle ages, and whether these sites should be regarded as exceptional or typical (Gelichi and Milanese 2002; Fenwick 2013; von Rummel 2016; Baratte 2018). I proposed that we tackle this methodological problem explicitly by taking a holistic approach that considers both old and new towns in the medieval period, by integrating urban successes and failures in the same narrative (Fenwick 2018, 2019). This chapter first discusses broader trends in urbanization across North Africa before briefly considering a handful of cases of North African cities, new and old, from which to derive a clearer image of the different possible urban trajectories in this vast region.

Urban dynamics across North Africa

One of the greatest challenges for archaeologists is how to understand urban change at the regional scale. Few have ventured to take on the task of examining cities or urbanization for medieval Africa (Khelifa 2004; Cambuzat 1982; Fenwick 2013). Mapping urban success and failure at a regional level reveals some significant patterns which I summarize here (Fig 1; Fenwick 2019). From the start, the Umayyad caliphate made interventions into the urban network. During the conquest era, around 670, the general 'Uqba b. Nafi established a settlement at Kairouan in central Tunisia as the base of his operations. Kairouan served as the provincial capital even after the capture of Carthage in 697–8, and remained the capital of North Africa for over a millennium. In the north, Tunis was built on the ruins of Thuni, near Carthage, in *c.* 705 to take on the role of district capital of northern Tunisia and to serve as the main port for the Muslim navy. Kairouan and Tunis became the most important medieval centres in Ifriqiya, but the old, large Byzantine cities formed the backbone of the urban network (Djaït 1973).

With few exceptions, all the largest administrative centres of the Roman period continued to be major centres in the early Islamic period (Fenwick 2019). Towns that continued share some characteristics: they had usually obtained the juridical status of *municipium* or *colonia* and in late antiquity became bishoprics. They are situated in strategic places on inland and coastal routes and had usually been fortified by town walls or intra-mural fortifications in the Byzantine period that were restored or rebuilt in the eighth and ninth centuries. As we saw in Chapter 2, most of these towns received a Muslim garrison (of Arab or, less frequently, Berber origin) in the caliphal period (Cambuzat 1982). The presence of a Muslim garrison seems to have driven economic demand and urban growth (Fenwick forthcoming a).

It would be foolhardy, however, to ignore the abandonment or retrenchment of many towns in this period. The marked drop in numbers of towns between the Roman and medieval period is a commonplace of the scholarly literature, and understandably so. If we compare towns in late antique Africa with those of ninth-century Ifriqiya, (Fig. 5), there is a significant reduction, especially in numbers of smaller towns which were abandoned far more frequently than large towns (Fenwick 2013). The densely urbanized Tunisian Tell was particularly affected: many of its small towns were abandoned or greatly reduced between the seventh and ninth centuries. Excavations at the sites of Uchi Maius, Musti, Althiburos and Chemtou found abandonment layers between late antique and medieval occupation of the ninth or tenth century (Gelichi and Milanese 2002; Kallala et al. 2011; Touihri 2014; von Rummel 2016). Whilst our archaeological knowledge of these sites is patchy, by the ninth or tenth century, these settlements were little more than fortified agricultural villages with no urban pretensions. In

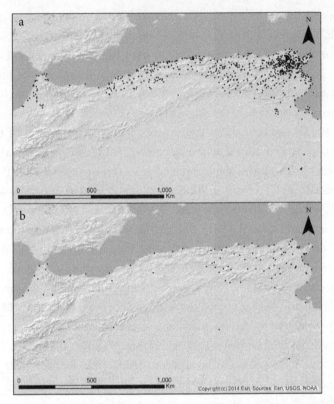

Fig. 5 Urban settlement distribution in (a) Roman and late antique North Africa and (b) early medieval North Africa (Corisande Fenwick).

southern Tunisia (anc. Byzacena) and eastern Algeria (anc. Numidia), small towns also disappear on the coast but large, fortified, urban sites on major routes and ports, such as Sousse, Sfax, Tobna and Biskra, continued to thrive. Further to the east, in Tripolitania and Cyrenaica, a similar picture emerges (King 1989). In antiquity, urban settlement was limited to a few good anchorages along the treacherous Libyan coast, and in the early middle ages there is no evidence for urban abandonment, although some cities such as Lepcis Magna diminish in size (Cirelli 2001). By the ninth century, the urban network in Ifriqiya had transformed from the dense post-Roman landscape of small and large towns to a sparsely urbanized landscape of large towns. These large towns benefited from the presence of soldiers, administrators and traders, and many towns show signs of growth and renewed investment which we can often see archaeologically from the mid-ninth century, though it is perhaps in the tenth and eleventh centuries that these towns seem to see the greatest period of growth.

Identifying when and why so many towns failed in Ifriqiya is difficult, and we must be wary of equating urban collapse with the Arab conquest. Some very famous cities were already severely depopulated in late antiquity. The huge port city of Utica, the first city to be founded by the Phoenicians in North Africa, was abandoned by the fifth century in response to the silting up of the harbour and a major earthquake (Chelbi et al. 1995). The coastal cities of Meninx and Cherchel seem to have faltered in the sixth century and been reduced to little more than villages (Fentress et al. 2009; Potter 1995). These are extreme examples, but my point is simple: some very large towns (and ones that archaeologists know very well) had already disappeared decades, if not centuries, before the first Arab raids.

In the central and western Maghreb, a very different pattern emerges. Between the late eighth and the eleventh centuries, many new cities and towns were founded in the fertile plains of Morocco and in the Saharan oases. This is a period of urban expansion, not retrenchment. Following the Arab conquest, garrisons seem to have been established at some of the few existing towns in the West, including Tangier (Tanja), Tlemcen (Pomaria) and probably Sebta (Ceuta), but not elsewhere. In the first two cases, new quarters were established outside the existing towns, and this may also be the case at Volubilis. Rather more common was the foundation of new urban centres in the ninth and tenth centuries: some of these were dynastic capitals that would have housed the rulers of the newly formed states, such as Tahart, founded by the Rustamids, or Fes, founded by the Idrisids. But the phenomenon was not restricted to capitals: in the most detailed survey of its kind, Patrice Cressier (1998) showed that between the ninth and eleventh centuries small new urban settlements were established in the fertile alluvial valleys of the Rif mountains, usually at important Berber markets or boundary points between different tribes. Urbanization was therefore not a top-down state-driven process but one in which local populations were involved.

Kairouan, Tunis and the new Muslim city

The city of Kairouan was founded by ʿUqba b. Nafiʿ in 670 as a *misr* (pl. *amsar*), a place to house the Arab-Muslim troops and their families away from the local conquered populations. It was where salaries were paid, in cash, to soldiers, courtiers and other government employees, and as such had a central economic importance (Kennedy 2002). Kairouan follows the model of *amsar* established several decades earlier at Basra (636), Kufa (637–8) and Fustat (641) during the conquests of Iraq and Egypt, where the founder was responsible for building a mosque, a governor's palace and assigning plots of lands to different tribal groups (Akbar 1989; Bacharach 1991; Kennedy 2010; Whitcomb 2007). The foundation of a city in a conquered territory is a symbolic act of imperial possession and mastering of the landscape; it is also a blank canvas to present imperial ideas of urbanism, society and civilization. According to one tradition, ʿUqba laid the foundations of Kairouan in a deserted wilderness covered in dense vegetation and frequented by reptiles and savage animals, while other traditions suggest that the camp was built on, or on the outskirts of, an existing town (probably that of Iubaltianae) (Mʿcharek 1999). Some textual traditions suggest that the town was only a camp of huts and tents at the start, while others state that ʿUqba built a mosque and a governmental residence (*dar al-imara*) and settled Arab troops in the different quarters of the city (Sakly 2000; Mahfoudh 2003).

Despite the political uncertainty of the caliphal period, Kairouan rapidly grew into a significant city. A substantial building programme took place under Hisham (r. 723–742) when the mosque was expanded because it was too small for the growing city. A *suq* was built and roofed on a long street along the west face of the Grand Mosque; like those built in Syria-Palestine, the street was probably colonnaded (Mahfoudh 2003: 75). Hisham is also credited with building fifteen reservoirs for the provision of water, one of which still survives today (the al-Dahmani basin). Here, we see clearly the role of the state in urban foundation: Kairouan was provided with a working infrastructure, including markets, a water supply and a congregational mosque of sufficient size for the believers. These building works in North Africa were part of a broader imperial building programme under Hisham that has not been sufficiently acknowledged by scholars: his reign also saw substantial investment in market and mosque construction in Syria-Palestine and beyond.

Immediately after the Abbasids reconquered North Africa in 761–2, the new governor built defensive walls in *pisé*. This was certainly for defence, but it may also be, as Mahfoudh (2003) has suggested, a symbol of caliphal authority. In 771, the Muhallabid governor Yazid b. Hatim demolished all but the *mihrab* of ʿUqbaʾs mosque and rebuilt it. At the same time, he reorganized the principle *suqs* and regulated the transactions taking place within. By the end of the caliphal period, Kairouan possessed a Great Mosque alongside dozens, if not hundreds, of smaller public and private mosques, a *dar al-ʿimara*, or governor's residence, several distinct cemeteries and *suqs* organized by the two main neighbourhoods of the Quraysh, the Meccan tribe of the Prophet, and the Ansar, the families of the Medinan tradesmen who supported the Prophet (Sakly 2000).

Most of what we know about the urban fabric of medieval Kairouan dates to the ninth century, when the Aghlabid emirs conducted a substantial building programme (Mahfoudh 2003). The Grand Mosque was demolished and rebuilt by Ziyadat Allah I in 836 on the same plan as the first mosque, keeping the original orientation of the *qibla* (141 degrees to the south). It was later enlarged and renovated in 862–3 by Ibrahim II, and today survives more or less in its ninth-century form of a large colonnaded prayer hall, courtyard and square minaret (Fig. 15a). Ibrahim II also built the immense cisterns, the 'Aghlabid Basins', on the outskirts of the town between 856 and 857 for the vast sum of

300,000 *dinars* (Solignac 1953): these were built as water reserves and to prevent flooding from the *sebkha* and surrounding *wadis* (Mahfoudh 2003: 286–8). Private monumental building also occurred in this period: the Mosque of the Three Doors was built by an Andalusi immigrant in 866 (Golvin 1970: 190–1). The Aghlabid rulers also founded palace-cities outside Kairouan (on which, see more below), first al-Abbasiyya in 800 in recognition of Abbasid sovereignty (Marçais 1925), and then Raqqada in 876 (Chabbi 1967–1968). By the ninth century, this newly founded city had become the biggest artisanal centre of Africa, renowned for its glazed green and brown ceramics on a yellow background, its large *suqs* and diverse population of Arabs, Persians, Berbers, Africans, Byzantines and Jews.

Around thirty years after the foundation of Kairouan, a second city, Tunis, was founded on the north-eastern coast to replace Carthage. It was not a *misr*, but it was built as a Muslim city. According to the sources, in 699, Hasan b. al-Nuʿman founded the new city and arsenal at the base of the lagoon, on the outskirts of Roman Thunes, a minor town and bishopric. As well as building or dredging a canal between the sea and lagoon, he imported Coptic labourers from Egypt to build an arsenal and ships for a new naval fleet (Lézine 1971: 141–54). Of the city itself little is known, though it seems Tunis was also transformed under Hisham; its mosque was expanded into a cathedral mosque, the shipyard was enlarged and new docks constructed. Further investment took place under the Aghlabid emirs when the Zaytuna mosque was re-built on a monumental scale in 864.

Kairouan and Tunis represent huge investments of labour, materials, money and time which no other North African city received under the caliphate. Their size remains unclear – wildly divergent figures from 14,000 to 300,000 inhabitants for the ninth century are suggested for Kairouan (Sakly 2000: 61) – but they were certainly the largest centres in the Maghreb in the eighth century. The large congregational mosques at the centre of both towns would have articulated a very different visual identity from the urban landscapes of old cities. Kairouan and

Tunis would also have been distinctive as much because of what they lacked of the old urban order as because of their new architectural forms. Occupied for centuries, other cities were a palimpsest of North Africa's complicated history, protected by defensive walls and intra-mural forts and filled by churches and monumental complexes such as theatres, baths and temples, many of the latter already in ruin and re-purposed for other functions.

Inherited cities

Most medieval cities were 'inherited cities' whose buildings and street plan – and their inhabitants – limited the possibilities for monumental building programmes. The fabric of the inherited towns had already undergone significant changes during late antiquity in response to changing patterns of public euergetism and the decline of the classical municipal system (Lepelley 1992). The fullest archaeological treatment of these issues is Anna Leone's *Changing Townscapes in North Africa from Late Antiquity to the Arab Conquest* (2007). She shows that major structural changes occurred in the cities of Tunisia and Tripolitania from the fifth century onwards: public spaces were adapted for other uses, industrial and agricultural activities moved into towns, peripheral zones and suburbs of towns were often abandoned; and there is limited evidence for monumental building beyond churches and fortifications.

In the early Islamic period, the inherited towns follow a variety of different trajectories: some expanded beyond their Byzantine limits, others retained the size and layout they had in the Byzantine period, others still contracted, or far less frequently, splintered into smaller settlements. Five sites – Carthage in Tunisia, Sousse in Tunisia, Lepcis Magna in Libya, Sbeïtla in Tunisia and Volubilis in Morocco – provide some sense of the great degree of urban variability in the early middle ages: each shows moments of continuity, crisis and recovery at different phases in their history.

Carthage

Carthage's history in the middle ages is exceptional (Fig. 6). The capital of Africa for over a thousand years under Punic, Roman, Vandal and Byzantine rule, it was one of the biggest port cities in the Mediterranean, and far larger and more densely populated than any other North African city. As we saw in Chapter 1, the seizure of Carthage in 697–8 had

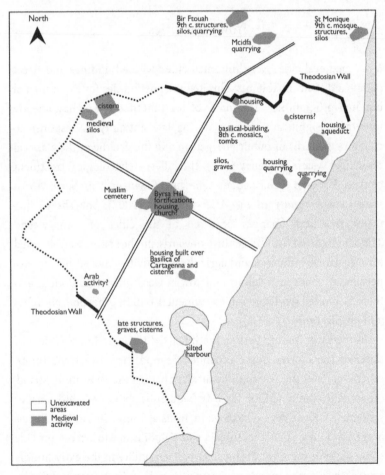

Fig. 6 Plan of Carthage, Tunisia (adapted from Hurst and Roskams 1984, 33, fig. 11).

immense symbolic weight and its capture, destruction and subsequent abandonment were described in stark terms by the Arab historians. Whilst the Arabic accounts were inflated for rhetorical effect, much of Carthage was reduced to little in this period: destruction or abandonment deposits dating to the late seventh century have been found in excavations across the city, and the large martyrial churches outside the walls were razed and robbed out between the seventh and ninth centuries (Fenwick 2019; Stevens 2016).

This was not the end of Carthage. The Byrsa Hill, the centre of Byzantine Carthage, was continuously occupied. It was fortified and may have housed a substantial church (perhaps the enigmatic 'monument with the basilica plan') and Christian community (Morel 1991: 32–3; Vitelli 1981: 18–39). A *ribat* may also have been located on the Byrsa, perhaps on the site of the Roman judicial basilica (Ennabli 1997: 87; Sebaï 2002). Terracing, houses and huts built over seventh-century destruction levels may represent the attempts of Carthage's community to re-establish themselves. North of the Odéon, excavations uncovered two houses built over a seventh-century destruction layer (Wells and Wightman 1980: 53–5). These houses of earthen floors and rubble walls were far simpler than the elaborate insulae clad with mosaics that Carthage was famed for in earlier centuries. With the notable exception of the harbour zone, which was abandoned by the sixth or seventh century (Hurst 1994: 12), most areas excavated reveal signs of medieval activity in the form of ceramics, pits or cisterns. Not all occupation was ephemeral. The monumental basilica-planned building, basin and mosaic at the Rotonde de l'Odéon has been re-dated to the late eighth century based on a coin of 759 in the make-up of a geometric mosaic pavement (Caron and Lavoie 2002). If this dating is correct, it suggests a degree of urban investment (as well as the continuity of mosaic-building traditions) during the eighth century that is so far unparalleled at other excavated sites in northern Tunisia.

Much of the walled city, some 400 hectares in size, was given over to agricultural use. After 650, people seem to have lived in huts and to have farmed in the ruins of the Basilica of Carthagenna (Ennabli 2000: 63).

The monastery of Bigua was also converted into an agricultural complex in the early medieval period, where the counterweight of a screw oil press (a press type only known in Tunisia and Libya after the Arab conquest) and basins to store the olives have been found (Ennabli 2000: 129–30). Outside the walls, small rural agricultural communities emerged in the late ninth century and tenth centuries around the old, now destroyed, basilicas of St Monique, Bir Ftouha and perhaps the Basilica Maiorum. Bir Ftouha, still in use as a church in the late seventh century, was systematically stripped of its marble and decorations between the ninth and twelfth centuries and transformed into an agricultural site (Stevens et al. 2005: 490–8). At St Monique, a nine-bay rhomboid structure, perhaps a small mosque, and two other substantial structures were found over the razed foundations of the basilica, together with several silos, hand-mills, a plaster cornice with Arabic characters and ninth- to eleventh-century lamps (Vitelli 1981: 9–10; Whitehouse 1983).

Quarrying also took place on a significant scale at Carthage in the early medieval period, as the Arabic sources make clear. Al-Bakri tells us 'the marble of Carthage is so abundant that if (all) the people of Ifriqiya were to assemble there to quarry the blocks, they would not fulfil their task' (1913: 43). As we shall see in Chapter 6, many of the churches (the Basilica Mcidfa, Bir Ftouah, Dermech, Basilica of Carthagenna) seem to have been deliberately dismantled for their materials, especially their columns, capitals and marble furnishings, which could be re-used as decorative features in mosques, *ribats* and palaces. Churches were not the only target of this activity, and earlier public buildings and houses would also have been dismantled for spolia. Some areas, such as the *frigidarium* (cold-room) of the Antonine baths, were workshops for the re-working of Roman and Byzantine marbles. Here, a deep destruction layer of clay and ashes with 'Christian' pottery was sealed by a layer containing medieval sherds and a large amount of debris from the re-working of Roman architectural elements, including granite columns, marble capitals and an inscribed slab (Lézine et al. 1956). Quarrying must have been quite an industry in the early medieval period – perhaps even a source of wealth for Carthage's inhabitants.

Columns from Carthage were apparently obtained at great cost in the tenth century for the palace of Madinat al-Zahra in Umayyad Spain (Ibn Ghalib (12th c.) trans. by Ruggles 2011: 116). By the ninth or tenth century, early medieval Carthage was a shadow of its former glory. The huge metropolis was covered by a series of small agricultural villages and its monuments used as a quarry with a *ribat* on the Byrsa hill watching over the sea. Carthage is a textbook example of the *città ad isole* model proposed for early medieval Italy which argues that in the middle ages the old monumental centre of cities like Rome weakened and the urban fabric fragmented into smaller settlement units typically centred around churches (e.g., Wickham 2005: 642–3). This model has also been proposed for North African cities in the seventh century, especially Sbeïtla (Duval 1990; Leone 2007:181–84), but it does not seem to be a common pattern: the enceinte of Carthage, like that of Rome, encompassed a much larger zone than any other North African city. We should be cautious of extrapolating urban trajectories from a megapolis like Carthage, which was always an exceptional case.

Sousse (Hadrumetum)

Little is known about the most important inherited towns of Ifriqiya like Sousse, Sfax, Béja, Tobna and Gafsa which were the principal military centres. None have been excavated, and only rarely has their medieval architecture been systematically recorded. Sousse shows the potential of examining medieval architecture in conjunction with the historical sources (Laporte 2015; Lézine 1971; Mahfoudh 2003). Known as Hadrumetum in the Roman period (and Justinianopolis under Byzantium), it was the provincial capital of Byzacena and was a prosperous, fortified port city when it was conquered. Sousse continued to serve as military and regional capital under the Umayyads and Abbasids, and in the late eighth century, a *ribat* (fort) was built to guard the interior port, near or on what was presumably the Roman *forum*, probably by the Muhallabid governor Yazid b. Hatim (r. 772–788) (Lézine 1956) (Fig. 7). This is the oldest known *ribat* in Ifriqiya and may

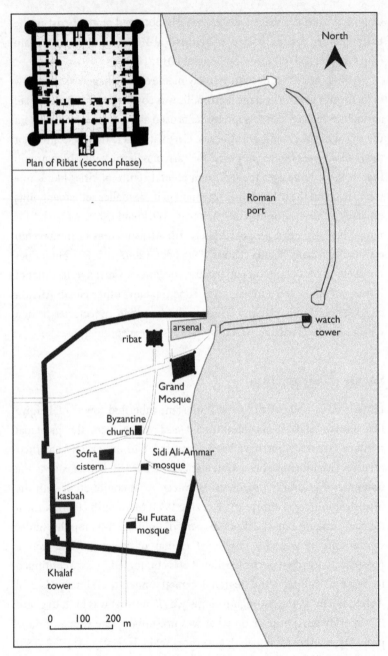

Fig. 7 Plan of Sousse (Hadrumetum), Tunisia (adapted from Lézine 1971, 92, fig. 92).

have been built on top of the foundations of an ancient church (Foucher 1964: 341).

Sousse was transformed in the ninth century, when it became the main naval base for Aghlabid expeditions to Sicily. The emir Ziyadat Allah I built an arsenal to build warships, preceded by an inner harbour basin that was protected within the walls. The *ribat* was rebuilt in its current form in 821 (Fig. 7). It has a square plan (38 x 38 m) comprising a central courtyard surrounded by rooms and an upper floor that housed a prayer hall, and is flanked by round towers at the corners, semi-circular towers half-way along the walls and a later cylindrical *manar* (watch-tower) added on the south-east side. In the following decades, the emirs further invested in Sousse: the Kasbah was built in 844–5; the grand mosque in 851; the tower of Khalaf was added to the Kasbah in 851; and finally, a massive defensive enceinte was built in 859 (or rebuilt following the line of Byzantine walls) that encircled 32 hectares and encompassed the entire city, including the arsenal and inner port (Lézine 1956: 54–5). Outside the walled city, several small fortifications were built to protect the main routes (Djelloul 1995).

The construction of the great mosque (851) in front of the *ribat* transformed the urban aesthetic of Sousse. Immense (59 x 51 m), its prayer hall is divided into thirteen naves and six bays. The mosque has no minaret, and the call of prayer would have been proclaimed from the top of the north-east tower. This was not the only mosque in Sousse. The earliest known is the prayer hall (821) on the upper floor of the *ribat*. In 838–41, the small nine-bay Bu Fatata mosque with a façade of three horseshoe arches was founded by the emir Abu Iqal al-Aghlab and his freedman Khidr. A small prayer room in the tower of Khalaf (851) was surely restricted to the use of the garrison. No churches or synagogues have yet been securely identified, but this was one of the biggest trading ports in the ninth century, and al-Ya'qubi (1892 I: 78) describes it as a mixed community with Persians, Syrians, Christians and Jews.

Sousse shows how rapidly a town could be transformed from a Roman city into a walled medieval Islamic city centred around mosque and *ribat*. Ninth-century investment in Sousse was paralleled at other towns, including Tunis, Monastir, Sfax and Hammamet, which also received mosques or *ribats* and fortifications under Aghlabid rule. From the mid-ninth century, Islam makes a visible imprint on the old towns of North Africa: archaeology and texts provide evidence of large-scale foundations of mosques across Ifriqiya by the emirs and local pious individuals, as we shall see in Chapter 6. In the same period, there is also significant investment in fortifications at large and small coastal centres in response to Byzantine raids on the African coastline (Talbi 1966). The Byzantines focused on sub-urban zones and unprotected coastal towns, notably in the Sahel and Cap Bon rather than the great port cities, most of which were already walled. At least twenty *ribats* are securely dated to this period, including the single-storey *ribat* at Leptiminus (Lamta) (860) and that of the isle of Ghedamsi (871) (Djelloul 1995; Hassen 2001). These new *ribats* look very different to the forts built by the Byzantines in the sixth and seventh centuries (Pringle 1981), as the famous examples of Sousse and Monastir show (Lézine 1970). Coastal and inland towns were further defended by a series of small forts or isolated towers that governed their approaches and transformed the appearance of towns significantly (Djelloul 1995: 38; Khelifa 2004). Sousse provides us with a tantalizing glimpse into the changes that many of the largest and most prosperous towns in Ifriqiya seem to have undergone in the mid to late ninth century, and is an important corrective to the image of decline evident in the handful of exceptional archaeological sites that we know so well.

Lepcis Magna (Lebda)

Lepcis Magna was one of the most prosperous North African cities in the Roman period, renowned for its wealthy urban elite and fertile hinterland producing olive oil and grain (Mattingly 1995: 116–22). In late antiquity, the city was affected by raids and earthquakes, and most significantly by massive flooding between the mid-fourth and mid-fifth centuries (Pucci et al. 2011). The dam collapsed and the *wadi* regained its former course, with devastating effects for the city. Huge amounts of alluvial sands were deposited throughout the city, perhaps causing buildings to collapse, and the harbour to silt up. These lend support to Procopius' statement that large parts of Lepcis Magna were buried in sand in the sixth century (Proc. *De Aed.* VI, iv.1). In the aftermath of the Byzantine reconquest, the town became the provincial capital, and a large wall circuit and several churches were built. By the seventh century, the harbour was filled in aside from the seasonal *wadi* cutting through to the sea, and the city was probably displaced as the central town in Tripolitania by Tripoli (anc. Oea).

Urban life and trade did not stop. Enrico Cirelli (2001) has ably pulled together the evidence for medieval Lebda and shown that a sizeable settlement continued to exist around the port area. The area inside the Justinianic enceinte (44 ha) remained occupied well into the ninth century, when the second smaller internal circuit was probably constructed, reducing the area to 28 hectares. Small pockets of medieval occupation have been identified outside the walls which were probably smaller farming communities outside the fortified core of the town but still offered protection by the earlier Roman enceinte and earthworks. Houses built with recycled materials were found on the docks, intermixed with an oil mill. Similar houses have been found around the Old Forum and the eastern side of the basilica. Over the Flavian temple, a ceramics workshop with a furnace was found that produced globular amphorae and jugs dating to the ninth to tenth centuries (Dolciotti 2007). The ceramics produced at this medieval kiln circulated in Lebda's hinterland (Cirelli et al. 2012: 772); the amphorae, presumably containing olive oil, would have also been exported by sea. Although the harbour was silted up, small ships could probably still moor near the end of the western dock, or perhaps be pulled up on the beach. Lebda remained a centre into the eleventh century and continued to trade, producing and importing globular amphorae and olive oil on some scale. The process of deurbanization took centuries but was linked to the city's declining importance as a port and its continued exposure to devastating floods.

Sbeïtla (Sufetula)

Sbeïtla in central Tunisia provides a striking example of urban continuity. Pioneering excavations and re-analysis of archival reports by Noël Duval in the 1980s produced a plan of a city reduced by the seventh century to a series of small inhabited nuclei comprising fortified complexes, a church and a production site, and surviving in this fragmented state until at least the ninth century (Duval 1982, 1990). However, excavations by Fethi Béjaoui in the 1990s revealed medieval occupation outside the clusters identified by Duval, suggesting that the fragmentation model needs to be revisited (Fig. 8).

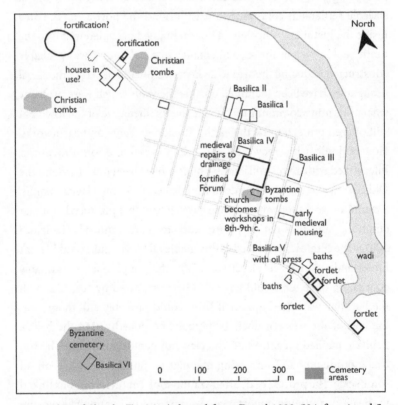

Fig. 8 Plan of Sbeïtla, Tunisia (adapted from Duval 1990, 504, figs. 4 and 5; integrating excavations described in Béjaoui 1996 and 1998).

Unusually, Sbeïtla was not fortified with a town wall or fortress in the Byzantine period. The absence of a major fort is surprising given the significant role the city played in the seventh century as a military base for the Byzantine army against the Arabs. It was the seat of the renegade exarch Gregory who was killed by the Arabs in 647 in the crucial battle of Sbeïtla. A wall had been erected around the forum (probably in the Roman period), and the amphitheatre and the 'temple anonyme' in the north-west of the town may have also been fortified (Duval and Baratte 1973: 73, 64). Fortified dwellings, built in the seventh century and occupied into the ninth century, line the southern entrance to the town. These typically contained an internal well, cisterns and stabling, and are reached by outside stairs leading up to the first storey.

In the centre of town, around the walled forum, houses were occupied into the ninth century, with their floors and thresholds raised from earlier levels (Béjaoui 1996). So far, only one block has been excavated, but Aghlabid ceramics are visible in unexcavated *insulae* throughout the town, particularly in the southern sector, which suggests continued occupation here too. All the churches (Basilicas I, II, IV and V) continued to be used after 650, and the latter two continued in use until the tenth to eleventh century (Duval 1982). The gridded street system seems to have survived relatively intact, with few signs of encroachment. The drainage system also continued to function, and was repaired in the post-conquest period (Béjaoui 1996). As in the Byzantine period, olives continued to be pressed in the town itself. Alongside these continuities, some religious or public spaces were converted to residential or industrial use. In the eighth or ninth century, a church was transformed into a series of subdivided rooms, perhaps serving as workshops since slag and kilns were found in the area (Béjaoui 1998). Inside the fortified forum, a series of domestic or commercial structures were erected at some juncture (Merlin 1912: 8, 15). Sbeïtla was a very different place by the ninth century than in the sixth or even seventh century, but still an ordered settlement on an orthogonal plan with churches, workshops, presses and a working drainage system.

Volubilis (Walila)

Finally, we turn to the western Maghreb and the site of Volubilis, an important anomaly in several ways (Fig. 9). It is one of the few towns that has been extensively excavated in the far western Maghreb, and it is the only site so far with secure archaeological evidence for the eighth century. Originally the provincial capital of Mauritania Tingitana, Volubilis was abandoned or reduced to very little in the late fourth or early fifth century after a major earthquake destroyed much of the city, covering it with a deep layer of destruction material (Fentress and Limane 2018: 57–9). In the late sixth century, the western third of the

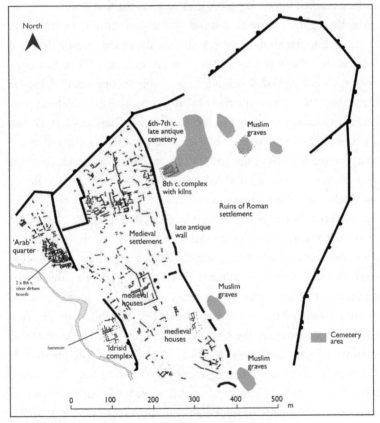

Fig. 9 Plan of Volubilis, Morocco (Corisande Fenwick).

original Roman settlement was reoccupied, protected by the addition of a new rampart running north–south (Akerraz 1983). Outside and to the east, much of the old Roman city was given over to burials, some with Christian inscriptions, which have been found in the ruins of many of the Roman houses (Akerraz 1998: 297).

After the Arab conquest, the town took on a new importance. Coins were minted there in the Abbasid period, some inscribed with the city's new name 'Walila' (Eustache 1956; El Harrif 2001). The Awraba tribe which settled there had converted to Islam, perhaps after serving in the conquest of al-Andalus. Within the late walls, three houses have been excavated; these were constructed in the seventh century, and replaced by similar units over time, before being abandoned by the mid-ninth century. Each was composed of a single small rectangular building, subdivided into domestic space and stabling/workrooms, with storage silos outside (Fentress and Limane 2018: 74–81). Outside the walls, in the old town and close to the late antique cemetery, pottery kilns were built in the shell of a Roman house (Maison au Compas), either as individual units or arranged around a central courtyard (Akerraz 1998). A later cemetery with skeletons laid out in accordance with Muslim funerary rites lay to the east; further Muslim graves have been found in the eastern and southern quarters of the old town.

On the other side of the settlement, outside the walls and near the *wadi*, is the so-called 'Arab quarter' which seems to be the location of an early Arab settlement, perhaps a garrison of soldiers. The plan of this area is unclear, but aside from a mysterious central tower built out of spoliated Roman blocks containing two graves, the zone contains densely packed housing and large amounts of Islamic bronze and silver coins (Eustache 1956). Also outside the town walls was a large eighth-to ninth-century complex consisting of a small bathhouse, a collective granary, and three substantial buildings with large courtyards and orthogonal plans (Fentress and Limane 2018: 82–95). The excavators suggest that this was a public and administrative complex, similar to the *dar al-imara* or governor's palace, built by Idris I in the late 780s as a headquarters for his newly formed state. Volubilis then provides a striking example of late antique abandonment and early medieval expansion, with new Arab-Muslim suburbs placed outside the walls of the existing city just as in the Middle East.

Dynastic foundations

The establishment of the successor states spurred a wave of city foundations that had not been seen for many centuries in North Africa. Some were established as dynastic seats to house the ruler, his troops and to act as the centre of government. Some such foundations, such as Fes or Sijilmasa (Messier and Miller 2015), thrived and became major hubs; however, the majority – such as al-Abbasiyya (Marçais 1925), Raqqada (Chabbi 1967–1968), Sedrata (Aillet et al. 2018; van Berchem 1954), or the later foundations of Achir (Carver and Souidi 1996; Golvin 1966), Sabra al-Mansuriya (Cressier and Rammah 2006) and the Qala of the Beni Hammad (De Beylié 1909) – boomed for several centuries and then disappeared. Unlike the abandoned Roman cities that have long attracted archaeologists, few of these medieval foundations have been properly excavated. This is a missed opportunity: these cities constitute an exceptional data-set for the medieval archaeologist.

The evocative descriptions of the foundations of these sites in later Arabic texts often mimic the narrative for Kairouan: the ruler or his representatives were responsible for identifying the site, building large palaces (including the *diwan*) and a congregational mosque, setting out the markets, constructing defensive walls and laying out – but not usually building – residential quarters (Valérian 2015). Frequently, the texts describe a glorified founder figure establishing a city out of a savage wildness and so reversing barbarity through the civilizing effect of Islam, a model established by the Prophet in Arabia at Yathrib and paralleled by ʿUqba at Kairouan (O'Meara 2007). However, most 'new' foundations were either established at locations with some form of earlier permanent or seasonal settlement or outside existing centres.

The earliest of these dynastic foundations is the Rustamid capital of Tahart in central Algeria, founded in 761 by Ibn Rustam, a Persian, who took refuge there (Aillet 2011). The northern part of the settlement is visible from the aerial photos: it occupies 8 hectares and was defended by a quadrangular enceinte of walls of *pisé* with bastions. Inside, there are houses separated by regular roads. On the southern plateau is a large building, which Marçais (1946b) identified as the early medieval fortress, but Cadenat (1977) more convincingly identifies as the fortress built by the rebel ʿAbd al-Kader in the nineteenth century. Medieval authors tell us that the site was known as Tahart al-jadida ('the new') because it was some 9 kilometres to the west of Tahart al-qadima ('the old'), a Romano-Christian centre (possibly Tingartia) at the height of a strategic mountain pass. This dual-town format is seen at other later sites in North Africa, most notably at Fes which was divided into *Madinat Fas* founded in 789 by Idris I and *al-Aliyya*, a second walled medina founded in 808 by his son, Idris II.

City foundation became a prerogative of Islamic rulers, though it follows several different patterns. At Nakur, for example, a city was founded in the early ninth century at an existing marketplace by Said b. Idris b. Salah b. Mansur, the grandson of the founder of the Hymarite dynasty (Cressier et al. 2001). No settlement seems to have existed before, but the Arabic sources suggest it was not a top-down process of urban foundation, but rather a convergence of interests between two local tribal groups (the Banu Warugal and the Timsaman). The survey and small-scale excavations confirm that the town followed the basic blueprint for dynastic centres laid out above: it has two substantial walls, as well as a mosque and hammam. Like other inland sites in Morocco, Nakur had its own port, al-Mazamma, on the Atlantic coast – the ceramics reveal connections with Ifriqiya and al-Andalus as well as local productions (Cressier 2017).

Some pre-Islamic towns in Morocco may have been substantial, though this is underplayed in archaeological reports. Al-Basra in Morocco, a 30-hectare walled, round town, was formally established by the Idrisid dynasty in *c.* 800 on the place of an earlier Berber settlement

(Benco 1987, 2004). Radiocarbon dates confirm that a large settlement consisting of stone and mudbrick buildings with tiled roofs and flagstone pavements existed there as early as the fifth or sixth century (Benco 2002). This settlement seems to have been abandoned, and then followed by a phase of ephemeral occupation, perhaps dating to the late seventh century. In the ninth century, the town was re-founded and is characterized by well-built courtyard houses with roof tiles in the centre and an industrial zone on the west; there may have been gardens and orchards housed within the walls.

Major urban centres were also established in the Saharan oases, as in the case of Sijilmasa, the famous caravan city established in the eighth century that subsequently became the principal centre of trans-Saharan trade. According to the legendary account of al-Bakri (1913: 282–90), the city was founded in 757–8 on an uncultivated plain where Berber pastoralists had grazed their flocks, and by the early ninth century had gained a mosque and walls (Capel 2017). Fire-pits dated by radiocarbon to the sixth to eighth century, as well as many large protohistoric cemeteries and hillforts in the oasis, hint at the possibility of earlier sedentary life (Bokbot 2019; Capel and Fili 2018; Messier and Miller 2015: 69–71). Despite extensive archaeological campaigns at the site, which remain largely unpublished, little is known of the early medieval settlement. It was certainly a prosperous settlement with strong ties to global trading networks in the ninth and tenth centuries. Excavations uncovered traces of several early residential buildings, including an elite residential complex, dated by radiocarbon to 785–875, consisting of several courtyards, a garden and a kitchen and decorated with ornate wall-plaster and wooden ceilings (Messier and Fili 2011). As is characteristic of Saharan architecture, the settlement was built in *pisé* and mud-brick and developed in a haphazard manner over the centuries (Fauvelle et al. 2014).

In Ifriqiya, the Aghlabids also built cities to house themselves and their retinues in the immediate vicinity of Kairouan: al-Abbasiyya (in honour of the Abbasids) in 800, which was later replaced by Raqqada in 876. These 'palace-cities' are rather different in form and function to

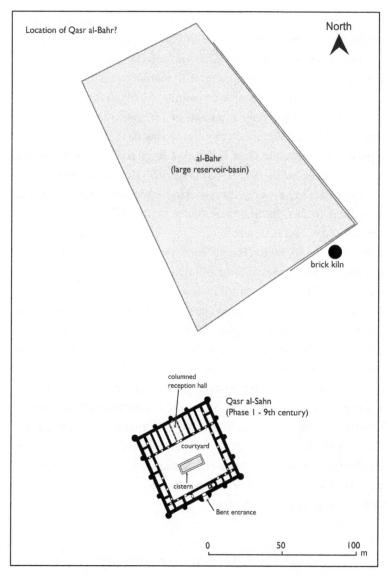

Fig. 10 Plan of Raqqada, Tunisia (adapted from Vaschalde et al. 2017).

the foundations in the western Maghreb and had a ceremonial function similar to the Abbasid foundations in Iraq (Goodson 2017). Medieval authors mention al-Abbasiyya's royal palaces and congregational mosque, built of brick and gypsum with marble columns and a seven-storey round minaret, as well as baths, inns and markets: excavations in the 1920s uncovered only a mound of *pisé* and mud-bricks and a reservoir (Marçais 1925). Excavations at Raqqada in the 1960s revealed a palace (probably the Qasr al-Sahn), a large reservoir and a brick-making kiln (Chabbi 1967–1968) (Fig. 10). This is the only ninth-century palace to have been excavated in the western Mediterranean to date. Built in *pisé*, its first phase dates to the Aghlabid period and consists of a walled enclosure (55 x 55 m) with round corner towers and additional round buttresses on each side, similar in form to the Umayyad desert castles of Syria and Iraq. A bent entrance in the south leads into a large courtyard with a reservoir, off which were a series of rooms and a columned reception hall in the north. It was subsequently extended in two successive phases (probably in the tenth and eleventh centuries) and eventually contained around 109 rooms, courtyards and annexes (Arnold 2017: 3–12). This is but a small fraction of the site: medieval texts describe at least five Aghlabid royal palaces and gardens, a congregational mosque, baths, markets, caravanserais, as well as barracks for the sub-Saharan military elite guard who defended the emirs. These descriptions of scattered palaces, gardens and barracks are redolent of the Abbasid palace-city Samarra in Iraq built in 836 and would be later mirrored at Fatimid Sabra al-Mansuriya (945–8) and the Qala of the Bani Hammad.

The transformation of the city

The spectacular ruined temples, churches and houses of a Carthage or Lepcis Magna, names that evoke the splendour and wealth of Roman cities in North Africa, were once taken as material proof of an urban crisis brought about by the collapse of Byzantine authority and the drawn-out conquest and consolidation of Mulim rule. A rather different urban history emerges when one combines analysis of broader patterns in urban success and failure with detailed study of individual towns. If the conquest was to all extents an invisible one, the North African urban network was transformed by the ninth century. New cities were founded to house the new rulers or as administrative centres, especially in the Maghreb al-Aqsa, which underwent a phase of urbanization in the ninth and tenth centuries. In Ifriqiya, for the most part, the Muslim authorities found North Africa's existing urban network adequate for their needs, but over time the largest and most prosperous inherited towns won out and many of the smaller towns that had characterized late antique Africa were abandoned or reduced to very little.

Urban trajectories varied enormously for both the old, inherited classical towns and the new Muslim foundations. Kairouan and Tunis, both built on or near existing settlements, mark the most obvious break with the old order. Established as new Muslim cities to house soldiers and the ever-growing Muslim community, they included new types of buildings including mosques and the *dar al-amara* (governor's residence) that had never before been seen in North Africa. The takeover of forts and the addition of extra-mural quarters to house the new Muslim community increased the size of other sites and introduced new forms of domestic architecture. Most changes in urban patterns, however, were not related to the direct intervention of the Muslim state, and their speed and chronology varied for individual towns.

The Roman and late antique heritage continued to shape the urban form of many of the old towns of Ifriqiya and differentiated them from the new Muslim foundations of Kairouan and Tunis. Churches and Byzantine-built forts and town walls were still dominant elements in many cityscapes, as were the Roman streets and water systems that underpinned their ability to function as urban centres. Many smaller towns disappeared or were transformed into villages at some point between the seventh and ninth centuries, perhaps more a reflection of shifting economic priorities than the difficulties of sustaining urban life. What urban life was like in the larger centres is much harder to say in the absence of detailed fieldwork, but on balance it seems likely to have continued much as before. These cities may have been reduced in the eighth century, but perhaps not markedly more than in the seventh century.

The late eighth and particularly the ninth century mark the emergence of a fully Islamic urban aesthetic. The act of urban foundation became a core component of Muslim rulership in North Africa. New cities and urban forms were established for the first time in centuries in the far west, where a series of urban foundations by different dynasties replicated the model of an Islamic city with mosque and walls. In Ifriqiya, the new palatine towns of al-Abbasiyya (800) and Raqqada (876) were also built along these lines, but on a grander and more ceremonial scale. At the same time, the appearance of the old cities of Ifriqiya also changed, with new congregational mosques, oratories, *ribats* and town walls built in the late ninth century along the Tunisian coastline and in the interior, much of it sponsored by state investment. The result was the emergence of a new, refashioned multi-religious and prosperous urban society in ninth-century North Africa still rooted in a Byzantine or tribal cultural inheritance but increasingly embracing Islamic norms and urban forms.

4

The Countryside

North Africa contains a bewildering array of different ecological niches which range from some of the most fertile zones of the Mediterranean to its Saharan regions, some of the most difficult in which to sustain human life. Between these extremes, most of the Maghreb is arid or semi-arid, and approximately 75 per cent of the region receives less than 350 millimetres of rainfall annually. These different ecological zones offer divergent possibilities for exploitation and settlement: the Mediterranean coast; an upland region of relatively fertile hills and valleys that is known as the Tell in Algeria and Tunisia and becomes the hilly plateau of the Gebel in Libya; the open plains and steppe known as the Sahel in Tunisia; the arid pre-desert and the oases of the Sahara itself. Enough rain falls on the coast and Tell to grow grain, olives, figs, fruit trees and vines. The more arid plains, pre-desert and Saharan oases require irrigation or the digging of wells to allow agriculture but support pastoralism and animal husbandry. Agricultural practices therefore varied throughout North Africa and adapted to the environmental conditions of low rainfall and high temperatures in arid and semi-arid environments.

The early Islamic Maghreb produced large amounts of olive oil, wine, wheat and barley, honey, saffron, dates, fruits, sesame oil, cotton as well as producing textiles, leather and other animal products that were exported all over the Islamic world, by the late ninth century when the earliest surviving Arabic geographies appear (Vanacker 1973). The astonishing agricultural productivity of certain regions of North Africa (the Medjerda valley, Cap Bon, the Sahel and the Saharan oases) and the large numbers of farming villages is frequently remarked upon. For al-Yaʿqubi (1892: 211), for example, the prosperity of Ifriqiya was due to the date palms of the Jarid and the olive groves of the Sahel 'where villages lie so thick on the ground that they all but touch one another'. Another common trope is the fertility of the oases and *wadis* on the northern fringes of the Sahara. Al-Bakri tells us that the wheat in the Wadi Soffegin in the Libyan pre-desert grew a hundredfold and that at Badis (Algeria), there were two harvests of barley a year (1913: 25, 175). There can be little doubt that the region was a major agricultural producer and exporter in the ninth to eleventh centuries (Jalloul 1998), even if it is sometimes difficult to see archaeologically.

The seventh and eighth centuries are even harder to see archaeologically, and as a result are often depicted as a moment of deep crisis for North Africa's countryside: the prosperous Roman rural landscape of villas, estates and olive oil-producing farms, replaced by an impoverished and depopulated late antique and medieval landscape characterized by pastoralism and scattered villages (e.g., Dietz 1995). For colonial scholars, this image of agrarian and demographic crisis was matched with one of a rural Berber population returning to their tribal and pastoral roots from the fifth century onwards (Courtois 1955; Frend 1952). These arguments are based on flawed assumptions about the astounding fertility of the 'granary of Rome' and its subsequent decline due to the incapability of the 'native' Berbers to farm, or the ravages of nomadic Arab invaders in either the seventh or eleventh centuries (Davis 2007).

Field survey supports a picture of late antique rural crisis, though at different times in different regions. In an important article, Anna Leone and David Mattingly (2004) compared the rural survey data from a range of projects and found that site numbers drop off from the fourth century in Tripolitania and the late fifth/early sixth century in southern Tunisia, while site numbers in northern Tunisia did not decrease until at least the late sixth century, though, as they note, this drop reflects our reliance upon African Red Slip ware and amphorae for dating. The late antique settlement hierarchy was markedly different from the villa and estate landscape of the high imperial Roman period. In northern Tunisia, a mixed settlement hierarchy of small and large farms, villages and towns endured until the seventh century, whilst in Tripolitania and southern Tunisia, people were living collectively in agglomerated settlements, often centred on a *ksour* (a fortified complex) by the sixth century, rather than in farms or villas scattered across the landscape. The reduction in site numbers and trend towards nucleation has led some to argue for a demographic shift of people towards the cities and northern Tunisia, linked with the growing insecurity of the interior (Fentress et al. 2004), and others to argue for a shift to pastoral or subsistence strategies (Hitchner 1994).

Archaeologists have found it difficult to identify rural activity in the medieval period because they have spent so little time looking for it. The great boom in field survey that took place in the 1980s, spearheaded by the ground-breaking UNESCO Libyan Valleys Survey, has not had a transformative effect on our understanding of the medieval rural landscape. Matters are exacerbated by our poor knowledge of medieval ceramics – particularly for the pivotal eighth century which is essentially invisible to field survey archaeologists. Those few studies which have dealt with the early Islamic countryside have begun and finished with the written evidence, since nothing else was available (Amara 2009; Benhima and Guichard 2009; Hassen 2000; Madani 2009; Talbi 1981). Yet, as historians know well, it is no easy task to reconstruct settlement organization, land ownership and land-management strategies or to reconstruct agricultural regimes and environmental change from the limited written sources. This chapter tackles debates about North Africa's agricultural productivity in the early middle ages by looking at rural survey evidence for settlement numbers, crop production and animal husbandry, and environmental evidence for climate change and exploitation.

Archaeological survey and the tyranny of African Red Slip ware

Only a handful of rural sites have been excavated, thus our archaeological knowledge of North African rural landscapes in all periods is derived from data collected in field survey. Field survey developed in North Africa during the Mediterranean-wide survey boom in the 1980s which sought to understand shifting patterns of rural settlement and agricultural strategies over the *longue durée* (Stone 2004). The UNESCO 'Farming the Desert' project in the Libyan pre-desert set a gold-standard for diachronic field survey examining landscape change from prehistory to the early modern period (Barker 1996), but its promise was not widely held up, and later surveys rarely included the Islamic or early modern periods. Subsequent surveys, primarily in Tunisia and Libya, explored the Roman landscape in a range of ecological niches, from coastal farming zones to inland steppe and pre-desert areas. In Morocco, by contrast, surveys mapped medieval urban and fortified sites but through extensive, rather than intensive, survey, and so smaller, rural settlements are poorly understood (Cressier 1992; Ennahid 2001; Redman 1983).

Methodologically innovative as so many of the North African surveys of the 1980s to 2000s were, by shining such a bright light on the busy Roman and late antique countryside, they made the medieval countryside darker still by comparison. Except in a few cases, published surveys end their analysis with the seventh century, which makes it impossible to assess the apparent boom of the agricultural sector in the ninth to eleventh centuries described in the medieval sources or to identify whether there is a continuity in site occupation or typology. This is not simply a product of our poor knowledge of unglazed medieval ceramics. When surveys have not ignored the medieval period completely, there is a near universal failure to date survey finds beyond the uselessly broad category of 'Islamic' for the period 700 to 1900. Sometimes this neglect of the medieval period was dictated in archaeological permits (the Punic period was also affected), but it more frequently reflects the dominance of Roman archaeology and the lack of medieval specialists. For example, the recent publication of the Leptiminus hinterland survey did not include any analysis of the medieval ceramics that were collected but remain unstudied (Stone et al. 2011).

A second issue arises from the intensity of survey methods. Even when medieval sites are deliberately sought, survey intensity affects our ability to recognize medieval settlement of a more ephemeral nature (especially if it is built in *pisé* or mud-brick). The Jerba survey provides a cautionary tale: in 2000, a block measuring 1 x 1.3 kilometres was discovered with a dense spread of medieval material, and when first surveyed twelve medieval sites were counted. When it was re-walked more intensively, an additional forty-five distinct sites of medieval date were identified, from locations previously recorded as background noise. In this example, larger sites and mosques were recognized the first time, but 'the finer detail was recoverable only by the more intensive approach' (Fentress et al. 2009: 30).

The issue of survey intensity is common to survey data in all periods, but there are additional challenges for reconstructing medieval landscape patterns. Sites are typically dated by ceramics (and less frequently masonry type or building function) which we understand poorly for the Byzantine and medieval periods. In North Africa, from the sixth century onwards there was a greater dependence on locally produced, coarser, handmade and more friable pottery which leaves less robust material signatures in the archaeological record (Bonifay 2004). Given our limited understanding of glazed, coarse and handmade wares, even those surveys with dedicated medieval ceramicists found it impossible to date sites to the eighth century. Does a lack of datable medieval pottery in some regions indicate a genuine absence of rural settlement, or simply a poor sample for the period, caused by limited regional access to more easily identifiable imported pottery and a dependence on local wares?

Medieval archaeologists in Europe have highlighted problems in deducing a decline in settlement from weak material signatures (e.g., Christie 2004), and there are good reasons to reject the argument that a drop in the amount of pottery necessarily equates to fewer people and rural settlements. The same is the case in North Africa: the Dougga project was able to construct a local coarseware chronology from their excavations at the sixth- to seventh-century farm of Aïn Wassal (De Vos

Raaijmakers and Maurina 2019). They found that in the seventh century, sites with only coarseware outnumbered sites with ARS three to one (De Vos 2000: 65–6, 71). Had they relied upon ARS alone, they would have observed a clear decline and substantial drop in site numbers from the sixth century, but instead, their nuanced study demonstrates a vibrant and connected countryside in the seventh and perhaps early eighth century. This cautionary case suggests that until we construct local ceramic chronologies for different regions, we may be severely underestimating rural settlement in North Africa, particularly from the late sixth century onwards. This is not to deny that some regions experienced a decline in rural settlement. The Jerba survey used coarsewares and amphorae, as well as finewares, to date sites and observed a decline in site numbers in their Late Antique II period (500–700), followed by a surge in site numbers in their Early Medieval I period (700–1050). If we move away from attempting to address demographic issues from survey evidence and instead focus on settlement morphology, agricultural practices and environmental evidence, we can see real changes in the medieval countryside and patterns of exploitation between the seventh and tenth centuries.

The medieval countryside

The Muslim conquest had a considerable impact on landholding practices. Immediately after the conquest, land grants in Ifriqiya were given to the Arab army and their Berber allies (this practice was not common elsewhere in the caliphate). These included substantial estates of one or more villages in northern and central Tunisia, and medium- and small-sized estates in the Sahel and the province of Tripoli (Talbi 1981: 208–14). Presumably, these estates had been owned by the state, church or local elites under the Byzantines and were confiscated by the Arabs as part of the spoils of the conquest. These estates were not only held by individuals, but could have been held collectively by tribal groups: later texts describe how the Abbasid takeover was accompanied

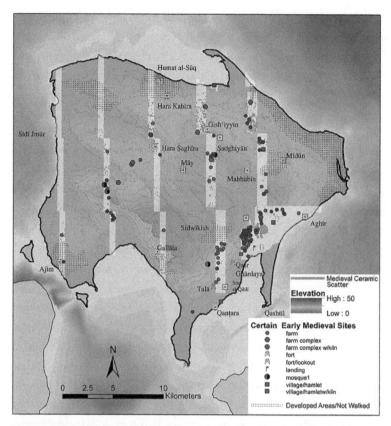

Fig. 11 Map of Jerba, Tunisia, showing medieval settlement distribution (copyright: Michael Frachetti).

by the demobilization of the Umayyad army which had contingents installed in the African countryside where they held collective lands (Bahri 1999: 2). Some of these estates were very large indeed and may have been cultivated by a large slave-labour force (Talbi 1981: 192, 198).

It has proven challenging to investigate the impact of Muslim rule on the countryside archaeologically because archaeologists have spent so little time examining rural landscapes. Three exceptions from Tunisia and Libya provide tantalizing glimpses into medieval rural settlement patterns, agricultural regimes and how the landscape was exploited. On the island of Jerba, surveyed between 1996 and 2000, the antique urban centres of Burgu, Ghizen, Haribus and Meninx on the island were more or less extinguished by the early seventh century when the island was dominated by a series of inland and coastal villages. Villages with kilns continued to produce a variety of vessels and containers, including amphorae for transporting olive oil, suggesting that trade networks were maintained, albeit on a smaller scale (Fentress et al. 2009: 197–200). In the middle ages, the settlement pattern changed again (Fig. 11): villages, towns and large farms occupied for centuries were abandoned, and replaced by clusters of new small single-family unit farms on slight rises, with the lowest grounds left for cultivation (Holod and Kahlaoui 2017). These farms are arranged in small groups around the *wadis*, often with an associated mosque. The most densely populated zone was the south-east of the island, a well-watered region whose fertile soils made it a prime zone for growing fruit trees, grapes, olives and grains (Fentress et al. 2009: 62). Large zones of the island's interior and north were set aside for plantations, perhaps large olive-growing estates, known later as *ghaba*, associated with larger isolated farm complexes. Holod and Cirelli (2011: 171) suggest that these new settlement patterns are connected to the mass influx of Ibadi settlers to Jerba in the ninth century described in the written sources. Intriguingly, new forms of jars in a whitish fabric appear for the first time in this period; these are very similar to those produced in the Rustamid capital of Tahart and, as they propose, they may reflect the movement of artisans and new ceramic techniques with the Ibadi settlers.

The Italian survey in the hinterland of Lepcis Magna (Lebda) conducted between 2007 and 2013 found a similar rise in settlement numbers in the medieval period (Cirelli et al. 2012; Munzi et al. 2014; Munzi et al. 2016). Tripolitania's towns and countryside were already suffering in the mid-fifth century. Although the coastal cities of Lepcis and Sabratha remained important, if diminished, a significant drop in rural settlement numbers and a decoupling of this region from broader trading circuits occurred in the sixth and seventh centuries, when only a few examples of the late production of Tripolitanian Red Slipware (mainly Hayes 8A and B) have been found. The seventh and eighth centuries, as elsewhere, are archaeologically invisible, though a handful of Umayyad bronze coins recovered in the Gasr el-Hammam area attest to a level of activity.

Between the eighth and eleventh centuries, there was a boom in rural settlement in the hinterland of Lepcis, perhaps related to its revival in the ninth century described in Chapter 3. Settlement here was very different from that of Jerba. The suburbs of the city contained open farms, often in the same places as earlier agricultural sites (a sign that there may not have been a break in occupation in the seventh and eighth centuries). Agriculture presumably focused on olive production, a practice attested by the eleventh-century geographer al-Idrisi (1866: 154), who describes a vast oil harvest produced from the territory of Lepcis. A different picture emerges in the arid interior in the Wadi Taraglat where the prevalence of fortified villages centred on one or more fortified granaries points to the importance of cereal and date-palm cultivation (Munzi et al. 2014: 226–31). Villages were complemented by new forms of open farms and isolated towers of two or three storeys which served a double function as watch-posts and granaries. Roman water-management systems were repaired and used to direct the flow of the *wadi* to cultivate the surrounding land. Here, we have an agricultural system based on both sedentary agriculture and semi-nomadic pastoralism which would have produced cheese, wool and leather.

The situation in the Libyan pre-desert is more difficult to assess. Here, rainfall drops below the minimum levels required for cereal, olive and vine cultivation, but using a simple system of floodwater management, farmers were able to cultivate crops in the *wadi*-beds (Fig. 12). The UNESCO Libyan Valleys Survey (ULVS) did not systematically record medieval ceramics but identified 141 definite or possible sites for the Islamic period (Barker 1996: 174). Isabella Sjöstrom (1993: 114) calculated that of a total of 482 settlements found in the survey, 130 were established in the Roman period and were occupied at least until the eleventh century, and an additional 80 settlements were

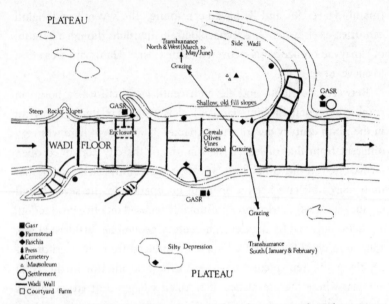

Fig. 12 A simplified schematic of a typical *wadi* sector in the Libyan pre-desert (copyright: Society for Libyan Studies, from Barker and Jones 1980: 36, fig. 11).

established in the Islamic period (broadly defined). *Ksour* were still being built in the ninth century and many sites continued to be occupied. By the eleventh century, the more remote and marginal *wadis* were no longer used for sedentary farming, and settlement concentrated in the wettest regions of pre-desert zone in the northern Beni Ulid, Merdum and Mansur *wadi* systems and atypical sites in the south such as the oasis village at Gheriat el-Gharbia (Barker 1996: 177–8). Transhumant cultivators and pastoralists presumably used the southern *wadis* as in recent times, and many of the undated hut and tent footings, enclosures, graves and simple walls may relate to their activity.

The superb preservation of the catchment systems, cross-*wadi* and edge walls, the associated sluices, drop structures, and cisterns permitted detailed reconstruction of these flood-water farming systems, many of which continued in use in the medieval period (Gilbertson et al. 1984). The geomorphological and pollen data suggests increased ploughing and intensified grazing in the medieval period, associated with widespread alluviation and repairs to *wadi* walls. Pollen data and sediment analysis revealed key shifts in agricultural exploitation between the Roman and late Islamic period (Barker 1996: 352–7). In the Roman period, olives were intensively cultivated for export to other areas of the Mediterranean. Large-scale oleioculture was replaced in the medieval period by an agricultural regime of cereal farming and pastoralism that clustered in the northern *wadi* belts. While tree-crops (grape, oil, fig, date, almond) remained important, they appear in far smaller quantities (especially grape) than in the Roman period, and olive presses are absent from the medieval villages. There were also shifts in animal husbandry: no pig was found, though there was a high preponderance of sheep/goats and limited amounts of game. As in the Roman period, the sheep/goats were usually killed as sub-adults and juveniles suggesting that they were bred for meat, rather than milk or wool production (Clark 1986: 56).

These surveys – all in ecologically or politically marginal zones – reflect a flourishing and increasingly connected countryside in the ninth or tenth century and have implications for other regions of the Maghreb which have not been studied in the same detail. The picture can be fleshed out by new evidence from excavations in northern Tunisia. From the late ninth century, small villages begin to re-appear at sites like Uchi Maius, Althiburos and Chemtou in the Tunisian Tell after a seeming hiatus in occupation. At Chemtou, a ninth-century agricultural settlement built over a deep debris layer in the forum lasted into the eleventh century and comprised modest, one-storied rectangular houses with walls of stone rubble and wood-and-clay roofs and deep storage pits between these houses (von Rummel 2016). At Uchi Maius, a contemporary settlement in and around the fortified citadel consisted of several houses, where they were pressing olives and often had bread ovens (*tabuna*) in their courtyards (Gelichi and Milanese 2002). Amidst the ruins of Utica, a substantial village of single-room *pisé* houses with silos for storing grain, perhaps as large as 2 hectares in size, was established in the forum area in the north of the city in the mid-tenth century, though here quarrying may have been a core function (Fentress et al. 2014). At Carthage too – the one city destroyed by the Arabs – its vast walled area had splintered into agricultural villages, as we saw in Chapter 3. This trend towards ruralization, rather than pastoralism, is also seen at Leptiminus, a town without a good natural harbour which seems to have faltered in Late Antiquity unlike its neighbours Sousse, Monastir, Bekalta and Salakta. Here, the town was replaced by much smaller land-facing villages which focused on cultivating olives, producing textiles and perhaps salt to the west of the ninth-century single-storey *ribat* (Stone et al. 2011: 279).

How accurate is this picture of a prosperous countryside in the late ninth century in Tunisia and Tripolitania, and does it represent a recovery from eighth-century crisis? A ninth-century anecdote is revealing. Ibn ʿAbd al-Hakam recounts that after the defeat and death of the Byzantine exarch Gregory at Sbeïtla in 647, the Arabs demanded a huge ransom. To their amazement, a heap of gold coins piled up in front of their leader's tent. He asked a local how his people could pay this amount. The man scratched the surface of the ground and produced an olive stone. 'The Roum', he replied, 'have no olives themselves, and therefore they come to us to buy the oil, which we sell to them. This is the source of our wealth' (Ibn ʿAbd al-Hakam 1942: 46–9). Although the story is unlikely to be true, it and contemporary texts recounting both Africa's past and present agricultural wealth, suggest relatively high levels of local oil production in the seventh and ninth centuries, especially in the main olive-growing region of central Tunisia. The situation in the eighth century is less clear, but it seems likely that most olive groves survived, but were perhaps less intensively exploited without the impetus of large-scale export trade to other areas of the Mediterranean (Wickham 2005: 720–94).

In distant Morocco and western Algeria, rural settlement is less well understood, though presumably the urbanization of the region was matched with investment in the countryside and a rise in agriculture to feed the inhabitants of the new towns. In the hinterland of the Idrisid foundation of al-Basra, for example, a field survey identified small medieval rural sites dated between the eighth and thirteenth centuries (Ennahid 2001). Elsewhere, earlier Roman sites were re-occupied, as at Rirha (Morocco) where there is a ninth-century settlement after a hiatus of almost five centuries (Callegarin et al. 2016: vol. 4). The rusticity of the buildings and the absence of coinage suggests that the site was of minor importance, perhaps an artisanal or commercial centre. Unlike the urban sites of al-Basra and Volubilis, there is no evidence of new crops like cotton or citrus appearing at Rirha: instead, the palaeobotanical evidence shows a great continuity in the crops produced (wheat, millet, grape, fava, olive, flax), though there is an increase in the proportion of barley (*hordeum vulgare L.*) at the expense of *triticum* and *emmer* wheat. Meat consumption shifts, with a greater emphasis on cattle, goats and birds, as well as fish and hunting of wild boar (Muller et al. 2016).

A striking phenomenon in Morocco and the western Maghreb is the upsurge and investment in oasis cultivation in the early middle ages. Around the Midrarid capital of Sijilmasa, the construction of an artificial channel (perhaps in the ninth century) to divert water from the Oued Ziz to the city and its hinterland would have enabled a significant expansion of oasis agriculture and settlement (Capel 2017). Survey in the neighbouring Wadi Draa, one of the largest and richest oasis belts in the Sahara, provides insight into the process (Mattingly et al. 2017a). The Draa is sustained by the only perennial river that runs into the Sahara from the north and in the medieval period was an important secondary corridor for caravans coming from the south to access the Atlas passes and reach Marrakech. In the early first millennium AD, a mixture of mobile and small-scale settled communities doing oasis agriculture or hill-land farming inhabited the region. A major shift takes place between the seventh and tenth centuries when many earlier hill-top sites were abandoned, new planned settlements were established and mud-brick was introduced for the first time. The careful mapping of an abandoned oasis system suggests this settlement shift coincides with the establishment of substantial canal networks for irrigated agriculture on the oasis floor in the eighth to tenth centuries.

The written sources we possess for the early medieval countryside are scattered but informative on landholding practices. Large estates dominated the settlement pattern in northern Tunisia until at least the seventh century, and it seems likely that this landholding pattern continued into the medieval period, with the seizure of already-existing estates by the conquerors. Abu'l-Mughira, *qadi* of Ifriqiya between 717 and 741, for example, owned two estates called Qasr Mughira and Qaryat al-Mughiriyin, each of which included a hamlet or village, left to him by his father, who had taken part in the conquest (Talbi 1981: 211). The latter – a large estate and village – is situated 10 kilometres to the west of Béja in the fertile grain-growing Medjerda valley of northern Tunisia (Bahri 1999: 1). The *ksour*/fortified village pattern around Lepcis Magna and in the pre-desert might well be considered as small estates, though the continuity of local building techniques suggests that these settlements remained in the hands of local elites who dominated trans-Saharan trade. The landscape of small farms on Jerba seems less likely to reflect an estate-based landowning pattern, but Jerba may be a special case because of its isolation and the Ibadi influence. The newly established large farm complexes in the north and centre of the island in the prime olive-growing zone suggests that here too there may have been large estates in the early medieval period. Whether these were in the hands of local Jerbans or the Ibadi settlers is difficult to assess, though the transformation in the organization in the landscape suggests major changes in the economy, landholding patterns and agricultural practices between the late antique and early medieval period. As well as these changes in land tenure, there seems to have been migration into less populated zones, as reflected in the movement of new Ibadi populations onto the island of Jerba, where they brought new areas of the island under cultivation (Holod and Kahlaoui 2017). The same may apply to the pre-desert regions of the Sahara such as in the Wadi Draa, which saw the extension of large-scale oasis cultivation in the eighth to tenth centuries alongside widespread sedentarization (Mattingly et al. 2017a).

Agriculture and animal husbandry

Medieval agriculture in much of North Africa focused on a 'Mediterranean triad' of cereals, olives and grapes, supplemented by pulses (lentils, chickpeas and beans), and in this sense had changed little since antiquity. The most common fruits were olives, grapes, figs, and dates. Despite prohibitions against wine for Muslims, viticulture remained important, especially on Cap Bon. The major cash-crop was olive oil, which was exported across the Mediterranean, and was a key product of Tunisia, as attested by the historical and agronomic literature and juridical records (Jalloul 1998). The medieval period represents an important phase in the development of agriculture in North Africa. Andrew Watson (1989) proposed that the early Islamic period witnessed a 'Green Revolution', with major agricultural innovations based on the use of new crops, including staple foodstuffs (durum wheat, sorghum) and various 'cash' crops, such as fibre crops (cotton), oilseeds and fruits, as well as the introduction of new irrigation technologies and farming practices. His thesis has proved controversial but has yet to be evaluated systematically in North Africa, where only limited archaeobotanical research has been conducted because of the challenges of collecting, floating and studying samples. In the dry Libyan pre-desert, for example, while seed preservation is often good, there was no water available to do flotation (Barker 1996: 230). Michael Decker (2009) has challenged Watson's model based on the presence of durum wheat and cotton in North Africa and elsewhere in late antiquity. But on balance of the evidence, I would suggest that several crop types already cultivated in Ifriqiya, and especially in the highly irrigated oases of the Libyan Fazzan, in late antiquity were introduced to the Maghreb al-Aqsa in the medieval period and became widespread.

Take durum wheat, which is particularly resistant in dry climates. Although it is recorded in the Libyan pre-desert and Fazzan in late antiquity (Pelling 2013; van der Veen et al. 1996), and there are possible identifications in seventh-century (but not earlier) layers at Leptiminus and Carthage in Tunisia, it only appears at Volubilis and al Basra

(Morocco) in the eighth century and Setif (Algeria) in the tenth century (Fuller et al. 2018; Mahoney 2004; Palmer and Jones 1991). In Morocco, einkorn and emmer wheat are attested in the Neolithic, but not subsequently, and seem to be re-introduced in the medieval period, perhaps related to increased connections with al-Andalus, where they were an important staple in antiquity (Fuller et al. 2018). Sorghum may be an even later introduction from sub-Saharan Africa: it has not yet been identified in Morocco before the tenth to thirteenth centuries, where it appears at the site of Igliz (Ruas et al. 2011).

'Thirsty' field crops such as cotton and sugar cane may also have been introduced to the western Maghreb in the middle ages. Cotton cannot be grown without irrigation in regions where rainfall drops below 500 millimetres during the growing season, but the highest yields are obtained in dry areas under irrigation. It was cultivated regularly in the highly irrigated Fazzan in the third and fourth centuries (Pelling 2008), but it has yet to be discovered at any other Roman-period site in the Maghreb. Cotton, imported as bolls from elsewhere, perhaps the Saharan oases south of the Atlas, was present at Volubilis by the eighth or ninth century (Fuller et al. 2018), and it is also attested at the Saharan sites of Tadmakka/Essouk (Mali), where it cannot have been cultivated (Nixon et al. 2011). Sugar cane was introduced, less successfully, to parts of Ifriqiya by the ninth century (and more successfully to Sicily by the Aghlabids where sugar moulds have been found), though it has yet to be identified in the archaeobotanical record. It is unclear when it was introduced to the Sus region of Morocco, where by the twelfth century it had become one of the most important export crops (Berthier 1966; Ouerfelli 2008: 141–9). Cultivation of cotton and sugar cane would have required the intensification of existing water irrigation networks, and in some places, the introduction of new ones.

Work in the Libyan pre-desert and Fazzan has highlighted the importance of irrigation (especially *foggara* or *qanat* technology) and floodwater control in arid zones in the Roman period (Mattingly 2003). This technology is not an Islamic innovation in North Africa as elsewhere in the Islamic world (Avni 2018), and already had spread westwards in late antiquity to Algeria from the Libyan Fazzan (Wilson 2006). In Morocco, and perhaps the oases of central Algeria, there are few *foggara*, but new canal-based systems were built at Sijilmasa and in the Wadi Draa for the first time in the eighth and ninth centuries, associated with a great expansion in oasis cultivation (Capel 2017; Mattingly et al. 2017). Not all oasis zones were fed by *foggara* technology, and *dalw* wells seem to be an Islamic introduction but of unknown date (Wilson and Mattingly 2003: 126–7). These consist of a *sanya*, a pulley apparatus operated by an animal which uses a skin bag (*dalw*) to collect water from a well and discharge it into a channel.

Water-storage systems are another under-explored area. In the 1950s, the geologist Solignac (1953) suggested that large circular, polygonal or quadrilateral reservoirs were built in the ninth century on the plains around Kairouan and Sfax, at least some of which were paid for by the state. These vary in size, sometimes reaching as much as 50 metres in diameter, and may be up to 6 to 8 metres deep, and were probably used for grazing animals. There are a variety of forms, but the reservoirs with semi-cylindrical buttresses, capped by a rounded top, are identical to the Aghlabid basins outside the town of Kairouan. Based on masonry, mortar and typology, Solignac suggested that most were constructed between the ninth to eleventh centuries and were related to the pastoral economy and provided water for animals. At Gigthis, for example, several large circular reservoirs lined with re-used Roman blocks are associated with large amounts of ninth-century glazed ceramics (Drine 1994). Many of these cisterns were fed periodically from run-off water from slopes, or by capturing floodwaters through drainage systems and small dams (Mahfoudh et al. 2004). Solignac's dating has been contested in recent years, and it is suggested that many of these reservoirs may also date to the Roman period.

The zooarchaeological evidence shows a continued reliance on sheep, goats, and cattle for milk, meat, wool, bone and leather. The North African scrub landscape is ideal for sheep and goat herding, and these animals dominate the faunal assemblages in the Roman and medieval periods (Fenwick 2013: 233–43 for overview of medieval faunal evidence). Proportions change between the Roman and late antique periods when caprines (sheep and goats) make up about half the total assemblage and increase to two-thirds (67 per cent) of the total assemblage in the medieval period. At all sites, however, sheep predominate over goats, and there is no change in the relative proportion of sheep to goats between the late antique and early medieval periods, suggesting that MacKinnon's (2010) model of environmental degradation needs to be modified for the early medieval period. Cattle husbandry was an important element of the economy in the wetter northern Morocco and Algeria, in contrast to sites further east in Tunisia and Libya. Chickens had become increasingly important in late antiquity for eggs and meat, and in coastal regions, fish and molluscs also formed an important part of the diet. There is a clear drop in pig husbandry in the early medieval period, surely connected to the spread of Islamic dietary rules. Particularly telling is the reintroduction of pigs at the coastal site of Qsar es-Seghir (Morocco) in the Christian Portuguese levels, whereas cattle, sheep and goats dominate the earlier Islamic levels (Redman 1986: 229–30). Nonetheless, at many sites, pig bones are present in small numbers, and some suggest these may be wild boar (Schwartz 1984: 326), which are a common sight in the forested regions of Algeria and Tunisia today and are still hunted (and eaten).

Meat production focused on sheep and goats: the mortality profiles of caprines at most sites show a gradual culling of young, juvenile and young adult sheep/goats, with only around 40 per cent kept to adulthood. This is consistent with a management structure focused mainly on meat production; the older animals were likely female and used for breeding and may also have provided milk and wool. Cattle, in contrast, were probably used primarily for traction and milk: at al-Basra, 75 per cent of the cattle survived beyond four years of age and many showed signs of arthritis (Loyet 2004: 24). The regional and seasonal movement of livestock by pastoral and semi-pastoral groups recorded in historical and modern sources is not immediately visible in the archaeological record. Faunal analysis at Lepcis Magna suggests that the Islamic settlement was producing and consuming its own livestock on a subsistence basis, presumably grazing it in the walled surrounds, whereas the Roman city seems to have been bringing in livestock from elsewhere (Siracusano 1994).

As Marijke van der Veen has noted (2010: 8), there is a significant difference between noting when a new crop or agricultural practice was first introduced, and when a new practice or package of new practices and techniques became embedded and had an impact on society at large. Key issues concern chronology and regional variation: were these changes in agriculture already underway during late antiquity, or do they post-date the Arab conquest? Do we see the new developments first in the Libyan Fazzan and only later in Morocco? And at what types of settlement do we see the first signs of innovation? Are these changes part of an 'Islamic package' which includes irrigation technology? Routine radiocarbon dating of botanical remains is needed, especially at sites that cross the Roman to medieval transition, to enable us to distinguish between continuing Roman agricultural practices and 'new' Islamic practices.

Climate change and ecology

Climate change is increasingly invoked as an explanatory factor in early medieval studies of the Mediterranean (Haldon et al. 2014; Izdebski et al. 2016; McCormick et al. 2012). Palaeoclimatic reconstruction of North Africa is complicated by the fact that standard techniques for climate reconstruction, including pollen cores and marine or lake laminae, require permanent bodies of standing water, which are rare in North Africa. Much of the evidence for climate change in the middle ages therefore comes from temperate Europe, and may not be relevant to the very different micro-ecologies of North Africa (Leveau 2018). In aggregate, however, climate, rainfall and hydrology were comparatively stable over the last two thousand years, with minor fluctuations at different points over the Late Holocene. These small shifts did not affect North Africa uniformly. The climates of the western and eastern Mediterranean experienced a see-saw effect during the Medieval Climate Anomaly (1000–1400 CE) and probably earlier periods (Roberts et al. 2012). Palaeoclimate proxy evidence suggests that as conditions in Morocco and Iberia became drier, Tunisia and Sicily became wetter (Lüning et al. 2018). There is a risk of overly deterministic models of the relation between climate change and agro-pastoral strategies: communities would have responded in different ways to the same environmental stresses, even within the same micro-region.

In a fundamental article, Annik Brun (1989), after conducting pollen analysis in the Gulf of Gabes in southern Tunisia, challenged the 'Arab invasion' hypothesis of deforestation favoured by many colonial scholars. Instead, she proposed a post-Roman aridification phase from the fifth century which reached its maximum around the fourteenth century. Small changes in inter-annual rainfall would have had substantial impact on unirrigated agriculture in those regions, such as the Tunisian steppe, where rainfall averages are close to the required margin for cereal crops. These zones are what Wilkinson (2014) has described as 'zones of uncertainty', where crop cultivation is a risky strategy. The Kasserine survey in the Tunisian steppe found much less evidence for permanent agricultural settlement after the early sixth century. This, linked with the shifting economic situation, may relate to this aridification phase (Hitchner 1994). Unfortunately, archaeologists have been less good at dating more ephemeral sites such as temporary camps or animal enclosures which might demonstrate a shift to pastoralist strategies.

More recent work from the *sebkhas* (periodically flooded salt flats) in the arid steppes of southern Tunisia provides further nuance (Jaouadi et al. 2016). The data from Sebkha Boujmel in the gulf of Gabes indicates a return to an arid climate between 550 and 850, followed by a humid period between 850 and 1450. Between 850 and 1150, there was both a rise in olive pollen and a peak in wormwood (*Artemisia absinthium*), a scrub vegetation that is not palatable and is usually avoided by grazing animals. Olive pollen is a particularly useful indicator of the scale of agricultural activity because cared-for olive trees produce large quantities of pollen, while abandoned trees do not (Langgut et al. 2014). The rise in olive pollen confirms the picture of a fertile and growing olive export industry from the mid-ninth century. The spread of wormwood may also be a response to increased exploitation: modern studies show that it occupies sandy steppes that have been degraded by over-grazing and vegetation clearance. Its spread here seems to be a response to decline in plant diversity under pressure from high levels of pastoral activity as well as heightened interannual and/or seasonal climatic instability. Attempts to redress the impact of over-grazing comes from the nearby Sebkha Mhabeul, which also revealed a series of fire events before 1100, suggesting that burning was used to improve the quality of pasture (Marquer et al. 2008).

Late antiquity is marked by unstable climatic conditions elsewhere in Tunisia and palaeo-ecological studies have revealed a rise in the frequency and intensity of flood events from 550 onwards at Sebkha Mhabeul (Marquer et al. 2008), as well as a series of flood events in the fertile Medjerda Valley (Faust et al. 2004). Flash floods, progressive coastal erosion and rising sea levels in late antiquity seem to have affected coastal sites and their rural hinterlands particularly. A 1990s survey of the Tunisian coastline identified only thirteen sites between 700 and 800, in contrast to ninety sites for the Byzantine period, which they explain in part by an erosive crisis in late antiquity pre-dating the Muslim conquests (Slim et al. 2004: 233–6). We can trace these processes at better-studied larger coastal towns like Carthage, Utica and Lepcis whose shallow ports had already become clogged with alluvium in late antiquity: rising sea levels would have brought flood water, sandblow and salt water into wells and the soil.

In the Libyan Sahara, palaeo-ecological data also supports a modest decrease in rainfall during the Islamic period; however, unlike the steppe regions of North Africa which required rainfall for agriculture, this would have had a minimal impact on oasis agriculture which is dependent upon irrigation using groundwater sources or springs

(Mattingly 2013: 507–8). The high investment costs of creating oasis gardens and the ongoing burden of maintaining irrigation systems and high labour inputs makes oasis agriculture inherently unsustainable (Scheele 2010). In the Wadi al-Ajal in the Fazzan, the mass expansion of *foggara* irrigation by the Garamantes in the early first millennium may have exacerbated a natural decline in the water table which prompted a move to well-based irrigation by the eleventh century (Wilson and Mattingly 2003: 272–5). This decline in the water table seems to be linked to a shrinking of oasis agriculture from the fourth to sixth centuries to a few scattered villages by the eleventh century in the lowest-lying parts of the landscape where groundwater would have remained most accessible to well agriculture.

In Morocco, palaeo-ecological records point to an intensification of human impact on the landscape in the north in the early Roman period (Cheddadi et al. 2015). In southern Morocco and the High Atlas, regions outside Roman rule, several studies suggest an expanding pastoral and agricultural base slightly before the Arab conquest of Morocco. Marine sediment cores show an abrupt increase in sedimentation rates between *c.* 650 and 850, most likely due to land erosion caused by increased cropping and livestock (sheep and goat) grazing (McGregor et al. 2009). The increasing importance of ovicaprines in the early middle ages meshes well with the rise of pine, oak and macquis pollen as goats, in particular, are ideally suited to forage in scrub landscape. In the southern High Atlas, sedimentary analysis in the Assif n'Imserdane valley confirms an increase in anthropogenic pressures (cutting, burning and grazing) between 725 and 940, a little earlier than at Oukaimeden, some 10 kilometres away, where there is an increase in grazing activity between 1010 and 1210 (Ruiz et al. 2014), perhaps in association with the growing importance of Aghmat and Marrakech in the eleventh century. Taken together with the compelling evidence from the Wadi Draa of a shift towards sedentarization from the sixth century and intensive oasis cultivation from the eighth century (Mattingly et al. 2017a), there was a significant increase in agricultural and pastoral activities in southern Morocco in the early Islamic period.

Conclusion

North Africa was an agrarian society, and most of its population would have lived in the countryside rather than in the city. Although it remains difficult to chart the impact of the Muslim conquest on landholding practices, or even to 'see' rural settlement in the eighth century, it is unlikely that agriculture completely collapsed or that the countryside was abandoned; we might rather view this as a period of less intensive agricultural exploitation. By the late ninth century, if not before, North Africa's agricultural sector was thriving. Both the archaeological evidence and literary sources support a picture of a prosperous countryside of estates, farms and villages. Indeed, the limited evidence we possess points to a significant increase in agricultural exploitation across North Africa to meet local and external demand that continued into the tenth and eleventh centuries. There is, as always, significant regional variety in the extent and timing of the changes. Local people had to deal with the changes brought about by fewer but larger cities in Ifriqiya and urbanization in the Maghreb al-Aqsa, as well as to the shifting needs of the economy and new land-management practices: some adapted their animal procurement strategy, while others moved to cultivate other areas, and perhaps in other cases, simply continued much as they had before.

Economic Life

Scholarship on the early medieval economy is dominated by the question of long-distance Mediterranean trade. In Pirenne's (1937) powerful model, it explains both the collapse of western European society and its re-establishment in the tenth and eleventh centuries. Pirenne countered ideas that the fifth-century barbarian invasions were responsible for the collapse of Roman institutions and cities, and instead argued that it was the Arab conquest and its disruption of Mediterranean trade which caused urban life to collapse and political institutions to disintegrate, a view that must be set alongside contemporary arguments displacing late antique collapse to the Arab conquest in North African colonial discourse. Since the 1980s, Pirenne's model has been challenged and modified, but scholars broadly agree that there was a significant drop in Mediterranean trade of bulk staple goods (grain, oil and ceramics) in the seventh and eighth centuries (Hodges and Whitehouse 1983; McCormick 2001). In contrast to the Islamic Middle East, North Africa is thought to suffer a particularly profound economic crisis in the seventh and eighth centuries from which it does not recover until the late ninth or even tenth century, because it was so dependent upon Mediterranean maritime exchange before 700 (Wickham 2005: 728). The latest research supports this image of North Africa already in economic crisis before the first Arab raids and less embedded in Mediterranean networks, though still a significant producer and exporter of goods (Bonifay 2004; Morrisson 2016; Reynolds 2016). However, North Africa is not only a Mediterranean region, it has another sea to its south: the sand sea of the Sahara, and Saharan trade was already developed in the Roman and late antique periods (Mattingly et al. 2017b).

This chapter explores the different spheres of economic life by building up a picture of the goods that were produced as well as traded and circulated, before moving to discuss regional, Mediterranean and Saharan trading networks. It examines the re-emergence of North Africa as an economic powerhouse in the ninth century and the development of new trade and commercial networks in the aftermath of the Arab conquest which linked North Africa to sub-Saharan Africa, Europe and Iraq (Goitein 1966; Marçais 1946a; Vanacker 1973). These networks were not created *ex nihilo*; goods and people moved over far greater distances than before, and in far larger quantities. These new trade links and the goods that were exchanged (many of which are difficult to see archaeologically) can be traced from the written evidence as well as the growing amount of archaeological evidence. Together with the urbanization of the Maghreb al-Aqsa, urban growth and monumental construction (Chapter 3) and the surge in rural settlement and agricultural exploitation (Chapter 4), they provide testimony to a thriving economy by the mid-ninth century, if not before.

Industry

North Africa was one of the most important ceramic producers in the Roman and late antique Mediterranean. Mass-produced, plain and decorated tablewares known as African Red Slip ware (ARS) were made in a red fabric and covered with a red slip and shipped across the Mediterranean. These fine ceramics served as an alternative to more expensive bronze, silver or gold dining sets. In the 1970s, John Hayes (1972) defined a typology which allowed some forms to be dated as closely as fifty years and suggested that the Muslim conquest of the Near East and North Africa caused a clear break in the production and circulation of ceramic in the Mediterranean. Michel Bonifay (2004) adjusted the dating for earlier forms, but the final phases of production remain contentious, in part because our assumptions about the end-date of different kinds of ARS come from tightly dated exports in other regions, rather than from the North African workshops themselves. ARS production at key workshop centres like Nabeul seems to continue into the early eighth century but was of a lower-quality standard, with a whitish fabric and dominated by a late, simpler form of the ubiquitous Hayes 105 plate (Bonifay 2004: 210). This simple form has a reduced distribution. Bowls such as Hayes 109 also continued to be produced until the end of the seventh century, and perhaps into the eighth (Reynolds 2016: 144).

Finewares only ever made up a small proportion of the ceramics in use. Already by the sixth century, handmade cookwares had replaced wheelmade cookwares for jars and cooking pots (Bonifay 2003). The prevalence of handmade ceramics in North Africa suggests a shift from the large workshops of the Roman period to production of handmade and wheel-turned pots at household or village level. There are also changes in the size and form of amphorae: the large Tunisian amphorae such as Keay 50 and 61A continued to circulate, but several new forms of small globular amphora (for wine?) and tiny *spatheia* (for salted fish or olives?) appeared in the seventh century and continued to be produced and to circulate until at least the ninth century (Reynolds 2016). At Lepcis, globular amphorae (alongside distinctive jugs) were produced in an industrial quarter in the area of the former Flavian temple between the late eighth and tenth centuries (Dolciotti and Ferioli 1984). The size of these amphorae would have been much easier to handle on smaller ships and landing places.

The appearance of the first Islamic glazed wares in the late ninth century marks a significant break with earlier ceramic traditions (Fig. 13). Their production required the mastery of new and technologically challenging glazing techniques, as well as the acceptance of new forms and decorative styles by consumers. The yellow ceramics of Raqqada (*jaune de Raqqada*) are extremely distinctive, with their mustard-yellow lead glaze and their abstract designs in green (copper) and brown (manganese). The new technique was accompanied by a new decorative repertoire of anthropomorphic and zoomorphic figures (especially birds) and the addition of certain Arabic formulae such as

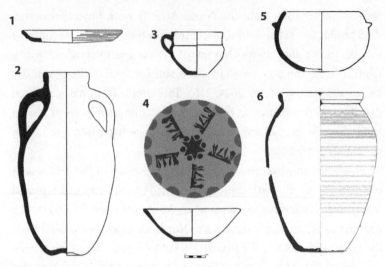

Fig. 13 A selection of diagnostic early Islamic pottery from North Africa.

(1) Plate, Jerba Survey (after Holod and Cirelli 2011: 180, fig. 12.1); (2) globular amphora, Lepcis Magna (after Dolciotti 2009: 261, fig. 24); (3) cup, Raqqada (after Gragueb-Chatti 2009, 341: fig. 9); (4) carinated bowl with white background and Kufic inscription '*al mulku lillah*', Raqqada (after Gragueb Chatti 2017: 357, fig. 17.3b and Louhichi 2010: 62); (5) handmade cooking pot (after Amoros Ruiz and Fili 2011: 30, fig. 12.1); (6) small storage jar, Volubilis (after Amoros Ruiz and Fili 2011: 36, fig. 12.1).

'*al-mulk*' (sovereignty) (Daoulatli 1994). It decorated carinated and flared bowls as well as cups, small bottles, pots and filter jugs, but there is substantial variety in form, suggesting different workshops. While forms and appearance apparently imitate wares from further east, the decoration expresses a more local aesthetic, employing epigraphy, or birds rather than the human figure. A second variant on a white background was much more limited in quantity and diffusion, and to date has only been found at Raqqada. The forms are restricted to bowls with flared rims, conical bowls and dishes with large rims, all of which have Eastern precedents. Unlike the first variant, there is no zoomorphic decoration and the décor is primarily geometric or epigraphic. The Arabic formulae are usually '*al-mulku lillal*' (the sovereignty of God) or simply '*al-mulk*'. Soundes Gragueb Chatti (2011, 2017) suggests that this was not for common use but a palatial production for the Aghlabid elite, inspired by Chinese Tang porcelain.

Lustreware ceramics are a much later introduction to North Africa. Lustre technology entails applying a lustre paint (based on copper and/ or silver) on an already glazed ceramic and then firing it for a second time at a low temperature. This second firing gives the ceramic its characteristic colour range and metallic shine. With the notable exception of the polychrome and monochrome tiles in the *mihrab* in Kairouan (see below), no imported ninth-century Iraqi lustrewares have yet been identified in Africa or Sicily, though they are widely dispersed in Egypt. Lustre ceramics first appear in North Africa in the tenth century, and were made locally as well as imported from Fatimid Fustat. Excavations at the first Fatimid capital of Sabra al-Mansuriya uncovered a kiln with lustreware wasters: scientific analysis shows the Tunisian potters used a different recipe with significantly less silver than that in Fustat (Waksman et al. 2014).

Almost nothing has been written about the monochrome green, brown and yellow glazed pottery that is found widely across North Africa (and the primary marker of medieval occupation). These ceramics of varying quality were produced at multiple regional workshops and distributed widely (see Cressier and Fentress 2011, for a summary). We might assume these follow the same chronology proposed for Sicily: green glazes from the end of the ninth or beginning of the tenth century followed by the introduction of less common brown and yellow monochrome glazes in the tenth or eleventh centuries (Ardizzone et al. 2015: 245–6). Unglazed tablewares, handmade wares, cooking wares, storage containers and lamps, which are the commonest forms, are even less well understood. At al-Basra (Morocco), for example, 80 per cent of all the ceramics found at the site were wheel-made buff-coloured pottery in a limited range of forms, including small and large storage jars, pitchers, bowls, cups and oil lamps which were produced in kilns at the site (Benco 1987). Most unglazed wares show a great deal of continuity with the late antique ceramic repertoire, though new forms such as filter jars and carinated bowls appear by the ninth century, surely linked to changing dietary habits (Amoros Ruiz and Fili 2011; Reynolds 2016). A particularly distinctive form of oil lamp (*qandil*) with a beaked spout, sometimes glazed, appears by the late ninth century, though circular lamps remain more common. Unlike the glazed forms, these utilitarian wares show a good deal of variation between areas, suggesting the continuity in local traditions of pottery production.

The spread of glaze techniques and new ceramic forms poses questions about technology transfer. During the ninth century, a ceramic repertoire emerged similar to that in Sicily and al-Andalus which suggests a shared vocabulary of forms and functions across the Islamic West. The close relationships between the earliest glazed wares of Palermo (*giallo di Palermo*) and Raqqada does seem to support the long-held notion that North African artisans brought glazing techniques to Sicily after the Aghlabid invasion (Ardizzone et al. 2017). However, a different pathway seems to be true for al-Andalus, where the use of yellow glaze is very rare (Salinas and Montilla 2017).

This period also saw technological change in glass production. Most glass used in the first millennium was made from sand and alkali in a small number of workshops in Egypt or the Levant. These were re-distributed in raw chunks and ingots in secondary workshops across the Mediterranean where they would be re-heated and shaped into vessels by blowing, moulding, casting or cold-working (Freestone 2006). Glass was also recycled and vessel cullet (waste glass) was moved around. At Carthage, for example, local workshops were supplied from several different production sites in Egypt and the Levant until the fifth century, when raw glass was more frequently imported from Egypt than the Levant (Schibille et al. 2017). A radical change in glass production occurred in the Levant during the late eighth and ninth centuries, when glass-makers stopped using Egyptian natron as a flux and started using plant ash instead (Henderson et al. 2004). The same pattern may be detected in North Africa, where seventh- to eighth-century glass from Tunisia continues to be of a natron (Levantine) composition (Foy 2003: 87). By the late ninth and tenth centuries, plant ash is used in Morocco at al-Basra (Robertshaw et al. 2010: 371–4), though more analyses of medieval glass are required to prove this hypothesis. In theory, the shift to plant ash would have allowed the emergence of primary workshops in North Africa, as raw natron no longer had to be imported, though artisans may still have imported fine sand or glass ingots from the Levant. Medieval glass workshops are attested at Volubilis, Morocco (eighth to ninth century), Surt, Libya (tenth century), Sabra al-Mansuriya, Tunisia (tenth to eleventh century), and several North African towns were known as being important production centres for different types of glass goods (Shatzmiller 1993: 224–6).

Vast quantities of glass are typically found in Islamic layers at urban sites in North Africa, though they have seldom been studied and thus precise dating is challenging. Everyday items include cups and goblets, beakers, lamps, perfume flasks and medicine bottles in similar styles to the late antique and Byzantine period (Foy 2003). Some new glass forms also appear in the ninth to eleventh centuries, including vessels with relief-cut and lustreware decoration, probably imported from Egypt. Glass was also used as window panes at palatial sites such as at Sabra al-Mansuriya and the Qala of the Beni Hammad, and its discovery in the Algerian Sahara at Sedrata (Aillet et al. 2018: 324) suggests that it may have been used widely in elite contexts. Glass beads and bangles were an important trade commodity and were shipped alongside bowls, dishes, bottles, goblets and 'window' glass into the Sahara, where they have been found at major trading entrepots such as Essouk, Gao and Tegdouast (Devisse and Robert-Chaleix 1983: 515–22; Insoll 1998; Nixon 2017: 152–91).

Metalworking was an important industry in North Africa. Artefacts made in precious metals such as silver or gold are rarely found because they would usually have been melted down and recycled. The same is true of large objects in bronze; however, smaller bronze items, especially jewellery and pins, are found in large quantities, as at Surt (Fehérvari et al. 2002). Everyday objects in iron and lead, such as agricultural implements, weapons, tools, nails and weights, are found in quantity in excavations but rarely studied.

Tantalizing hints about the metalworking industry come from the spectacular objects which have been found in mosques. One well-known and precisely dated example from the eleventh century is the hanging 'lantern of al-Mu'izz' from Kairouan, a large shallow hammered-brass bowl perforated with many small holes and a six-point star at the base to enable the light to shine through. It was hung with three chains with elaborate geometric and floral decoration (Marçais and Poinssot 1948: 411–33). Inscriptions in Kufic script give us information about the artisan who made it, and his patron: 'the work of Muhammad, son of Ali al-Qaysi al-Saffar [the metalworker] for al Mu'izz [the Zirid prince, r. 1016–62]'. This lantern was preserved in the library store-room of the Great Mosque of Kairouan along with a number of cast-bronze chandeliers of similar date. Whilst metalwork is often thought to be imported from al-Andalus, this find suggests that there was a luxury metalworking industry in Kairouan by the eleventh century, if not earlier. In the tenth and eleventh centuries, excavations at the palace sites of Raqqada and Sabra al-Mansuriya revealed cast-bronze items including fountain-heads (*aquamaniles*) in the shapes of rams, but casual finds at small towns such as Beni Khalled (Cressier and Rammah 2006) suggest that these may well have been more widely dispersed in houses. These are very similar to those found in al-Andalus and Egypt but are likely to also have been produced in North Africa.

Textiles were an important North African export as well as import, though they rarely survive. One of the earliest known Islamic textiles, the 'Marwan *tiraz*', was embroidered in Ifriqiya in the mid-eighth century in a silk workshop (a *dar al-tiraz*). The silk was probably imported from Central Asia (Moraitou et al. 2012). Silk was not produced in Tunisia except at Gabes; however, the textile industry of Tunisia processed Spanish and Sicilian silk just as it did Egyptian flax and Sicilian cotton (Vanacker 1973: 677). Woven silk was such an important export that it is mentioned in almost every business letter sent to, or from, the region by the tenth century (Goitein 1967: 102). Cotton was imported into Egypt from Tunisia and Sicily in raw, but more frequently processed, form. Vast quantities of Egyptian flax were imported to Tunisia, where it was then processed and embroidered (sometimes mixed with local-grown cotton) and then sent eastwards as finished pieces. By the tenth century, textiles in the forms of carpets and embroidered cloth were one of the most important exports of Tunisia (Goitein 1967). At Ghirza in the arid Libyan pre-desert, a group of almost eighty textiles of flax, cotton and wool dated to the tenth century has been recovered (Brogan and Smith 1984). Most are made of a clockwise twist (Z-twist) or S2Z-plied yarns and are either undyed or decorated in multi-coloured bands with woven or embroidered designs. The threads of these textiles are spun in a different direction from the majority of Egyptian and Middle Eastern textiles which are anti-clockwise (S-twist) and attest to local North African textile workshops (Bender Jørgensen 2017).

North Africa was also an important centre of manuscript production, as befitted Kairouan's role as one of the leading intellectual centres in the eighth- and ninth-century Islamic West (Fez became increasingly important from the late ninth and tenth centuries). Early manuscripts were copied onto folded parchment and gathered loosely into leather covers or protective wooden boxes or sewn together, several of which are still preserved in Kairouan. Parchment was made from animal skins that have been scraped, soaked and dried; the hair colour of the animal affected the colour of the parchment. The finest skins came from young or even fetal animals (the seizure of fetal lambs was a factor in the Kharajite revolt of 739–40). Paper was introduced to the Islamic world via central Asia only in the eighth century, when it was used for government documents, before becoming widespread from the second half of the tenth century. In North Africa, parchment rather than paper continued to be the main medium for manuscripts and Qurans until the fourteenth century, written in the characteristic Maghrebi (western) script. Scribes also used parchment for private letters and accounts sent from Tunisia to Egypt, and these have been found in the Geniza archives into the middle of the eleventh century, even though Egyptians had already transitioned to paper (Bloom 2001: 85–9).

Little is known about the workshops where these goods were produced, though certain activities such as ceramic production, metalworking and fulling may have concentrated on the outskirts of towns, presumably due to their smell and polluting nature. The medieval pottery kilns at Volubilis, for example, are located in the abandoned area of the Roman town, immediately north of the wall that bounded the medieval settlement (Akerraz 1998). Similarly, work at al-Basra has identified an industrial sector in the western zone of the site, in which they have excavated two updraft kilns producing pottery and roof-tiles and a metalworking area, where large concentrations of slag, charcoal and burned animal bone and bone tools for working metal were found (Benco et al. 2002). At Lepcis Magna too, in addition to kilns in the harbour area, there is some evidence of industrial production (glass-making?) outside the walls in the Hunting Baths, which probably dates to the medieval period (Laronde 1994: 1002). At Thuburnica, large amounts of Arab ceramics and debris indicating a kiln were found in the Sanctuary of Saturn, also located on the edge of the settlement (Carton 1907: 381–2).

Trade and exchange

The emphasis on long-distance trade and Mediterranean exchange networks in literature on the medieval economy is driven by the evidence that we are able to draw upon. Archaeologists usually rely on ceramics as a proxy for movement and circulation of goods, since they survive so well. In the early medieval period, however, ceramics are quite simply not the right proxy to explore economic complexity, to trace routes or to understand the relative importance of local, regional and inter-regional networks. This is not only because the study of ceramics is far behind that of the Middle East, Spain or Sicily, though this is an important factor. The expense and difficulty of transporting pottery in inland North Africa, a region without any navigable rivers, means that we rarely find imported ceramics in inland regions, even in late antiquity (Bonifay 2013). Ceramics were much less important goods than grain, olive oil and wine – which would have often been transported in skins, sacks or barrels. It is not until the tenth and especially the eleventh century that we have anything so convincing as ARS – for this is the moment when lead-glazed ceramic appears everywhere. This phenomenon continued: as Derek Kennet (1994: 276) points out, lead-glazed wares are rarely found on sites until the late tenth century, when they begin to appear across North Africa and Sicily, even penetrating the pre-desert and Sahara. And just as in late antiquity, this phenomenon does not reflect long-distance trade in ceramics but rather the emergence of regional production centres producing a relatively homogenous repertoire of glazed forms.

In the early medieval period, North Africa was a mix of regional economies, some of which were more linked into Mediterranean or Saharan networks than others. Most trade and exchange was regional and operated within the same localized exchange networks as in the Byzantine period (see Bonifay 2004: 201), though on a significantly smaller scale. Excavations at Sidi Jdidi, Pupput and Neapolis show that northern Tunisian workshops continued to distribute ARS well into the eighth century (Bonifay 2003: 563; Duval et al. 2002: 190). Tablewares manufactured in central and southern Tunisia continued to circulate in medieval Jerba as they had done in earlier periods (Fontana 2000: 100). At Lepcis Magna, the globular amphorae and jugs produced at the medieval kiln circulated to the village and *ksour* sites in the town's immediate hinterland and along the *wadis* along the route linking Ghat, Jarma and Sogna to Lepcis Magna (Cirelli et al. 2012: 772). The amphorae, a type produced in the central Mediterranean, were widely circulated and presumably contained olive oil produced in the olive groves that made the Lepcitanian elite so famously wealthy in the Roman period.

A compelling picture of the small-scale nature of regional networks comes from al-Basra in Morocco. Here, excavations revealed two rectangular updraft kilns which produced a limited range of buff wheel-made ceramics for the town's inhabitants and consisted of 80 per cent of the urban ceramic assemblage (Benco 1987). The residents of the town therefore purchased the bulk of their ceramics locally, rather than importing them from elsewhere. Survey in the town's hinterland identified a number of small rural sites defined by ceramic scatters, roof-tiles and grinding stones (Ennahid 2001). Chemical compositional analysis showed that the buff-vessels produced at al-Basra were traded to these hinterland sites up to 40 kilometres from the town (Benco et al. 2009). The pattern of distribution reflects a network dispersed through a weekly market system, which continues to form an integral part of the rural Moroccan economy: each region has a central market with a radius of 40 to 50 kilometres (or a 10- to 12-hour walk), with smaller markets servicing an area of 7 to 22 kilometres, or a 2-hour walk. This system of periodic markets may be inferred from Roman and medieval sources which describe weekly rural, or tribal, markets where people met to trade a variety of products (Shaw 1991; Cressier 1992). Some of these marketplaces were named after a tribe or important person, or day of the week, and many were located at route intersections so that a number of villages and hamlets could have access to the products. Others were found at the boundaries of ecological zones to facilitate the trade between farmers and pastoralists (Cressier 1992).

Significantly, chemical analysis identified two other compositional groups of ceramics which were probably made elsewhere and brought to al-Basra. The first of these were glazed bowls and cups which required a different firing technology to the buff-ware; these made up only 2 per cent of the al-Basra assemblage and must have been imported from elsewhere. The second compositional group relates to a cream-ware fabric (often red or brown painted) used primarily for pitchers and oil lamps, very similar to Berber pottery produced in northern Morocco today. Here, we see that local production was sufficient to satisfy local markets, but the long-distance movement of ceramics was restricted to high-prestige ceramics like the glazed wares and perhaps to specialist forms like jugs and lamps.

The pattern observed at al-Basra is reproduced elsewhere. Initially, the glazed ceramics produced at Kairouan had a very localized distribution within Tunisia (Louhichi 1999: 675; Louhichi and Picon 1983: 45). In contrast, the late ninth-century 'Raqqada ware' with a yellow background and green and brown decoration were diffused across North Africa and Sicily, and are attested in many centres: Tunis, Bulla Regia, Oudna, Sbeïtla, Mactar, Haïdra, Dougga, Belalis Maior, Uchi Maius, Thysdrus and Zama, and unpublished reports from Rougga, Borjine and Souar (Gragueb Chatti 2017). Similar examples have been found at Ajdabiya, Sidi Khebrish and Madinat Sultan in Cyrenaica, and in the Libyan Fazzan. Far to the west, a similar form and decoration has been found at Tahart and even as far south as Tegdaoust in Mauretania (Louhichi and Picon 1983). The widespread adoption, and perhaps imitation, of these eastern-inspired forms reflect the scale of land and maritime trading networks for prestige goods such as glazed ceramics.

A compelling example of the new trading connections that were opening comes from Volubilis in Morocco, which had become almost completely disembedded from Mediterranean trading networks by the fourth century. Even the most widely circulated African Red Slip wares seem to have stopped reaching Volubilis and the Oued Sebou valley by the middle of the fifth century (Rebuffat 1986: 651), when much of the city was destroyed by an earthquake. The numismatic assemblage is even more telling: only one coin has been found for each of the fifth, sixth and seventh centuries in a hundred years of excavations. The only imported goods in the sixth and seventh centuries are a handful of ornate Byzantine bronze censers and lamps, some marked with crosses, perhaps to perform Christian liturgical needs (Villaverde Vega 2001: 157–74). Our picture of the late antique settlement, then, is of a place that was largely disconnected from Mediterranean or Atlantic trading routes and of an urban elite, strongly rooted in the Moorish cities of the west, who could perhaps afford a restricted range of high-status, prestige goods made elsewhere in the Mediterranean for funerary or liturgical uses, but not for everyday purposes. The sorts of imported goods that we find at late antique Volubilis are exotic goods, but of a restricted type.

In the eighth century, everything changes. In contrast to a single coin of Constans II (r. 641–88) from the seventh century, there are hundreds of gold, silver and bronze coins for the eighth century, some minted at Volubilis itself (under its new name of Walila) (Eustache 1956, 1966). The large amount of coins found at the site reveals a degree of wealth that is very different to the preceding centuries and reflects the town's new-found role as an economic hub. The coins suggest that Islamic Volubilis was emerging from its localism by extending north and east in its trading activities, even though this is not reflected in bulk goods such as ceramics. Coin finds at the workshop in the *maison au compas*, discarded where commercial exchanges take place, suggest that craft specialists such as potters and metalworkers were accepting money in exchange for goods and services and saving their earnings in small caches (Akerraz 1998). Small, overlapping urban and regional networks such as these were more broadly linked by longer-reaching Mediterranean and Saharan trade networks for more valuable goods such as gold, slaves, textiles, spices, glass and precious metals, all of which are difficult to identify archaeologically.

We know very little archaeologically about the actual spaces of exchange – markets, *suqs* and shops – frequently described in the Arabic geographies. As in the Levant, caliphs and rulers invested in building markets as well as maintaining a regulated weight and measure system. A *suq* was built in Kairouan under Hisham's orders (r. 724–43) on a long street along the west face of the Grand Mosque; like those built in Syria-Palestine, the street was probably colonnaded (Mahfoudh 2003: 75). At Tocra (in Cyrenaica), shops were added onto the wide paved *decumanus maximus* outside the Byzantine fort in the mid-seventh century or immediately after (Jones 1983), similar to the shops at Jerash or Palmyra (Walmsley 2007). At other sites such as Sétif, markets may have been situated on the edge of the town. Here, excavations uncovered a possible market area suggested by massive silos below a tenth- to eleventh-century residential quarter (Mohamedi et al. 1991).

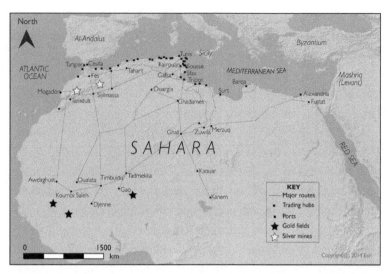

Fig. 14 Map of Mediterranean ports and Saharan trade routes (Corisande Fenwick).

Mediterranean trading networks

The Arab conquests, as in so many other instances, did not bring an end to Mediterranean trade, though it was much reduced from the fourth to sixth centuries onwards. Trade and exchange continued even during the fighting and insecurity in North Africa in the latter half of the seventh century. Significant quantities of ARS and amphorae were traded to major entrepots across the Mediterranean in the second half of the seventh century, particularly Rome, Tarragona, Marseille, Corinth, Paphos, Chios and Constantinople (Reynolds 2016: 143–7). Trade crossed political boundaries: North African links with the eastern Mediterranean continued into the latter half of the seventh century, as is shown by the presence of many Tunisian amphorae (probably containing olive oil or perhaps fish sauce) in a church at Ostrakine on the coast of Sinai, which burned between 668 and 685 but had been under Muslim rule (Oren and Arthur 1998: 203–11). Tantalizing hints of the links between North Africa and the wider Mediterranean world come from one of the earliest known letters in Arabic, sent from a merchant in Kairouan to another merchant in the Nile Valley of Egypt in the mid to late seventh century and before the capture of Carthage (Raghib 1991). The letter attests to a significant trade in wine, clothing and other goods (probably by sea) between the two regions, as well as the existence of a large Arabic-literate merchant community and a complex credit system. After the capture of Carthage, trade with the caliphate and Byzantine Mediterranean continued by land and by sea, though it remains poorly understood due to the absence of clear chronological markers and the under-development of maritime archaeology in the southern Mediterranean. As in antiquity, trade connections between Tunisia, Sicily and southern Italy remained strongest despite ongoing hostility with the Byzantine empire. Our best evidence for interaction comes from letters between Rome and the African church on ecclesiastical matters and accounts of merchants moving between Africa, Europe and Byzantium (McCormick 2001). The Crypta Balbi and San Clemente assemblages in Rome reveal continued trade between Muslim Africa and Byzantine Italy in the eighth century (Reynolds 2016), whilst on Jerba, globular amphorae dating to the eighth to tenth centuries found on many sites and produced in local kilns closely resemble amphorae produced in south Italy and along the North African coast (Holod and Cirelli 2011: 174). Links with the western Mediterranean continued, perhaps connected to the Muslim conquest of southern France. At Sant-Peyre (Gard, France), an Umayyad seal was found alongside Tunisian amphorae (Keay 50, 61) and a Tunisian lamp (Bonifay 2004: 485), suggesting that maritime exchange continued with southern France, which Muslim troops briefly held in the early eighth century.

We should not downplay links with the Middle East and Iraq, although only the most valuable and precious goods reached North Africa from such a distance. The Marwan *tiraz* from Central Asia (Moraitou et al. 2012) indicates that already by the mid-eighth century, Abbasid-appointed governors in North Africa were receiving the most luxurious commodities from the Islamic East. Slaves and booty were certainly travelling the other way in considerable numbers, but to date, there is no evidence of mass-produced ceramics such as Coptic or Iraqi glazed wares or Chinese porcelains which would reflect wide-scale exchange of artisanal goods for a wider market. Even in the late ninth century, the polychrome and monochrome lustre tiles from Iraq that decorate the *mihrab* (Bobin et al. 2003) and the teakwood panels of the *minbar* from the Great Mosque of Kairouan are some of our only examples of imported Middle Eastern luxury materials, surely linked to caliphal gift-giving and diplomacy.

Research in Sicily and al-Andalus reinforces the picture of highly regionalized trading networks in the Islamic West where low-cost everyday goods such as ceramics tended not to circulate over large distances and, when they did, were restricted to certain routes. Nonetheless, over time, ceramic forms become standardized thanks to the mobility of artisans and the spread of new ceramic technologies. In Sicily, for example, locally produced versions of the *jaune de Raqqada* appeared soon after the Aghlabid conquest of Sicily, suggesting a movement of artisans to Palermo, the new capital, where they produced the ware which was itself then circulated on the island (Arcifa and Bagnera 2017). Analysis of tablewares and lamps, cooking wares and amphorae confirms strong trading and cultural links between western Sicily and Tunisia in the ninth and tenth centuries, visible in the similarity of certain ceramic forms as well as some imports from Ifriqiya (Ardizzone et al. 2017). Amphorae which would have contained olive oil, wine or other sorts of goods were more widely traded, and Sicilian amphorae have been identified at several North African sites.

Just as Sicily and Tunisia were closely connected by trade, the straits of Gibraltar linked Morocco and al-Andalus – much more closely than Morocco and Ifriqiya. No Aghlabid ceramics have yet been found at the ninth-century towns of Fes, Nakur or Volubilis, though ceramics imported from the central Maghreb or al-Andalus are present (El Baljai et al. 2017). At Nakur, ninth- and tenth-century glazed ceramics from al-Andalus (probably from Bayyana or Málaga in al-Andalus) reveal links across the straits; however, the evidence supports a local western Mediterranean economy for tin-glazed ceramics decorated with green-and-brown glaze

(Cressier 2017). Direct exchange is difficult to discern in ceramics in this period, most of which were produced and consumed at local level.

In the mid to late ninth century, the increasing visibility of a countryside of estates, farms and fortified villages goes hand in hand with increasing evidence for local and long-distance trade in agricultural produce, particularly in olive oil. Both Ibn Hawqal and al-Bakri tell us that the olive oil consumed in Egypt came from Sfax, al-Bakri adds that African oil was exported throughout the Maghreb, Sicily and Europe, and that merchants came from far to negotiate the best price. A tantalizing hint to the scale of the growing export industry in olive oil, comes from a salvage excavation near Borjine in the olive plains of the Sahel, where a large ninth-century amphorae kiln was found next to an olive press building (Louhichi 2010: 18–19). This is a clear example of large-scale olive oil production geared at an export market; the amphorae were presumably being produced in order to ship the olive oil by sea.

A further hint to increasing maritime trade and exchange from the late ninth and tenth centuries comes from ports and harbours (Fig. 14), which were often protected by the *ribats* founded along North Africa's coast (Djelloul 1995; Valérian 2012). Anchorages did not need to have deep harbours or jetties: ships could be moored in the shallows and unloaded directly onto the beach. In Morocco and Algeria, we see a phenomenon of port towns being built on the northern Mediterranean coast in association with inland towns in the ninth and tenth centuries (Cressier 1992). Sailors from al-Andalus also settled in various North African ports or established their own outposts, such as Ténès, Oran and Bégaïa. By the tenth and especially the eleventh century, goods, people and ideas were moving across the Mediterranean on a phenomenal scale, though there was never again any equivalent to African Red Slip ware as a proxy for Mediterranean trade.

Saharan trading networks

While goods and people have always crossed the Sahara, the medieval period was a rare time when large-scale profits could be made from long-distance trade, as well as the more usual patterns of trans-Maghrebi or desert-to-Mediterranean/desert-to-Sahel exchange. A substantial Saharan trading network existed in the Roman period, probably initially channelled through Jarma in the Libyan Fazzan, but later via a number of different Saharan routes (Mattingly et al. 2017b). By the early medieval period, there were three predominant routes, one in the east running south from Tripoli through Fazzan, a second from the Ouargla and Ghardaia oases in southern Algeria via In Salah to Gao in Niger, the third in the Moroccan Sahara running south from Sijilmasa to Awdaghust (Fig. 14). Intermediate routes also existed, including one running south–west from Egypt through the Fazzan towards the Niger (Savage 1997: 84–5).

Trade within the Sahara, like the Mediterranean, functioned within a series of interlocking networks and smaller connections. Goods (including slaves) were rarely moved directly across the Sahara, but rather were moved between series of intermediaries in response to demand by Saharan communities as well as major North African hubs (Wilson 2012). A merchant's house at Ghirza, an important cult site in the Libyan pre-desert that was reoccupied in medieval times, provides an intimate glimpse into the goods that were traded around the Libyan pre-desert. Here, the Roman-period temple (Building 32) was rebuilt and transformed into a house 'of Saharan aspect' between the tenth and twelfth centuries, before burning down (Brogan and Smith 1984: 274). The porch was covered in graffiti, in Libyan script as well as figures of horses and ostriches, and a possible *mihrab* outlined in stones was found outside. The house contained Abbasid and Fatimid coins alongside glazed ceramics, imported and locally produced fabrics (flax, silk, cotton and wool), elaborate mirror boxes, goat and gazelle horns, ostrich feathers and horsehair (from cushions?), datestones, figs, bronze beads, loom-weights, some locally made, others imported (Brogan and Smith 1984: 272, 82–3, 91–309). Many of these reflect short- and medium-distance trading networks, but the imported cloth and mirror boxes may have been exchanged for slaves and salt.

Gold, slaves, dates, spices, salt and precious stones were the main Saharan exports in the early medieval period. Of these, gold in the form of coins minted in Africa provides a possible clue to the levels of trans-Saharan trade in the seventh and eighth centuries. Byzantine Carthage was a mint of great importance, and its output of gold was large (Morrisson 1999, 2004). The provenance of the gold is hotly debated, but Timothy Garrard's (1982) argument that African gold was being used from the late third century AD remains convincing when combined with the evidence from the Fazzan and sub-Saharan Africa for the movement of goods from the fourth century onwards (Wilson 2012). The Byzantine mint at Carthage stopped producing in 695 and was immediately replaced in 698 by Arab gold coins minted at Kairouan. Umayyad coinage is characterized by similar high-platinum gold content to Byzantine coinage in North Africa and the Eastern empire, which suggests that the Arabs melted down and recycled Byzantine gold (Gondonneau et al. 2000). There is another possible explanation: that the Arabs continued to use a sub-Saharan African source which has yet to be identified. In the 730s, shortly after the conquest of Morocco, an expedition was dispatched south of the Atlas 'as far as the land of the blacks' to bring back 'as much gold as wanted' (Ibn ʿAbd al-Hakam 1954: 195–6). Strikingly, Gondonneau and Guerra (2002: 582, table 4) found that the platinum/gold ratios in *dinars* changes under the Abbasids, and claim that this corresponds to a change in the ore used around 750. There are problems with both the sample size and our limited knowledge of sub-Saharan gold sources, but this shift may reflect increasing caliphal investment in North African trading routes rather than a change in dynasty. For example, between 747 and 755, the governor ʿAbd al-Rahman ordered wells to be dug between southern Morocco and West Africa (al-Bakri 1913: 156). The 740s is also when weights and measures start to be widely distributed, suggesting increasing state control of trade and market activity.

The Saharan slave trade is trickier to reconstruct. North Africa was one of the most important exporters of slaves in the medieval world. Hundreds of thousands of slaves were seized during the conquest and in various expeditions into the interior and against the Mediterranean islands: slaving of Berber Muslim populations in Morocco was one of the stimuli for the Kharajite revolt in 739–40. The need for slaves to supply the Abbasids was so huge that governors were dismissed from their posts for not providing enough. The caliph al-Mansur (r. 754–75) sent an army to Ifriqiya to seize it from ʿAbd al-Rahman b. Habib who had claimed that he could not send a tribute in slaves because all the people he ruled had become Muslim and could not be lawfully enslaved (Talbi 1966: 25–35). In the late eighth century, there was already a thriving Saharan trade in slaves via Tripoli, Zuwila and the Lake Chad area, and by the late ninth century, traders from Khurasan (modern Iran), Basra and Kufa (both in modern Iraq) were operating in the slave-trading centre of Zuwila (Savage 1997: 67–87). Staggering estimates as high as 1,320,000 slaves for the period between 600 and 1000 have been proposed for the slave trade from the scanty written evidence (Austen 1992). Problematic as these figures are, they reflect what we know to have been a steady demand for labour from sub-Saharan Africa within the Islamic world. A promising avenue for research on the medieval trans-Saharan slave trade and its impact on Mediterranean societies lies with genetic and isotopic analyses.

By the ninth century, there is a significant rise in the quantities of goods and people traded within and across the Sahara, accompanied with new investment at major oasis nodes on the trading routes. Sijilmasa, the most important northern Saharan node, became a substantial trading centre in the eighth to tenth centuries, with elite housing and imported ceramics (Capel 2017; Messier and Miller 2015). In precisely the same period, many tell sites in the south-west Sahara expand significantly in size and complexity, including Tegdaoust, Koumbi Sale, Gao Ancien, Gao Saney and Tadmekka. Where archaeologists have actually managed to get below early modern or medieval phases – the tells are extremely deep – there is often evidence of temporary occupation and tent-holes from the early first millennium as well as rock art and burials. All of these sites were nodes in Saharan trading networks long before the Arab conquest of the Maghreb, but there is a distinct boom on both shores of the Sahara that seems to relate to increasing demand in the early medieval period.

The site of Tadmekka (modern Essouk, Mali) provides insight into this process from the other side of the Sahara (Nixon 2017). Excavations uncovered gold coin moulds and crucibles dating to 850–900, our earliest physical evidence for the gold trade. These were presumably exchanged for the North African goods found at Tadmekka in this period, including copper, glass, pottery (including a coucoussiere), durum wheat, dates, cotton, silk and semi-precious stones, goods that could only have come from long-distance trade. Similar evidence comes from the double settlement of Gao, a capital of one of the African kingdoms, where mud architecture first appears in the late ninth/early tenth century together with increasing evidence for long-distance trade (Insoll 1996, 2000). Agricultural and animal products (cereals, flax and hides), metals (copper and silver) and glass were traded, and a mid-tenth- to eleventh-century cache of over fifty hippopotamus tusks was found, presumably destined for workshops in North Africa (Insoll 1995). The startlingly large quantities of imported glass and metal from the Mediterranean, and glass and carnelian beads of Middle Eastern provenance, found at the ninth-century site of Igbo Ukwu in the forests of southern Nigeria reveal the immense reach of Saharan trading networks from a very early period (Shaw 1970). At both Tadmekka and Gao, however, significant amounts of glazed pottery and glass from the Islamic world (including Spain, Maghreb and Egypt) only appeared in the eleventh and twelfth centuries. North African glazed wares have been found at a number of sub-Saharan sites: chemical analysis found that more than half of the glazed wares at Tegdouast were produced in Sijilmasa (Cressier and Picon 1995: 392). While these may have been used by Muslim traders, rather than being objects of trade in their own right, they testify to meaningful mercantile contact.

The role of Muslim (and Jewish) traders in Saharan exchange remains a subject of debate. Large diaspora communities of Muslim traders were established throughout the Maghreb and sub-Saharan

Africa between the eighth and tenth centuries in separate quarters or even settlements outside existing ones. Scholars once assumed that these traders catalysed the urbanization of West Africa, an outdated and inaccurate model known as the 'Arab stimulus paradigm', which in its most extreme form held that cities such as Jenné-jeno and Timbuktu were North African Arab trading colonies placed on the far side of the desert to help control the trans-Saharan trade (e.g., Bovill 1958). Over the past three decades, archaeologists have categorically overturned this problematic model, and at the same time challenged the validity of imposing models of urbanism developed elsewhere onto sub-Saharan African history (e.g., McIntosh 2005). Another cautionary tale comes from the Libyan Fazzan where scholars once assumed that Ibadis founded Zuwila, the main Saharan entrepot in the medieval Fazzan. Field survey has revealed that Zuwila was thriving in late antiquity and had already displaced Jarma by the time of the first Muslim raids of the Fazzan to become the main conduit for trade in sub-Saharan goods and slaves (Mattingly et al. 2015). Ibadi and other Berber groups were not responsible for establishing trans-Saharan trade *ex nihilo*: their activities in the desert oases in the late eighth and ninth centuries built on pre-existing networks, which still need to be unravelled for other regions of the Sahara.

Conclusion

On the eve of the conquests, North Africa was a mix of overlapping regional economies, some of which were more linked to Mediterranean or Saharan networks than others. The eighth century is difficult to see, and in much of North Africa this was a time of retrenchment into micro-regional economies, but this was only temporary. On the current evidence, widespread economic revival and a major expansion of commercial activity seems to date to the mid to late ninth century. As we saw in Chapter 4, the archaeological and written evidence support a picture of a prosperous countryside of estates, farms and villages, and a significant increase in agricultural exploitation across North Africa to meet local and external demand that grew significantly into the tenth and eleventh centuries. At the same time, high-prestige items such as slaves, glazed ceramics, metalwork and textiles were produced and circulated, and trade and commercial networks flourished, linking North Africa to new markets in sub-Saharan Africa, Europe and Iraq. The complex web of commercial exchanges that linked the Mediterranean with the desert and sub-Saharan Africa was not linked to a single state system, but rather worked through relationships of trust and kinship enshrined in Islamic law.

Social Life

What was the impact of Muslim rule and the spread of Islam on the people of North Africa and daily life? The much-abused term of 'Islamization' is often used to describe this process, though in very different ways (Peacock 2017). In much scholarship, Islamization is taken as synonymous with conversion to Islam and the development and spread of specifically Muslim institutions and material culture (e.g., Levtzion 1979), whilst for other scholars, especially archaeologists, it is used to refer to the spread of Islamic lifeways, that is, cultural, political and social practices which might not be confined to Muslims alone (Carvajal 2013; Gutiérrez Lloret 2011).

Islamization is distinct from Arabization, the process by which the Arabic language spread. In a celebrated article, William Marçais (1938) argued that the Arabic spoken in North African cities may derive from that spoken by the Arabs in the seventh and eighth centuries, but that the vernacular Arabic of the countryside was closer to Bedouin dialects introduced by the Banu Hilal from the eleventh century onwards. Very early Arabic graffiti and inscriptions from the seventh and eighth centuries have been found in Cyrenaica and Tripolitania, marking the walls of churches, temples, arches and door lintels, which bear witness to the widespread use of Arabic in daily life in Libya by some portions of society, but these have yet to be fully studied (e.g., Harrison et al. 1964: 19–20). A series of Kufic tombstones from Kairouan show that by the tenth and eleventh centuries, even Christians were commemorating their dead in Arabic (Roy and Poinssot 1950). It is extremely difficult to establish the rhythms of written and linguistic Arabization, which was never complete, for a large part of North Africa still speak Berber dialects today.

Both Arabization and Islamization are typically, though almost always tacitly, understood as the process by which something – be it people, actions or things – 'became' something other. Latin, Greek or Berber languages were replaced by Arabic, churches by mosques, and Christian dietary practices by Muslim ones. Problematically, these models assume both a unilinear process of cultural change and that consensus-building is the principal means by which social, cultural or religious change happens. This chapter takes a different stance and focuses on what the most recent archaeological discoveries can tell us about social life in North Africa. It looks at three different aspects: the spread of Islam and religious life; housing and domestic life; and diet and culinary practices.

Religious life and the spread of Islam

On the eve of the Muslim conquest, North Africa was divided into the Christian north, approximately the territory ruled by the Byzantines (modern-day western Algeria, Tunisia and coastal Libya) and the polytheistic Berber zones of the Sahara and western Mauretanias. The Christian north was densely occupied by a web of churches in urban and rural areas (Baratte et al. 2014; Gui et al. 1992). Judaism was also an important religion, though it is difficult to identify archaeologically (Stern 2007). In contrast, while there was a Christian presence in the Berber zones, there are few securely identified churches, and most of our evidence comes from a handful of gravestones, Christian lamps and bronzeware, capitals and carvings (Euzennat 1974). The far west also contained Jewish communities, though the evidence is slim and reliant on later references in Ibn Khaldun and others (Hirschberg 1963). Much of the population seems to have practised polytheistic religions, particularly ancestor worship, or religion associated with the ram (Benhima 2011). These very different religious landscapes had implications for the spread of Islam in North Africa, which proceeded at different paces in Ifriqiya and the Maghreb al-Aqsa.

A variety of models for the spread of Islam have been proposed from the written evidence (Brett 1992; Cressier 1998; Valérian 2011a). Traditionally, scholars of medieval Africa conflated military conquest with conversion. Drawing on the much later conquest narratives, the Arabs were seen as conquering the various Berber tribes and Islamizing the Berber world (Mercier 1875: 64). For some scholars, Islamization occurred quickly, and the majority converted within fifty years of the conquest, with a few pockets of Christians and Jews remaining (Marçais 1946a: 35–40). For others, conversion took place between the seventh century and the incursions of the Banu Hilal in the eleventh century (Gautier 1927).

Richard Bulliet (1979) was the first to quantify conversion in a far-reaching study of the different regions of the Islamic world that has many advocates for its chronology if not its methodology. He produced a statistical curve, derived from a sample of ancestral names found in biographical dictionaries and concluded that mass conversion took place during the tenth century under the Fatimids (Bulliet 1979: 92–103). He argued that the primary factor governing the rate of conversion to Islam was that of contact between Muslims and non-Muslims. Thus, immediately after the Arab conquests, when there were relatively few Muslims compared to non-Muslims, the rate of new conversions was slow because of the low levels of contact between the two groups. As more conversions occurred, the probability of new conversions increased, and from the mid-ninth century onwards, the conversion rate increased exponentially, until most of the population was Muslim. In a provocative article, Michael Brett (1992) suggested that this increased contact came from two waves of trade-driven 'colonization' of the North African interior by Muslims and Arabs. The first sprung out of the garrison cities of the conquest – Barqa, Tripoli, Kairouan, Tlemcen and Tangier – connected by road and sea to Egypt and the East. The second wave affected the far west and dates to the 770s when the Idrisids and Rustamids established new towns on the east–west and Saharan trade routes within and beyond the Roman *limes*. These new towns were peopled in part with immigrants from al-Andalus and Ifriqiya, and for

Brett, 'it seems appropriate to speak of the colonisation of a largely rural region by urban Muslim communities springing up in the midst of an agricultural and pastoral native population' (1992: 61).

In contrast to a trade-driven model of Islam, Allaoua Amara (2011) emphasizes the close links between state power, religion and conversion in a compelling four-stage model of conversion for urban and rural communities in the central Maghreb (i.e., Algeria). The first stage dates to the immediate aftermath of the conquests when some communities converted. The next phase (late seventh to early eighth century) is characterized by the large-scale conversion of rural Berber communities. The third phase (ninth century) saw the urban Christian populations of the Zab and Aurès convert. Finally, in the tenth century, the alliance between political and religious authorities enforced Sunni orthodoxy on the diverse rural communities in southern Algeria. Amara's model thus proposes for Algeria an earlier date for when the minority became a majority.

Archaeology has played no part in these discussions about religious change. This is a missed opportunity, for whilst we may never know why people chose to convert, archaeology may be able to identify when Islam became the dominant religion. It is, of course, perilous to argue about the size of the Muslim community from the size of mosques, or the presence of funerary inscriptions and burial practices, but archaeology can trace the increasing visibility of the materiality of Muslim religious practice in different settings – urban, rural and domestic spheres. Timothy Insoll (1999, 2003) has suggested some material correlates for tracking conversion to Islam: the presence of mosques, burial practices, changes in dietary habits and housing. The last two are more difficult to associate with conversion to Islam rather than changes in cultural practices which might be shared between multiple religious groups. For example, the ban on consuming pork is a tenet of Judaism as much as Islam, and one's religion need not dictate the architectural plan of one's house.

During the reigns of 'Abd al-Malik (685–705) and al-Walid (705–15), a standard visual tool-kit of Muslim imperial power had emerged in

Syria-Palestine which could be deployed within the provinces (Grabar 1987). The monumentalized hypostyle mosque was the most visible sign of the new order: new towns were defined by the conjunction of mosque and *dar al-amara* (government house) at their centres, emphasizing the religious implications of Muslim rule (Bacharach 1991). Differences between Muslim and Christian beliefs were explicitly articulated on the most famous early Islamic monument, the Dome of the Rock (691/2), and repeated in coins, monumental inscriptions, milestones, weights and seals which regularly proclaimed the existence of one God rather than the Christian Trinity. The conquest of Africa thus came exactly at the time when assertions of Islam become more overt in inscriptions in the Middle East, and North African coinage has monotheistic statements opposing Trinitarian concepts.

In Ifriqiya, the link between Islam and the state was made explicit from the earliest days of the conquest. The first mosques were built in the new towns of Kairouan, Tunis and perhaps Tripoli. Of these, the earliest was reportedly that built in Kairouan by 'Uqba b. Nafi in 670 which established the direction of the *qibla* (an angle of 141 degrees), and this remains the dominant orientation of mosques in Tunisia. It was remodelled under Hasan b. al-Nu'man (*c.* 689), under the caliph Hisham (723–42), who gave it a minaret, and under Yazid b. Hatim in 771. Various construction dates and builders are given for the Zaytuna mosque in Tunis, ranging from 84/703 to 731, though an earlier date seems most likely. Nothing precise is known about their appearance before they were rebuilt in an expanded form under the Aghlabids in the ninth century, though presumably both conformed to the architectural template of Umayyad congregational mosques in the Middle East which had been established by 700 (Johns 1999). Such mosques comprised a narrow *riwaq*, or arcade, surrounding a rectangular courtyard on three sides and a hypostyle or pillared prayer hall with multiple bays was placed at the end of the courtyard.

Outside Kairouan and Tunis, the Muslim community in Ifriqiya was a minority in the eighth century. Muslim rule in this period meant military rule by small garrisons of the *jund* who were stationed in the major towns of Tunisia and eastern Algeria, most often in the Byzantine forts but also in extra-mural quarters. Religion seems to have played a significant role in differentiating between the conquerors and conquered in many towns. Early mosques are found only in the new forts or extra-mural quarters rather than in the old Christian towns, where churches continued to operate on some scale. The earliest of these, if the dating is correct, is a small prayer room in the early eighth-century fortress at Belalis Maior. The room (10.70 x 6 m) is divided into two naves and three transepts by re-used columns and contains a platform in front of a recess cut into the southern wall, oriented to the south-east, probably a *qibla* (Mahjoubi 1978: 384). The room opposite contains a channel and could have been used for ritual ablutions. Mosques or prayer rooms have been identified in multiple forts and citadels, including Haïdra, Ain Tuburnuc, Bagaï, Tobna, Laribus, Bordj Hallal and Tigisis, though the dating is ambiguous. Although we know little about these fort-mosques, which are small and typically decorated with spoliated columns, capitals and bases, they share parallels with prayer rooms inside later *ribaṭ*s, such as the prayer room inside the ninth-century Sayyida *ribaṭ* in Monastir (Marçais 1954: 110–12). The absence of evidence for mass construction of mosques or the abandonment of churches suggests that the initial impact of the conquest on religious practices was limited in Ifriqiya: mosques seem to be largely confined to fortresses, presumably for the Arab garrison troops, and to the provincial capitals, where we might expect large numbers of incoming Arabs to live.

A very different picture emerges in the central and southern Maghreb. Conquest chronicles and later judiciary texts make clear that the Berbers made their *islam*, or submission, as pagans rather than People of the Book. In name, at least, they were regarded as Muslim and paid the alms (*sadaqat*) of believers (Brett 1992). The Kharajite revolts about taxation and inequality in the 740s reveal that there were tensions between the converted Berbers and the Umayyad military aristocracy, but the rapid spread of the insurrection suggests that, at least nominally, Islam had spread quickly but perhaps superficially in the rural outbacks of central and southern Maghreb, on the outskirts of the effective rule of the caliphate (see Amara 2011).

Little fieldwork has been conducted in this region, but the site of Volubilis in the far western Maghreb, as so often, provides a good example of what we might expect to see. In the sixth and seventh centuries, the town may have had a Christian community amongst its inhabitants, one of the few isolated Christian pockets in the western Maghreb. Although no church has yet been identified at the site, a small group of tombstones inscribed in Latin containing Christian lamps and crosses is suggestive (Lenoir 2003: 176–8). The written sources relate the local Awraba tribe had already converted to Islam when Idris I arrived in 788, as they declared him imam shortly afterwards (Siraj 1995: 513–17). No mosques have yet been securely identified, though two much disputed possibilities have been suggested: one in the Umayyad/Abbasid quarter (Eustache 1956: 134, n.2), and the other in the ruins of the Roman town, where a 10 x 15 metre rectangular three-naved building containing columns and a small protruding apse (a possible *mihrab*?) was found surrounded by graves, one of which contained a ring inscribed in Arabic (Euzennat 1974: 183–6). Close by, eighth-century burials laid out in accordance with Muslim funerary rites were found in, and around, the late antique cemetery (Akerraz 1998). Excavations reveal a distinct absence of pig bones in eighth-century layers, in stark comparison with late Roman layers, indicating a shift in eating habits in line with a Muslim proscription of pork (King 2018). The visibility of Islam comes through a change in diet, the presence of (possible) mosques and new burial practices.

The religious landscape was transformed under the successor states in the late eighth and ninth centuries. In Tunisia, the Aghlabids built or rebuilt several congregational mosques which still survive today, including the Great Mosque in Kairouan (862), Tunis (856–63), and they also constructed, presumably for the first time, congregational mosques in the major coastal towns of Sfax (849), Sousse (851) and Monastir (ninth century) (Fig. 15: a–d). The biggest buildings in these new and inherited cities, these mosques dominated the cityscape, and

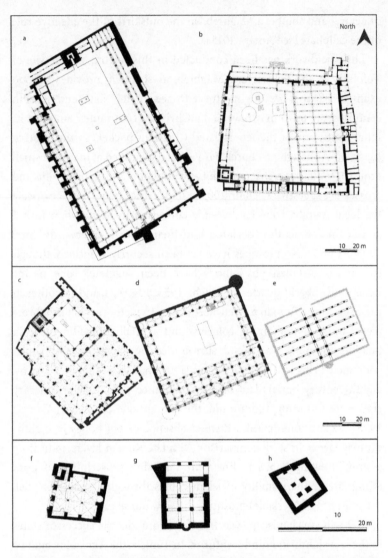

Fig. 15 A selection of early mosque plans from North Africa (Corisande Fenwick). (a) Great Mosque of Kairouan (862); (b) Zaytuna Mosque, Tunis (856–63); (c) Aghlabid mosque, Sfax (849); (d) Aghlabid mosque, Sousse (ninth century); (e) Qarawiyyin Mosque, Fes (ninth century phase); (f) Bu Fatata mosque, Sousse (830–41); (g) The Mosque of the Three Doors, Kairouan (866); (h) possible mosque at the Basilica of St Monique (ninth century?).

their scale and design differentiated them from earlier public and religious buildings in North African cities. They enclosed areas several times greater than the biggest of the martyrial churches of Carthage. The Great Mosque of Kairouan, for example, covers a massive area of roughly 9,000 square metres, and that of the Zaytuna Mosque in Tunis roughly 5,400 square metres. These buildings boast of resources, material and labour, and investment. Besides their religious functions, mosques were central to social and intellectual life in medieval North Africa. Institutions such as the Great Mosque of Kairouan and the Qarawiyyin mosque of Fes built by the Idrisids (Fig. 15e) were among the most prestigious intellectual centres of the medieval world, with rich libraries and centres of teaching.

The Aghlabid congregational mosques are all built on a considerable scale, carefully planned, and use carefully selected spolia to enhance the appearance of the mosques (Harrazi 1982; Saadaoui 2008). A T-shaped hypostyle plan became popular, comprising a central aisle distinguished from the rest of the prayer hall by greater width and height, and a second aisle immediately parallel to the *qibla* wall, whose juncture was usually marked by a dome. The *maqsura*, a reserved space for the ruler, is a standard feature and often appears as a distinct structure, as in the ornate ninth-century wooden *maqsura* of the Great Mosque of Kairouan, the earliest known from the Islamic world. Architectural ornament, carved in stone, wood, plaster or executed in brick, combines motifs familiar from antiquity, such as vine scrolls and other vegetal motifs, with Quranic verses carved or painted in a Kufic script.

While each of the Aghlabid mosques has its own distinct character, the Great Mosque of Kairouan was the model (Mahfoudh 2017b). The formerly square structure was given an elongated rectangular footprint measuring between 125 and 127 metres long by 73 to 78 metres wide overall (Fig. 15a). Within the courtyard, the central axis was emphasized on the prayer-hall façade by the greater elevation of the central nave, and by a triple-arched portal with a monumental central arch, visually surmounted by the impressive ribbed dome that marks the bay immediately fronting the *mihrab*. The *mihrab* (836–63) is the focus of the prayer hall: its horseshoe arch is supported by two spoliated red marble columns with matching Byzantine capitals, and covered by a half cupola dome in intricately painted manchineel wood imported from Equatorial Africa. The interior of the prayer niche is ornamented with twenty-eight openwork marble panels in floral and geometric vine designs. These were re-used Roman marble slabs, probably imported into Africa from Greece or Turkey in the second or third century, and then re-carved in the ninth century by an Andalusi craftsmen who inscribed his work (Mahfoudh 2017b). Behind this pierced marble screen, remains of the mosque's original *mihrab* are preserved. The surface of the *qibla* wall immediately surrounding the *mihrab* is decorated with square polychrome (green, yellow and brown) and monochrome (green) lustreware tiles imported from Iraq, set in a lozenge pattern (Bobin et al. 2003). Immediately outside is a teak *minbar* (856–63), the oldest in the world. Simple in form, its decoration is extremely intricate and consists of numerous panels carved with elaborate representations of trees, leaves and fruits.

The prayer hall and arcades of the Great Mosque contain a staggering 412 re-used capitals and columns, and this was evocatively described by the architectural historian Georges Marçais (1954: 8), as 'a museum of pagan and Christian art'. Al-Bakri tells us that Hasan b. al-Nu'man seized the red porphyry columns for Kairouan's mosque from a church (1913: 195). We can be certain that the imported Byzantine capitals (212!) in the mosque at Kairouan came from churches built or renovated in the sixth and seventh centuries; the same is likely to be true of local made imitation capitals dating to the fifth century or later (Hazzari 1982; Pensabene 1986). Although church buildings were probably the main source of spolia (on which more below), we should be wary of reading this solely as a gesture of religious supremacy. The elements required for mosques were essentially those in North African churches: columns, capitals and marble panels, many of these themselves recycled from earlier monumental Roman buildings (see Leone 2013).

In the late ninth and tenth centuries, small mosques were also founded in urban and rural settings. Diminutive, they usually have a square plan with nine bays and are roofed with domes or vaults. Some are relatively austere, such as the Bu Fatata mosque in Sousse (830–41) which was built on the order of the Aghlabid emir (Lézine 1970: 35–43; Fig. 15f). Others are extremely elaborate, including the Mosque of the Three Doors in Kairouan – founded in 866 by the Andalusi Ibn Kharyun – with its decorative façade of Kufic epigraphy (with Quranic verses and a dedicatory inscription) and floral and vegetal motifs arranged in bands above the triple-arched entrance (Fig. 15g). David Whitehouse (1983) has identified another possible and much simpler mosque above the ruins of the Basilica of St Monique (also called St Cyprian), in Carthage. Here, a rhomboid structure (12.1 x 14.3 m) was found on a very different orientation, and he suggests that it may be an early mosque on the basis of its nine-bay plan, the thickness of its walls (1.6 m), the orientation of the south (*qibla*) wall, and the 'projection' on its outer face which might mark the foundations of the *mihrab* (Fig. 15h). The ubiquitous presence of this type throughout the Islamic lands in the ninth and tenth centuries suggests a prominent metropolitan model, perhaps originating in Abbasid Baghdad.

The new Muslim states in the West also built congregational mosques in their new dynastic capitals and cities in the eighth and ninth centuries, though we know very little about the plan and size of these in their earliest phases. At Fes, for example, rescue excavations have discovered part of the ninth- and tenth-century foundations of the Qarawiyyin mosque, founded, according to tradition, by a Kairouanese woman, Fatima al-Fihriyya, in 857 and enlarged by the Umayyads of Cordoba in 958 (Ettahiri 2014; Fig. 15e). These excavations also found stucco fragments with Quranic inscriptions from the wall of either the ninth- or tenth-century mosque, probably from the wall of the *qibla* that was destroyed by the Almoravids during a later expansion in 1134. An inscribed ninth-century wooden beam dedicated by one of the Idrisid princes indicates that the décor of Idrisid mosques in Morocco was similar to that in Tunisia and al-Andalus, unsurprising given the level of mobility in this period, especially in Fes.

Mosques, tombs and Muslim cemeteries would also have been established in towns and oases to cater for the Muslim merchants and traders who moved there in the eighth and ninth centuries. At Zuwila in the Libyan Fazzan, for example, there is good evidence for a large Ibadi population as early as the eighth century, and a recently obtained radiocarbon date (cal. 670–857) points to the presence of an earlier mosque below the tenth-century White Mosque excavated in the 1960s and 1970s (Mattingly et al. 2015: 51). This would make the mosque of Zuwila one of the earliest mosques known in Libya, and one of only a handful of early mosques known archaeologically in North Africa.

Another early mosque in the West is that of Djamaa El Atiq found at Agadir-Tlemcen, and apparently constructed in 790 by Idris II. Unfortunately, it was excavated before the age of stratigraphic excavation, and we know little more than its plan (Bel 1913). The mosque had an irregular trapezoidal plan (48 x 45 m), at least four bays, with the *mihrab* on the eastern side, and had a bath complex that lay to the north-east (Charpentier et al. 2011; Dahmani and Khelifa 1980). Dahmani (1983) suggests that the mosque straddled the late Roman city wall of Pomaria, acting as the interface between the new communities of Agadir and the inhabitants of Pomaria. The location of this mosque, literally bridging the walls between the new and old town, reflects a major transformation in the way that Islam was used as a tool of state authority. No longer was Islam used to differentiate the incoming Muslims and Arabs from the North Africans, but as a mechanism to build bridges between communities.

Christianity

The limited evidence for construction of mosques in Ifriqiya before the ninth and tenth centuries is matched by a wealth of written evidence for the continuity of Christianity into the fourteenth century (Handley 2004; Prévost 2007; Savage 1997; Talbi 1990; Valérian 2011b). North

African Christians are mentioned in medieval European and Byzantine texts well into the fifteenth century, and there were close links with the Byzantine East, and most strongly with Italy and Sicily and the papacy at Rome (Conant 2012: 367–70). It has proven challenging to identify these Christian populations archaeologically. Of the churches identified as being occupied in the Byzantine period, we know the approximate date of abandonment or conversion for very few. All too often, the date of church abandonment is presumed to be that of the Arab conquest without real archaeological corroboration (Handley 2004). It would be unfair to tar all archaeologists with the same brush; nonetheless, there is a need to interrogate presumed dates of abandonment and move away from assuming in the absence of objective data that the Arab conquest acts as a *terminus post quem non* for Christian buildings.

The stability of Christian institutions is particularly clear at Sbeïtla (anc. *Sufetula*) in central Tunisia, where a diminishing Christian community existed until at least the tenth or eleventh century (Fig. 7). In late antiquity, this town had eight churches, including a cathedral complex with two large churches, five other churches and a cemetery church on the southwest outskirts of the site. The pioneering work of Noel Duval in the 1980s showed that at least four of the churches (Churches I, II, IV and V) continued to be used after 650, and the latter two continued in use until the tenth or eleventh century (Duval 1982: 625, 1999). Basilica II, the Church of Vitalis, even seems to have gained a new altar after 647, five years after the defeat of the exarch Gregory outside the town; people continued to be buried nearby in the early medieval period, including a small group of three tombs on the cardo to its north, one of which uses a Byzantine inscription as a tomb wall (Béjaoui 1996: 43; Duval 1971b: 145–298). In two of the ninth-century insulae, lintels decorated with a chi-rho symbol were used as thresholds (Béjaoui 1996: 42–3, figs. 13 and 5). One wonders whether this deliberate re-use and display of an explicitly Christian symbol reflects the religious affiliation of these houses' inhabitants. Doors, thresholds and gateways represent dangerous permeable openings into safe, domestic spaces and need additional protection (Gonnella 2010: 108–9), but it is unlikely that Muslim occupants would have used a Christian symbol to do this. Not all churches at Sbeïtla survived, however, and in the eighth or ninth century, Church VIII was transformed into a series of subdivided rooms, perhaps serving as workshops, as slag and kilns were found in the area (Béjaoui 1998).

Sbeïtla is unusual in that we have a reasonably good idea of its churches after the seventh century. Elsewhere, the archaeological evidence is not as clear, though many churches retained their Christian function for centuries after the conquest, as in Syria-Palestine (Schick 1995). Islamic lamps are reported in Church 1 at Henchir Seffan in Algeria (Berthier 1943: 79–84). At Bulla Regia, the tomb of an infant was placed inside the southern basilica in the early middle ages accompanied by a small hoard of Umayyad coins (Duval 1971a: 50). Christian graves near churches have been dated to the early medieval period, showing that the churches remained in use at Mactar and Sabratha (Bartoccini 1964: 38; Picard 1954). In Tripoli's hinterland, the Latin inscriptions of cemeteries of Aïn-Zara and En-Ngila reveal the long-term survival of Christianity in the Tripoli oasis as late as the tenth or eleventh centuries (Bartoccini and Mazzoleni 1977). Churches may also have served as important religious spaces for the new Muslim community, at least in Greek-speaking Cyrenaica which was captured much earlier than the rest of North Africa and may have been ruled from Egypt. Intermingled with Christian graffiti (in Greek) supplicating for intervention, the church at Ras el Hilal contains eighth-century Arabic graffiti quoting from the Quran: the earliest is dated to 722 and may mention a monastery (Harrison et al. 1964: 19–20). Other Arabic graffiti (as yet unpublished) has been found inside the apse of the west church at Ptolemais (Ward-Perkins et al. 2003: 181). Christians did not simply continue to use existing churches, but also built new ones. At Kairouan, Qustas (Constans) was granted permission to build a church in the city in the late eighth century (Talbi 1990: 319). Eleventh-century funerary epitaphs in Arabic mentioning a *senior* (d. 1050–1) and a *lector* (d. 1048) attest to clergy at Kairouan, though these tombs were not found in association with any church (Mahjoubi 1966).

The destruction and re-use of churches over time must reflect a gradual decline in the size of Christian communities: at Sbeïtla, for example, while some churches continue into the tenth century, others were given over to secular purposes. Pinpointing when these transformations occurred is of the utmost importance. What little stratigraphic evidence we have suggests that it is a phenomenon of the ninth century or later, coinciding with the construction of mosques in many of the biggest towns. Our clearest example of early destruction comes from the seventh-century basilica at Belalis Maior, which was destroyed and replaced by a fort in the eighth century. Churches were also converted for secular purposes, such as the second church at Belalis Maior, transformed into an oil-pressing facility (Mahjoubi 1978: 242–53), or the sixth-century church at Berenice, which after being damaged in the early medieval period was given over to residences and light industry (Lloyd 1977: 187–94), or Church III at Tipasa, which became a market (Gui et al. 1992: 25). We thus seem to have an initial phase in which churches and mosques co-existed, followed by an increased abandonment or re-use of churches as the numbers of Christians declined and the attitudes of Muslim rulers to Christian communities changed.

A small minority may have been transformed into mosques, including the Zaytuna mosque at Tunis, which was apparently built in the early eighth century on the remains of a Christian basilica, a legend supported by the discovery below the minaret of an earlier Roman building with a capital with a Byzantine cross (Gauckler 1907: 794). Conversion of mosques from churches, where it occurred, seems to have been a later phenomenon which took place several decades or centuries after the church had fallen out of use, rather like the earlier Christian conversion of pagan temples into churches in late antiquity (Sears 2011). Thus, the mosque of Sidi 'Uqba near Sbiba in the Tunisian high steppe seems to have been converted from a church in the Fatimid period (Bahri 2003: 169–77). Another candidate for conversion is that of El Kef (Sicca Veneria), where a building consisting of a domed cruciform-plan room with niches and an atrium is of the enigmatic 'monument à auges' type – broadly characterized as a building containing basins of disputed function – but almost certainly served a Christian function (Mahfoudh 2017a). At some point in the middle ages, it was converted into a mosque: the atrium was extended to the north to create a prayer hall of five naves and six bays; the *qibla* wall was mounted by a dome above the *mihrab*, while the cruciform room was converted into an open courtyard with a minaret in one chamber and a room for ablutions on the exterior of the building (Gauckler 1913: pl. VI–VII).

Many more churches, however, were dismantled for their materials. At Carthage, a city that was severely affected in the aftermath of the conquest, many of the basilicas were systematically stripped; the excavators of Bir Ftouha have shown that the main basilica was dismantled to collect the marble decorative elements, and to create lime (Stevens et al. 2005: 490–1). Excavations at the Basilica of Carthagenna also found few intact architectural elements, but many fragments of chancel marble, capitals and fenestration, pieces of stucco and burnt sandstone in pits and robbing trenches (Ennabli 2000: 45, 73). Within the Basilica Mcidfa, traces of Arab quarrying were found, including an (unpublished) marble column fragment with an Arabic graffito (Delattre 1907: 119), whilst capitals from the basilica at Dermech inside the walls were used in the construction of the Sidi ʿUqba mosque in Kairouan (Vitelli 1981: 10–11). Two Roman columns probably from Carthage in the Great Mosque of Kairouan are even inscribed 'for the mosque', in an elegant ninth-century script (Marçais 1954: 8), indicating a highly organized spolia industry (Fenwick 2013).

By the eleventh century, most churches seem to have been abandoned, and the Christian community was much reduced. Islam had become the dominant religion and mosques of all different sizes and shapes were built in towns and the countryside across North Africa, even in the remotest oases and hill-top refuges. These patterns visible in the material evidence seem to be reflected by two clear peaks in references to African Christianity in Western sources, the first in the ninth century and the second in the eleventh century. Jonathan Conant has suggested that the first reflects the initial large-scale acceptance of Islam in North

Africa in the ninth century, and thus the first awareness of a major threat to North African Christianity, whilst the second corresponds to the period when the Christian community was already a minority (Conant 2012: 369).

Housing and domestic life

Houses provide an intimate glimpse into how the people of North Africa lived through the rapid political changes of the medieval period. Archaeologists have excavated far more houses in North Africa than any other medieval structure, notwithstanding the prominent place given to palace-cities, mosques and *ribats* in modern scholarship. They have excavated houses of all shapes and sizes, from town-houses, farms, huts to the castle-like *ksour* and palaces, and in the different landscapes of desert oases, hilly uplands and the Mediterranean coast. Many of these houses were dug without care or documentation to reach the richly decorated Roman houses or monumental public buildings they covered – but in the last forty years many more have been excavated to modern stratigraphic standards. Houses and, by extension, the domestic sphere and the household, make up the bulk of the evidence that we have for the medieval period and offer an exceptional opportunity to move beyond the monumental mosque-palace-*ribat* focus of earlier generations and to examine how ordinary, everyday people lived.

There are multiple housing types from the early medieval period, ranging in size and quality from huts to *pisé* housing to substantial stone-built compounds. Housing becomes simpler from the mid-sixth century onwards, though there is a great variety in form and size. At Volubilis in the far west, small houses with one or two rooms were found (Fentress and Limane 2018: 116–20). Elsewhere, timber post-built structures have been identified, as in the forum areas of Cherchel (Potter 1995), or *pisé* housing, as in the forum area at Utica (Kallala et al. 2011: 23–4). Scholarly preoccupation with Roman monumental architecture means that the bulk of excavated evidence for early medieval housing is that which was installed in, or converted from, earlier buildings. In late antiquity and the early middle ages, public buildings such as temples and theatres, as at Thuburbo Maius, Lepcis, Belalis Maior, Sabratha and Dougga, or public spaces as the fora at Rougga, Cherchel and Utica were subdivided and given over to housing and industry (Leone 2007). Assessing, or even finding, physical evidence for such conversions is challenging; quite apart from the difficulty of identifying what was going on, we often have to reckon with the wholesale demolition of such phases by earlier archaeologists, intent on 'liberating' the Roman structures.

Houses were not always ephemeral or small-scale constructions. Fortified dwellings, like those at Sbeïtla built between the seventh and ninth centuries, are substantial structures of re-used ashlar blocks (Duval 1990). At Sbeïtla, the Roman insulae continue to be occupied into at least the ninth century (Béjaoui 1996), and it seems likely that the continued use of late antique residential types was more widespread. Other spectacular examples of elite housing survive. At Sijilmasa, an elite residential complex dated by radiocarbon to AD 785–875 is interpreted as an early *dar al-imara*. Certainly, the partially excavated complex is very large, consisting of rooms off a courtyard, a garden and a kitchen. The kitchen contained fire pits, silos filled with ceramic cooking utensils and a mass of animal bones. The house was lavishly decorated with painted and carved plaster, some with Quranic verse, and a fragment of wooden ceiling painting with geometric patterns in an Eastern style (Messier and Fili 2011).

The 'Arab house' (Fig. 16) – a modular courtyard plan with a bent entrance – seems to be a wholly new phenomenon, imported from the East after the conquest, as Elizabeth Fentress has argued in a series of articles (Amamra and Fentress 1990; Fentress 1987, 2000, 2013). Based upon her work at Sétif in Algeria and Volubilis in Morocco, Fentress developed a functional and symbolic reading of housing to trace differences between Berber and Arab populations. The 'Arab house' is defined by a right-angled entrance leading to a large central courtyard off which modular rooms opened. For Fentress, this reorganization of

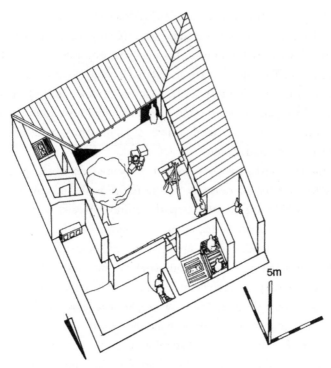

Fig. 16 Reconstruction of an eleventh-century 'Arab' house at Sétif, Algeria (Elizabeth Fentress).

domestic space is symbolic: the entrance protected the domestic space, and the organization of the dwelling reflects a spatial control by the paternal figure and a rigorous separation between men and women. She has convincingly argued that this new house type has its origins in the pre-Islamic Near East and reflects Arab-Muslim patriarchal family organization. Initially, she proposed this model based on her excavations of tenth- to eleventh-century housing at Sétif (see Mohamedi et al. 1991), and argued that these changes in housing and domestic space became widespread in the ninth or tenth centuries as Arabization of cities occurred. The equation of this plan with newcomers of Middle Eastern origin finds confirmation in the recent discovery at Volubilis of a large residential courtyard complex dating to the end of the eighth century, perhaps the palatial complex of Idris I, an Alid emigrant from the East and the founder of the Idrisid state (Fentress and Limane 2018: 120–65). Eventually, this housing became the norm, especially in urban settings, as at Tébessa (Lequément 1968), Honaine (Khelifa 2008) and Jama (Ferjaoui and Touihri 2005), establishing new kinds of privacy and gender organization. The spread of this house form to urban and rural sites by the ninth or tenth centuries is thus seen as a reflection of the Islamization of daily life.

Although most analysis to date has focused on house plan, an interesting avenue of research for the future is the organization of activities within the house. Internal features typically survive well, whether beaten-earth floors, cisterns, ovens or hearths. At Surt, for example, all the tenth-century houses had bread ovens (Fehérvari et al. 2002: 45–66), but in earlier periods, cooking was done outside in the yard using braziers or open hearths – this is deduced from the sooting on cooking pots (Bonifay 2004: 295–8). Storage silos are a common feature of medieval houses: once abandoned, these were typically used to dispose of rubbish. The excavation of these silos has often produced ceramics, animal bones and botanic samples which offer insights into daily life and consumption practices (e.g., Fentress and Limane 2018; Stevens et al. 2005).

Food and diet

Diet and culinary practices offer great potential to identify certain social-economic groups (wealthy/poor), incomers and locals, or religious observances (Christianity/Islam/Judaism). The traditional view of the Mediterranean diet emphasizes the essential triad of wheat, wine and olives, although animal products, fruits, vegetables, pulses and legumes would have also played an important part. Spices probably became more important in the Islamic period (Van der Veen and Morales 2015), along with the appearance of bread wheat (*triticum aestivum sl*), sorghum and emmer in some regions. Recipe books highlight the extensive use of spices in cooking by the thirteenth century and regularly list *atraf al-tib*, a spice mixture used in meat, fish and sweet dishes which was made of lavender, betel, bay-leaves, nutmeg, mace, cardamom, rosebuds, beech-nuts, ginger and pepper (Rodinson 2001: 132). The spread of sugar-cane in the ninth and tenth centuries could substitute for honey as a sweetener.

Several medieval Islamic cookbooks have survived from Morocco and the Iberian Peninsula, mostly concerned with courtly cuisine. Thirteenth-century cookbooks from Morocco and al-Andalus are heavily influenced by local culinary traditions and very different from those of the East (Perry 2007). Moroccan cuisine is more meat-based, while coastal Tunisia (like Iberia) developed a wide repertoire of dishes based on fresh seafood. The cookbooks show that variety was important, not simply in the range of different dishes that could be prepared, but in the number of variants of the same dish. We know, for example, that the Persian musician Ziryab who travelled via Kairouan brought the latest Baghdad dishes to Cordoba, and several Eastern recipes show up in North African cuisine. Easterners were less interested in Maghrebi cuisine, but thirteenth-century eastern cookbooks often include North African recipes for *murri* (a kind of fish sauce) and *mograhbiyyeh* or couscous ('the North African dish') from the twelfth century. Other signs of changes in diet related to the movement of new people might be visible in Morocco, where hulled wheats (einkorn and emmer) dominate in the Islamic levels after they have disappeared elsewhere in North Africa, perhaps because they were associated with the movement of people from Iberia (or Berbers returning) (Fuller et al. 2018).

Religious and cultural food preferences and prohibitions are often more pronounced in animal than in plant foods. Lamb, kid and chicken were the most highly regarded meats in medieval North Africa; wild game was consumed where available, and eggs and dairy products such as sheep and goats' milk, cheese and yogurt were commonly consumed. Fish was not a high-status food, but was frequently consumed along the coasts, as well as being dried and salted for trade inland, though it is difficult to quantify their importance relative to other foods from either textual or archaeological sources. As is well known, pork is not *halal*, or permitted for Muslims; the spread of Islamic dietary prohibitions about pig consumption is reflected in the zooarchaeological record, as we saw in Chapter 4. The noticeable absence of pig bones in medieval assemblages contrasts markedly with Roman and Vandal-Byzantine assemblages, and supports a ninth- to tenth-century date for the spread of Muslim dietary habits across Ifriqiya, with an earlier date for the western Maghreb at least at urban sites such as Volubilis (e.g., King 2018). Strikingly, a ninth- to eleventh-century midden excavated inside the walls at Carthage at the so-called 'Ecclesiastical Complex' contained 20 per cent pig bones, supporting the presence of the Christian community at Carthage described in the written sources (Reese 1977). Outside Carthage's walls, however, no pig bones were found in the contemporary silos of the site of Bir Ftouah (Stevens et al. 2005: 528–33). Wine continued to be produced and consumed. Amphorae from Sicily, surely for wine, are very common at tenth- to eleventh-century Bir Ftouah and Sabra Mansouriya, and have been found in various shipwrecks (Reynolds 2016: 153).

Changing habits in communal dining and service practices associated with Islam are also suggested by the rapid spread of new ceramic forms – conical bowls, platters, pitchers – in the late ninth century. These mark a profound change in consumers' tastes and preferences, and become common in the mid to late tenth century. The one- (or two-) handled *jarrito*, with a wide cylindrical neck and flat base, is a typical western Islamic form, characteristic of North Africa, Spain and Sicily (Reynolds 2016: 155). These are usually unglazed and display considerable variation in fabric, form and decoration. Paul Reynolds suggests that these may have been used for storing cold yogurt or milk (and perhaps for making yogurt, as many of the Spanish examples are charred), a practice common today in Berber Morocco.

Conclusion

Archaeology is ideally placed to explore the everyday spaces of daily life, the domestic sphere, diet and consumption, as well as to understand how religious change was materialized. At this stage, we can say most about the transformation of the religious landscape. The chronology differs significantly between those regions that were under Byzantine rule (eastern Algeria, Tunisia, coastal Libya), and those ruled by Berber chiefdoms in late antiquity. Although our evidence is partial, it does support the early spread of Islam into the central and western Maghreb (and perhaps pockets of the Sahara) in the eighth century, though of course it would never have been complete. This early conversion was an important factor in the collapse of the caliphate in North Africa and the emergence of successor states that used Islam as the main idiom through which to establish and legitimize their right to rule. In Ifriqiya, the rise of the Aghlabids marks a widespread transformation of the religious landscape, with widespread mosque construction and the re-use or abandonment of many churches in the ninth century. In the same period, changing burial rites, diet and culinary practices as well as new forms of privacy reflect the spread of habits associated with Islam. Even at this early stage, it is evident that mosque construction, new culinary practices, food preferences and house types spread at different rates across North Africa, as early as the eighth century in some regions, but increasingly in the ninth and tenth centuries. The next stage must be to analyse, publish and compare the results to understand when and how socio-cultural change occurred at the level of the household, and whether changes may be related to the spread of Islam or broader socio-cultural trends.

Epilogue
North Africa and the Islamic World

*[the Prophet said] 'The image of the world is made up of five parts,
like the head of a bird, its two wings, its chest, and its tail. Medina,
Mecca and the Yemen and the head. The breast is Egypt and Syria.
The right wing is Iraq . . . The left wing is Sind. . . . Its tail is from
Dhat al-Humam to the Maghreb,* **and the worst part of a bird is
its tail.'**

Ibn 'Abd al-Hakam, in Torrey 1909: 19

*The Maghreb was mentioned once in the presence of the Commander
of the Faithful. One of those present said, 'we have been told that the
world has been likened to a bird. The Orient is its head, the Yemen is
one of its wings and Syria is the other. Iraq is its chest and the
Maghreb is its tail.' Now in the assembled gathering there was a man
from the Maghreb . . . He said to them, 'you have spoken the truth.*
The bird is a peacock!'

Mafakhir al-barber, translated in Norris 1982: 2

This book began by drawing attention to the problems that overlooking
North Africa poses to scholarship on the early Islamic world; this
marginalization dates back to some of the very earliest written sources
that we possess. The image of the world as a bird with the Maghreb as
its tail – the worst part – is first attributed to 'Abd Allah b. 'Amr ibn
al-'As, the conqueror of Egypt who led the first raids against Cyrenaica,
Tripolitania and the Fazzan in the 640s and had firsthand knowledge of
the region. It appears in the work of Ibn 'Abd al-Hakam (d. 870) who
was writing about the conquest of North Africa long after the region
was lost to the caliphate and had splintered into an array of Islamic
states, some more powerful than others, who offered alternatives to the

political and spiritual authority of Baghdad. It is the centre's view of a treacherous neighbour that posed a sizeable threat.

A North African view on the Islamic world is naturally very different. The anonymous Maghrebi writer of the fourteenth-century *Mafakhir al-barber* ['The Boasts of the Berbers'] wittily turns the criticism into a compliment, for naturally the tail of the peacock is its most splendid feature. And indeed, whilst North Africa may be situated on the western edge of the Islamic world, it was not an undeveloped or impoverished periphery in the early medieval period. North Africa was the gateway to Europe and the Middle East for gold, slaves and precious items from sub-Saharan Africa. But it was also a prosperous region in its own right, legendarily fertile and wealthy in olive oil, grain and livestock. This wealth in trade and agriculture underwrote a golden age for North Africa from the ninth century and underpinned the dominance of Maghrebi states in the western Mediterranean. Throughout the early Islamic period, North African armies conquered al-Andalus, and repeatedly raided and sometimes settled in Sicily and the western Mediterranean islands, paving the way for the age of North African empires that was to follow under the Fatimids, Almoravids and Almohads.

For too long, the history of the Islamic world has been written from the perspective of the 'centre' – Syria-Palestine and Iraq – those regions which are more frequently described by the Arabic sources and have until recently been the focus of scholarly attention. Today, the study of the early Islamic world is at a crossroads. Our view of the caliphate is being de-centred by new work by historians and archaeologists on the edges – in Spain, Central Asia, Sind, East Africa and beyond. There are a growing number of excellent regional studies on the early Islamic world, but few have ventured out of their chosen region and even fewer have looked to the Islamic West from the East, or vice versa. Comparative research is not one of the strengths of Islamic archaeology (or history). But as the field expands, there is a danger that we will not examine bigger questions from a comparative perspective: What was the impact of Muslim rule and the spread of Islam on the diverse peoples and societies of this vast region? How and at what pace did new forms of

'Islamic' urbanism, architecture, goods, technologies and agricultural techniques develop in different regions? And how did goods and people circulate in and beyond the world that was united by Islam but often divided politically?

This short book has charted the key developments and debates in the archaeology of early Islamic North Africa as a starting point for comparative research on these questions. The Arab conquests of North Africa have all too often been viewed through the lens of the 'end' of the ancient world, rather than examined in their own right. While it remains difficult to trace the shifts in this pivotal period on the ground, the length of the conquest of North Africa – a process that spanned nearly six decades – is a salutary reminder that 'ends' are rarely as neat as scholars might like to imagine. There can only have been a handful of people who, when Carthage finally fell in 697–8, were old enough to remember the initial raids into Byzantine Africa from Egypt five decades earlier. Regime change did not mean the 'end' of the old cities, towns and villages or the sudden abandonment of traditional ways of life: people did not suddenly depopulate the countryside or the towns; they did not stop eating their meals off African Red Slipware or speaking Latin, Punic and Berber. They did not renounce their religions – Christianity, Judaism and various pagan cults – all of which survived and thrived for centuries after the conquest. Two hundred years after the Arab conquest, the townscapes and countryside of North Africa looked very different, but there is no reason to suppose that the changes at the moment of conquest were any less or any more catastrophic for the peoples of North Africa than the transformation of Africa into a Roman province.

With continuity came significant change. The new Muslim rulers attempted to integrate Byzantine and Berber Africa into one vast new province: they imposed new laws, taxation systems, a new currency and administrative language. They constructed a new inland capital city, Kairouan, that displaced Carthage, the capital for many centuries. By the early ninth century, North Africa was ruled by an array of Muslim states but not by the caliphate. These new dynasties succeeded in transforming North Africa's landscape in a way that the caliphate could not. Many of the trends outlined in this book – urban expansion, monumental construction, rural exploitation, the introduction of new technologies, long-distance trade, the spread of Islam – had already begun in the late eighth century when parts of Africa were still under Abbasid rule. But it is only from the mid-ninth century, with the successor states, that archaeologists are able to 'see' wide-scale investment in urbanization, rural landscapes, towns and monumental construction, much of it sponsored by the new North African rulers. At the same time, the introduction of new technologies and the spread of glazed ceramics to many towns provides a visible marker of regional and long-distance exchange that had not been seen since the sixth or early seventh century. Large-scale building programmes of mosques and fortifications, investment in ports and harbours, and a rise in the numbers of rural settlements reveal a prosperous North Africa that thrived outside the caliphate.

Early Islamic North Africa needs to be understood within broader historical narratives and scholarly debates. On one level, it must be viewed within the framework of the early Islamic caliphate and its modes and mechanisms of power. The late conquest of North Africa was a significant Umayyad achievement that brought much of the western Mediterranean under caliphal control: it provides a compelling opportunity to analyse how Muslim imperialism worked (e.g., Fenwick forthcoming a). It is on the edges that political, cultural and military systems change most quickly and radically, as they face new challenges, new peoples and environments. Ifriqiya was a frontier province held by military force. The spatial segregation of the soldiers and their families in the new foundations of Kairouan and Tunis, extra-mural quarters and forts, reinforced distinctions between the military and local populations. What made the North African situation unique was both the quantity of soldiers and the tense relations between the Arab military and the Berber populations – the only peoples to be incorporated into the Umayyad armies and to convert to Islam on such a large scale in the conquest era. Ifriqiya was one of the last regions to be conquered by the Arabs, and it was also one of the first to leave the caliphate, precisely because of these stark divides drawn up under Umayyad rule.

As the caliphate's most notorious failure, North Africa also provides an ideal opportunity to explore how and why the power vacuum was filled by successor states that were Islamic and used an explicitly Islamic rhetoric of power. Islamic structures of power were sophisticated and sufficiently flexible to act as a model for ambitious rulers in North Africa. Yet the centre was not powerful enough to rule the periphery. The rapid collapse of caliphal power and the establishment of new Muslim successor states in North Africa must be read within the emergence of a range of other Muslim states on its frontiers such as the Umayyads in al-Andalus, the Taharids in Khurusan (820), the Saffarids of Sihistan (867), the Tulunids in Egypt (868), and the Samanids in Transoxiana (874), a comparative history of Islamic state formation that has yet to be undertaken.

Finally, the diversity of the region and its peoples must also be emphasized in the histories that we tell. Distinctions between Byzantine and Berber Africa were particularly important in the early medieval period, and in part explain the different trajectories of Ifriqiya and the central and far western Maghreb. This is a very crude level of distinction, and future work needs to be attentive to regional and micro-regional peculiarities, as well as the shifting patterns of connectivity that linked parts of North Africa with each other and the broader world. For this reason, it is essential to consider North Africa within *both* its Mediterranean and Saharan context. As in the Roman period, North Africa was always more closely connected with the western Mediterranean, particularly Iberia, Sicily and southern Italy. The middle ages mark a significant increase in the rise of trade links with sub-Saharan Africa, bringing slaves, gold and other goods to the Maghreb and beyond, that we are only now beginning to understand. At the same time, the Islamic *koine* strengthened links with the Levant by land and sea, particularly with Egypt and Syria, which were also critical staging points on the Hajj route to Mecca. It is only by remaining simultaneously attentive to local and regional diversity and tracing these different connections – caliphal, Maghrebi, Saharan and Mediterranean – that we can appreciate the significance of North Africa and its role in the early Islamic world.

Timeline

Table 1 Empires and states in North Africa between 600 and 1000 CE.

Region	600	700		800	900
Ifriqiya	Byzantium 533–698		Abbasids 750–800	Aghlabids 800–909	
Central Maghreb	???	Umayyads 698–750	Rustamids 776–909		Fatimids 909–1048
Maghreb al-Aqsa	???	Nakur (710–1020) Midrarids (750–976) Barghawata (744–1058) Idrisids (788–974)			

533–4	Byzantine reconquest of Africa
632	Death of the Prophet Muhammad
642	First raid on Cyrenaica from Egypt
647	Battle of Sbeïtla
661	Establishment of Umayyad Caliphate
670	Foundation of Kairouan
696–7	ʿAbd al-Malik's coinage reforms
697/8	Capture of Carthage and Byzantine Africa
c. 710	Emirate of Nakur established in northern Morocco
711	Invasion of al-Andalus (Iberian Peninsula)
739–40	Kharajite revolt breaks out across North Africa
744	Barghawata confederacy established on Atlantic Coast of Morocco
750	Abbasid Caliphate established
757–8	Midrarid state established at Sijilmasa, Morocco
762	Abbasid Capital established in Baghdad by al-Mansur
762	Abbasid armies recapture Ifriqiya
776	Establishment of Rustamid (Ibadi) emirate at Tahart, Algeria

788   Establishment of Idrisid state at Volubilis (Walila), Morocco
800   Establishment of Aghlabid emirate in Ifriqiya
827   Aghlabid conquest of Sicily commences
909   Establishment of Fatimid Empire

Glossary

amsar see *misr*

caliph from *khalifa*, the supreme head of the Muslim communities in the line of the Prophet's successors

dar al-imara urban residence of the caliph or governor, usually on *qibla* side of the mosque

dinar Islamic gold coin (equivalent to the Byzantine *solidus*)

dirham Islamic silver coin (equivalent to the Sassanian *drachm*)

fals/fulus Islamic copper coinage (based on the Byzantine *follis*)

foggara underground conduit for water (known as *qanat* in the Middle East)

hadith sayings attributed to the Prophet or his companions

hammam bathhouse

Ibadi a school of Islam that elects its leader through an assembly of the leading elders rather than by tribal or familial descent

imam one who presides over Islamic prayer; a cleric or leader

kasbah fortress, citadel

Kharajite literally 'the outsiders/outcasts', militant, religious Muslim sect in the eighth century

ksar (ksour) a fortified tower or building common throughout North Africa; examples vary enormously in size and function

madinah/mudun a 'city', which usually had a mosque, a palace, markets, hammam and water utilities

maqsura royal enclosure within the prayer hall of a congregational mosque: it includes the *mihrab* and *minbar*

masjid a mosque or place of worship

mihrab niche or plaque placed in the *qibla* wall (sometimes outlined in stones in open-air mosques)

minbar pulpit used for delivering a weekly sermon (*khutba*)

misr (pl. *amsar*) garrison towns founded during the conquest period

pisé rammed earth or clay used to make walls or floors

qibla direction of prayer (normally towards Mecca)

ribat fortresses built in frontier zones housing religious warriors who defended the faith

shahada muslim profession of faith

suq market

umma muslim community
wadi temporary stream of water in arid regions

Further information can be found in *The Encyclopedia of Islam*, second edition (Leiden: Brill).

Bibliography

Abdeljaouad, L. (2017a), 'Étude épigraphique des graffiti de la grande mosquée de Kairouan', in S. Bouderbala, S. Denoix and M. Malcycki (eds.), *New Frontiers of Arabic Papyrology: Arabic and Multilingual Texts from Early Islam* (Leiden: Brill): 113–37.

Abdeljaouad, L. (2017b), 'Le coufique des inscriptions monumentales et funéraires aghlabides', in G. Anderson, C. Fenwick and M. Rosser-Owen (eds.), *The Aghlabids and Their Neighbors* (Leiden: Brill): 294–320.

Abdussaid, A. (1964), 'Early Islamic Monuments at Ajdabiyah', *Libya Antiqua* I: 115–19.

Abdussaid, A. (1971), 'Barqa, modern el-Merj', *Libya Antiqua* VIII: 121–6.

Aillet, C. (2011), 'Tāhart et l'imamat rustumide (c. 160/777-296/909)', *Annales Islamologiques* 45: 47–78.

Aillet, C., Cressier, P. and Gilotte, S. (2018), *Sedrata: Histoire et archéologie d'un carrefour du Sahara médiéval* (Madrid: Casa de Velázquez).

Akbar, J. (1989), 'Khaṭṭa and the Territorial Structure of Early Muslim Towns', *Muqarnas* 6: 22–32.

Akerraz, A. (1983), 'Note sur l'enceinte tardive de Volubilis', *Bulletin du Comité des travaux historiques et scientifiques* 19B: 429–36.

Akerraz, A. (1998), 'Recherches sur les niveaux islamiques de Volubilis', in P. Cressier and M. García-Arenal (eds.), *Genèse de la ville islamique en al-Andalus et au Maghreb occidental* (Madrid: Casa de Velázquez): 295–304.

Alaoui, A., Ettahiri, A. and Fili, A. (2014), 'L'archéologie islamique au Maroc, les acquis et les perspectives', *Maroc médievale* (Paris: Louvre éditions): 44–7.

Amamra, A.-A. and Fentress, E. (1990), 'Sétif: évolution d'un quartier', in J. Bermúdez López and A. Bazzana (eds.), *La casa hispano-musulmana: aportaciones de la arqueología* (Grenada: Patronato de La Alhambra y Generalife): 163–76.

Amara, A. (2011), 'L'islamisation du Maghreb central (VIIe-XIe siècle)', in D. Valérian (ed.), *Islamisation et Arabisation de l'Occident Musulman Médiéval (VIIe – XIIe siècle)* (Paris: Publications de la Sorbonne): 103–30.

Amara, A. (2009), 'Communautés rurales et pouvoirs urbains au Maghreb central (vii–xive siècle)', *Revue des mondes musulmans et de la Méditerranée* 126: 185–202.

Amoros Ruiz, V. and Fili, A. (2011), 'La céramique des niveaux islamiques de
    Volubilis (Walīla) d'après les fouilles de la mission maroco-anglaise', in
    P. Cressier and E. Fentress (eds.), *La céramique maghrébine du haut moyen
    âge, VIIIe–Xe siècle: état des recherches, problèmes et perspectives* (Paris:
    École française de Rome): 23–47.
Anderson, G. D. (2014), 'Integrating the Medieval Iberian Peninsula and
    North Africa in Islamic Architectural History', *Journal of North African
    Studies* 19: 83–92.
Anderson, G., Fenwick, C. and Rosser-Owen, M. (2017), 'The Aghlabids and
    their Neighbors: An Introduction', in G. Anderson, C. Fenwick and M.
    Rosser-Owen (eds.), *The Aghlabids and their Neighbors* (Leiden: Brill).
Arcifa, L. and Bagnera, A. (2017), 'Palermo in the Ninth and Early Tenth
    Century: Ceramics as Archaeological Markers of Cultural Dynamics', in
    G. Anderson, C. Fenwick and M. Rosser-Owen (eds.), *The Aghlabids and
    Their Neighbors: Art and Material Culture in Ninth-Century North Africa*
    (Leiden: Brill): 382–404.
Ardizzone, F., Pezzini, E. and Sacco, V. (2015), 'The Role of Palermo in the
    Central Mediterranean: The Evolution of the Harbour and the Circulation
    of Ceramics (10th–11th Centuries)', *Journal of Islamic Archaeology* 2:
    229–57.
Ardizzone, F., Pezzini, E. and Sacco, V. (2017), 'Aghlabid Palermo: Written
    Sources and Archaeological Evidence', in G. Anderson, C. Fenwick and
    M. Rosser-Owen (eds.), *The Aghlabids and Their Neighbors: Art and
    Material Culture in Ninth-Century North Africa* (Leiden: Brill): 362–81.
Arnold, F. (2017), *Islamic Palace Architecture in the Western Mediterranean:
    A History* (Oxford: Oxford University Press).
Austen, R. A. (1992), 'The Mediterranean Islamic Slave Trade Out of Africa:
    A Tentative Census', *Slavery and Abolition* 13: 214–48.
Avni, G. (2014), *The Byzantine–Islamic Transition in Palestine: An
    Archaeological Approach* (Oxford: Oxford University Press).
Avni, G. (2018), 'Early Islamic Irrigated Farmsteads and the Spread of Qanats
    in Eurasia', *Water History* 10: 313–38.
Bacharach, J. L. (1991), 'Administrative Complexes, Palaces and Citadels:
    Changes in the Loci of Medieval Muslim Rule', in I. Bierman, R. Abou-El-
    Haj and D. Preziosi (eds.), *The Ottoman City and Its Parts: Urban Structure
    and Social Order* (New Rochelle, NY: A. D. Caratzas): 111–28.
Bahri, F. (1999), 'Histoire de la ville de Béja de l'avènement de l'Islam à la
    conquete ottomane', *Africa* XVII: 1–10.

Bahri, F. (2003), 'Sbiba entre deux conquêtes à travers trois sites islamiques: de la conquête musulmane à l'invasion hilalienne au milieu du ve-xie siècles', in F. Béjaoui (ed.), *Histoire des hautes steppes, Antiquité-Moyen Âge* (Tunis: Institut National du Patrimoine Tunisie): 163–201.

al-Bakri (1913), *Description de l'Afrique septentrionale*, ed. and trans. M. de Slane (2nd edn) (Algiers: Adolphe Jourdan).

Baratte, F. (2018), 'Les villes du nord de l'Afrique entre Antiquité tardive et conquête arabe. Historiographie récente et nouvelles perspectives', in S. Panzram and L. Callegarin (eds.), *Entre civitas y madīna: El mundo de las cuidades en la Península Ibérica y en el norte de África (siglos IV–IX* (Madrid: Casa de Velázquez): 191–202.

Baratte, F., Béjaoui, F., Duval, N., Berraho, S., Gui, I. and Jackquest, H. (2014), *Basiliques Chrétiennes D'Afrique du Nord. II Monuments de la Tunisie* (Bordeaux: Ausonius éditions).

Barker, G. (1996), *Farming the Desert: The UNESCO Libyan Archaeological Survey* (London: The Society for Libyan Studies).

Bartoccini, R. (1964), 'Il tempio Antoniniano di Sabratha', *Libya Antiqua* 1: 21–42.

Bartoccini, R. and Mazzoleni, D. (1977), 'Le iscrizioni del cimitero di En-Ngila', *Rivista di Archeologia Cristiana* 53: 157–97.

Bates, M. (1995), 'Roman and Early Muslim Coinage in North Africa', in M. Horton and T. Wiedemann (eds.), *Antiquity to Islam: The Papers of a Conference Held at Bristol, October 1994* (Bristol: Centre for Mediterranean Studies, University of Bristol).

Bazzana, A., Cressier, P., Erbati, L., Montmessin, Y. and Touri, A. (1983), 'Première prospection d'archéologie médiévale et islamique dans le Nord du Maroc (Chefchaouen-Oued Laou-Bou Ahmed)', *Bulletin d'archéologie marocaine* 15: 367–450.

Béjaoui, F. (1996), 'Nouvelle données archéologiques à Sbeïtla', *Africa* XIV: 37–64.

Béjaoui, F. (1998), 'Une nouvelle église d'époque byzantine à Sbeïtla', *Africa Romana* XII: 1172–83.

Bel, A. (1913), 'Fouilles faites sur l'emplacement de l'ancienne mosquée d'Agadir', *Revue Africaine*: 27–47.

Benabbès, M. (2004), *L'Afrique Byzantine face à la conquête Arabe* (PhD dissertation, Université de Paris X).

Ben Cheneb, M. (1920), *Classes de savants de l'Ifriqiya* (Algiers: Alger Jules Carbonel).

Benabou, M. (1977), *La resistance africane a la romanisation* (Paris: Maspéro).

Benco, N. L. (1987), *The Early Medieval Pottery Industry at al-Basra, Morocco* (Oxford: British Archaeology Reports).

Benco, N. L. (2002), '1990 Archaeological Investigations at al-Basra, Morocco', *Bulletin d'archéologie marocaine* 19: 293–340.

Benco, N. L. (2004), *Anatomy of a Medieval Islamic town: Al-Basra, Morocco* (Oxford: Archaeopress).

Benco, N. L., Ennahid, S., Blackman, M. J., Glascock, M. D., Neff, H. and Speakman, R. J. (2009), 'Chemical Analyses of Pottery and Clays from the Islamic City of al-Basra and Its Hinterland in Northern Morocco', *Actas del VIII Congreso Internacional de Cerámica Medieval. Ciudad Real* 2: 673–84.

Benco, N. L., Ettahiri, A. and Loyet, M. (2002), 'Worked Bone Tools: Linking Metal Artisans and Animal Processors in Medieval Islamic Morocco', *Antiquity* 76: 447–57.

Bender Jørgensen, L. (2017), 'Textiles and Textile Trade in the First Millennium AD: Evidence from Egypt', in D. J. Mattingly, V. Leitch, C. N. Duckworth, A. Cuénod, M. Sterry and F. Cole (eds.), *Trade in the Ancient Sahara and Beyond* (Cambridge: Cambridge University Press): 231–58.

Benhima, Y. (2011), 'Quelques remarques sur les conditions de l'islamisation du Maghreb al-Aqsā: aspects religieux et linguistiques', in D. Valérian (ed.), *Islamisation et arabisation de l'Occident musulman médiéval* (Paris: Presses de la Sorbonne): 315–30.

Benhima, Y. and Guichard, P. (2009), 'De la tribu à la ville: un essai d'approche "régressive" de l'histoire du peuplement de la région de Tébessa', *Revue des mondes musulmans et de la Méditerranée* 126: 91–115.

Berthier, A. (1943), *Les vestiges du christianisme antique dans la Numidie centrale* (Alger: Maison-Carrée).

Berthier, P. (1966), 'Les plantations de canne à sucre et les fabriques de sucre dans l'ancien Maroc', *Hespéris-Tamuda* 7: 33–40.

Bloom, J. M. (2001), *Paper before Print: The History and Impact of Paper in the Islamic World* (New Haven: Yale University Press).

Bobin, O., Schvoerer, M., Ney, C., Rammah, M., Daoulatli, A., Pannequin, B. and Gayraud, R. (2003), 'Where Did the Lustre Tiles of the Sidi Oqba Mosque (AD 836–63) in Kairouan Come From?', *Archaeometry* 45: 569–77.

Bokbot, Y. (2019), 'Protohistory and Pre-Islamic Funerary Archaeology in the Moroccan Pre-Sahara', in M. C. Gatto, D. J. Mattingly, N. Ray and M. Sterry (eds.), *Burials, Migration and Identity in the Ancient Sahara and Beyond* (Cambridge: Cambridge University Press): 315–40.

Bonifay, M. (2003), 'La céramique africaine, un indice du développement économique', *Antiquité Tardive* 11: 113–28.

Bonifay, M. (2004), *Etudes sur la céramique romaine tardive d'Afrique* (Oxford: Archaeopress).

Bonifay, M. (2013), 'Africa: Patterns of Consumption in Coastal Regions versus Inland Regions. The Ceramic Evidence (300–700 A.D.)', in L. Lavan (ed.), *Local Economies? Production and Exchange of Inland Regions in Late Antiquity* (Leiden: Brill): 529–66.

Boone, J. L. (2009), *Lost Civilization: The Contested Islamic Past in Spain and Portugal* (London: Duckworth).

Boone, J. L., Myers, J. E. and Redman, C. L. (1990), 'Archeological and Historical Approaches to Complex Societies: The Islamic States of Medieval Morocco', *American Anthropologist* 92: 630–46.

Borrut, A. (2011), *Entre mémoire et pouvoir: l'espace syrien sous les derniers Omeyyades et les premiers Abbassides* (Leiden: Brill).

Bovill, E. (1958), *The Golden Trade of the Moors* (Oxford: Oxford University Press).

Brett, M. (1978), 'The Arab Conquest and the Rise of Islam in North Africa', in J. D. Fage (ed.), *Cambridge History of Africa* (Cambridge: Cambridge University Press): 490–555.

Brett, M. (1992), 'The Islamisation of Morocco: From the Arabs to the Almoravids', *Morocco* I: 57–71.

Brogan, O. and Smith, D. J. (1984), *Ghirza: A Libyan Settlement in the Roman Period* (Tripoli: Department of Antiquities).

Broughton, T. (1929), *The Romanization of Africa Proconsularis* (Baltimore: Johns Hopkins University Press).

Brun, A. (1989), 'Microflores et paléovégétations en Afrique du Nord depuis 30 000 ans', *Bulletin de la Société géologique de France*: 25–33.

Bulliet, R. (1979), *Conversion to Islam in the Medieval Period: An Essay in Quantitative History* (Harvard, MA: Harvard University Press).

Buzaian, A. (2000), 'Excavations at Tocra (1985–1992)', *Libyan Studies* 31: 59–102.

Cadenat, P. (1977), 'Recherches à Tihert-Tagdempt 1958–1959', *Bulletin d'archéologie algerienne* VII: 393–462.

Cagnat, R. (1913), *L'armée romaine d'Afrique et l'occupation de l'Afrique sous les Empereurs* (Paris: E. Leroux).

Callegarin, L., Kbiri Alaoui, M., Ichkhakh, A. and Roux, J.-C. (2016), *Rirha: site antique médiéval du Maroc. Vol IV: Période médiévale islamique (IXe-XVe siécle)* (Madrid: Casa de Velázquez).

Cambuzat, P.-L. (1982), *L'évolution des cités du Tell en Ifrîḳiya du VIIe au XIe siècle* (Alger: Office des publications universitaires).

Cameron, A. (2000), 'Vandal and Byzantine Africa', in A. Cameron, B. Ward-Perkins and M. Whitby (eds.), *Cambridge Ancient History, Volume 14: Late Antiquity: Empire and Successors, AD 425–600* (Cambridge: Cambridge University Press): 552–69.

Camps, G. (1983), 'Comment la Berberie est devenue le Maghreb arabe', *Revue de l'Occident musulman et de la Mediterannee* 35: 7–24.

Camps, G. (1984), 'Rex gentium Maurorum et Romanorum. Recherches sur les royaumes de Maurétanie des VIe et VIIe siècles', *Antiquités africaines* 20: 183–218.

Capel, C. (2017), 'Sijilmasa in the Footsteps of the Aghlabids: The Hypothesis of a Ninth-Century New Royal City in the Tafilalt Plain (Morocco)', in G. Anderson, C. Fenwick and M. Rosser-Owen (eds.), *The Aghlabids and Their Neighbors: Art and Material Culture in Ninth-Century North Africa* (Leiden: Brill): 531–50.

Capel, C. and Fili, A. (2018), 'Sijilmāsa au temps des Midrārides: nouvelles approches historiques et premier bilan archéologique', in C. Aillet (ed.), *L'ibadisme dans les sociétés de l'Islam médiéval: Modèles et interactions* (Berlin: De Gruyter): 137–68.

Carcopino, J. (1943), *Le Maroc antique* (Paris: Gallimard).

Caron, B. and Lavoie, C. (2002), 'Les recherches canadiennes dans le quartier de la "Rotonde de l'Odéon" à Carthage: un ensemble paléochrétien des IVe-Ve siècles ou une phase d'occupation et de construction du VIIIe siècle', *Antiquité Tardive* 10: 249–62.

Carton, L. (1907), 'Note sur la découverte d'un sanctuaire de Saturne dans la «Colonia Thuburnica»', *Comptes-rendus des séances de l'Académie des Inscriptions et Belles-Lettres* 51: 380–4.

Carvajal, J. C. (2013), 'Islamicization or Islamicizations? Expansion of Islam and Social Practice in the Vega of Granada (South-East Spain)', *World Archaeology* 45: 109–23.

Carver, M. and Souidi, D. (1996), 'Archaeological reconaissance and evaluation in the Achir basin (Algeria)', *Archeologique islamique* 7: 7–44.

Chabbi, M. (1967–1968), 'Raqqada (résumé)', *Africa* 2: 349–52.

Chapoutot-Remadi, M. (1997), 'Thirty Years of Research on the History of the Medieval Maghrib', in M. Le Gall and K. J. Perkins (eds.), *The Maghrib in Question: Essays in History and Historiography* (Austin, TX: University of Texas Press).

Charpentier, A. (2018), *Tlemcen médiévale: Urbanisme, architecture et arts* (Paris: De Boccard).

Charpentier, A., Negadi, S. M. and Terrasse, M. (2011), 'Une mission de coopération en archéologie islamique à Tlemcen (Algérie)', *Les nouvelles de l'archéologie*: 53–8.

Cheddadi, R., Nourelbait, M., Bouaissa, O., Tabel, J., Rhoujjati, A., López-Sáez, J. A., Alba-Sánchez, F., Khater, C., Ballouche, A. and Dezileau, L. (2015), 'A History of Human Impact on Moroccan Mountain Landscapes', *African Archaeological Review* 32: 233–48.

Chelbi, F., Paskoff, R. and Trousset, P. (1995), 'La baie d'Utique et son évolution depuis l'Antiquité: Une réévaluation géoarchéologique', *Antiquités africaines* 31: 7–51.

Christie, N. (2004), *Landscapes of Change: Rural Evolutions in Late Antiquity and the Early Middle Ages* (Aldershot: Ashgate).

Cirelli, E. (2001), 'Leptis Magna in età islamica: fonti scritti e archeologiche', *Archeologia Medievale* XXVIII: 423–40.

Cirelli, E., Felici, F. and Munzi, M. (2012), 'Insediamenti fortificati nel territorio di Leptis Magna tra III e XI secolo', in P. Galetti (ed.), *Paesaggi, Comunità, Villaggi Medievali. Atti del Convegno internazionale di studio, Bologna, 14–16 gennaio 2010* (Spoleto: Fondazione Centro Italiano di Studi sull-Alto Medieovo): 763–7.

Clark, G. (1986), 'ULVS XIV: archaeozoological evidence for stock-raising and stock-management in the predesert', *Libyan Studies* 17: 49–64.

Conant, J. P. (2010), 'Europe and the African Cult of Saints, circa 350–900: An Essay in Mediterranean Communications', *Speculum* 85: 1–46.

Conant, J. (2012), *Staying Roman: Conquest and Identity in Africa and the Mediterranean, 439–700* (Cambridge: Cambridge University Press).

Courtois, C. (1955), *Les Vandales et l'Afrique* (Paris: Arts et métiers graphiques).

Cressier, P. (1992), 'Le développement urbain des côtes septentrionales du Maroc au Moyen Âge: frontière intérieure et frontière extérieure', in J.-M. Poisson (ed.), *Castrum 4: Frontière et peuplement dans le monde méditerranéen au Moyen Âge* (Madrid: Casa de Velázquez): 173–87.

Cressier, P. (1998), 'Urbanisation, arabisation, islamisation au Maroc du Nord: quelques remarques depuis l'archéologie', in P. Cressier, J. Aguadé and Á. Vicente (eds.), *Peuplement et arabisation au Magreb occidental. Dialectologie et histoire* (Madrid: Casa de Velázquez): 27–39.

Cressier, P. (2013), 'Ville médievale au Maghreb. Recherches archéologiques', in P. Senac (ed.), *Histoire et Archéologie de l'Occident musulman (VIIe–XVe siecles), Al-Andalus, Maghreb, Sicile* (Toulouse: Maison de la Recherche): 117–40.

Cressier, P. (2017), 'Nakur: un émirat rifian pro-omeyyade contemporain des Aghlabides', in G. Anderson, C. Fenwick and M. Rosser-Owen (eds.), *The Aghlabids and Their Neighbors: Art and Material Culture in Ninth-Century North Africa* (Leiden: Brill): 491–513.

Cressier, P. (2018), 'Quelques remarques sur la genèse des villes islamiques au Maghreb occidental', in S. Panzram and L. Callegarin (eds.), *Entre civitas y madīna. El mundo de las ciudades en la Península Ibérica y en el norte de África (siglos IV-IX)* (Madrid: Casa de Velázquez): 317–30.

Cressier, P., Erbati, L., Acién Almansa, M., El Boudjay, A., González Villaescusa, R. and Siraj, A. (2001), 'La naissance de la ville islamique au Maroc (Nakūr, Aġmāt, Tāmdult). Résultats préliminaires de l'approche archéologique du site de Nakūr (capitale d'un émirat du haut Moyen Âge)', *Actes des Premières journées nationales d'archéologie et du patrimoine* 3: 108–19.

Cressier, P. and Fentress, E. (eds.) (2011), *La céramique maghrébine du haut moyen âge, VIIIe-Xe siècle: état des recherches, problèmes et perspectives* (Rome: École française de Rome).

Cressier, P. and Picon, M. (1995), 'Céramique médiévale d'importation à Azelik-Takkada (République du Niger)', *Actes du Ve Colloque International: La Céramique Médiévale en Méditerranée Occidentale* (Rabat: INSAP): 390–8.

Cressier, P. and Rammah, M. (2006), 'Sabra al-Mansuriya. Une nouvelle approche archéologique', *Comptes-rendus des séances de l'Académie des Inscriptions et Belles-Lettres* 150: 613–33.

Creswell, K. A. C. (1989), *A Short Account of Early Muslim Architecture* (Cairo: The American University in Cairo Press).

Crone, P. and Cook, M. A. (1977), *Hagarism: The Making of the Islamic World* (Cambridge: Cambridge University Press).

Dahmani, S. (1983), 'Note sur un exemple de permanence de l'habitat et de l'urbanisme', *BCTH* N.S. 19B: 439–47.

Dahmani, S. and Khelifa, A. (1980), ' Les fouilles d'Agadir. Rapport préliminaire. 1973-1974', *Bulletin d'Archéologie Algérienne* VI: 243–65.

Daoulatli, A. (1994), 'Le IXe siècle: le jaune de Raqqada', *Couleurs de Tunisie: 25 siècles de céramique* (Paris: Société Nouvelle Adam-Biro): 95–6.

Davis, D. K. (2007), *Resurrecting the Granary of Rome: Environmental History and French Colonial Expansion in North Africa* (Athens: Ohio University Press).

De Beylié, L. (1909), *La Kalaa des Béni Hammad* (Paris: E. Leroux).

De Miguel Ibáñez, M. P., Fontecha Martínez, L., Izagirre Arribalzaga, N. and De la Rua Vaca, C. (2016), 'Paleopatología, ADN y diferenciación social en la maqbara de Pamplona: límites y posibilidade', in J. A. Quirós Castillo (ed.), *Demografía, paleopatologías y desigualdad social en el noroeste peninsular en época medieval* (Bilbao: Universidad del País Vasco): 163–81.

De Vos, M. (2000), *Rus Africum: Terra acqua olio nell'Africa settentrionale. Scavo e ricognizione nei dintorni di Dougga (Alto Tell tunisino)* (Trento: Università degli studi di Trento).

De Vos Raaijmakers, M. and Maurina, B. (2019), *Rus Africum IV. La fattoria Bizantina di Aïn Wassel, Africa Proconsularis* (Oxford: Archaeopress).

Decker, M. (2009), 'Plants and Progress: Rethinking the Islamic Agricultural Revolution', *Journal of World History* 20: 187–206.

Delattre, A.-L. (1907), 'L'area chrétienne et la Basilique de Mcidfa à Carthage', *Comptes-rendus des séances de l'Académie des Inscriptions et Belles-Lettres* 51: 118–27.

Delattre, A.-L. (1916), 'Une grande basilique près de Sainte-Monique à Carthage', *Comptes-rendus des séances de l'Académie des Inscriptions et Belles-Lettres* 60: 150–64.

Delattre, A.-L. (1922), 'Fouilles sur l'emplacement d'une basilique près de Douar-ech-Chott à Carthage', *Comptes rendus des séances de l'Académie des Inscriptions et Belles-Lettres* 66: 302–7.

Devisse, J. and Robert-Chaleix, D. (1983), *Tegdaoust III: Recherches sur Aoudaghost* (Paris: Editions Researches sur les Civilisations).

Diehl, C. (1896), *L'Afrique byzantine: histoire de la domination byzantine en Afrique (533–709)* (Paris: E. Leroux).

Dietz, S. (1995), *Africa Proconsularis: Regional studies in the Segermes Valley of Northern Tunisia* (Aarhus: Aarhus University Press).

Djaït, H. (1967), 'La Wilāya d'Ifrīqiya au IIe/VIIIe siècle: Étude institutionnelle', *Studia Islamica* 27: 77–121.

Djaït, H. (1968), 'La Wilāya d'Ifrīqiya au IIe/VIIIe siècle: Étude institutionnelle (suite et fin)', *Studia Islamica* 28: 79–107.

Djaït, H. (1973), 'L'Afrique arabe au VIIIe siècle: (86–184 H./705–800)', *Annales: économies, sociétés, civilisations* 28: 601–21.

Djaït, H. (1975), 'L'Islam ancien récupéré à l'histoire', *Annales: économies, sociétés, civilisations*: 900–14.

Djaït, H. (2004), *La fondation du Maghreb islamique* (Sfax: Amal editions).

Djelloul, N. (1995), *Les fortifications côtières ottomanes de la régence de Tunis (XVIe–XIXe siècles)* (Zaghouan: Fondation Temimi pour la recherche scientifique et l'information).

Dolciotti, A. M. (2007), 'Una testimonianza materiale di età tarda a Leptis Magna (Libia). La produzione islamica in ceramica comune', *Romula* 6: 247–66.

Dolciotti, A. M. and Ferioli, P. (1984), 'Attività archeologica italo-libica a Leptis Magna in funzione della formazione professionale per il restauro e la conservazione', *La presenza culturale italiana nei paesi arabi: storia e prospettive* (Rome: Istituto per l'oriente): 329–32.

Dondin-Payre, M. (1991), 'L'exercitus Africae inspiration de l'armee francaise: ense et aratro', *Antiquités Africaines* 27: 141–9.

Donner, F. M. (1981), *The Early Islamic Conquests* (Princeton: Princeton University Press).

Drine, A. (1994), 'Les installations hydrauliques de *Gigthi*', *Africa Romana* XI: 683–92.

Duval, N. (1971a), *Les églises africaines à deux absides, recherches archéologiques sur la liturgie chrétienne en Afrique du Nord* (Paris: E. de Boccard).

Duval, N. (1971b), *Sbeïtla et les églises africaines à deux absides recherches archéologiques sur la liturgie chrétienne en Afrique du Nord* (Paris: E. de Boccard).

Duval, N. (1982), 'L'urbanisme de Sufetula-Sbeïtla en Tunisie', *Aufstieg und Niedergang der römischen Welt* 10.2: 596–632.

Duval, N. (1990), 'Sufetula: l'histoire d'une ville romaine de la haute-steppe à la lumière des recherches récentes', *L'Afrique dans l'Occident romain (Ier siècle av. J.-C. - IVe siècle ap. J.-C.)* (Rome: École française de Rome): 495–535.

Duval, N. (1999), 'L'église V (des Saints-Gervais-Protais-et-Tryphon) à Sbeïtla (Sufetula), Tunisie', *Mélanges de l'Ecole française de Rome. Antiquité* 111: 927–89.

Duval, N. and Baratte, F. (1973), *Les ruines de Sufetula-Sbeïtla* (Tunis: Société Tunisienne de Diffusion).

Duval, N., Slim, L., Bonifay, M., Piton, J. and Bourgeois, A. (2002), 'La céramique africaine aux époques vandale et byzantine', *Antiquité Tardive* 10: 177–98.

El Baljai, K., Ettahiri, A. S. and Fili, A. (2017), 'La céramique des niveau idrisside et zénète de la Mosqué al-Qarawiyyin de Fès (IXe-Xe siècles)', in G. Anderson, C. Fenwick and M. Rosser-Owen (eds.), *The Aghlabids and Their Neighbors: Art and Material Culture in Ninth-Century North Africa* (Leiden: Brill): 405–28.

El-Harrif, F. Z. (2001), 'Monnaies islamiques trouvées à Volubilis: liberté locale et pouvoir abbaside', *Actes de Ières journées nationales d'Archéologie et du patrimoine, Rabat, 1–4 juillet 1998* (Rabat: Société Marocaine d'Archéologie et du Patrimoine): 142–59.

Ennabli, L. (1997), *Carthage, une métropole chrétienne du IVe siècle à la fin du VIIe siècle* (Paris: CNRS).

Ennabli, L. (2000), *La basilique de Carthagenna et le locus des sept moines de Gafsa: nouveaux édifices chrétiens de Carthage* (Paris: CNRS).

Ennahid, S. (2001), *Political Economy and Settlement Systems of Medieval Northern Morocco: An Archaeological-Historical Approach* (Oxford: Archaeopress).

Ettahiri, A. S. (2014), 'A l'aube de la ville de Fès. Découvertes sous la mosquée alQarawiyyin', *Dossiers de l'Archéologie* 365: 42–9.

Ettahiri, A. S., Fili, A. and Van Staëvel, J.-P. (2013), 'Nouvelles recherches archéologiques sur la période islamique au Maroc: Fès, Aghmat et Îgîlîz', in P. Senac (ed.), *Histoire et Archéologie de l'Occident musulman (VIIe–XVe siecles), Al-Andalus, Maghreb, Sicile* (Toulouse: Maison de la Recherche): 157–82.

Ettinghausen, R., Grabar, O. and Jenkins, M. (2001), *Islamic Art and Architecture 650–1250* (New Haven: Yale University Press).

Eustache, D. (1956), 'Monnaies musulmanes trouvées à Volubilis', *Hespéris* 43: 133–95.

Eustache, D. (1966), 'Monnaies musulmanes trouvées dans la Maison du Compas, Volubilis', *Bulletin d'archéologie marocaine* 6: 349–64.

Euzennat, M. (1974), 'Les édifices du culte chrétiens en Maurétanie tingitane', *Antiquités africaines* 8: 175–90.

Faust, D., Zielhofer, C., Escudero, R. B. and del Olmo, F. D. (2004), 'High-resolution fluvial record of late Holocene geomorphic change in northern Tunisia: climatic or human impact?', *Quaternary Science Reviews* 23: 1757–75.

Fauvelle, F.-X., Erbati, L. and Mensan, R. (2014), 'Sijilmâsa: cité idéale, site insaisissable? Ou comment une ville échappe à ses fouilleurs', *Les études et essais du centre Jacques Berque* 20: 1–17.

Fehérvari, G., Hamdani, A., Shaghlouf, M. and Bishop, H. (2002), *Excavations at Surt (Medinat al-Sultan) between 1977 and 1981* (London: Society for Libyan Studies).

Fentress, E. (1987), 'The House of the Prophet: North African Islamic Housing', *Archeologia medievale*: 47–69.

Fentress, E. (2000), 'Social Relations and Domestic Space in the Maghreb', *Collection de l'Ecole française de Rome* 105: 15–26.

Fentress, E. (2013), 'Reconsidering Islamic Housing in the Maghreb', in I. Grau Mira and S. Gutiérrez Lloret (eds.), *De la estructura domestica al espacio social. Lecturas arqueologicas del uso social del espacio* (Alicante: Publicaciones de la Universidad de Alicante): 237–44.

Fentress, E., Drine, A. and Holod, R. (2009), *An Island through Time: Jerba Studies* (Portsmouth, RI: Journal of Roman Archaeology).

Fentress, E., Fontana, S., Hitchner, R. B. and Perkins, P. (2004), 'Accounting for ARS: Fineware and Sites in Sicily and Africa', in S. E. Alcock and J. F. Cherry (eds.), *Side-by-Side Survey: Comparative Regional Studies in the Mediterranean World* (Oxford: Oxbow): 147–62.

Fentress, E., Ghozzi, F., Quinn, J. and Wilson, A. (2014). *Excavations at Utica by the Tunisian-British Utica Project 2013*. https://www.academia. edu/8035031/Excavations_at_Utica_by_the_Tunisian-British_Utica_ Project-2013_E._Fentress_F-Ghozzi_J._Quinn_and-A._Wilson (accessed 21 October 2019).

Fentress, E. and Limane, H. (eds.) (2018). *Fouilles de Volubilis 2000–2005* (Leiden: Brill).

Fentress, E. and Wilson, A. (2016), 'The Saharan Berber Diaspora and the Southern Frontiers of Byzantine North Africa', in S. T. Stevens and J. Conant (eds.), *North Africa under Byzantium and Early Islam* (Washington, DC: Dumbarton Oaks): 41–63.

Fenwick, C. (2008), 'Archaeology and the Search for Authenticity: Colonialist, Nationalist, and Berberist Visions of an Algerian past', in C. Fenwick, M. Wiggins and D. Wythe (eds.), *TRAC 2007: Proceedings of the 17th Annual Theoretical Roman Archaeology Conference* (Oxford: Oxbow): 75–88.

Fenwick, C. (2013), 'From Africa to Ifrīqiya: Settlement and Society in Early Medieval North Africa (650–800)', *Al-Masāq* 25: 9–33.

Fenwick, C. (2018), 'Early Medieval Urbanism in Ifrīqiya and the Emergence of the Islamic City', in S. Panzram and L. Callegarin (eds.), *Entre civitas y madīna. El mundo de las ciudades en la península ibérica y en el norte de África (ss. IV-IX)* (Madrid: Casa de Velázquez): 283–304.

Fenwick, C. (2019), 'The Fate of the Classical Cities of North Africa in the Middle Ages', in R. Bockmann, A. Leone and P. von Rummel (eds.), *Africa – Ifriqiya: Cultures of Transiton in North Africa between Late Antiquity and the Early Middle Ages* (Rome: Deutsches Archäologisches Institut): 137–55.

Fenwick, C. (forthcoming a), 'Archaeology, Empire and the Arab Conquest of North Africa', *Past and Present*.

Fenwick, C. (forthcoming b), 'The Umayyads and North Africa: Imperial Rule and Frontier Society', in A. Marsham (ed.), *The Umayyad World* (London: Routledge).

Ferjaoui, A. and Touihri, C. (2005), 'Présentation d'un îlot d'habitat médiéval à Jama', *Africa* III: 87–112.

Fierro Bello, I. (2017), 'Writing and Reading in Early Medieval Ifriqiya', in G. Rahal and H.-O. Luthe (eds.), *Promissa nec aspera curans* (Toulouse: Les Presses Universitaires): 373–93.

Fili, A. (forthcoming), 'The Maghreb al-Aqsa', in B. Walker, T. Insoll and C. Fenwick (eds.), *Oxford Handbook of Islamic Archaeology* (Oxford: Oxford University Press).

Flood, F. B. and Necipoglu, G. (2017), 'Frameworks of Islamic Art and Architectural History: Concepts, Approaches, and Historiographies', in F. B. Flood and G. Necipoglu (eds.), *A Companion to Islamic Art and Architecture* (Oxford: Wiley Blackwell): 1–56.

Fontana, S. (2000), 'Un 'immondezzaio' di VI secolo da Meninx: la fine della produzione della porpora e la cultura materiale a Gerba nella prima età bizantina', *Africa Romana* XIII: 95–114.

Foucher, L. (1964), *Hadrumetum* (Tunis: Publications de l'Université de Tunis).

Foy, D. (2003), 'Le Verre en Tunisie: L'Apport des fouilles récentes tuniso-françaises', *Journal of Glass Studies* 45: 59–89.

Freestone, I. C. (2006), 'Glass Production in Late Antiquity and the Early Islamic Period: A Geochemical Perspective', *Geological Society, London, Special Publications* 257: 201–16.

Frend, W. H. C. (1952), *The Donatist Church: A Movement of Protest in Roman North Africa* (Oxford: Clarendon Press).

Fuller, D., Pelling, P. and De Varailles, A. (2018), 'Plant Economy: Archaeobotanical Studies', in E. Fentress and H. Limane (eds.), *Volubilis après Rome* (Leiden: Brill): 349–68.

Garrard, T. F. (1982), 'Myth and Metrology: The Early Trans-Saharan Gold Trade', *Journal of African History* 23: 443–61.

Gauckler, P. (1896), *L'archéologie de la Tunisie* (Paris: Berger-Levrault).

Gauckler, P. (1907), 'Les thermes de Gebamund à Tunis', *Compte-rendus des séances de l'Academie des Inscriptions et Belle-Lettres* 51: 790–5.

Gauckler, P. (1913), *Basiliques chrétiennes de Tunisie (1892–1904)* (Paris: A. Picard).

Gautier, E. F. (1927), *L'Islamisation de l'Afrique du Nord. Les siecles obscurs du Maghreb* (Paris: Payot).

Gelichi, S. and Milanese, M. (2002), 'The Transformation of the Ancient Towns in Central Tunisia during the Islamic Period: The Example of Uchi Maius', *Al-Masaq* 14: 33–45.

Gilbertson, D. D., Hayes, P. P., Barker, G. W. and Hunt, C. O. (1984), 'The UNESCO Libyan Valleys Survey VII: An Interim Classification and Functional Analysis of Ancient Wall Technology and Land Use', *Libyan Studies* 15: 45–70.

Goitein, S. D. (1966), 'Medieval Tunisia: The Hub of the Mediterranean', *Studies in Islamic History and Institutions*: 308–28.

Goitein, S. D. (1967), *A Mediterranean Society: The Jewish Communities of the Arab World as Portrayed in the Documents of the Cairo Geniza* (Berkeley: University of California Press).

Golvin, L. (1966), 'Le Palais de Zīrī à Achîr (Dixième Siècle JC)', *Ars Orientalis*: 47–76.

Golvin, L. (1970), *Essai sur l'architecture religieuse musulmane* (Paris: Klincksieck).

Gondonneau, A. and Guerra, M. (2002), 'The Circulation of Precious Metals in the Arab Empire: The Case of the Near and the Middle East', *Archaeometry* 44: 573–99.

Gondonneau, A., Roux, C., Guerra, M. F. and Morrisson, C. (2000), 'La frappe de l'or à l'époque de l'expansion musulmane et les mines de l'ouest de l'Afrique: l'apport analytique', in B. Kluge and B. Weisser (eds.), *XII. Internationaler Numismatischer Kongress Berlin 1997* (Berlin: Staatliche Museen zu Berlin): 1264–74.

Gonnella, J. (2010), 'Columns and Hieroglyphs: Magic "Spolia" in Medieval Islamic Architecture of Northern Syria', *Muqarnas* 27: 103–20.

Goodchild, R. G. (1967), 'Byzantines, Berbers and Arabs in Seventh Century Libya', *Antiquity* 41: 114–24.

Goodson, C. (2017), 'Topographies of Power in Aghlabid-Era Kairouan', in G. Anderson, C. Fenwick and M. Rosser-Owen (eds.), *The Aghlabids and Their Neighbors: Art and Material Culture in Ninth-Century North Africa* (Leiden: Brill): 88–105.

Grabar, O. (1987), *The Formation of Islamic Art* (New Haven: Yale University Press).

Gragueb Chatti, S. (2011), 'La céramique vert et brun à fond blanc de Raqqāda', in P. Cressier and E. Fentress (eds.), *La céramique maghrébine du haut moyen âge, VIIIe-Xe siècle: état des recherches, problèmes et perspectives* (Rome: École française de Rome): 181–95.

Gragueb Chatti, S. (2017), 'La céramique aghlabide de la Raqqada et les productions de l'Orientislamique: parenté et filiation', in G. Anderson, C. Fenwick and M. Rosser-Owen (eds.), *The Aghlabids and Their Neighbors: Art and Material Culture in Ninth-Century North Africa* (Leiden: Brill): 341–61.

Guéry, R. (1981), 'L'occupation de Rougga (Bararus) d'après la stratigraphie du forum', *Bulletin archéologique du Comité des Travaux Historiques et Scientifiques* 1: 17.

Guéry, R. (1985), 'Survivance de la vie sédentaire pendant les invasions arabes en Tunisie Centrale: l'exemple de Rougga', *BCTH n.s.* 19B: 399–410.

Guéry, R., Morrisson, C. and Slim, H. (1982), *Recherches archéologiques franco-tunisiennes à Rougga. III. Le trésor de monnaies d'or byzantines* (Rome: École française de Rome).

Gui, I., Duval, N. and Caillet, J.-P. (1992), *Basiliques chrétiennes d'Afrique du Nord (inventaire et typologie)* (Paris: Institut d'Études Augustiniennes).

Gutiérrez Lloret, S. (2011), 'Histoire et archéologie de la transition en al-Andalus: les indices matériels de l'islamisation à Tudmīr', in D. Valérian (ed.), *Islamisation et arabisation de l'Occident musulman médiéval: VIIe-XIIe siècle* (Paris: Publications de la Sorbonne): 195–246.

Gutron, C. (2010), *L'archéologie en Tunisie (XIXe–XXe siècles): jeux généalogiques sur l'Antiquité* (Paris: Édition KARTHALA).

Haldon, J., Roberts, N., Izdebski, A., Fleitmann, D., McCormick, M., Cassis, M., Doonan, O., Eastwood, W., Elton, H. and Ladstätter, S. (2014), 'The Climate and Environment of Byzantine Anatolia: Integrating Science, History, and Archaeology', *Journal of Interdisciplinary History* 45: 113–61.

Handley, M. A. (2004), 'Disputing the End of African Christianity', in A. H. Merrills (ed.), *Vandals, Romans and Berbers: New Perspectives on Late Antique North Africa* (Aldershot: Ashgate): 291–310.

Hannoum, A. (2001), *Colonial Histories, Post-Colonial Memories: The Legend of a North African Heroine, the Kahina* (Portsmouth: Heinemann).

Hannoum, A. (2003), 'Translation and the Colonial Imaginary: Ibn Khaldun Orientalist', *History and Theory* 42: 61–81.

Harrazi, N. (1982), *Chapiteaux de la grande Mosquée de Kairouan* (Tunis: Institut national d'archéologie et d'art).

Harrison, R., Reynolds, J. and Stern, S. (1964), 'A Sixth-Century Church at Ras El-Hilal in Cyrenaica', *Papers of the British School at Rome* 32: 1–20.

Hassen, M. (2000), 'Villages et habitations en Ifrīqiya au bas Moyen Âge. Essai de typologie', in A. Bazzana and É. Hubert (eds.), *Castrum 6, Maisons et espaces domestiques dans le monde méditerranéen au Moyen Âge* (Madrid: Casa de Velázquez): 233–44.

Hassen, M. (2001), 'Les ribât du Sahel d'Ifrîqiya. Peuplement et évolution du territorie au Moyen Âge', in J.-M. Martin (ed.), *Castrum 7: zones côtières littorales dans le monde méditerranéen au Moyen Âge* (Madrid: Casa de Velázquez): 147–62.

Hayes, J. W. (1972), *Late Roman Pottery* (London: British School at Rome).

Heidemann, S. (1998), 'The Merger of Two Currency Zones in Early Islam: The Byzantine and Sasanian Impact on the Circulation in Former Byzantine Syria and Northern Mesopotamia', *Iran* 36: 95–112.

Henderson, J., McLoughlin, S. and McPhail, D. (2004), 'Radical Changes in Islamic Glass Technology: Evidence for Conservatism and Experimentation with New Glass Recipes from Early and Middle Islamic Raqqa, Syria', *Archaeometry* 46: 439–68.

Hirschberg, H. J. (1963), 'The Problem of the Judaized Berbers', *The Journal of African History* 4: 313–39.

Hitchner, R. B. (1994), 'Image and Reality: The Changing Face of Pastoralism in the Tunisian High Steppe', in J. Carlsen, P. Ørsted and J. E. Skydsgaard (eds.), *Landuse in the Roman Empire* (Rome: "L'Erma" di Bretschneider): 29–43.

Hodges, R. and Whitehouse, D. (1983), *Mohammed, Charlemagne and the Origins of Europe: Archaeology and the Pirenne Thesis* (London: Duckworth).

Holod, R. and Cirelli, E. (2011), 'Islamic Pottery from Jerba (7th–10th Century)', in P. Cressier and E. Fentress (eds.), *La céramique maghrébine du haut moyen âge, VIIIe-Xe siècle: état des recherches, problèmes et perspectives* (Rome: École française de Rome): 159–79.

Holod, R. and Kahlaoui, T. (2017), 'Jerba of the Ninth Century: Under Aghlabid Control?', in G. Anderson, C. Fenwick and M. Rosser-Owen (eds.), *The Aghlabids and Their Neighbors: Art and Material Culture in Ninth-Century North Africa* (Leiden: Brill): 449–69.

Hoyland, R. G. (1997), *Seeing Islam as Others Saw It: A Survey and Evaluation of Christian, Jewish, and Zoroastrian Writings on Early Islam* (Princeton, NJ: Darwin Press).

Hoyland, R. G. (2002), *Arabia and the Arabs: From the Bronze Age to the Coming of Islam* (London: Routledge).

Hurst, H. R. (1994), *Excavations at Carthage: The British Mission*. Vol. II, *The Circular Harbour, North Side*. 1, *The Site and Finds Other than Pottery* (Oxford: Oxford University Press).

Ibn ʿAbd al-Hakam (1942), *Conquête de l'Afrique du Nord et de l'Espagne*, trans. A. Gateau (Algiers: Éditions Carbonel).

Ibn ʿIdhari (1983), *Al-Bayan al-mughrib fi akhbar al-Andalus wa-al-Maghrib*, ed. G. Colin and E. Lévi-Provençal (Leiden: Brill).

al-Idrisi (1866), *Description de l'Afrique et de l'Espagne*, ed. and trans. R. Dozy and M. J. de Goeje (Leiden: Brill).

Insoll, T. (1995), 'A Cache of Hippopotamus Ivory at Gao, Mali; and a Hypothesis of Its Use', *Antiquity* 69: 327–36.

Insoll, T. (1996), *Islam, Archaeology and History: Gao Region (Mali) ca. AD900–1250* (Oxford: BAR).

Insoll, T. (1998), 'Islamic Glass from Gao, Mali', *Journal of Glass Studies* 40: 77–88.

Insoll, T. (1999), *The Archaeology of Islam* (Oxford: Blackwell Publishers).

Insoll, T. (2000), *Urbanism, Archaeology and Trade: Further Observations on the Gao Region (Mali), the 1996 Fieldseason Results* (Oxford: BAR).

Insoll, T. (2003), *The Archaeology of Islam in Sub-Saharan Africa* (Cambridge: Cambridge University Press).

Izdebski, A., Pickett, J., Roberts, N. and Waliszewski, T. (2016), 'The Environmental, Archaeological and Historical Evidence for Regional Climatic Changes and Their Societal Impacts in the Eastern Mediterranean in Late Antiquity', *Quaternary Science Reviews* 136: 189–208.

Jalloul, N. (1998), 'Permanences antiques et mutations médiévales: agriculture et produits du sol en Ifriqiya au haut moyen âge (ixe–xiie s.)', *Africa Romana* XII: 485–511.

Jaouadi, S., Lebreton, V., Bout-Roumazeilles, V., Siani, G., Lakhdar, R., Boussoffara, R., Dezileau, L., Kallel, N., Mannai-Tayech, B. and Combourieu-Nebout, N. (2016), 'Environmental Changes, Climate and Anthropogenic Impact in Southern-Eastern Tunisia during the Last 8 kyr', *Climate of the Past* 12: 1339–59.

Johns, J. (1999), 'The "House of the Prophet" and the Concept of the Mosque', in J. Johns (ed.), *Bayt al-Maqdis: Jerusalem and Early Islam* (Oxford: Oxford University Press): 59–112.

Jones, G. D. B. (1983), 'Excavations at Tocra and Euesperides, Cyrenaica 1968–1969', *Libyan Studies* 14: 109–21.

Jones, G. D. B. (1984), 'The Byzantine Bath-House at Tocra: A Summary Report', *Libyan Studies* 15: 107–11.

Jones, G. D. B. (1985), 'Beginnings and Endings in Cyrenaican Cities', in G. Barker, J. Lloyd and J. Reynolds (eds.), *Cyrenaica in Antiquity* (Oxford: BAR): 27–41.

Jonson, T. M. H. (2014). *A Numismatic History of the Early Islamic Precious Metal Coinage of North Africa and the Iberian Peninsula* (PhD dissertation, University of Oxford).

Julien, C. A. (1951), *Histoire de l'Afrique du Nord: des origines à la conquête arabe*, 2nd edn (Paris: Payot).

Kadra, F. (1983), *Les Djedars: monuments funéraires Berbères de la Région de Frenda* (Algiers: Office des Publications Universitaires).

Kaegi, W. E. (2010), *Muslim Expansion and Byzantine Collapse in North Africa* (Cambridge: Cambridge University Press).

Kallala, N., Fentress, E., Quinn, J. and Wilson, A. (2011). *Survey and Excavation at Utica 2010* [Online]. Available: http://utica.classics.ox.ac.uk/index.php?id=20 (accessed 25 April 2012).

Kennedy, H. (1985), 'From Polis to Madina: Urban Change in Late Antique and Early Islamic Syria', *Past and Present* 106: 3–27.

Kennedy, H. (2002), 'Military Pay and the Economy of the Early Islamic State', *Historical Research* 75: 155–69.

Kennedy, H. (2004), *The Prophet and the Age of the Caliphates: The Islamic Near East from the Sixth to the Eleventh Century*, 2nd edn (Harlow: Longman).

Kennedy, H. (2010), 'How to Found an Islamic City', in C. Goodson, A. E. Lester and C. Symes (eds.), *Cities, Texts and Social Networks 400–1500* (Aldershot: Ashgate): 45–63.

Kennedy, H. (2017), 'The Origins of the Aghlabids', in G. Anderson, C. Fenwick and M. Rosser-Owen (eds.), *The Aghlabids and Their Neighbors: Art and Material Culture in Ninth-Century North Africa* (Leiden: Brill): 31–48.

Kennet, D. (1994), 'Pottery as Evidence for Trade in Medieval Cyrenaica', *Libyan Studies* 25: 275–85.

Khelifa, A. (2004), 'L'urbanisation dans l'Algérie médiévale', *Antiquités africaines* 40: 269–88.

Khelifa, A. (2008), *Honaine: ancien port du royaume de Tlemcen* (Algiers: Édition Dalimen).

King A. C. (1981), 'Animal Bones', in A. Mohamedi, A. Benmansour, A. Amara and E. Fentress (eds.), *Fouilles de Sétif, 1977–1984* (Alger: Agence Nationale d'Archéologie et de Protection des sites et Monuments Historiques): 247–58.

King, A. C. (2018), 'The Faunal Remains', in E. Fentress and H. Limane (eds.), *Volubilis après Rome* (Leiden: Brill): 369–86.

King, G. R. D. (1989), 'Islamic Archaeology in Libya 1969–1989', *Libyan Studies* 20: 193–207.

Langgut, D., Lev-Yadun, S. and Finkelstein, I. (2014), 'The Impact of Olive Orchard Abandonment and Rehabilitation on Pollen Signature: An Experimental Approach to Evaluating Fossil Pollen Data', *Ethnoarchaeology* 6: 121–35.

Laporte, J.-P. (2015), 'D'Hadrumète à Sousse, des années 350 à 859', *RM2E – Revue de la Méditerranée édition électronique* II: 3–34.

Laronde, A. (1994), 'Nouvelles recherches archéologiques dans le port de Lepcis Magna', *Comptes-rendus des séances de l'Académie des Inscriptions et Belles-Lettres* 138: 991–1006.

Laroui, A. (1977), *The History of the Maghrib* (Princeton: Princeton University Press).

Lenoir, E. (2003), 'Monuments du culte chrétien en Maurétanie Tingitane', *Antiquité Tardive* 11: 167–80.

Leone, A. (2007), *Changing Townscapes in North Africa from Late Antiquity to the Arab Conquest* (Bari: Edipuglia).

Leone, A. (2013), *The End of the Pagan City: Religion, Economy, and Urbanism in Late Antique North Africa* (Oxford: Oxford University Press).

Leone, A. and Mattingly, D. J. (2004), 'Vandal, Byzantine, and Arab Rural Landscapes in North Africa', in N. Christie (ed.), *Landscapes of Change: Rural Evolutions in Late Antiquity and the Early Middle Ages* (Farnham: Ashgate): 135–62.

Lepelley, C. (1992), 'The Survival and Fall of the Classical City in Late Roman Africa', in J. Rich (ed.), *The City in Late Antiquity* (London: Routledge): 50–76.

Lequément, R. (1968), *Fouilles a l'amphithéâtre de Tébessa (1965–1968)* (Alger: Ministere de l'information et de la culture).

Leveau, P. (2018), 'Climat, sociétés et environnement aux marges sahariennes du Maghreb une approche historiographique', in S. Guédon (ed.), *La frontière méridionale du Maghreb. Approches croisées (Antiquité-Moyen Âge)* (Bordeaux: éditions Ausonius): 271–357.

Levtzion, N. (1979), *Conversion to Islam* (New York: Holmes and Meier).

Lewicki, T. (1957), 'La répartition géographique des groupements ibadites dans l'Afrique du Nord au moyen-âge', *Rocznik orientqlistyezny* 21: 301–43.

Lézine, A. (1956), *Le ribat de Sousse suivi de notes sur le ribat de Monastir* (Tunis: Imprimerie La Rapide).

Lézine, A. (1966), *Architecture de l'Ifriqiya: recherches sur les monuments aghlabides* (Paris: Klincksieck).

Lézine, A. (1970), *Sousse: les monuments musulmans* (Tunis: Éditions Cérès productions).

Lézine, A. (1971), *Deux villes d'Ifriqiya, Sousse, Tunis: études d'archéologie, d'urbanisme, de démographie* (Paris: P. Geuthner).

Lézine, A., Picard, C. and Picard, G.-C. (1956), 'Observations sur la ruine des Thermes d'Antonin à Carthage', *Comptes-rendus des séances de l'Académie des Inscriptions et Belles-Lettres* 100: 425–30.

Lloyd, J. A. (1977), *Excavations at Sidi Khrebish, Benghazi (Berenice)* (Tripoli: Dept. of Antiquities).

Lorcin, P. M. E. (2002), 'Rome and France in Africa: Recovering Colonial Algeria's Latin Past', *French Historical Studies* 25: 295–329.

Louhichi, A. (1997), 'La céramique fatimide et ziride de Mahdia d'après des fouilles de Q'sar Al-Qaïm', *Africa* 15: 123–38.

Louhichi, A. (1999), 'La céramique de l'Ifriqiya du IXe au XIe siècle d'après une collection inédite de Sousse', in Bakirtzis (ed.), *Actes du VIIe Congrès International dur la Céramique Médiévale en Méditérannée* (Athens: Caisse des Recettes Archéologiques): 11–16.

Louhichi, A. (2010), *Céramique Islamique de Tunisie: École de Kairouan, École de Tunis* (Tunis: Éditions de l'Agence de mise en valeur).

Louhichi, A. and Picon, M. (1983), 'Importation de matériel céramique ifriqiyen en Mauritanie', *La Céramique Médiévale en Méditerranée. Actes du VIe Congrès de l'AIECM, Aix-en-Provence, 13–18 novembre 1995* (Rome: École française de Rome): 45–58.

Loyet, M. (2004), 'Food, Fuel and Raw Material: Faunal Remains from al-Basra', in N. Benco (ed.) *Anatomy of a Medieval Islamic Town: Al-Basra, Morocco* (Oxford: Archaeopress): 21–30.

Lüning, S., Gałka, M., Danladi, I. B., Adagunodo, T. A. and Vahrenholt, F. (2018), 'Hydroclimate in Africa during the Medieval Climate Anomaly', *Palaeogeography, Palaeoclimatology, Palaeoecology* 495: 309–22.

M'charek, A. (1999), 'De Zama à Kairouan: la Thusca et la Gamonia', *Frontières et limites géographiques de l'Afrique du Nord antique. Hommage à Pierre Salama*: 139–83.

MacKinnon, M. (2010), '"Romanizing" Ancient Carthage: Evidence from Zooarchaeological Remains', in D. Campana, P. Crabtree, S. D. deFrance, J. Lev-Tov and A. Choyke (eds.), *Anthropological Approaches to Zooarchaeology* (Oxford: Oxbow): 168–77.

Madani, T. (2009), 'De la campagne à la ville: échanges, exploitation et immigration dans le Maghreb médiéval', *Revue des mondes musulmans et de la Méditerranée* 126: 155–71.

Magness, J. (2003), *The Archaeology of the Early Islamic Settlement in Palestine* (Winona Lake, IN: Eisenbrauns).

Mahfoudh, F. (2003), *Architecture et urbanisme en Ifriqiya Médiévale* (Tunis: Centre de Publication Universitaire).

Mahfoudh, F. (2017a), 'Commerce de Marbre et Remploi dan les Monuments de L'Ifriqiya Médiévale', in S. Altekamp, C. Marcks-Jacobs and P. Seiler (eds.), *Perspektiven der Spolienforschung 2* (Berlin: Edition Topoi): 15–42.

Mahfoudh, F. (2017b), 'La Grande Mosquée de Kairouan: textes et contexte archéologique', in G. Anderson, C. Fenwick and M. Rosser-Owen (eds.), *The Aghlabids and Their Neighbors: Art and Material Culture in Ninth-Century Africa* (Leiden: Brill): 161–89.

Mahfoudh, F., Baccouch, S. and Yazidi, B. (2004). *L'histoire de l'eau et des installations hydrauliques dans le bassin de Kairouan* [Online]. Available: http://www.iwmi.cgiar.org/assessment/files/word/ProjectDocuments/ Merguellil/Histoire%20eau%20Kairouan.pdf (accessed 1 July 2015).

Mahjoubi, A. (1966), 'Nouveau témoinage épigraphique sur la comunauté chrètienne de Kairouan au Xe siècle', *Africa* I: 85–103.

Mahjoubi, A. (1978), *Recherches d'histoire et d'archéologie à Henchir el-Faouar, Tunisie: la cité des Belalitani Maiores* (Tunis: Université de Tunis).

Mahjoubi, A. (1997), 'Reflections on the History of the Ancient Maghrib', in M. Le Gall and K. J. Perkins (eds.), *The Maghrib in Question: Essays in History and Historiography* (Austin: University of Texas Press): 17–34.

Mahoney, N. (2004), 'Agriculture, Industry, and the Enviroment: Archaeobotanical Evidence from Al-Basra', in N. Benco (ed.), *Anatomy of a Medieval Islamic Town: Al-Basra, Morocco* (Oxford: Archaeopress): 31–44.

Manzano Moreno, E. (2006), *Conquistadores, emires y califas: los Omeyas y la formación de Al-Andalus* (Barcelona: Crítica).

Manzano Moreno, E. (2010), 'The Iberian Peninsula and North Africa', in C. Robinson (ed.), *The New Cambridge History of Islam, Volume 1* (Cambridge: Cambridge University Press): 581–621.

Marçais, G. (1913), *Les Poteries et Faiences de la Qal'a des Beni Hammad* (Constantine: Braham).

Marçais, G. (1925), 'Fouilles à Abbâssîya, près de Kairouan', *Bulletin archéologique du Comité des Travaux Historiques et Scientifiques*: 293–306.

Marçais, G. (1946a), *La Berbérie musulmane et l'Orient au moyen Âge* (Paris: Aubier).

Marçais, G. (1946b), 'Tihert-Tagdempt', *Revue Africaine* 90: 24–57.

Marçais, G. (1954), *L'architecture musulmane d'occident: Tunisie, Algérie, Maroc, Espagne et Sicile* (Paris: Arts et métiers graphiques).

Marçais, G. and Lévi-Provencal, E. (1937), 'Note sur un poids de verre du VIIIe siècle', *Annales de l'Institut d'Etudes Orientales* III: 6–18.

Marçais, G. and Poinssot, L. (1948), *Objets kairouanais, IXe au XIIIe siècle: reliures, verreries, cuivres et bronzes, bijoux* (Tunis: Tournier).

Marquer, L., Pomel, S., Abichou, A., Schulz, E., Kaniewski, D. and Van Campo, E. (2008), 'Late Holocene High Resolution Palaeoclimatic Reconstruction Inferred from Sebkha Mhabeul, Southeast Tunisia', *Quaternary Research* 70: 240–50.

Masqueray, E. (1886), *Formation des cités chez les populations sédentaires de l'Algérie: Kabyles de Djurdjura, Chaouâ de l'Aourâs, Beni Mezâb* (Paris: Leroux).

Mattingly, D. J. (1995), *Tripolitania* (London: B.T. Batsford).

Mattingly, D. J. (1996), 'From One Colonialism to Another: Imperialism and the Maghreb', in J. Webster and N. Cooper (eds.), *Roman Imperialism: Post-Colonial Persepectives* (Leicester: Leicester Archaeology Monographs): 49–69.

Mattingly, D. J. (ed.) (2003), *The Archaeology of Fazzan: Volume 1, Synthesis* (London: Society for Libyan Studies).

Mattingly, D. J. (2011), *Imperialism, Power, and Identity: Experiencing the Roman Empire* (Princeton: Princeton University Press).

Mattingly, D. J. (ed.) (2013), *The Archaeology of Fazzan: Volume 4, Survey and Excavations at Old Jarma* (London: Society for Libyan Studies).

Mattingly, D. J., Bokbot, Y., Sterry, M., Cuénod, A., Fenwick, C., Gatto, M. C., Ray, N., Rayne, L., Janin, K. and Lamb, A. (2017a), 'Long-Term History in a Moroccan Oasis Zone: The Middle Draa Project 2015', *Journal of African Archaeology* 15: 141–72.

Mattingly, D. J., Leitch, V., Duckworth, C. N., Cuénod, A., Sterry, M. and Cole, F. (2017b), *Trade in the Ancient Sahara and Beyond* (Cambridge: Cambridge University Press).

Mattingly, D. J., Sterry, M. J. and Edwards, D. N. (2015), 'The Origins and Development of Zuwīla, Libyan Sahara: An Archaeological and Historical Overview of an Ancient Oasis Town and Caravan Centre', *Azania: Archaeological Research in Africa* 50: 27–75.

McCormick, M. (2001), *Origins of the European Economy: Communications and Commerce, A.D. 300–900* (Cambridge: Cambridge University Press).

McCormick, M., Büntgen, U., Cane, M. A., Cook, E. R., Harper, K., Huybers, P., Litt, T., Manning, S. W., Mayewski, P. A. and More, A. F. (2012), 'Climate Change during and after the Roman Empire: Reconstructing the Past from Scientific and Historical Evidence', *Journal of Interdisciplinary History* 43: 169–220.

McGregor, H. V., Dupont, L., Stuut, J.-B. W. and Kuhlmann, H. (2009), 'Vegetation Change, Goats, and Religion: A 2000-Year History of Land Use in Southern Morocco', *Quaternary Science Reviews* 28: 1434–48.

McIntosh, R. J. (2005), *Ancient Middle Niger: Urbanism and the Self-Organizing Landscape* (Cambridge: Cambridge University Press).

Mercier, E. (1875), *Histoire de l'établissement des Arabes dans l'Afrique septentrionale* (Paris: L. Marle).

Mercier, E. (1895–1896), 'La population indigène de l'Afrique sous la domination romaine, vandale et byzantine', *Recueil des notices et mémoires de la Société archéologique de Constantine* 30: 127–211.

Merlin, A. (1912), *Forum et églises de Sufetula* (Paris: E. Leroux).

Merrills, A. (2018), 'Invisible Men: Mobility and Political Change on the Frontier of Late Roman Africa', *Early Medieval Europe* 26: 355–90.

Merrills, A. and Miles, R. (2010), *The Vandals* (Chichester: Wiley-Blackwell).

Messier, R. and Fili, A. (2011), 'The Earliest Ceramics of Sijilmasa', in P. Cressier and E. Fentress (eds.), *La céramique maghrébine du haut moyen âge, VIIIe-Xe siècle: état des recherches, problèmes et perspectives* (Rome: École française de Rome): 129–46.

Messier, R. A. and Miller, J. A. (2015), *The Last Civilized Place: Sijilmasa and Its Saharan Destiny* (Austin, TX: University of Texas Press).

Metcalfe, A. (2002), 'The Muslims of Sicily under Christian Rule', in G. Loud and A. Metcalfe (eds.), *The Society of Norman Italy* (Leiden: Brill): 289–317.

Miles, R. (2006), 'British Excavations at Bir Messaouda, Carthage 2000–2004', *BABesch* 81: 199–226.

Modéran, Y. (2003), *Les Maures et l'Afrique Romaine (IVe–VIIe siecle)* (Rome: École Francaise de Rome).

Mohamedi, A., Benmansour, A., Amamra, A. A. and Fentress, E. (1991), *Fouilles de Sétif, 1977–1984* (Alger: Agence Nationale d'Archéologie et de Protection des sites et Monuments Historiques).

Molinari, A. (forthcoming), 'Sicily', in B. Walker, T. Insoll and C. Fenwick (eds.), *The Oxford Handbook of Islamic Archaeology* (Oxford: Oxford University Press).

Moraitou, M., Rosser-Owen, M. and Cabrera, A. (2012), 'Fragments of the So-Called Marwan Tiraz', *Byzantium and Islam: Age of Transition* (London: Yale University Press): 238–41.

Morel, J.-P. (1991), 'Bref bilan de huit années de fouilles dans le secteur B de la colline de Byrsa à Carthage', *CEDAC Carthage Bulletin* 12: 30–40.

Morrisson, C. (1980), 'Un trésor de solidi de Constantin IV de Carthage', *Revue numismatique* 6: 155–60.

Morrisson, C. (1999), 'La diffusion de la monnaie de Carthage hors d'Afrique du Ve au VIIe siècle', in S. Lancel (ed.), *Numismatique, langues, écritures et arts du livre, spécificité des art figurés* (Paris: Éditions du Comité des travaux historiques et scientifiques): 109–18.

Morrisson, C. (2004), 'L'atelier de Carthage et la diffusion de la monnaie frappée dans l'Afrique vandale et Byzantine (439–695)', *Antiquité Tardive* 11: 65–84.

Morrisson, C. (2016), 'Regio dives in omnibus bornis ornata. The African Economy from the Vandals to the Arab Conquest in the Light of Coin Evidence', in S. T. Stevens and J. Conant (eds.), *North Africa under Byzantium and Early Islam* (Washington, DC: Dumbarton Oaks): 173–200.

Morrisson, C. and Seibt, W. (1982), 'Sceaux de commerciaires byzantins du VIIe siècle trouvés à Carthage', *Revue numismatique* 6: 222–41.

Muller, S. D., Ruas, M.-P., Ivorra, S. and Ouestali, T. (2016), 'L'environnement naturel et son exploitation aux époques antique et médiévale', in L. Callegarin, M. Kbiri Alaoui, A. Ichkhakh and J.-C. Roux (eds.) *Rirha: site antique et médiéval du Maroc I* (Madrid: Casa de Velázquez): 35–124.

Munzi, M. (2001), *L'epica del ritorno: archeologia e politica nella Tripolitania italiana* (Rome: L'Erma di Bretschnedier).

Munzi, M., Felici, F., Matoug, J., Sjöström, I. and Zocchi, A. (2016), 'The Lepcitanian Landscape across the Ages: The Survey between Ras el-Mergheb and Ras el-Hammam (2007, 2009, 2013)', *Libyan Studies* 47: 67–116.

Munzi, M., Felici, F., Sjostrom, I. and Zocchi, A. (2014), 'La Tripolitania rurale tardoantica, medievale e ottomana alla luce delle recenti indagini archeologiche territoriali nella regione di Leptis Magna', *Archeologia medievale* 41: 215–46.

al-Muqaddasi (2001), *The Best Divisions for Knowledge of the Regions*, trans. B. Collins, (Reading: Garnet Publishing).

Nef, A. (2017), 'Reinterpreting the Aghlabids's Sicilian Policy (827–910)', in G. Anderson, C. Fenwick and M. Rosser-Owen (eds.), *The Aghlabids and Their Neighbors: Art and Material Culture in Ninth-Century North Africa* (Leiden: Brill): 76–87.

Nixon, S., Murray, M. A. and Fuller, D. Q. (2011), 'Plant Use at an Early Islamic Merchant Town in the West African Sahel: The Archaeobotany of Essouk-Tadmakka (Mali)', *Vegetation History and Archaeobotany* 20: 223–39.

Nixon, S. (2017), *Essouk-Tadmekka: An Early Islamic Trans-Saharan Market Town* (Leiden: Brill).

Norris, H. T. (1982), *The Berbers in Arabic Literature* (London: Longman).

O'Meara, S. (2007), 'The Foundation Legend of Fez and Other Islamic Cities in Light of the Life of the Prophet', in A. K. Bennison and A. L. Gascoigne (eds.), *Cities in the Pre-Modern Islamic World: The Urban Impact of Religion, State and Society* (London: Routledge): 27–41.

Oren, E. and Arthur, P. (1998), 'The N Sinai Survey and the Evidence of Transport Amphorae for Roman and Byzantine Trading Patterns', *Journal of Roman Archaeology* 11: 193–212.

Ouerfelli, M. (2008), *Le sucre: production, commercialisation et usages dans la Méditerranée médiévale* (Leiden: Brill).

Oulebsir, N. (2004), *Les usages du patrimoine: Monuments, musées et politique coloniale en Algerie (1830–1930)* (Paris: Éditions de la Maison des sciences de l'homme).

Palmer, C. and Jones, M. K. (1991), 'The Botanical Remains', in A. Mohamedi, A. Benmansour, A. Amara and E. Fentress (eds.), *Fouilles de Sétif, 1977–1984* (Alger: Agence National d'Archéologie et de Protection des sites et Monuments Historiques): 260–7.

Panzram, S. and Callegarin, L. (eds.) (2018), *Entre civitas y madīna. El mundo de las ciudades en la Península Ibérica y en el norte de África (siglos IV–IX)* (Madrid: Casa de Velázquez).

Peacock, A. C. S. (2017), 'Introduction: Comparative Perspectives on Islamisation', in A. C. S. Peacock (ed.), *Islamisation: Comparative Perspectives from History* (Edinburgh: Edinburgh University Press): 1–18.

Pelling, R. (2008), 'Garamantian Agriculture: The Plant Remains from Jarma, Fazzan', *Libyan Studies* 39: 41–71.

Pelling, R. (2013), 'The Archaeobotanical Remains', in D. J. Mattingly (ed.), *The Archaeology of Fazzan: Volume 4, Survey and Excavations at Old Jarma* (London: Society for Libyan Studies): 473–94.

Pensabene, P. (1986), 'La decorazione architettonica, l'impiego del marmo e l'importazione di manufatti orientali a Roma, in Italia e in Africa (II-VI d.C.)', in A. Giardina (ed.), *Società romana e impero tardoantico. III. Le merci, gli insediamenti* (Roma-Bari: Laterza): 285–429.

Pentz, P. (1992), *The Invisible Conquests: The Ontogenesis of Sixth and Seventh Century Syria* (Copenhagen: National Museum of Denmark).

Pentz, P. (2002), *From Roman Proconsularis to Islamic Ifriqiyah* (Göteburg: Götesborgs Universitet).

Perry, C. (2007), 'Foreword', in L. Zaouali (ed.), *Medieval Cuisine of the Islamic World* (Berkeley, CA: University of California Press): ix–xx.

Picard, C. (2011), 'Islamisation et arabisation de l'Occident musulman médiéval (VIIe–XIIe siècle): le contexte documentaire', in D. Valérian (ed.), *Islamisation et arabisation de l'Occident musulman médiéval (VIIe–XIIe s.)* (Paris: Publications de la Sorbonne): 35–61.

Picard, C. (2016), *La Mer des Califes: Une histoire de la Méditerranée musulmane (VIIe–XIIe siècle)* (Paris: Le Seuil).

Picard, G.-C. (1954), 'Mactar', *Bulletin Economique et Social de la Tunisie* 90: 3–18.

Pirenne, H. (1937), *Mohammed and Charlemagne* (London: Unwin).

Potter, T. W. (1995), *Towns in Late Antiquity: Iol Caesarea and Its Context* (Sheffield: Sheffield University Press).

Prevedorou, E., Díaz-Zorita Bonilla, M., Romero, A., Buikstra, J. E., Paz de Miguel Ibáñez, M. and Knudson, K. J. (2010), 'Residential Mobility and Dental Decoration in Early Medieval Spain: Results from the Eighth-Century Site of Plaza del Castillo, Pamplona', *Dental Anthropology* 23: 42–52.

Prévost, V. (2007), 'Les dernières communautés chrétiennes autochtones d'Afrique du Nord', *Revue de l'histoire des religions* 224: 461–83.

Prévost, V. (2008), *L'aventure ibāḍite dans le Sud tunisien (VIIIe-XIIIe siècle): effervescence d'une région méconnue* (Helsinki: Academia Scientiarum Fennica).

Pringle, D. (1981), *The Defence of Byzantine Africa from Justinian to the Arab Conquest* (Oxford: British Archaeological Reports).

Pucci, S., Pantosti, D., De Martini, P. M., Smedile, A., Munzi, M., Cirelli, E., Pentiricci, M. and Musso, L. (2011), 'Environment–Human Relationships in Historical Times: The Balance between Urban Development and Natural Forces at Leptis Magna (Libya)', *Quaternary International* 242: 171–84.

Raghib, Y. (1991), 'La plus ancienne lettre arabe de marchand', in Y. Raghib (ed.), *Documents de l'Islam médiéval: nouvelles perspectives de recherches* (Cairo: Institut Français d'archéologie orientale): 2–9.

Rebuffat, R. (1986), 'Recherches sur le bassin du Sebou (Maroc)', *Comptes rendus des séances de l'Académie des Inscriptions et Belles-Lettres* 130: 633–61.

Redman, C. L. (1983), 'Survey and Test Excavation of Six Medieval Islamic Sites in Northern Morocco', *Bulletin d'archéologie marocaine* 15: 311.

Redman, C. L. (1986), *Qsar es-Seghir: An Archaeological View of Medieval Life* (New York: Academic Press).

Reese, D. S. (1977), 'Faunal Remains (Osteological and Marine Forms) 1975–76', in J. H. Humphrey (ed.), *Excavation at Carthage 1976 Conducted by the University of Michigan, Vol. 3* (Ann Arbor, MI: University of Michigan Press): 131–65.

Reynolds, P. (2016), 'From Vandal Africa to Arab Ifriqiya', in S. T. Stevens and J. P. Conant (eds.), *North Africa under Byzantium and Islam* (Washington, DC: Dumbarton Oaks): 129–72.

Roberts, N., Moreno, A., Valero-Garcés, B. L., Corella, J. P., Jones, M., Allcock, S., Woodbridge, J., Morellón, M., Luterbacher, J. and Xoplaki, E. (2012), 'Palaeolimnological Evidence for an East–West Climate See-Saw in the Mediterranean since AD 900', *Global and Planetary Change* 84: 23–34.

Robertshaw, P., Benco, N., Wood, M., Dussubieux, L., Melchiorre, E. and Ettahiri, A. (2010), 'Chemical Analysis of Glass Beads from Medieval Al-Basra (Morocco)', *Archaeometry* 52: 355–79.

Rodinson, M. (2001), 'Studies in Arabic Manuscripts Relating to Cookery', in M. Rodinson, A. J. Arberry and C. Perry (eds.), *Medieval Arab Cookery* (Devon: Prospect Books): 91–163.

Rosser-Owen, M. (2014), 'Andalusi Spolia in Medieval Morocco: Architectural Politics, Political Architecture', *Medieval Encounters* 20: 152–98.

Rossi, E. (1953), *Le iscrizioni arabe e turche del Museo di Tripoli (Libia)* (Tripoli: Department of Antiquities).

Roy, B. and Poinssot, P. (1950), *Inscriptions arabes de Kairouan* (Paris: C. Klincksieck).

Ruas, M.-P., Tengberg, M., Ettahiri, A. S., Fili, A. and Van Staëvel, J.-P. (2011), 'Archaeobotanical Research at the Medieval Fortified Site of Îgîlîz (Anti-Atlas, Morocco) with Particular Reference to the Exploitation of the Argan Tree', *Vegetation History and Archaeobotany* 20: 419.

Ruggles, D. F. (2011), *Islamic Art and Visual Culture: An Anthology of Sources* (Oxford: Wiley-Blackwell).

Ruiz, B., Gil, M. J. and Duque, D. (2014), 'Vegetation History in the Oukaïmeden Valley: Human Action and the Evolution of the Landscape', *Complutum* 25: 123–37.

Saadaoui, A. (2008), 'Le remploi dans les mosquées ifrīqiyennes aux époques médiévale et moderne', *Lieux de cultes: aires votives, temples, églises, mosquées* (Paris: CNRS Éditions): 295–304.

Sakly, M. (2000), 'Kairouan', in J.-C. Garcin (ed.), *Grandes Villes Méditerranéennes du Monde Musulman Médiéval* (Paris: École Française de Rome): 57–85.

Saladin, H. and Migeon, G. (1907), *Manuel d'art musulman* (Paris: Picard et fils).

Salinas, E. and Montilla, I. (2017), 'Material Culture Interactions between al-Andalus and the Aghlabids', in G. Anderson, C. Fenwick and M. Rosser-Owen (eds.), *The Aghlabids and Their Neighbors: Art and Material Culture in Ninth-Century North Africa* (Leiden: Brill): 429–50.

Sato, K. (2007), 'The Fihrids and Early Arab Settlers in Eighth Century al-Andalus and Ifrīqiya', *Memoirs of the Research Department of the Toyo Bunko* 65: 113–30.

Savage, E. (1997), *A Gateway to Hell, a Gateway to Paradise: The North African Response to the Arab Conquest* (Princeton: Darwin Press).

Scheele, J. (2010), 'Traders, Saints and Irrigation: Reflection on Saharan Connectivity', *Journal of African History* 51: 281–300.

Schibille, N., Sterrett-Krause, A. and Freestone, I. C. (2017), 'Glass Groups, Glass Supply and Recycling in Late Roman Carthage', *Archaeological and Anthropological Sciences* 9: 1223–41.

Schick, R. (1995), *The Christian Communities of Palestine from Byzantine to Islamic Rule: A Historical and Archaeological Study* (Princeton: Darwin Press).

Schwartz, J. H. (1984), 'The (Primarily) Mammalian Fauna', in H. Hurst (ed.), *Excavations at Carthage: The British Mission. Vol. 1, pt. 1, The Avenue du Président Habib Bourguiba, Salammbo: The Site and Finds Other than Pottery* (Sheffield: The British Academy): 229–56.

Sears, G. (2011), 'The Fate of the Temples in North Africa', in L. Lavan and M. Mulryan (eds.), *The Archaeology of Late Antique 'Paganism'* (Leiden: Brill): 229.

Sebaï, L. (2002), 'Byrsa au Moyen-âge: de la "basilique Sainte-Marie" des rois vandales à la *Mu'allaqa* d'Al-Bakri', *Antiquité Tardive* 10: 263–8.

Sénac, P. and Cressier, P. (2012), *Histoire du Maghreb médiéval: VIIe-XIe siècle* (Paris: Armand Colin).

Shatzmiller, M. (1993), *Labour in the Medieval Islamic World* (Leiden: Brill).

Shaw, B. D. (1981), 'Rural Markets in North Africa and the Political Economy of the Roman Empire', *Antiquités Africaines* 17: 37–83.

Shaw, T. (1970), *Igbo-Ukwu: An Account of Archaeological Discoveries in Eastern Nigeria* (London: Faber and Faber).

Sijpesteijn, P. M. (2013), *Shaping a Muslim State: The World of a Mid-Eighth-Century Egyptian Official* (Oxford: Oxford University Press).

Siracusano, G. (1994), 'The Fauna of Leptis Magna from the IVth to the Xth c. AD', *ArchaeoZoologia* 6: 111–29.

Siraj, A. (1995), *L'image de la Tingitane. L'historiographie arabe médiévale et l'Antiquité nord-africaine* (Rome: École française de Rome).

Sjöström, I. (1993), *Tripolitania in Transition: Late Roman to Islamic Settlement* (Aldershot: Avebury).

Slim, H., Trousset, P., Paskoff, R. and Oueslati, A. (2004), *Le littoral de la Tunisie: étude géoarchéologique et historique* (Paris: CNRS éditions).

Smith, D. and Crow, J. (1998), 'The Hellenistic and Byzantine Defences of Tocra (Taucheira)', *Libyan Studies* 29: 35–82.

Solignac, M. (1953), *Recherches sur les installations hydrauliques de Kairouan et des steppes tunisiennes du VIIe au XIe siècle J.C.* (Alger: Institut d'études orientales).

Stern, K. (2007), *Inscribing Devotion and Death: Archaeological Evidence for Jewish Populations of North Africa* (Leiden: Brill).

Stevens, S. T. (2016), 'Carthage in Transition: From Late Byzantine City to Medieval Villages', in S. T. Stevens and J. P. Conant (eds.), *North Africa under Byzantium and Islam* (Washington, DC: Dumbarton Oaks): 89–104.

Stevens, S. T. and Conant, J. P. (eds.) (2016), *North Africa under Byzantium and Islam* (Washington, DC: Dumbarton Oaks).

Stevens, S. T., Kalinowski, A. V. and vanderLeest, H. (2005), *Bir Ftouha: A Pilgrimage Church Complex at Carthage* (Portsmouth, RI: Journal of Roman Archaeology).

Stone, D., Mattingly, D. J. and Ben Lazreg, N. (2011), *Leptiminus (Lamta) Report no. 3: The Field Survey* (Portsmouth, RI: Journal of Roman Archaeology).

Stone, D. L. (2004), 'Problems and Possibilities in Comparative Survey: A North African Perspective', in S. E. Alcock and J. Cherry (eds.), *Side by Side Survey: Comparative Regional Studies in the Mediterranean World* (Oxford: Oxbow): 132–43.

Talbi, M. (1966), *L'Émirat Aghlabide* (Tunis: Maisonneuve).

Talbi, M. (1973), 'Hérésie, acculturation et nationalisme des berbères Bargawata', in M. Galley (ed.), *Premier congrès des cultures Méditerranéennes d'influence arabo-berbère* (Algiers: Société nationale d'édition et de diffusion): 217–33.

Talbi, M. (1981), 'Law and Economy in Ifrīqiya (Tunisia) in the Third Islamic Century: Agriculture and the Role of Slaves in the Country's Economy', in A. L. Udovitch (ed.), *The Islamic Middle East, 700–1900: Studies in Economic and Social History* (Princeton: Darwin Press): 209–49.

Talbi, M. (1990), 'Le Christianisme maghrébin de la conquête musulmane à sa disparition: une tentative d'explication', in M. Gervers and R. J. Bikhazi (eds.), *Conversion and Continuity: Indigenous Christian Communities in Islamic Lands, Eighth to Eighteenth Centuries* (Toronto: Pontfical Institute of Mediaeval Studies): 313–51.

Terrasse, M. (1976), 'Recherches archéologiques d'époque islamique en Afrique du Nord', *Comptes-rendus des séances de l'Académie des Inscriptions et Belles-Lettres* 120: 590–611.

Thébert, Y. and Biget, J.-L. (1990), 'Afrique après la disparition de la cité classique', *L'Afrique dans l'Occident romain. Actes du colloque de Rome, 3–5 décembre 1987* (Rome: École française de Rome): 575–602.

Touihri, C. (2014), 'La transition urbaine de Byzance à Islam en Ifriqiya depuis l'archéologie. Quelques notes préliminaires', in A. Nef and F. Ardizzone (eds.), *Les dinamiche dell'islamizzione nel mediterraneo centrale e in sicilia: nuove proposte e scoperte recenti* (Paris: L'École Française): 131–40.

Valérian, D. (ed.) (2011a), *Islamisation et arabisation de l'Occident musulman médiéval (VIIe–XIIe siècle)* (Paris: Publications de la Sorbonne).

Valérian, D. (2011b), 'La permanence du christianisme au Maghreb: l'apport problématique des sources latines', in D. Valérian (ed.), *Islamisation et arabisation de l'Occident musulman médiéval (VIIe–XIIe siècle)* (Paris: Publications de la Sorbonne): 131–49.

Valérian, D. (2012), 'Réseaux d'échanges et littoralisation de l'espace au Maghreb (VIIIe–XIe siècle)', in A. Malamat and M. Ouerfelli (eds.), *Les échanges en Méditerranée médiévale* (Aix-en-Provence: Presses Universitaires de Provence): 87–105.

Valérian, D. (2015), 'Récits de fondations et islamisation de la mémoire urbaine au Maghreb', in C. Aillet and B. Tuil Leonetti (eds.), *Dynamiques religieuses et relation au sacré dans le Maghreb médiéval. Éléments d'enquête* (Madric: CSIC): 151–68.

van Berchem, M. (1954), 'Sedrata. Un chapitre nouveau de l'histoire de l'art Musulman. Campagnes de 1951 et 1952', *Ars Orientalis* 1: 157–72.

Van der Veen, M. (2010), 'Agricultural Innovation: Invention and Adoption or Change and Adaptation?', *World Archaeology* 42: 1–12.

Van der Veen, M., Grant, A. and Barker, G. (1996), 'Romano-Libyan Agriculture: Crops and Animals', in G. Barker (ed.), *Farming the Desert: The UNESCO Libyan Valleys Archaeological Survey. Vol. 1: Synthesis* (London: Society for Libyan Studies).

Van der Veen, M. and Morales, J. (2015), 'The Roman and Islamic Spice Trade: New Archaeological Evidence', *Journal of Ethnopharmacology* 167: 54–63.

Vanacker, C. (1973), 'Géographie économique de l'Afrique du Nord selon les auteurs arabes du IXe siècle au milieu du XIIe siècle', *Annales. Histoire, Sciences Sociales*: 659–80.

Vaschalde, C., Thiriot, J., Chéhaibi, Z. and Durand, A. (2017), 'Le combustible du four de briquetier aghlabide de Raqqāda (Kairouan, Tunisie) à la lumière de l'anthracologie', *Campagnes et archéologie rurale au Maghreb et en Méditerranée, Actes du sixième colloque international, Kairouan : 14, 15 et 16 avril 2016* (Kairouan: Université de Kairouan): 281–95.

Vernoit, S. (1997), 'The Rise of Islamic Archaeology', *Muqarnas* 14: 1–10.

Villaverde Vega, N. (2001), *Tingitana en la antigüedad tardía (siglos III-VII). Autoctonía y Romanidad en el extremo occidente mediterráneo* (Madrid: Real Academia de la historia).

Viré, F. (1956), 'Dénéraux, estampilles et poids musulmans en verre en Tunisie: collection HH Abdul-Wahab', *Cahiers de Tunisie* 4: 17–90.

Vitelli, G. (1981), *Islamic Carthage: The Archaeological, Historical and Ceramic Evidence* (Carthage: Centre d'Etudes et de Documentation Archéologique de Carthage).

von Rummel, P. (2016), 'The Transformation of Ancient Land- and Cityscapes in Early Medieval North Africa', in S. T. Stevens and J. Conant (eds.), *North Africa under Byzantium and Islam* (Washington, DC: Dumbarton Oaks): 105–18.

Waksman, Y., Capelli, C., Pradell, T. and Molera, J. (2014), 'The Ways of the Lustre: Looking for the Tunisian Connection', in M. Martinón-Torres (ed.), *Craft and Science: International Perspectives on Archaeological Ceramics* (Doha: Bloomsbury Qatar Foundation): 109–16.

Walmsley, A. (2007), *Early Islamic Syria: An Archaeological Assessment* (London: Duckworth).

Ward-Perkins, J. B., Goodchild, R. G., Harrison, R. M., Dodge, H. M., Gibson, S. and Reynolds, J. M. (2003), *Christian Monuments of Cyrenaica* (London: Society for Libyan Studies).

Watson, A. M. (1989), *Agricultural Innovation in the Early Islamic World: The Diffusion of Crops and Farming Techniques, 700–1100* (Cambridge: Cambridge University Press).

Wells, C. and Wightman, E. M. (1980), 'Canadian Excavations at Carthage, 1976 and 1978: The Theodosian Wall, Northern Sector', *Journal of Field Archaeology* 7: 43–63.

Whitcomb, D. (2007), 'An Urban Structure for the Early Islamic City: An Archaeological Hypothesis', in A. K. Bennison and A. L. Gascoigne (eds.), *Cities in the Pre-Modern Islamic World: The Urban Impact of Religion, State and Society* (London: Routledge): 15–26.

Whitehouse, D. (1983), 'An Early Mosque at Carthage?', *Annali. Istituto Orientale di Napoli Roma* 43: 161–5.

Wickham, C. (2005), *Framing the Middle Ages* (Oxford: Oxford University Press).

Wilkinson, T. J., Philip, G., Bradbury, J., Dunford, R., Donoghue, D., Galiatsatos, N., Lawrence, D., Ricci, A. and Smith, S. L. (2014), 'Contextualizing Early Urbanization: Settlement Cores, Early States and Agro-Pastoral Strategies in the Fertile Crescent during the Fourth and Third Millennia BC', *Journal of World Prehistory* 27: 43–109.

Wilson, A. (2006), 'The Spread of Foggara-Based Irrigation in the Ancient Sahara', in D. Mattingly, S. McLaren, E. Savage, Y. al-Fasatwi and K. Gadgood (eds.), *The Libyan Desert: Natural Resources and Cultural Heritage* (London: The Society of Libyan Studies): 205–16.

Wilson, A. (2012), 'Saharan Trade in the Roman Period: Short-, Medium- and Long-Distance Trade Networks', *Azania: Archaeological Research in Africa* 47: 409–49.

Wilson, A. and Mattingly, D. (2003), 'Irrigation Technologies: Foggaras, Wells and Field Systems', in D. J. Mattingly (ed.), *The Archaeology of Fazzan* (London: Society for Libyan Studies): 235–78.

al-Yaʿqubi, (1892) *Kitab al-Buldan*, ed. M. de Goeje (Leiden: Brill).

Index

Note: Page numbers in **bold** refer to figures.

It happe

LANCASHIRE

IN CONCILIO CONSILIUM

Malcolm Greenhalgh

Merlin Unwin Books

First published in Great Britain by Merlin Unwin Books, 2012
    Reprinted 2015, 2020
Text © Malcolm Greenhalgh, 2012

Merlin Unwin Books Ltd
Palmers House
7 Corve Street
Ludlow
Shropshire SY8 1DB UK
www.merlinunwin.co.uk

The author asserts his moral right to be identified with this work.
Designed and set in Bembo by Merlin Unwin.
Printed in the UK by Short Run Press.
ISBN 978-1-906122-39-3

ABOUT THE AUTHOR: MALCOLM GREENHALGH
The Lancastrian name of Greenhalgh comes from the hamlet of that name between Kirkham and Poulton-le-Fylde (a de Greenhalgh was there in about 1270). Malcolm Greenhalgh was born in Bolton, and educated at Kirkham Grammar School and Lancaster University. He moved to Tarleton, working and lecturing on wildlife on the Ribble. Then from his home at Lowton, he worked as a freelance writer, spending much time researching books about north-west England. His first book was *Wildfowl of the Ribble Estuary* (1975), and more recent ones include *Flavours of Lancashire* and *The Ribble: River and Valley*. He died in 2019. He always said:
    'I am proud to have the Queen as Duke of my County Palatine!'

CONTENTS

ACKNOWLEDGEMENTS

I would like to thank Karen McCall and Merlin Unwin for allowing me to write the volume on The County Palatine in their County series. I must also acknowledge help in the provision of photographs by Mike Hewitt/Getty Images, US Congress Library, Jon Ward Allen, Ray Ball, Mike Harding and the wonderful Ken Dodd; also to R.F.G Hollett & Son, Wigan History Shop, Leigh Library, Bolton Library and Art Gallery, Manchester Central Reference Library and the Harris Library and Art Gallery. Our County is so fortunate in its wealth of libraries and art galleries (see page 217). Visit them!

Malcolm Greenhalgh

The publishers would like to thank Malcolm's son, Peter, for updating this edition.

THE COUNTY PALATINE OF
LANCASHIRE

*Formerly Lancashire-over-the-Sands
now administered by Cumbria*

Ulverston

Leighton Moss Reserve

*Formerly
Yorkshire West Riding
now administered
by Lancashire*

Barrow

Morecambe

Heysham   Lancaster

Fleetwood

**IRISH
SEA**

Wycoller

Clitheroe

Burnley

Blackpool   Lytham
St Annes   Preston   Blackburn

Martin Mere Reserve

Southport

*Formby
Red Squirrel Reserve*

Rochdale

Bolton   Bury

Oldham

Wigan

*Now administered
as Merseyside*

St Helens

Salford

MANCHESTER

LIVERPOOL   *River Mersey*

*Now administered as
Greater Manchester*

For Izzy, Alex and Charlotte,
Joe, William and Edward

FOREWORD

In 1974, Edward Heath decided to demolish over 800 years of our history. He savaged our traditional counties and replaced them with new artificial ones that few wanted. Lancashire was particularly badly hit. The southwest was hived off with Wirral to make Merseyside. The southeast was tacked onto a bit of Cheshire to form Greater Manchester. To the north, all Furness that was once Lancashire-over-the-Sands (the sands of Morecambe Bay) was taken, along with all Cumberland and Westmorland, to create Cumbria. Finally, a chunk of south Lancashire, including the towns of Widnes and Warrington, was ceded to Cheshire.

I live in the village of Lowton St Luke which is (just) in Heath's Greater Manchester. My postal address is Lowton, Warrington, Cheshire, and the postal sorting office is in Newton-le-Willows, Merseyside! Yet I am a Lancastrian, and proud of it.

A Yorkshire tyke writing a similar book about their county would similarly protest. Indeed, they did protest and had Heath's ridiculous Cleveland obliterated. Before 1974 the River Hodder was part of the border between Lancashire and Yorkshire, and then the Fairsnape ridge, putting most of the Forest of Bowland in the County of the White Rose. Further south, the old boundary put villages like Sawley and Gisburn, Barnoldswick and Earby firmly in Yorkshire. No longer, officially. Heath plonked them into Lancashire along with some fells in the Lune valley.

The effect on our county has been great and often laughable. Up to 1974 the Lancashire coastline was 216 miles long; the new Lancashire has a coastline of only 118 miles. Today the most southerly point in official Lancashire is near the villages of Sefton and Kirkby, where most people speak with a scouse accent, whereas the most northerly point of Merseyside is the north end of Southport, which is by the Ribble, not Mersey!

Up to 1974, Coniston Water was Lancashire's largest lake; today it is Stocks Reservoir that, up to 1974, was in Yorkshire! Until 1974, Lancashire's highest point was the Old Man of Coniston (at 3,631'); today it is Leck Fell (at 2,057'). And if you are into cricket, most clubs in the Lancashire League are not now in Lancashire, nor is Old Trafford, HQ of Lancashire Cricket Club.

Greater Manchester! Ugh!

Away with it all, I say. This book deals with The County Palatine of Lancaster, and its boundaries are the pre-1974 ones (forgive me if I stray into what was Yorkshire, but if I do there will be a good reason). There are other Counties Palatine, but Lancashire is the only *The* County Palatine. The County Palatine has, at its head, the Duke of Lancaster, and the dukedom is held by the Crown. So when drinking the Loyal Toast, whilst non–Lancastrians say, 'The Queen', we raise our glasses to 'The Duke of Lancaster!'

An awful lot has happened in Lancashire and to include it all would require several big tomes. I have therefore had to be highly selective. I hope that you enjoy what I have selected, and that it makes you proud to be a Lancastrian (or extremely jealous if you are not).

Malcolm Greenhalgh
Lowton, Lancashire

PS. Since this book was first published, many affected by the 1974 reorganisation have lobbied to have our traditional counties recognised by Government. In response, the Government has agreed that the traditional counties, with their boundaries and local cultures, ***do still exist,*** and that the 1974 boundary changes and inventions such as Greater Manchester, Merseyside and Cumbria were and are solely for administrative purposes. So, though you may still be administered by one of these, you are still a LANCASTRIAN!

INTRODUCTION

Lancashire vied with Cornwall for the title, Poorest County in England, up to the 18th century. Let me give an instance from 1515, in terms of wealth per 1000 acres of land. That year the average for all English counties was £66/1000 acres, our near neighbour the West Riding of Yorkshire was pretty poor at £11.30/1000 acres, but Lancashire... a pathetic £3.80/1000 acres.

The reason for this dreadful state of affairs was the nature of the countryside. Nine estuaries (Mersey, Alt, Ribble, Wyre, Lune, Keer, Kent, Leven and Duddon) dominate the coastline, the Wyre, Lune, Keer, Kent and Leven entering Morecambe Bay. They greatly hindered movement in a north-south direction and were crossed at the travellers' peril (see page 186). Inland, the coastal plain that dominates the hinterland south of the Lune and continues in a broad swathe on either side of the Mersey as far as Manchester, was largely treacherous peat bog that we call 'moss' or 'mossland' after the sphagnum moss that dominates these 'raised bogs'. Beyond the mosslands, the land quickly rises in inhospitable steep-sided moorland. So there were only scattered patches of ground with good, well-drained soil where farmsteads and villages could be built. Nothing illustrates this topographical problem better than transport systems passing north-south through the county, especially between Preston and Lancaster. On a band of well-drained land, often only a quarter of a mile wide, a road was built by the Romans around 80AD, and parallel with this Roman road are now the A6 trunk road, the M6 motorway, the West Coast railway lines, and part of the Lancaster Canal. To the west are mosslands, and to the east steep fellsides.

So what happened in Lancashire in the 200 years between 1750 and 1950, to turn what was an impoverished county into one of the wealthiest?

Anthony Gormley's sculpture 'Another Place' on the Mersey estuary at Crosby. It consists of 100 cast iron figures: naked males, scattered over an area 2 miles by half a mile. They all stand to attention and look seawards as the tide ebbs and flows, the bodies rising and sinking beneath the tide in eerie fashion

First of all, after several failed attempts, techniques were developed to reclaim the mosslands. This involved digging deep channels and pumping the water away to the nearest river. Rank vegetation was then burned, marl or lime scattered over the land to reduce the acidity of the peat, and then the drying moss was ploughed. Fertiliser was then incorporated. Often this was 'night soil' – human excrement – brought from the dung heaps of the growing towns. Today we can still see signs of this process, in the form of tiny shards of broken pottery scattered on the surface of newly-ploughed fields. When the town dweller broke a cup or plate, it was thrown onto the dung heap and became part of the night soil.

Mosslands provide very fertile soil for growing vegetables and cereals: so productive that the cost of reclamation was more than covered by the income from the first year's crop. And these mosslands provided much of the food needed by the growing townships.

The second factor was the huge increase in the exploitation of locally available raw materials and the perfect position of the growing port of Liverpool for Atlantic trade. And not only Liverpool, but also Lancaster (with its sub-ports of Heysham, Glasson Dock and Sunderland Point) and Poulton-le-Fylde (whose ships docked in the Wyre estuary at Wardley's Creek and at Skippool). Through the 18th and first part of the 19th century, as the Industrial Revolution was gathering steam, ships headed off to West Africa loaded with goods manufactured in the growing Lancashire towns: pots and pans, rope, sail cloth, clothing and so on. These were off-loaded and a cargo of slaves brought aboard. The ships then headed west, to the West Indies and southern states of the USA, where the poor slaves were made to work the plantations. Then the ships returned to Lancashire with cargoes of rum, cane sugar and cotton (page 37). That is why Liverpool was, at one time, the wealthiest city in England, if not the world, and has more beautiful listed buildings than any other outside London.

Lancashire had plenty of its own raw materials. South Lancashire sits on coal, lots of coal. It is reckoned that there is more coal left underground than was ever brought to the surface (page 42). North Lancashire, especially Furness, had massive seams of haematite, a rich iron ore, and in south Furness and around Carnforth are outcrops of Carboniferous limestone, essential in the blast furnace (page 51). So the iron and steel was on hand to manufacture mill looms, railway lines, railway and other essential engines, and so on.

Lancashire is also wet. Did not John Arlott once remind his listeners, when rain interrupted play at Old Trafford, that 'Manchester is the only city in the world where they have lifeboat drill on the buses!'

As the towns grew, so this rain was increasingly collected in reservoirs built in the nearby moorlands. The moors have a peat covering over a rock called millstone grit, and these render the water collected to be slightly acidic and very soft, which was ideal for use in the steam engines that drove the Industrial Revolution,

11

and in the production and dyeing of cotton fabrics. It also makes the perfect cup of tea.

The final factor that brought wealth to Lancashire was its human population. In 1700, 98% of Lancastrians lived on the land and in times of famine many died. During the 18th and 19th centuries, many tenant smallholders lost their plots which became incorporated into the larger farms we have today. These displaced people moved into the towns, just as the owners of mills, factories and mines needed more labour. By our standards these workers' lives were incredibly hard, but they were easier than when they scratched a living from the land. So they bred more successfully and the population of towns and cities exploded. The first official census was taken in 1801, when population growth had already begun. Then, the population of Burnley was 5,200; by 1921 it was over 103,000. In 1801 Accrington was a village of fewer than 2,000 souls; by 1921 it had grown to 44,975. Let us take one more example, Blackburn. In 1801 it had already grown to a small town with 11,980 inhabitants, but only 60 years later, in 1881, there were 120,064 and Blackburn was described at the 'cotton weaving capital of the world.'

Lancashire was a very dynamic county. Besides iron, coal and cotton, the county's closeness to the salt mines of Cheshire (not forgetting its own salt deposits by the Wyre estuary around the village of Stalmine = salt mine), was the base on which a huge chemical industry was founded, mainly in the Warrington-Widnes region. Below the peat of the West Lancashire mosslands are deposits of clear sand, blown there at the end of the last Ice Age, and ideal for making top quality glass. So St Helens (and the Pilkington company) became a major centre of glass manufacture.

Throughout this period one major problem had to be overcome: effective, inexpensive transport of large quantities of raw materials and finished products. In the 17th and early 18th century Lancashire's road system was dreadful. After harrying an army of Royalists along the road from Preston to Wigan (page 160), Oliver Cromwell wrote in his diary that the road was 'twelve miles of such ground as I have *ever* rode on in all my life.' Such appalling roads would never have allowed for the industrial development that occurred. So it was in Lancashire that canals and navigations were pioneered (page 54) and where the first commercial railways operated (page 60). Canals and railways can carry bulk materials far more easily than a horse and cart on a pothole-ridden road. Today, of course, motorway and air carry most goods; Lancashire was there too, at the start.

As the county's wealth increased, so leisure time appeared for even the lowliest worker. People worked five and a half long days in the mill or down the mine. What about Saturday afternoon? In winter, watch football. Lancashire provided half the founding members of the Football League (see page 94 for the list). In summer? Watch Lancashire League cricket, or tend the allotment. Then along came Wakes Week, when the mill towns closed down for an annual fixed holiday and one could not even buy a newspaper! What to do in Wakes Week? Go to Southport, Blackpool or Morecambe. These resorts flourished through the

Cromwell's Bridge crosses the River Hodder near Whalley. Cromwell's army crossed here on its way to the Battle of Preston (p159)

19th and first half of the twentieth century. But now they have lost out to the guaranteed sun of Benidorm.

Times have changed. And perhaps not for the better. King Cotton died a death in the 1950s and 1960s, King Coal in the 1970s and 1980s. Thanks in part to Mr Heath, Fleetwood's deep sea trawler fleet went in the 1970s. Leyland Motors (call it British Leyland if you want) has gone and the car manufacturing by the Mersey at Halewood is far from healthy. Up in Furness, the Vickers shipyard has laid off a large number of its workers, and the iron and steel works are defunct. The consequence is unemployment amongst the young of our Lancashire towns and cities; the army of NEETS (not in employment, education or training) for whom there is no job in t' mill or down t' pit.

But now let us see in a little more detail what happened in Lancashire, for believe me, it is still the best county in England... nay the World...nay, lads and lasses, the Universe!

100 FACTS ABOUT LANCASHIRE

1. Lancashire Day is on 27 November; it was on that date in 1295 that representatives from the county travelled to London as members of Edward I's parliament.

2. Lancashire's flag is of a red rose on a gold background.

3. Lancashire's motto is *In Concilio Consilium*, which translates as 'In Council is Wisdom'; local authority councils often try to prove that this is not so!

4. The largest English town lacking a railway station is Leigh.

5. Lancashire has two Open Championship golf courses, Royal Birkdale and Royal Lytham & St Annes. Incidentally, Samuel Ryder whose name is remembered in a great golfing competition, was a Lancastrian. He was born in Walton-le-Dale.

6. Wigan was called Coalopolis and Manchester Cottonopolis at the height of the Industrial Revolution.

7. The first Friends' Meeting House was built in 1692 at Yealand Conyers, near Carnforth.

8. Liverpool does not appear in the Domesday Book, but it was once the wealthiest city in the United Kingdom.

9. The centre of the British Isles is now officially in Lancashire, a mile north-east of Dunsop Bridge. Up to 1974 it was in the West Riding of Yorkshire.

10. There is a Bare Women's Institute in Morecambe. Bare was an ancient village that is now part of the seaside town.

11. The Norse-Viking words 'fell' meaning a hill and 'beck' meaning a stream can be found nowhere south of Lancashire (the actual boundary is the River Ribble).

12. Uncle Joe's Mintballs are made in Wigan by William Santus.

13. Whalley churchyard has grave stones with the following dates inscribed on them: April 31st 1752 and February 30th 1819!

14. Arthur Ransome (author of *Swallows and Amazons*, and many more books) is buried in St Paul's churchyard, Rusland.

15. The Tibet Buddhist Manjushri Mahayana Centre is at Conishead, near Ulverston.

16. Levens Hall is world famous for its topiary.

17. There is no pier at Wigan Pier, despite George Orwell. Some have claimed that a barge-loading structure that juts out from the towpath is the pier, but that is just nonsense.

18. The drink Vimto was invented by Lancastrian John Nichols.

19. Blackpool's famous illuminations were first switched on in 1912. Every year a 'celebrity' switches them on, and they have included George Formby in 1953 (see page 69), Gracie Fields in 1964 (Page 68), Ken Dodd in 1966 (page 72), a Canberra bomber in 1969 (the great plane was manufactured in Preston), Red Rum in 1977 (page 112), and Les Dawson in 1986 (page 78). In recent years the list has been dominated by people seemingly nominated by BBC pop radio and TV.

20. Colne's Wallace Hartley was the band leader on the Titanic; he kept the band playing as the liner sank.

21. The actor Ian McKellen was born in Burnley.

22. Westhoughton is called 'Cow Head City' because, when a cow got its head stuck in a five-barred gate, the residents freed it by cutting off its head!

23. The unit of energy, 'joule', is named after J.P. Joule who was born in Salford on Christmas Eve 1818.

24. The world's greatest steeplechase is the Grand National. The first was won by Lottery in 1839, and the only horse to win it three times (and second twice) was Southport's Red Rum (in 1973, 1974 and 1977, see page 112).

25. The first bale of cotton to reach Lancashire was landed at Sunderland Point.

26. The biggest hoard of Viking silver (975oz, plus 7,000 coins) was discovered by the Ribble at Cuerdale.

27. Bradshaw, whose guides to the railway network became so famous, was born in Pendleton in 1801.

28. After he lost the Battle of Hexham, Henry VI wandered through northern England until he was arrested at Clitheroe and taken to the Tower of London where he was later executed.

29. The Co-operative Movement was founded in Rochdale, the first Co-op store opening on Toad Lane on 21 December 1844.

30. Mr Rolls and Mr Royce first met and agreed to build cars together in Manchester's Midland Hotel in May 1904.

31. Until 1974 Coniston Water was Lancashire's biggest lake. It was still 'officially' in the County when Donald Campbell's boat Bluebird crashed at 320mph in 1967.

32. James Lofthouse invented Fisherman's Friends in his chemist shop in Fleetwood in 1865.

33. 'Iron Mad' John Wilkinson, who was born at Lindale (now south Cumbria), built the first iron boat and the castings for the Iron Bridge in Coalbrookdale.

34. Barton Aerodrome is Britain's oldest municipal airport and has the world's oldest operational control tower.

35. Ferndean Manor, in Charlotte Brontë's Jane Eyre, was based on Wycoller Hall near Nelson.

36. The last Temperance Bar is to be found in Rawtenstall.

37. It was at Hoole that Jeremiah Horrocks calculated when the transit of Venus across the sun's disc would occur and then observed it happen.

38. In 1617, at a dinner in Hoghton Tower, James I is reputed to have knighted a loin of beef, saying, 'Rise Sirloin'!

39. Richmal Crompton, author of the *Just William* books, was born in Ramsbottom in 1890.

40. As the cotton industry collapsed in Lancashire in the 1950s, the mill-worker had a 50-hour week. That was a great deal less than at the start of the cotton industry in the 1790s: 72 hours per week!

41. The first Blackpool rock was made in Dewsbury, Yorkshire in 1887! It has been manufactured in Blackpool since 1902.

42. Blackburn MP Barbara Castle brought in the law that insists that we all wear seat belts in the car. She didn't drive!

43. Salford opened the first public library in 1850.

44. The first public parks were opened in 1846 at Preston (Avenham Park) and Salford (Peel Park, which features in the great film *Hobson's Choice*).

45. In 1935 the Duke of Gloucester launched a ship at Barrow-in-Furness, with the words, 'I name you Orion', whilst standing in Brisbane, Australia. He used telegraph!

46. Lancastrian Richard Owen, who worked as a zoologist at the British Museum, coined the word 'Dinosaur'.

47. Stan Laurel was born in Ulverston, where there is a Laurel and Hardy Museum.

48. Antony Gormley's sculpture *Another Place* consists of life-size sculptures of his naked body set out across the beach at Crosby.

49. Brindle Church has five fonts.

50. With 49 arches, Whalley Viaduct, across the Calder Valley, is the longest in Britain.

51. The Clog Dancing Festival is held every year in Accrington.

52. The World Record bag of red grouse was shot on 12 August 1915 at Abbeystead, when eight guns bagged 2,929 grouse in the day.

53. The Scottish kilt, as distinct from the plaid that extends over the shoulder, was invented in the 18th century by Lancastrian Thomas Rawlinson. The men cutting wood for Rawlinson's iron-smelting furnaces fround the full Highlad dress made them too hot, and found thekilt hanging from the waist far cooler.

54. The great comedian and writer Eric Sykes was born in Oldham in 1923.

55. Chipping Post Office is Britain's oldest shop still serving customers. It first opened in 1668.

56. The first town to be lit by gas was Preston.

57. Stonyhurst is the UK's leading Jesuit public school. Its Old Boys include Arthur Conan Doyle (who based the arch villain Moriarty on another pupil) and actor Charles Laughton ('I'll see you hanging from the tallest yardarm, Mr Christian!'). Poet Gerard Manley Hopkins taught there for a short while.

58. A Manchester grocer called Arthur Brooke founded the famous Brooke Bond tea company. There never was a Mr Bond!

59. Britain's first motorway was the M6 Preston by-pass, the second Lancaster by-pass.

60. England's first paper mill was in Euxton, near Chorley.

61. Liverpool has the largest number of listed buildings of any city outside London.

62. Blackpool Pleasure Beach is still Britain's Number One attraction, drawing in over six million visitors every year.

63. At over 120 miles in length, the Leeds and Liverpool Canal is the longest in the British Isles (see page 58).

64. Manchester United has won more trophies than any other English football team.

65. Trencherfield Mill, Wigan, has the world's largest working steam engine.

66. The world record Bury black pudding was made by Chadwick's in December 1998. It was 40" long and weighed 115lbs.

67. Manchester Central is the largest municipal library in Britain.

68. The Hallé, founded by Sir Charles Hallé in 1858 is Britain's oldest symphony orchestra.

69. The world's first fish and chip shop was opened by Mr Lees of Mossley in 1863. By 1888 there were 10,000 in Britain.

70. The most extensive sand dunes in Britain are at Formby-Ainsdale.

71. The first regular passenger railway in the world was between Liverpool and Manchester (*see page* 61).

72. The shortest street in the world is Elgin Street, Bury, at 17 feet.

73. Europe's largest city centre indoor shopping 'mall' is the Arndale Centre in Manchester. Why do we use Americanisms?

74. The UK's first council houses were built in Liverpool in 1869.

75. Leonard Rossiter, star of *Rising Damp* and *The Rise and Fall of Reginald Iolanthe Perrin*, was born in Liverpool in 1926.

76. The UK's biggest motorway interchange is NOT Spaghetti Junction! It is the Worsley Interchange, involving M60, M61, M602, M62, A580 and A666.

77. Britain's longest preserved railway (as distinct from commercial railway) is the Rawtenstall–Bury–Heywood line.

78. The United Cattle Products factory in Levenshulme was the world's largest producer of tripe.

79. One of Charlie Chaplin's first stage appearances was with the Lancashire Clog Dancing Team in London. One of the team was ill and Chaplin took his place.

80. The world's first electric railway ran from Crossens (South-port) to Liverpool; it opened in 1905.

81. The Runcorn-Widnes road bridge that crosses the Manch-ester Ship Canal is the longest steel arch bridge in the UK.

82. Beetham Tower in Manchester is the tallest residential building in western Europe. It is 171 metres tall.

83. Carnforth Railway Station 'starred' in the film *Brief Encounter*.

84. Goodison Park was the world's first purpose-built football stadium.

85. The Manchester Evening News Arena, opened in 1995, is Europe's largest indoor concert arena.

86. The largest clock faces in the UK are on the Royal Liver Building. The dials are 25' in diameter and the minute hands 14' in length.

87. Most would have expected Liverpool's *The Beatles* to have sold more records than any other act in 1965, but that year Manches-ter's *Herman's Hermits* beat them to it.

88. Coronation Street is the UK's most popular soap opera. It was based on a real street, Archie Street in Salford.

89. The first service station on the M6 was Charnock Richard.

90. Accrington Stanley, Blackburn Rovers, Bolton Wanderers, Burnley, Everton and Preston North End were six of the twelve founder members of the Football Association in 1888. Bolton is the oldest club, founded in 1874.

91. And while we are on football, the first floodlit match ever was between Blackburn Rovers and Accrington Stanley in 1878.

92. The hot-pot is, of course, one of Lancashire's most famous dishes. The World Record was made at Garstang in 2007. It contained 220lbs potatoes, and about 80lbs each of onions and lamb, and weighed a total of 460lbs.

93. Professor Eric Laithwaite, born in Atherton and educated at Kirkham Grammar School, invented the magnetically levitated train. Like many inventions, it was turned down by the UK administration, but profitably sought elsewhere in the world. Typical!

94. In 1959 *The Manchester Guardian* became just The Grauniad (sorry, *Guardian*).

95. Roy Chadwick, who invented the Lancaster bomber, famed for carrying the 'bouncing bombs' in the Dambuster raid, was born in Farnworth.

96. There is a clock at Worsley that strikes thirteen when the time is one o'clock. The reason is that the Duke of Bridgewater's workers returned to work late after their dinner ('luncheon' for non-Lancastrians) on the basis that they didn't hear the clock strike one.

97. Suffragette Emmeline Pankhurst was born Emmeline Goulden in Moss Side, Manchester in 1858. She married Richard Pankhurst who supported her campaign for women's suffrage.

98. Henry Tate, refiner of sugar and great philanthropist, after whom the Tate Galleries in London and Liverpool are named, was born in Chorley in 1819.

99. Bolton is the largest town in the UK that is not a city.

100. A balanced diet in Wigan, the Land of the Pie-eaters, is a potato pie in each hand. Incidentally, the name 'pie-eater' comes from the General Strike of 1926 in which starving Wigan workers returned to their jobs, thereby eating 'humble pie'.

Chapter One

LANCASHIRE SINCE THE ICE AGE

In the Introduction we saw how Lancashire was transformed by the Industrial Revolution from a sparsely populated, relatively inhospitable and poor county into one of the wealthiest, industrial counties in the United Kingdom. It is therefore not very surprising to find that, in contrast with the counties of the Midlands and south and east of England, prehistory and early history have left few marks. But marks there most certainly are.

Lancashire in the Old Stone Age

A band of Old Stone Age (Palaeolithic) hunters stalked an elk across the rolling grassy plain that we call the Fylde. One of them managed to hurl a spear into one of the elk's legs, but the elk managed to escape. Later it floundered into a sticky bog and died. Its skeleton was found in the 1970s near Poulton-le-Fylde, with flint barbs from the spear still embedded in the bone. Radiocarbon dating indicated that the elk and hunting party met 13,000-11,500 years ago when the Ice Age in northwest England was nearing its end. Today Poulton-le-Fylde is only a short distance from the tide. But then, with so much water trapped in the immense ice sheets and snow-fields, the sea level was very much lower (some estimates suggest over 30 metres lower), and the coastline of northwest England was far away in the west, on an approximate line between the Lleyn peninsula of North Wales, the Isle of

Man and the Mull of Galloway. The coastline probably reached approximately its present position about 9,000 years ago, at about the time that Middle Stone Age people settled here (see below).

Other Palaeolithic remains, in the form of crude flint tools, dating from 10,700 years ago, have been found close to the northern shore of Morecambe Bay (which would then be a boggy, grassy plain extending out into what is now the Irish Sea) in Lindal Low Cave and Kirkhead Cave.

Lancashire through the Prehistoric Era

Traces of Middle and New Stone Ages (Mesolithic and Neolithic), and of Bronze Age and Iron Age have been found throughout much of Lancashire, but most of what seem to be more permanent settlements were by the coast. This is to be expected. Most food that can be gathered inland, such as hazelnuts and a wide variety of berries and flightless, moulting wildfowl are seasonal. In contrast, many foods can be gathered on the coast every day of the year, such as crabs, mussels and cockles, shrimps and sea fish. So places like Walney Island, Urswick and Heysham Head, that are naturally well-drained compared with most coastal sites then, were chosen.

The Stone Circle at Birkrigg Common which is about 4,500 years old. It commands a striking view over Morecambe Bay

There, concentrations of flints and crude pottery of styles from Mesolithic to Iron Age have been unearthed, indicating that such sites were occupied perhaps continuously from 7,000 years ago until at least the arrival of the Romans.

Another major prehistoric site is the Formby-Freshfield area. Today the coast here is dominated by a broad belt of sand dunes which developed, at the earliest, about 4,600 years ago. Before that this coastline was a series of mud-bottomed shallow lagoons surrounded by reeds and scrub. Red and roe deer, and the huge wild cattle known as aurochs, came down to drink. Wading birds, including cranes, paddled, in the shallows, catching their prey. Wolves lay in wait for these. And not only wolves. Neolithic family parties hunted these lagoons. In summer when the water level fell, beasts and humans left their footprints in the glutinous mud, and the sun baked these footprints as hard as rock. Then, the following winter, the preserved footprints were protected by newer sediments and, later, the development of the dunes.

Since the 1980s the dunes of Formby Point have retreated and left behind, on the shore, the ancient clay beds and preserved footprints. These footprints, of deer, auroch, wolf, crane and humans have been dated to between 5,750 and 6,650 years ago. One of the most incredible Lancashire experiences is of putting one's own feet next to Neolithic footprints, and to follow the track of a Neolithic hunter down what is now the sea shore.

Inland there are a few pre-Roman human traces including the remains of a Neolithic chambered cairn (called Pikestones) on Anglezarke Moor and a passage grave at Calderstones near Liverpool, a Bronze Age wood henge at Bleasdale, a stone circle on Turton Moor, a flint-knapping site at Chorlton-on-Medlock, and Iron Age hillforts at Skelmore Heads, Castle Heads and Warton Crag (all overlooking Morecambe Bay)and at Portfield and Castercliffe (in East Lancashire).

Footprints of a running child preserved in the mud around 6,000 years ago and only now revealed by erosion of dunes at Freshfield

Perhaps the most interesting remains, from late Bronze Age and early Iron Age, are of ancient trackways built over the mosslands. Timber posts were laid in two parallel lines over the ground and held in place by pegs. Then across these foundation timbers was laid the roadway of split logs, which gave the surface of the track a ridged effect; for that reason we know them as 'corduroy roads'. It seems that they were laid down when, through increased rainfall, the peat mosslands were growing upwards very quickly. So quickly that reports of these corduroy roads noted that the cut marks on the timbers appeared quite fresh, without any wear.

This suggests that their construction was a vain attempt to keep tracks across the country, used before the peat developed, open. One such road was found crossing Pilling Moss, and was misnamed the Danes' Pad. Another was found at Hightown, and another, Foulshaw Moss, on the north side of Morecambe Bay.

Roman Lancashire

When the Romans arrived in Lancashire in 78AD most of the north of England was governed by a celtic Iron Age tribe called the Brigantes, and we still use names derived from those that they gave to some geographical features, such as the rivers Darwen (meaning river where oak trees can be seen), Douglas (black stream), Keer (dark river) and Lune (healthy river), Mellor (bare hill), Penketh (high wood) and the area of central south Lancashire known as Makerfield (open land with ruins or a wall). Pendle Hill is an interesting name, for 'pen' means hill in the old celtic tongue and 'hyll' is from the Anglo-Saxon. Both these are incorporated in Pendle, which thus means 'hill hill' and so Pendle Hill, as it appears on the Ordnance Survey maps, means 'hill hill hill'!

Names from this time are very few, for what became Lancashire was then something of an outpost of the Brigantian empire, was sparsely inhabited and was mostly bog or fell. So the Romans came to Lancashire to pass through it rather than settle. We can see this from the scattered 'staging-post' Roman villas, which were established as farms to provide food and horses for the Roman army. Cheshire and Yorkshire had many villas. Inhospitable Lancashire had none.

So in 78-79AD Agricola built a road from Middlewich, in Cheshire, that crossed the Mersey at Wilderspool (Warrington) and went north through Coccium (Wigan), a Roman camp/industrial site at Walton-le-Dale and onto a fort at Lancaster. This road then passed up the Lune valley to a fort at Calacum (Burrow) and then north down the Eden valley to Carlisle. The southern part of this road, from Warrington to Walton-le-Dale is closely followed by the modern A49, and the second part, from Walton-le-Dale to Lancaster is followed by the A6 (also M6 and the West Coast main railway line). The Romans pioneered a route through difficult terrain that we have adopted today!

Later a second road began at Deva (Chester) and headed northeastwards to Condate (Northwich) and on into Lancashire and a fort at Mamucium (Manchester). This road then headed due north through Radcliffe, Tottington and Blackburn (none of which then existed) to a major fort by the Ribble at Bremet-

27

ennacum (Ribchester). From there the road continued through Bowland to the fort by the river Lune at Burrow.

The major east-west Roman road began in Ilkley in West Yorkshire and passed into Lancashire via the most accessible Aire-Ribble Pennine gap. It continued on to the fort at Ribchester and then followed the top of the north bluff of the lower Ribble valley to Fulwood (north of Preston), where its straightness can still be seen in today's Watling Street Road and Lytham Road. This road continued on to a camp at Kirkham. It is likely that the road forked here, one branch heading to the Ribble estuary at Freckleton (where a Roman fleet could anchor in the lee of the Naze), the other to a port called Sentantiorum. This port has not been located. One theory is that it was west of what is now Rossall Point near Fleetwood and was lost to erosion by the sea, and another that it was in the Wyre estuary, probably at Skippool.

All these roads had one purpose: to get troops and supplies through Lancashire as quickly as possible to garrisons manning the frontier of the Scottish border, Hadrian's Wall (built 122-128) and the extension of the wall along the Solway coast south to Whitehaven. The east-west route serviced ships moving north from Chester to the frontier.

But it was not to last. By the end of the third century part of this network had been abandoned and, although Lancaster, Ribchester and Manchester were occupied to at least 380, early in the fifth century the Romans quit northwest England and Lancashire entered what has been called the Dark Ages.

Dark Lancashire

The Dark Ages are not all that dark. Convention has it that when the Romans left, waves of Anglo-Saxon warriors overwhelmed Lancashire, killing the entire small Romano-British population, and bringing their language. It seems, however, that the change was not of people, but of culture. Some Anglo-Saxon farmers certainly settled here and they influenced the remaining Romano-British to adopt their way of life including language. They also gave their names to many of our towns and villages. Ashton, Bolton, Bootle, Burscough, Clifton, Kirkham, Lytham and Preston are all derived from Old English (Anglo-Saxon). Then, England was split up into Kingdoms, and Lancashire below the Ribble was part of the Midlands kingdom of Mercia, above the Ribble the southwesterly outpost of Northumbria.

Sometime after 874 Danes overran much of the Midlands and northeast England. Some of them reached and settled in Lancashire, especially the southeast, judging from names of Danish origin, such as Flixton, Hulme and Urmston. Then, in 910 Norsemen, who had left Norway to settle in Ireland, the Isle of Man and western Scotland, reached the coast of northwest England. Many settled here in Lancashire, choosing the most sparsely inhabited places on the coast or in the hills. Place names like Altcar, Anglezarke, Birkdale, Formby, Norbreck, Scaris-brick and Warbreck are all from Old Norse. They have also left

The Cuerdale Viking Hoard was found on the left bank of this stretch of the river Ribble. It is the largest hoard ever to be found in the British Isles (page 30)

us tangible remains, including ornate, carved wheel-head stone crosses at Halton (in the Lune valley), Lancaster, Urswick and Winwick, and, at Heysham, a hogback tomb lid from about 1000, that includes both Norse pagan and Christian elements in its intricate carving. Most staggering was the Norse-Viking hoard of about 7,500 silver coins and 88lbs of silver ingots and ornaments discovered in May 1840 by workmen repairing the bank of the Ribble at Cuerdale, near Preston. The hoard had been buried sometime after 950 (the latest minting date on the coins). We shall never know why those who buried it never retrieved it. Only one larger similar Viking hoard has been found: in Russia!

Christianity almost certainly arrived in Lancashire before the Romans departed, but the only SURE evidence comes from Whalley, where a Celtic Christianity flourished, probably from late in the fifth century, before the Anglo-Saxons were converted in the sixth century. In 625 Lancashire became part of Paulinus's diocese, and then the county north of the Ribble was amalgamated into the diocese of York, south of the Ribble, of Lichfield. Tradition also has it that St Patrick, who worked as a missionary in Ireland (from where he ousted all the snakes), was shipwrecked at Heysham in Morecambe Bay sometime during the fifth

The ruins of St Patrick's Church, Heysham overlook Morecambe Bay. It was built in the 9th century

Graves excavated from the sandstone bedrock of Heysham Head, one of them around 1,200 years old

century, and may even have been born at Urswick, in the Furness district. However the chapel that bears his name, together with the small grave carved out of the sandstone of Heysham Head (they were probably ossuaries for storing skeletons of the dead), have been dated to the ninth century. It is also possible that St Helen's Church at Overton, overlooking the Lune estuary, is even older, for we know that the doorway is early Norman and that the four-feet thick western wall predates that by perhaps a couple of hundred years.

Norman Lancashire

Christianity apart, what is now Lancashire was a turbulent place at the end of the Dark Ages, at the start of the eleventh century, and the turbulence all came to a stop with the Norman conquest. By 1055, eleven years before Hastings, England was united under one crown, that of Edward the Confessor, but the northern boundaries were unsettled. North of the River Duddon (in what became Cumberland) was part of Scotland and Lancashire north of the Ribble was part of the earldom of Northumbria, the earldom granted to Tostig, the son of Earl Godwin. Tostig was a hated

31

man and temporarily he had to flee abroad to escape death. Whilst he was away, Edward the Confessor died and, although Tostig would have sought the crown, his half-brother Harold Godwinsson was declared king. So the furious Tostig made alliance with the Norwegian king Harold Hardrada and they invaded northeast England to oust King Harold. They overcame a northern force at York, but then faced Harold and his army at Stamford Bridge on 25 September 1066. Tostig was killed and his army routed. But then King Harold heard of William's arrival on the south coast. So he marched south and faced the Norman army at Hastings on 14 October.

The outcome was that Harold reputedly got an arrow in his eye and that William became the King of England. Of course, previous leaders thought that they could continue to fight their corner, and uprisings occurred in the North which led, in 1068-9, to William 'harrying the north' into submission. It seems that many farmsteads and hamlets were destroyed, for of 64 settlements recorded in 1068 in Ribblesdale, when the Domesday Survey was carried out in 1086, only 16 were recorded, and the overall population density was tiny: four people per square mile compared with an average of 32 people per square mile over all England.

After ousting the Old English rulers, William gave much lands to his Norman lords. For instance, Roger de Poitou, who had fought well at Hastings, was granted all Northumbria (which included Lancashire-across-the-Sands) and the land between Mersey and Ribble. He thus controlled much of Lancashire. He built motte and bailey castles on either side of the head of the Ribble estuary at Penwortham and Tulketh (the Penwortham one can still be seen, though overgrown, in Penwortham churchyard) and a castle at Lancaster. Over the next ninety years the northern boundary of Lancashire was fiercely contested by the Scots, but during the reign of King John (1199-1216) the pre-1974 boundaries became fixed and Lancashire became a legal and administrative county.

Because of the sparseness of population, and poor nature of the countryside for agriculture, much was given over to royal hunting forests. The word 'forest' does not imply tracts of woodland; it simply means an area of land where deer were protected and stiff penalties were imposed on those that broke forest law. For instance, anyone found guilty of shooting a deer with a bow and arrow might lose a hand to prevent the crime being repeated. And dogs above a certain size, which might be used to course a deer, would have their hind legs broken (the Bowland dog-gauge survives at Browsholme Hall).

The forests included Fulwood and Myerscough (in the Hundred of Amounderness), Bleasdale, Over Wyresdale, Roeburndale and Quernmore (Lonsdale), and Accrington, Rossendale, Trawden and Pendle (Blackburn); in other words, most of central Lancashire that was not mossland. Before 1974, most of the Forest of Bowland, which was administered from Whitewell, was in Yorkshire; it is 'officially' now all in Lancashire. The strict forest laws were allowed to go into abeyance during the reign of Elizabeth I and repealed during

The Chapter House of Cockersand Abbey overlooks the Lune estuary. This is the only building that remains of the Abbey

the reign of James I, early in the 17th century and the lands settled by farmers. Many old Lancashire farmhouses in former hunting forests date from this time.

Despite their cruelty to the vanquished English inhabitants, Norman lords were deeply religious and concerned for the afterlife. So many of them established abbeys and priories in the county, presumably so that St Peter would let them in at the Gate. Cartmel and Conishead Priories and Furness Abbey were granted lands north of the Sands, Cockerham and Lancaster Priories and Cockersand Abbey in south Lonsdale, Lytham Priory in the Hundred of Amounderness, Whalley Abbey in the Blackburn Hundred, Penwortham Priory in the Leyland Hundred, and Warringon, Burscough and Upholland Priories in the West Derby Hundred. Salley Abbey, in the Ribble valley between Clitheroe and Gisburn, was until 1974 in Yorkshire.

Besides the land on which the religious buildings were built, the abbeys and priories were also granted vast tracts of land, often in the hills, where they raised huge flocks of sheep to produce wool for export. The enormous sums of money thus generated from wool production paid for the beautiful buildings. To see how fantastically ornate these old religious houses were, go to Furness Abbey and Cartmel Priory, for they are the best preserved, though Whalley (and Salley) and Cockersand are worth a visit. Of course, their demise came about when Henry VIII fell out with the Pope and the Roman Catholic Church, made himself Supreme Ruler of the Church of England and then, when the religious houses protested, ordered their dissolution.

In the autumn of 1536 northern English protest turned to revolt in what is known as the Pilgrimage of Grace. The uprising was quickly put down and, in early 1537, leading clergymen, such as John Paslew, abbot of Whalley, and William de Trafford, abbot of Salley, were executed, and the priories and abbeys ruined. Cartmel Priory escaped ruin, for it was also a parish church and parish churches were exempt from dissolution. As with the hunting forests, the lands owned by the abbeys and priories were sold, many to wealthy people who then let the land to farmers.

Lancashire continued to be a relatively poor rural county until the 18th century. The two English Civil Wars, and the 1715 and 1745 Jacobite rebellions provided trauma (see page 156), but the biggest change was just around the corner...

Chapter Two

LANCASHIRE AND THE INDUSTRIAL REVOLUTION

The Port of Liverpool

When talking of the history and development of Lancashire up to the start of the Industrial Revolution in the 18th century, it is essential to bear in mind that the population was then growing very slowly and that what towns and cities there were, were very small. Liverpool is a prime example. It was founded by King John in August 1207 and initially had seven streets: High, Castle and Old Hall Streets ran in parallel north-south, Chapel and Water Streets ran east-west and continued as Tithebarn and Dale Streets respectively. The King encouraged people to settle in Liverpool New Town with a Royal Declaration:

John by the grace of God King of England, Lord of Ireland, Duke of Normandy and Aquitaine, Count of Anjou, to all his loyal subjects who wish to have burgages [i.e. a cottage with land for producing food] in the township of Liverpool, greeting. Know ye that we have granted to all our loyal subjects who shall take burgages in Liverpool that they shall have all the liberties and free customs in the township of Liverpool which any free borough on the sea has in our land. And therefore we command you that in safety and in our peace ye come hither to receive and occupy our burgages. And in testimony hereof we transmit to you our letters patent.

Witness Simon de Pateshill. At Winchester the 28th day of August in the 9th year of our reign [1207].

John founded Liverpool to provide a safe anchorage for his ships that would take troops and supplies to Ireland, but it was little used for that purpose, Chester being more accessible from London. So well into the 17th century Liverpool remained a 'town' of seven streets. Then, after the Civil Wars, when Cromwell was subjugating Ireland during the Commonwealth, Liverpool came to the fore in the transport of Parliamentarian soldiers. By 1660 the town's population was probably about 1,500; perhaps double what it was in 1300. By 1700 the population was about 5,000; in 1720 about 12,000; in 1801, 78,000; and in 1831, 165,000. Growth was about providing the burgeoning industries of south and east Lancashire with raw materials (especially cotton) and commodities such as tobacco and cane sugar, and the slave trade.

The first slave boat left Liverpool in 1700; incredibly, it was called *The Blessing!* At its peak, in the ten years from 1783, Liverpool ships made 878 trips to West Africa, and then crossed the Atlantic before returning to Liverpool. And on the 878 legs from Africa to the West Indies or southern states of the US they transported 303,737 slaves and generated a profit of £15,186,850. And the slaves grew the cotton, ships brought it back to Liverpool, and the cotton was turned into cloth in south and east Lancashire. And there too, we see a parallel increase in the populations of towns and cities.

Lancashire Cotton Towns

In James I's time, Preston consisted mainly of four streets: Church Street, Lancaster Road, Fishergate and Friargate. And behind those streets, where today the city is a mass of buildings, there were plots where people grew their food. In 1631 the plague hit Preston, and 1,069 people died from a population of about 3,000, and many had fled the town leaving, on 16 August, only

887 behind (according to a survey carried out by the mayor). In 1642, just before the English Civil Wars broke out (page 158), the population of people living in the town was about 1,500, and in 1663 still at least 1,300 and probably more. By today's standards, Preston was then only a village. But in the next 138 years, Preston's population grew to 11,887 in 1801, and then to 69,361 in 1851 and by 1921 to over 120,000. This was almost entirely because of the cotton industry.

Similarly Blackburn. In the late 1600s the population stood at around 1,500 and was based in what are now the town centre streets, Church Street, Darwen Street, Northgate and King Street. Imagine small cottages with vegetable plots, and chickens running hither and thither where now are banks, shopping centres, the cathedral grounds and Radio Lancashire's HQ! And

Butts Spinning Mill at Leigh was typical of so many Lancashire's cotton mills, well built of top quality bricks and with ornate decorations

the now culverted Black Burn flowing by. By 1780 the population had grown to 5-6,000, in the first official census of 1801, to 11,980, by 1851 to 46,538, and it peaked at 133,052 in 1911. Again, the growth here, and in other towns such as Accrington, Burnley, Bolton, Oldham and Rochdale, was because of cotton mills bringing people in from the countryside.

The centre of the cotton industry was, of course, Manchester.

Mediaeval Manchester was a small market town with an annual fair on Acresfield (now occupied by St Anne's Square) and a royal charter from 1301. Its mid-sixteenth century population has been estimated at about 2,000 suggesting no more than about 400 families living both in and around the town centre as well as in the countryside around the town. In today's terms, this would be the population of a medium-sized modern housing estate.

However by 1700 the population of Manchester (plus Salford) was about 8,000. By 1773 it had grown to 43,000. Between 1801 and 1851 the population of Manchester alone increased fourfold, from 76,788 to 316,213 and of Salford from about 35,500 to 213,100. That this increase of population was fuelled to at least some extent by a movement of people from country to town is borne out by the following estimates: in 1801 at least 74% of the south Lancashire population lived in the countryside and worked on the land and a maximum of 26% lived and were employed in towns and cities; by 1891 only 6% lived in the countryside and 94% were concentrated in towns and cities.

This change in population distribution was matched by the growth of urban cotton mills. The first big cotton-spinning mill opened in Manchester in 1783 and by 1816 there were 86 in Manchester and Salford alone. In 1819 there were 344 cotton mills in the whole of Lancashire, 1,815 by 1839. By 1850, 1,235 of the 1,753 cotton mills in the whole of the UK (70%) were in Lancashire, and of 292,862 workers in cotton mills in the UK, 215,983 (74%) were in Lancashire.

Cotton imports, mostly through Liverpool, matched the growth in the number of mills.

The profit was immense. In 1751 £46,000 worth of cotton cloth was exported from Lancashire mills, £355,000 in 1780 and a massive £15 million in 1835 (perhaps equivalent to nearer £50 billion in today's money).

It wasn't only the manufacture of cloth from raw cotton that employed those living and working in Manchester. In 1841 less than twenty percent of Manchester workers were actively involved in manufacture. In contrast the figures for other towns were much higher: for instance Oldham (40%), Bolton (45%) and Ashton-under-Lyne (50%). Manchester was the centre. Here were the vast warehouses that stored the raw cotton and the finished cloth: in 1815 Canon Street alone had 57 such warehouses. Manchester also had the carriers, who distributed the raw cotton to satellite towns and brought back the finished cloth. It shared carriers with Liverpool, carrying stuff

Tons of raw cotton imported into Lancashire for cloth manufacture:	
1700	<450
1751	1350
1764	1760
1780	3050
1800	25,460
1823	85,105
1845	329,000
1854	346,500

Manchester City Hall, the centre of Cottonopolis. The building of so many grand town halls in south and east Lancashire was funded by cotton

(cotton and cotton products) between port and manufacturing centres. There were also accountants, bookkeepers, checkers, clerks and, of course, the mill owners.

Today the cotton industry has almost vanished. Its decline began in 1919 when Japan began to produce cotton goods much cheaper than they could be made in Lancashire. The decline accelerated after 1949 when other Far East countries, such as India and China, began to export cheap cloth and finished garments.

As a boy in the late 1940s and early 1950s I can recall the mill hooters going to announce the start or end of a shift, and the cobbled streets of Bolton and Rochdale resounding to the clatter of thousands of pairs of iron-shod clogged feet, as men with blue

Castle Street, Liverpool is one of the original seven streets built by King John in 1207

overalls and women wearing 'pinnies' and hiding their curlers beneath headscarves walked the short distance between mill and terraced cottage. That is no more. Despite the *Cotton Industry Act* of 1960, which attempted to reorganize and make Lancashire's cotton mills more efficient, by 1970 the carding, spinning and weaving of cotton in Lancashire were largely history. But the south Lancashire conurbation and its now diverse industry is a testament to those times.

The Lancashire Coalfield

Although there is some evidence that the Romans may have mined coal at one or two sites in the region (for instance at Arley near Westhoughton), up to the beginning of the fourteenth century, wood and peat appear to be the main fuels for heating homes and cooking meals. The first mention of mining in legal documents comes from Wigan in about 1330, though for well over 200 years after that mining appears to have been a small-scale parochial affair. The reasons are clear. Until the seventeenth century there was little demand. It was only when the big cotton mills needed huge quantities for powering their steam engines, and the workers living in the dense rows of terraced streets needed fuel for heating and cooking that coal became essential. Second, most coal in this region is deep underground, requiring the development of deep-mining technology. It was not until well into the eighteenth century that this technology allowed mining to reach the now relatively shallow depth of 300 feet.

The Lancashire coal-field extends in area from Colne, south to north-eastern Cheshire and continues in a block westwards between Mersey and Ribble to Skelmersdale and St Helens. The coal measures are generally up to about 2,500 feet deep, though a shaft at Parsonage colliery at Leigh was sunk to about 3,300 feet making it the deepest in the British Isles. This is, of course, not the depth of coal; within that thickness of strata there will be an average of about 75 feet of coal. The coal occurs in seams, each one usually being up to six feet thick, and between the seams are much thicker layers of 'dirt': shales, sandstones and mudstones. For instance, at Astley Green colliery the first seam (the Worsley four-foot seam) was 780 feet from the surface at the top of the shaft (it dipped at a gradient of 1:5 to the south, so mining the coal took the miners deeper in that direction), and there were a further eleven seams to the bottom, 2,670 feet from the surface.

There were vertical shafts, down which men and machinery descended and up which the coal was brought, together with the series of passages leading far beyond the shaft, which led to the coalfaces. The passage at the coalface would be no thicker than the coal seam; if it were thicker then large amounts of dirt would be brought to the surface as well as coal and would have to be sorted by hand. The only dirt deliberately brought to the surface was that mined during the sinking of a shaft or the excavation of a new roadway, and this was piled up to produce the characteristic 'slag-heaps' or 'pit-rucks' still visible in the Wigan, St Helens, Leigh and Bolton areas.

Though relatively thin, the seams often extended in a broad swathe so that the coalface being mined might be many yards in length. One coal face that I visited at Parkside near Newton-le-Willows, four years before that mine was closed down, was

The last pit-head in Lancashire at Astley Green. It is now a mining museum

around 100 yards in length and less than five feet in thickness. Two men, wearing only their helmets and underpants in the intense heat, worked what appeared like a huge bacon-slicer that moved to and fro along the coalface, sheering off black coal. The coal fell onto a wide moving belt that carried it away to the bottom of the shaft almost three miles away. From there it was swiftly brought to the surface; for example, at Worsley Green the engine was capable of lifting nine tons of coal up to 2,600 feet to the surface every two minutes.

As the coalface retreated so there moved forwards the transport-belt and a bank of automatic hydraulic roof-props. For me (I'm six feet tall), simply moving, with back painfully bent, along the coalface and through the props was hard work in itself. The potential danger was evident. The hydraulic props creaked as hundreds of feet of strata above pressed down on them, and behind, from where the props had moved, already the unsupported roof was falling. I was a visitor, at the face for only a few minutes. Men worked here, five shifts per week through their working lives, in a claustrophobic blackness lit only by a headlamp, and in air laden with coal dust that ground away the lungs.

It is easy to forget the short-term effects of exposure to coal dust: in the shower, trying to wash it from every nook and cranny; an hour later, noticing the eyelids and lashes that seemed to be coated in black mascara and wiping a black-running nose. In the long term, very many miners died from lung disease. And of course, from accidents (see page 198).

Coal from the Lancashire coalfield drove the nineteenth century industrial boom. In 1861 the Wigan area had around 45 mines, employing 9,000 miners and producing four million tons. In 1874 there were 588 collieries in Lancashire and they brought to the surface 16 million tons of coal. By 1907 there were fewer pits – only 360 – but they raised 26 million tons. However, as the most accessible seams became exhausted, so the cost of getting the coal soared. One problem was the flooding of deep mines, for they were perfect soak-aways for the surrounding countryside; by 1947, when the industry became nationalised, it is estimated that to raise every single ton of coal to the surface, four tons of water had to be pumped out of the mines.

There were other problems. Coal is a dirty fuel, its acid smoke darkening and corroding buildings and producing dense smogs in cold damp winter days. Smogs are now a thing of the past, but through to the late 1950s and early 1960s those sulphurous yellow-grey fogs with a visibility of less than ten yards were quite common.

Even on the high moors, the effects of smoke pollution from burning coal are still evident, and not only in blackened rock-faces. Oil, natural gas and nuclear energy are significantly cleaner to use, and it is so much easier to have the central heating automatically switch on in the morning than struggle out of a warm bed to clean a grate and light a fire!

But the kiss of death to the Lancashire coalfield was political. The coal industry subsidy from government was increasing and the National Union of Mineworkers was considered too militant. Arthur Scargill lost a war with Margaret Thatcher and, with the exception of the odd opencast working, by 1992 the coal industry in Lancashire was gone. It has been said that the Wigan coalfield produced a total of at least 700 million tons of coal, and that there are more than 700 million tons still down there!

With the exception of museums, signs of the coal industry have mostly gone. Pit-head winding gear, as characteristic a feature of the industrial Lancashire skyline as the cotton-mill chimney, is with one exception (the mining museum at Astley) no more. Slag-heaps have been landscaped and, as I write this, the extensive heaps of Bickershaw colliery on the Pennington side of Leigh are being taken away in wagons. Soon, perhaps, the only vestige of mining in this area will be the shallow pools or 'flashes',

the result of subsidence where the land has sunk after the coal has
been taken away.

Lancashire's Water

The only natural lakes in pre-1974 Lancashire were Coniston
Water and Esthwaite, and both are a long way from the major
towns and cities. But there are many reservoirs in the Pennine
moors that tap river headwaters to provide the vast human population with water to slake thirsts, cook food, wash, clean clothes
and cars, use in manufacturing industries, flush loos, and water
gardens and golf courses.

A significant proportion of this water (reckoned to be up to
50 percent by some green activists, but more probably about 20
percent) is lost through leaking pipework, bursts, dripping taps
and taps that have not been switched off properly. It is now so easy
to turn on a tap without appreciating that every pint wasted is one
pint that should be flowing down a river. Indeed, it is likely that,
save for following spells of heavy rain, a high proportion of water
flowing down Irwell and Mersey at their confluence, and down
the Calder and Darwen as they enter the Ribble has already been
through some industrial process, washing machine, bath, shower
or sink, or someone's kidneys!

To state the fact that a significant proportion of the water
gathered by the host of reservoirs is wasted does not imply that
these reservoirs were not and are not needed. We have seen that
there was a tremendous growth of population and industry in
the county from the mid-eighteenth, through the nineteenth and
into the twentieth century. The initial population explosion in
the towns and cities was catered for by poor quality housing,
consisting of streets of one-up and one-down back-to-backs or
tenements built round a courtyard. These were not the back-to-
backs as shown in the introduction to Coronation Street. They

had no backyards or even backdoors. They were literally back-to-back, where the back wall of one was back wall to the other. This saved in costs and in space. As these appalling dwellings spread through the centres of towns and cities, so those who could afford it moved out to more salubrious properties. Larger houses were then let, room by room and cellar by cellar to the poor incomers.

These early nineteenth century buildings had no indoor sanitation. There might be only one privy, usually draining into a cesspit but sometimes directly into a stream, shared between the occupants of twenty houses, though in some Liverpool housing schemes there were two privies for sixteen houses (though that might mean upwards of 200 people). There was no tapped clean water in the home. Water came from standpipes or pumps in the street. The source in Fountains Street in Manchester was once guarded to prevent people polluting it by washing themselves and their clothes in its clean water. Open buckets were used to carry water from the street into the dwelling. There would be enough for drinking and cooking, but not sufficient for regular washing of body or clothing or bedding.

In one particularly dreadful corner of Manchester, the middle of which is now occupied by Oxford Road station and known then as Little Ireland because of the concentration of Irish immigrants living there, each privy served at least 220 people. F. Engels described the scene there in his book *The Condition of the Working Classes in England* (1844): 'two hundred cottages.....four thousand human beings.....the cottages are old, dirty, and of the smallest sort.....streets uneven, fallen into ruts, and in part without drains or pavements; masses of refuse, offal and sickening filth lie among standing pools in all directions; the atmosphere is poisoned by the effluvia from these, and ladened and darkened by the smoke of a dozen tall factory chimneys.....the race that lives in these ruinous cottages.....must really have reached the lowest stage of humanity.'

The consequence of such dreadful conditions faced by the majority of town and city dwellers was a higher-than-average death rate. In 1841-50 the national death rate was 22 per 1,000; in Manchester it was 33 and in Liverpool 36 per 1,000. Epidemics of diseases like influenza and measles killed many who had avoided typhus (a disease borne by the then common body louse), pulmonary tuberculosis (a bacterium transmitted in droplets in coughs and sneezes), and typhoid and cholera generated by sewage-contaminated water. In 1845, 1846 and the first half of 1847, 300,000 Irish refugees arrived in Liverpool, many suffering from typhus, measles, smallpox and scarlet fever. In 1846, 53 percent of children under the age of five years died in the city. There were large outbreaks of cholera in 1836, 1849, 1854 and 1866. The 1849 epidemic arrived in December with a mass immigration from Ireland: it killed 5,000 in Liverpool alone. A Manchester report on that epidemic to the General Board of Health described how, '*Innumerable privies.... [at] the back of long terrace ranges [terrace streets]... empty themselves into the filthy ditch [the River Medlock]*'. At the same time almost half of Lancashire's town dwellers (49 percent) still had no near access to a supply of clean

The Liver Building, with the famous Liver birds topping its domes, adorns the Mersey shore

water whether inside or within a few yards of their dwelling place. That latter statistic may seem dreadful, but only three decades earlier 88 percent of households had to walk to gather their buckets of water.

Clearly something had to be done about housing, sewage treatment and water supply. In 1844 the old style back-to-back was outlawed and regulations on the use of cellars for habitation were introduced in 1853. Sewage schemes were introduced from the late 1840s that reduced the risk of contaminating drinking water. But there was no easy solution to the provision of clean water, as the water supplies within town and city were inadequate and certain to be contaminated with 'gut flora' and industrial effluent. Supplies would have to be piped in from the countryside. And, because Pennine rivers are spate rivers, running almost dry in summer droughts and in wasteful flood during winter rains, there would have to be storage. So reservoirs were built to gather and to store river water that could then be piped to town.

The chain of reservoirs in Longdendale was built, at a cost of £1,167,428, during the 1850s to supply Manchester and Salford with 62 million gallons of water per day. The first piped water reached Manchester from Longdendale in 1857. Soon, demand exceeded supply for not only were population and industry growing, but as soon as water became readily available so too did individual consumption increase.

In 1832 Manchester consumed the equivalent of 33.6 pints of water per person per day; by 1852 this had grown to 99.3 pints per day, in 1868 to 236.9 pints per day and in 1878 to 261.7 pints per day. Today, besides industrial usage, when the washing of clothes is a daily routine, when every day is a bath day, when the car needs washing on Sunday mornings and when the garden sprinkler must be switched on if rain hasn't fallen for a week, water consumption in Manchester is equivalent to 670 pints of water per person per day.

In 1894 the aqueduct from a deepened Thirlmere was completed to carry water the 98 miles to Manchester. By 1900 the City of Manchester was consuming 99 million gallons of water per day and demand still growing. In 1920 that demand was satisfied by the piping of water from a deepened Haweswater, again in the Lake District.

Liverpool obtained its first Pennine water from the Anglezarke-Rivington complex of reservoirs, built in the hills above Bolton, in 1857. When this supply could not fulfil the demand, Liverpool turned to lakes in North Wales. Other developing Lancashire towns built similar reservoirs by putting dams across Pennine streams.

The largest, Stocks reservoir, was built in 1930 by damming the headwaters of the Hodder to supply the growing Fylde coast holiday resorts. Sometimes a series of dams was constructed on one river so that, in wet periods, if one reservoir overflows, the excess is gathered by another dam further downstream (for instance, Bolton has three reservoirs: Entwistle, Wayoh and Jumbles on Bradshaw Brook to the north of the town; and Wigan has three Worthington reservoirs on the river Douglas). Sometimes surplus capacity is piped down to lowland storage reservoirs: examples include the triple Audenshaw Reservoir just north of Denton; Heaton Park Reservoir between Prestwich and Whitefield (Manchester); and Prescot Reservoirs (Liverpool).

Water is still in small supply compared with demand. United Utilities, the company that now supplies the towns and cities of Lancashire, has to play a precarious balancing act in getting water to where it is needed. It also has to face the politically difficult prospect of taking more water from the Lake District and North Wales that have a high rainfall, low human population and are National Parks. Because the water falling as rain on rain-soaked Lancashire cannot fulfil the demands of those living there.

Lancashire's Iron and Steel

Cotton and coal were the major industries in south Lancashire, but in the north of the country it was iron and steel. Beneath Furness and west Cumberland to the north were immense beds of an iron-rich ore called haematite. In the 17th and 18th and early 19th centuries the iron was extracted from this ore at 'bloomeries', using charcoal produced from the south Lakeland forests. So much charcoal was produced that the forests were wiped out, until the 1780s when iron ore was exported to other parts of the county where there were still forests, and charcoal produced in Galloway was exported to Furness bloomeries.

Today, if you travel the lanes of Furness, it is difficult to spot these once major industrial sites at, for instance, Duddon Bridge, Penny Bridge, Nibthwaite and Backbarrow, or the forges that turned the raw iron into tools and machines at Spark Bridge, Rusland Pol or Burblethwaite. Or the quays around the northern shore of Morecambe Bay (such as Greenodd, Baycliffe and Louzey Point in the lee of Walney Island) from which iron or tools were exported in tiny ships.

In the late 19th century the iron industry became centred on a new town called Barrow-in-Furness. In 1856 The Dukes of Buccleuch and Devonshire and Sir James Ramsden funded the construction of blast-furnaces that would use the Bessemer process, invented the previous year (1885), for turning iron into steel. They also produced docks, through which extra iron ore from Cumberland and coal from south Lancashire could be imported, and steel and steel products exported. And they built a large shipyard to build iron ships, the first two being the Duke of Devonshire, the second the Duke of Buccleuch and the third the Duke of Lancaster (who at the time was Queen Victoria). And in only fifty years the tiny village of about a hundred inhabitants had grown to a town of 70,000.

Soon, Barrow was building ships for the Royal Navy, the first a gun-boat HMS *Foxhound*, and then it became involved with the building of submarines. Through the two World Wars the shipyard was hard at work, providing the essential vessels. Then, after the last war and with the onset of the Cold War, there was a need for big submarines that could remain submerged and undetected, driven by nuclear power and being capable of delivering missiles carrying nuclear warheads.

The peak of achievement came in 1992 when the Trident submarine HMS *Vanguard* was launched. But by then the Cold War was all but over. Demand for very expensive warships fell, and as it did, unemployment in Barrow-in-Furness rose, rapidly. By then, 305 submarines had been built at Barrow, and nearly a hundred surface ships for the Royal Navy. There are currently (2011) none on the record books, and iron production in north Lancashire has ceased.

Transport In and Through Lancashire

The towns and cities of Lancashire evolved from what were mostly villages from the eighteenth century. This would not have been possible unless an efficient transport system had evolved at the same time. In 1700 the Mersey was navigable to Warrington and Widnes, the Ribble to Preston and the Lune to Lancaster for the very few hours each day when the tide was in. At low water the extensive mudflats and shallow braided channel made shipping dangerous.

In 1700 the state of the roads was abysmal. Deep potholes, filled with muddy water, caused heavily-laden wagons and stagecoaches to crash over, making the only effective means of transporting goods the slow and expensive packhorse trains.

The following is the advertisement for the first direct stagecoach service between Manchester and Liverpool:

> ### By coach, if God permit
>
> A machine sets out on Monday, Septr. 1st, 1760, and on every Monday and Tuesday morning at 6 o'clock, from the Bull's Head Inn at Manchester; will Call at the Red Lyon Inn at Warrington, and at Mr Reynolds's, the Old Legs Of Man Inn at Prescot, and lies at the Golden Fleece in Liverpool. Returns from thence every Tuesday and Friday morning at 6 o'clock, and calls at the same places on the way back to Manchester.
> Performed (if God permit).
> John Stonehewer & James France – Drivers.

Even when a faster 'Diligence' coach came into service in 1775, the journey took a full day and was broken by breakfast at Irlam, lunch at Warrington, and tea at Prescot.

The first effort to improve transport throughout the region was by Turnpike Acts of Parliament. The earliest of these, the 1727 Warrington-Wigan Act, stated that the road (now the A49) was 'becoming ruinous and in many places impassable in the winter season and some parts thereof are so narrow that coaches and carriages cannot pass by one another'. Yet because there were so many roads – really dirt or muddy tracks – needing upgrading in the increasingly productive area between Mersey and Ribble and in East Lancashire, the cost was too great and the improvements were too long in coming. Instead of roads linking the towns, canals were built. However stagecoaches persisted well into the nineteenth century for transporting people and the mail; the last London-Derby-Manchester stagecoach arrived in Manchester on 2 October 1858.

Lancashire Pioneers the Canal Era

In March 1745 an Act of Parliament allowed for the construction of one of England's first canals, the Sankey Navigation, to run from St Helens to Fiddler's Ferry on the Mersey (a distance of seven miles); it was later extended to the Mersey at Widnes (a total of 13 miles). The plan initially was to make Sankey Brook navigable, but this was not possible over the entire length. Instead a canal was dug alongside the brook, using water from the river. In case the brook failed to hold enough water to keep the canal topped up, extra water was provided by a reservoir (Carr Mill Dam) constructed at the head of Sankey Brook. The Sankey Navigation carried coal from the mines around St Helens to the Mersey and onto Liverpool and Runcorn. A similar navigation had already been cut further north under a 1719 'Act for the making of the River Douglas, alias Asland, navigable, from the River Ribble to Wigan' that from 1742 had allowed laden coal barges to go from Wigan to Preston. Note that these are 'navigations', based on rivers, and not true 'canals'.

Britain's first true canal at Worsley was built by the Duke of Bridgewater to carry coal from his mine at Worsley to Salford

Earlier, in 1720, an Act had been passed allowing for the Mersey and Irwell to be made navigable between Liverpool and Manchester at all states of the tide. This was extended in 1736 by an Act enabling Worsley Brook to be made navigable between Worsley Mill and the River Irwell. On 25 November 1758, Francis Egerton, third Duke of Bridgewater (1736-1803) approached Parliament to point out that the proprietors of the Mersey and Irwell Navigation had failed to carry out the work and that, 'though upward of twenty years are elapsed', Worsley Brook had not been made navigable. Therefore the Duke proposed that he should build, under a new Act, a canal to carry coal from his mines at Worsley to Salford and thence on to Hollin Ferry west of Caddishead on the Mersey. This would allow coal to be carried at relatively low cost – therefore bringing down greatly the cost of fuel – both to the Salford and Manchester conurbation and to Lymm, Thelwall and neighbouring areas of Cheshire. Despite opposition the Act was given Royal Assent on 23 March 1759 and the Duke, aided by his land agent and the water engineer James Brindley, began his 'cut'. This was Britain's first true canal.

However, as the canal was being built, the Duke realised that a more profitable venture would be to take his canal, not to Salford, but across the River Mersey at Barton and then on into the centre of Manchester. Such a revised plan would later allow an extension of the canal system south, to the developing industrial region of the Midlands. So on 12 March 1760 a second Act was passed, permitting the re-routing which would involve the construction of Barton Aqueduct, carrying the Bridgewater Canal 40 feet over the Irwell. When the Manchester Ship Canal was constructed many years later, the aqueduct was replaced by the Barton Swing Aqueduct.

The Duke's next step was to extend his canal to link Manchester, the canal terminus under the 1760 Act, with the Mersey Estuary and Liverpool. The company that was responsible

Lock gates on the Ulveston Canal. At just over a mile, this is the world's shortest canal, connecting the sea at Morcambe Bay with Ulverston town

for the Mersey and Irwell Navigation under the 1720 Act had failed in getting ships through the upper tidal reaches, for at low water, sandbanks impeded transport and following heavy rain the river was in fast flood. Bridgewater used this failure as a stick with which to beat the Mersey-Irwell proprietors and used his new proposal as a carrot to bring parliament on his side. A third Act sponsored by the Duke of Bridgewater was passed on 24 March 1762 and the Bridgewater Canal now headed west through north Cheshire, reaching Preston Brook in 1771 and the vastness of the Mersey estuary at Runcorn Lock in 1776.

This enabled relatively rapid and inexpensive transport between Manchester and Liverpool, and in 1788 a packet-boat (a fast boat carrying mail as well as passengers) was set up. Packet-boats left Runcorn and Manchester at 8am every morning. The boat heading to Manchester from Runcorn reached Preston Brook at 11am (where it was met by a coach carrying mail and passengers from Chester), Stockton Heath/Warrington at 1pm (where it was met by a coach from Liverpool), Lymm at 2.30,

Altrincham at 4pm and Manchester at 6pm. The boat leaving Manchester at 8am reached Altrincham at 10am, Lymm at 11am, Stockton Heath/Warrington at 1pm (where it connected with the Liverpool coach) and reached Runcorn at 4.30pm. A boat also linked Runcorn with Liverpool, depending upon the state of the tide.

Manchester, Worsley and many towns close to the Mersey Estuary were now served by canal. However the Duke of Bridgewater had a wider vision that was realised on 14 May 1766 when Parliament approved an Act for the cutting of the Trent & Mersey Canal that, in 1772, joined Bridgewater Canal at Preston Brook. Now the Duke's canal system reached south as a network to the growing Midlands, and from thence the canal system would continue on south to London and Bristol and east to the Humber ports.

Other local canals were built to serve satellite towns in the Mersey Basin: the Rochdale Canal (completed 1804), the Peak Forest (completed 1800) and Macclesfield Canals, the Bolton & Bury Canal. Before Bridgewater cut his canals, the price of coal transported overland was £2 per ton; when carried by canal six shillings (30p) per ton. This cheap coal powered the textile boom years from 1760.

However Liverpool, that vital port, was still linked to the canal system only by the tidal estuary of the Mersey or by the dreadful road system; but plans had already been formulated to solve that problem. In 1767 John Longbotham surveyed a canal route linking Liverpool with Leeds and the West Riding woollen mill-towns. James Brindley resurveyed and amended the route the following year and in 1770 Parliament passed an Act for 'The making and maintaining a navigable Cut or Canal from Leeds Bridge in the County of York, to the North Lady's Walk in Liverpool in the County Palatine of Lancaster, and from thence to the Mersey'. On 5 November 1770 the first sod was cut at Halsall, ten miles north of Liverpool, at the junction between the flat peat mosslands and boulder clay slope, at about 60 feet above sea level. Constructing this canal would be a vast undertaking, taking 46 years to complete (the Leeds & Liverpool canal was opened on 23 October 1816), at a cost of over £1¼ million, covering 127 miles and including 91 locks and two tunnels, and the building of seven reservoirs to provide water. The length of time taken to complete the job would mean that the shareholders would have a long wait for any return on their investments. Yet there was some profit made before the entire canal was completed.

In 1783 a new Act enabled 'the Company of Proprietors of the Leeds and Liverpool Canal to purchase the said River [Douglas] navigation'. Thus a canal link was cut from the Leeds & Liverpool Canal at Burscough north to the Douglas mouth and into the Ribble Estuary. This provided a link between Liverpool and both Preston and the coal-producing town of Wigan.

The canal link to Wigan made a profit with the introduction of a speedy packet-boat service. On 9 July 1775 the first boatload of race-goers departed from Gathurst, upstream of Wigan, at eight o'clock in the morning, for the afternoon races at Aintree. By 1790 the service carrying mail and passengers operated daily, Mondays excepted, on a fixed and very rapid service for the late eighteenth century:

> Depart 8.00am Liverpool
> 10.30am arrive Red Lion, Maghull
> 12 noon arrive Halsall
> 1.15pm arrive Burscough
> 2.30pm arrive Appley Bridge
> 4.00pm arrive Wigan

There was a parallel service departing Wigan at 8am and arriving Liverpool at 4pm.

In 1819, three years after the Leeds & Liverpool Canal had been completed, an Act of Parliament allowed the building of the

Leigh branch linking the Leeds-Liverpool with the Bridgewater Canal. This opened in 1821, allowing barges from Liverpool and Wigan to travel directly throughout the network of English canals. It allowed also a packet-boat to ply its trade swiftly, with mail and passengers, between Manchester and Liverpool. Every day a boat departed from both cities at 6.15am. At 11am the boat from Manchester reached Wigan, at which time the boat from Liverpool reached the Lion Inn at Scarisbrick. The boat from Liverpool then went on to Wigan (arrival at 3pm) and Manchester (arrival at 8pm), whilst the boat from Manchester reached Scarisbrick at 3pm and Liverpool at 8pm. Passengers leaving the boats at Scarisbrick could take a coach to the Union Hotel or Hesketh Arms (these are now the Prince of Wales and Scarisbrick Hotels respectively) in Southport.

Yet despite its revolutionary effect, the canal age was short-lived. From the 1830s, barely fifteen years after the completion of the Leeds & Liverpool Canal and only a decade after the Leigh Branch was completed, the railway system was born and then flourished. It was not only the speed by which trains could transport goods and people. In severe drought (as happened in the 1880s) the canals had to close down for want of water. In severe winter weather (as, for instance, in 1895) the canals were frozen solid for over a month. Canals ceased to be profitable.

Today canals have a quite different function. They are used for pleasure boating and fishing and are a wildlife haven.

There was one exception, the last canal to be built. As early as 1720 Parliament had passed, 'An Act for making the Rivers Mersey and Irwell navigable from Liverpool to Manchester'. This did not happen. But following Acts in 1794 and 1888 a navigation was cut and in 1894, at a cost of £1.7 million, the Manchester Ship Canal opened. Beginning at Eastham Locks on the south side of the Mersey Estuary, near Bromborough, the canal runs parallel with the shore to Runcorn, where it is joined by the

Weaver Navigation. From Runcorn the canal heads straight for Warrington where, at Bollin Point, the Mersey flows into the canal, providing top-up water. Now canal and river bypass Irlam, Partington and Eccles before reaching the Salford Quays and Manchester.

The building of the Ship Canal, a waterway capable of taking ocean-going cargo vessels 35 miles beyond Liverpool to the heart of the city, opened up an industrial corridor that was ripe for exploitation. On the Cheshire side, Ellesmere Port, Stanlow and Carrington grew into immense oil terminals and refineries. Trafford Park became a huge industrial complex. It contributed to the growth of Widnes and Runcorn as centres of the chemical industry, and Warrington as a multi-industrial centre. But even the Ship Canal had a limited life span....

Lancashire Pioneers of the Railway Era

In October 1829 the Rainhill Trials took place between five locomotives built by five rail sponsors to ascertain which of them should run a railway from Liverpool to Manchester. *The Perseverance*, built by Mr Burstall of Edinburgh, broke down on its way to the start, so it did not take part. Dr Brandreth's *The Cycloped*, built in Liverpool, was disqualified because it broke the rules: it was powered, not by an engine, but by a horse on a treadmill!

The Novelty (built by Messrs Braithwaite and Ericsson of London) made the top speed in the Trials, but then its engine blew up. Mr T. Hackworth's *The Sans Pareil* (Darlington) completed the Trials, but its heavy build and lack of springs did not meet the rules and its boiler leaked badly.

The winner of the event, ten runs over a course of a mile and a half, followed by time off for refuelling before a second set of ten, mile-and-a-half runs was Mr Robert Stephenson of Newcastle-on-Tyne and his steam engine *The Rocket*. Although some have implied that some skulduggery was afoot, his speed and reliability could not be matched and, with the Trials over, Mr George Stephenson carried a coach-load of passengers thirty times along the course at speeds up to a giddy 30mph!

The following year, on 15 September 1830, the railway linking Liverpool and Manchester was opened. Building it had given the Stephensons great problems. A viaduct had to be constructed near Newton-le-Willows over the Sankey Navigation, which included nine arches each spanning eighteen yards. Between Newton-le-Willows and Manchester the line had to cross Chat Moss: heather and birch logs were used to 'float' the line across the wettest five miles. The opening day not only heralded the opening up of Britain by a rail network, but it also saw the world's first ever railway casualty when William Huskisson, MP for Liverpool, took one stride back onto the track and was knocked down by the train and killed!

Quickly the railway system spread through the industrialised

This plaque commemorates William Huskisson, the first man ever to be killed by a train

The current Liverpool-Manchester railway line precisely follows the 1830 route. The white marble memorial on the right of the picture is to William Huskisson (previous page)

Lancashire and then further afield. A line was opened on 25 July 1831 from the Liverpool–Manchester line at Newton-le-Willows to Warrington, and on 8 July 1837 that line was extended across the sandstone Twelve Arches Viaduct over the Mersey linking Warrington with Birmingham. In 1838 lines linking Liverpool and London Euston, via Warrington, and Preston with London Euston, also via Warrington, were completed. The line from London reached Lancaster in 1840 and Carlisle in 1846.

This infant railway system became the Grand Junction Railway and then, having absorbed other smaller companies (Lancaster-Carlisle in 1844, Leigh & Kenyon and Bolton & Leigh in 1845, and London & Birmingham and Manchester & Birmingham in 1846), became London & North West Railways (LNWR). By 1848 the London Euston-Glasgow Central line opened, with Warrington roughly midway. By 1858 an east-west main line was completed, running from Garston (later Liverpool City centre at Lime Street) through Manchester and Sheffield before linking with the new East Coast main line connecting Edinburgh and Kings Cross. During the 1860s the Liverpool –

London service was speeded up with a crossing of the Mersey at Runcorn Gap.

Canals were now redundant. But soon even the mighty railways would face stern competition... from the roads.

Lancashire Pioneers the Ascendancy of Road Transport

By the late 1940s, transport by road began increasingly to take custom from the railways. And just as the Liverpool–Manchester canal and rail links had been pioneers, so too did a new road linking the two cities pioneer the modern road system. By the late 1920s the East Lancashire Road (A580) had been built between Liverpool and Manchester. It was a new type of road; the first of its kind in Britain; a sort of motorway that bypassed intervening towns and cities by going almost in a straight line (the shortest route) across country but with junctions through which older roads could link other nearby towns and villages with the two main cities and each other. It was, as it were, an artery between Liverpool and Manchester, with offshoot smaller arteries feeding other lesser organs. Now a manufacturer could send his wagon to the docks at Liverpool and bring raw materials directly and speedily to his warehouse; and he could transport finished goods directly to dock or other towns in the region. This type of road could make railway stations and goods-yards redundant. By the 1970s it had almost done so.

As a network of good roads started to develop after the Second World War, so the railways went into decline. In an attempt to make the railway system profitable, Dr Beeching was given the task of deciding which lines should go and which should remain open. The axe fell heavily. And as most of Lancashire's railway lines were closed, so were built a massive network of motorways. The first British motorway was the M6 Preston bypass, the second the Lancaster bypass. When it was completed, the M6 linked Scotland with the Midlands through Lancashire. Then the M62 was built that runs west to east and links Liverpool with Manchester and Manchester with the West Riding towns and cities. Now Manchester has a motorway orbital road, the M60, whilst coastal Liverpool has a bypass, the M57. Shipping has adapted to road transport with the container ship: imports reach Liverpool in containers and exports are taken away in containers. At Seaforth is one of the world's biggest container terminals, and a dual carriageway links port and the northern end of the M57.

Today, when they are not clogged with too much traffic, the motorway network in Lancashire south-of-the-Sands enables a Lancastrian to travel in less than an hour from home to anywhere else in the county. And a container arriving at Liverpool's Seaforth dock can be loaded onto a wagon, reach the M57 in ten minutes

The M6, Britain's first motorway, here takes traffic on a 'bypass' around the city of Preston

and hurtle at 60 miles per hour to the M57 junction with the M62 and be in Manchester less than an hour later. Or it can continue for another hour and be in any Yorkshire West Riding town.

People born in the 21st century will come to think the pre-motorway age as primitive, in the same way as those born in the twentieth century think of the canal age. During the Lancashire Wakes Weeks, when towns were almost deserted for a summer fortnight, the better-off drove A49 and A449 to Worcester, then along the A38 through Bristol and onto West Country holiday towns that were a little more genteel than Blackpool. It is approximately 280 miles from Manchester and Liverpool to Plymouth. In the pre-motorway 1950s it took my family about twelve hours to complete that journey. Today, the drive can be made in four hours along the M6 and M5 to Exeter and the dual carriageway A38 provided there are no traffic-jams! But in less than twelve hours we can leave home, check in at Manchester International Airport, and be whisked across the Atlantic to Jamaica's Montego Bay!

Such is progress. It is important, however, to remember that without the canals, then the railways and now the roads, the Industrial Revolution in Lancashire would have stalled. Instead of a massive industrial conurbation, all there would have been, today, would be just a scattering of villages and market towns.

Chapter Three

FAMOUS LANCASHIRE ENTERTAINERS

Lancashire has produced more entertainers – actors, comedians, musicians and so on – than any other county in the kingdom. There are three reasons for this.

Firstly, Lancashire in its truest sense has a large population, and the more people, the more entertainers will be generated. Secondly, Lancashire is traditionally a working class county, and the old adage 'work hard, play hard' applies; there was a great demand for entertainment, especially during the 20th century. Thirdly, when times are hard, laugh at hardship! Amongst the wittiest people I have ever met were coal miners, dockers and mill hands in the cotton industry. In this respect, it is interesting to note that most entertainers produced by the county have been of working class stock. There are exceptions:

Sir Thomas Beecham (1879-1961) was the son of Ormskirk chemist Joseph Beecham, creator of Little Liver Pills. During the first World War he was conductor of the Hallé, Manchester's own orchestra, and in 1932 he moved on to establish the London Symphony Orchestra. From 1946 he was conductor of the Royal Philharmonic. He was a very witty man, one of his classics being, 'The sound of a harpsichord is that of two skeletons copulating on a tin roof during a thunderstorm!'

The actor Rex (Reginald) Harrison was another for whom performing was never about keeping the wolf from the door. Born at Huyton on 5 May 1908, he was educated at Birkdale and at Liverpool College. He began his acting career with the Liverpool Playhouse before making his West End debut in 1931 (in the play *Getting George Married*), and his Broadway debut in 1936 (in *Sweet Aloes*). In 1946 he signed a contract with Hollywood's 20th-Century Fox, and from 1956–58 he starred in *My Fair Lady* on Broadway. He made over 50 films (my favourite is *Blythe Spirit*, written by Noel Coward and produced by David Lean). In true Hollywood fashion he married six times and had a torrid affair with the actress Carole Landis, who ended up committing suicide.

Both Beecham and Harrison, together with actors Robert Shaw (born Westhoughton, 1927) John Thaw (born Manchester, 1942) and Robert Powell (born Salford, 1944), the operatic contralto Kathleen Ferrier (born Higher Walton, 1912) and the jazz singer and raconteur George Melly (born Liverpool, 1926), were born in the county but made their names elsewhere. And they lost their Lancashire roots. Similarly, to some extent, the wonderful Bernard Cribbins, who was born in Oldham on New Year's Day 1928 and starred in a host of films (my favourites *Two Way Stretch, Carry On Jack* and *The Railway Children*), narrated the Wombles, read stories on *Jackanory* and appeared as a spoon salesman in *Fawlty Towers*. The other performers I have chosen had different backgrounds and remained true Lancastrians.

DAME THORA HIRD

A typical example was Dame Thora Hird. She was born to theatrical parents in 1913 in Morecambe and she appeared for the first time on stage in the town's Royalty Theatre when only eight weeks old. She appeared in over 100 films, including *Two*

Thousand Women (1944), *The Courtneys of Curzon Street* (1947) and *A Kind of Loving* (1962). In the 1960s she became a regular face on television when she starred with comedian Freddie Frinton in the programme *Meet The Wife*. She performed two of Alan Bennett's *Talking Heads* on TV: *Cream Cracker Under The Settee* (1988) and *Waiting For The Telegram* (1998). She will be fondly remembered by more recent audiences for her role as Edie Pegden, wife of the hen-pecked Wesley Pegden, in *Last Of The Summer Wine* (1986-2003). Up to her death in 2003 she retained her broad Morecambe accent... 'Wesley...cum 'ere NOW!'

All-Round Entertainers

GRACIE FIELDS

Gracie Fields is a classic example of a working class 'lass' who became a great star but never forgot her background. She was born in Rochdale on 9 January 1898 as Grace Stansfield. She left school to work in a cotton mill, but in her spare time performed in local amateur shows and revues. In 1918 she was talent-spotted for the part of Sally Perkins in a musical *Mr Tower of London*, which ran for seven years, during which time she married producer Archie Pitt. In 1928 she recorded her first song and by 1933 had sold over four million records. In 1931 her fame was assured when she starred in the film *Sally In Our Alley*, with the song *Sally*, from the film, becoming her trademark. Throughout the hard times of the 1930s people thronged to the cinema to see her many films, making her the most famous performer and greatest celebrity in the country.

In 1940 she divorced Pitt and married an Italian comedian called Monty Banks. When they moved to the USA for the rest of the Second World War people back home questioned her patriotism, but when the war ended, through the late 1940s and early 1950s, she was as popular as ever in both UK and USA. She married her third husband Boris Alperovic, and went into semi-retirement on the island of Capri. Many of her fans sought her out when they were on holiday on the island and she was famous for spending time chatting with them. Gracie Fields was made a CBE in 1938, and Dame Commander of the British Empire in 1979, just before her death.

She appeared in ten Royal Command Shows, the last in 1978. Of her songs, *Sally*, *The Biggest Aspidistra In The World*, and *Wish Me Luck As You Wave Me Goodbye* are still well known. She did much for charities, including the Gracie Fields Orphanage. Some of her private papers are deposited at the University of Lancaster.

She made a last visit to Blackpool a couple of years before she died. That evening at her hotel, she was told that the restaurant was closed but that a chef would prepare fish and chips for her. Eventually a bone china plate appeared, with bone-handled fish knife and fork, and a serving dish with fish and chips obviously brought in from a nearby chippie. 'Aye lad,' Gracie said to the waiter. 'Tha ought not to 'ave gone to all that trouble. Tha could 'ave left 'em in t'newspaper!'

GEORGE FORMBY

There were two George Formbys. Father and son. And though the father was a famous music hall comedian early in the 20th century, the son was what today would be called a 'megastar'. He was born as George Hoy Booth on 26 May 1904 in Wigan. When he was seven years old he left school to train as a jockey, but when his father died in 1921 he turned to the stage as a singer-comedian playing the ukulele. At the same time he changed his surname to Formby. In September 1924 he married the infamous Beryl Ingham who completely dominated and controlled his life.

His stage and film persona was what most Lancastrians might call that of a 'gormless imbecile', with a face dominated by a mouthful of teeth and an inane grin, and a flat Lancashire accent typical of the Wigan coalfield. He recorded many songs, the most famous being *When I'm Cleaning Windows, Grandad's Flannelette Nightshirt, Leaning on a Lamp Post, Chinese Laundry Blues,* and *With My Little Ukulele In My Hands*; most of them had a touch of saucy innuendo which appealed to the working man and woman. He made his first film *Boots, Boots* in 1934, and starred in a further nineteen up to and including 1946, the best known being *It's In The Air, Let George Do It, George In Civvy Street,* and *Trouble Brewing.* Though most of his films include romance with some demure actress, Beryl crossed from the script any kiss and chaperoned him away from temptation as soon as filming was over for the day.

During the Second World War, George travelled widely through North Africa, the Middle East and Europe entertaining British troops, and for that he was awarded the OBE. In 1951 his career peaked when he starred in the West End show *Zip Goes A Million,* but then he suffered from a heart attack and had to quit. On Christmas Day 1960 Beryl died and within weeks he had become engaged to a young Preston schoolteacher, Pat Howson. They were due to wed in May 1961, but George died that March.

MIKE HARDING

I hope that he will not shout at me for putting him in the same category as George Formby, but Mike Harding is one of the county's greatest all-round performers. It may surprise some readers to find that he was born on 23 October 1944 in Crumpsall, Manchester, for Mike is also known as the *Rochdale Cowboy.* But that name came from his song *Rochdale Cowboy,* which made the top 30 in 1975. When he was 14 years old, he joined a skiffle

Mike Harding is one of Britain's greatest all-round performers, and a man of many talents

group, *The Irk Valley Stompers* and then the *Stylos*. A qualified teacher, Mike preferred performing to a wider audience, writing his own folksongs and some jokes, crazy stories and monologues (such as *Napoleon's Retreat From Wigan*) for his one-man show. He has performed in countless theatres in the British Isles, and for serving troops around the world.

Mike's versatility and output have been prodigious. He appeared in *The Mike Harding Show* on BBC television, and in *The Harding Trail*, in which he cycled along the Appalachian Trail recording the people and their music on his way. He has presented programmes for children on TV, and written scripts for cartoons (such as *Danger Mouse, Duckula, The Reluctant Dragon*), plays such as *Last Tango In Whitby*, volumes such as *When The Martians Landed In Huddersfield* (in 1984 this was Number 1 in *The Sunday Times* bestseller list), and *The Unluckiest Man In The World And Similar Disasters*. His travel books include *Footloose In The West Of Ireland, Footloose In The Himalaya*, and *Walking The Dales* (he was once

President of the Ramblers' Association). He has recorded many albums, including *Mrs 'Ardin's Kid, A Lancashire Lad, Captain Paralytic* and *The Brown Ale Cowboy,* and *Plutonium Alley.* For many years he had a folk music show on BBC Radio 2, foolishly now axed.

Comedians

Lancashire has produced many great comics. Some are long gone, such as Ted Ray and Frank Randle from Wigan, Hylda Baker from Farnworth, Al Read from Salford and Tubby Turner from Preston, and the list is endless. So here is my selection of Lancashire's greatest comedians.

KEN DODD

Ken Dodd has, for over half a century, been the greatest Lancashire comic and, arguably, Britain's Number One. He was born on 8 November 1927 at 76 Empire Street, Knotty Ash, the son of coal merchant Arthur Dodd, who was a semi-professional saxophonist and clarinet player, and his wife Sarah. Doddy left school aged fourteen and worked for his father by day and developed his skills as ventriloquist, singer and comedian in his spare time. In 1954 he became a full time professional, appearing at the Nottingham Empire, and the following year had his first summer season (alongside Morecambe & Wise) in Blackpool. He made his first TV appearance on 11 March 1955 in BBC's *The Good Old Days.*

Ken Dodd has two outstanding physical features that have contributed greatly to his performance as a comedian: his long unkempt hair and his protruding front teeth. As he has said, 'By jove Missus! I'm the only one who can kiss a girl and nibble her ear at the same time!' He has also exploited an outrageous imagination, creating Diddymen, jam butty mines, the operatic tenor and sausage-knotter Rufus Chucklebutty (also Professor Yaffle

Chuckabutty), and expressions like 'tattifilarious', 'plumptious' and 'nicky-nocky-noo!'

Though he has made many appearances on radio and TV (including his own shows such as *An Audience With Ken Dodd*), it is, in my opinion, as a live stand-up performer that Doddy beats all. He has had summer shows in eight Blackpool theatres and five in Liverpool, and over the years his *Happiness* Show has been taken to most theatres in the UK.

In 1965 he was booked to appear at the London Palladium, two shows per day, three on Saturdays: his show ran for a record 42 weeks. Whilst comedy dominates his show, Doddy has also exploited his fine tenor voice. In fact, two of his recorded songs were big hits: *Love Is Like A Violin* (1960) reached Number 8 in the charts, and *Happiness* (1964) was 'top of the pops' for four weeks in 1965 and in the top thirty for six months.

Ken Dodd has for over half a century been the UK's number one comedian. The best, bar none!

In 2000, the year before the great foot-and-mouth outbreak, I took the train from Formby and walked back along the shore to Southport. I stopped when I saw a sign advertising Ken Dodd's *Happiness* Show and made my way to the theatre. Yes there were a few tickets still available. 'But before I can sell you them, I must warn you that we cannot say when the show will finish. Almost certainly it will be after the last public transport!' said the girl in the ticket office.

We took our seats at 7.20 and at 7.30 prompt Ken Dodd appeared on stage, opening with, 'If you don't laugh at my jokes, I'll follow you home and shout them through your letterbox!' We laughed and laughed until, at 8.55 he walked offstage and a lady, dressed in a sombre evening gown, came on to play the piano. 'Must be the interval,' said my wife, and like many others she nipped out to the loo. Back came Doddy, who proceeded to hurl jokes at us rather like bullets from a machine gun. And then, at 9.55 he announced, 'The interval now follows. Be back in twenty minutes. Do not attempt to leave the theatre, for the doors are padlocked, and underfed guard dogs are on patrol outside!' He returned to the empty stage at 10.15, and he remained there for exactly two hours and twenty-two minutes, continuing to regale us with hysterical stories and one-liners, until, with arms raised and a tickling stick in each hand, he yelled, 'Tatty-bye Southport!' and we all stood, with tears of mirth rolling down our cheeks, and yelled back, 'Tatty-bye!'

I have never experienced such an evening. We all felt utterly wasted through laughing so much for so long, and I have never witnessed such a happy audience leaving a theatre. [It is reported that at a show at Manchester's Opera House a man laughed so violently that he broke a rib!]

But Doddy's world was darker when the Tax Man came. The Tax Man had already hit one major celebrity for tax evasion. Jockey Lester Piggott had been sentenced to three years in jail over a £3 million fraud. The Tax Man also moved against Doddy and on 6 June 1989 he appeared in the dock at Liverpool's Crown Court. He had the best lawyer defending him, Lancastrian George Carman QC, whose father had been a furniture salesmen in Blackpool. Carman had already successfully defended people like Elton John, Imran Khan and Richard Branson. Now he had a mega-case to defend. Ken Dodd faced 23 charges relating to his income and tax paid back to 1972.

The jury was told of bundles of cash at Doddy's Knotty Ash home. That, of an income in the period in question of £1,154,566, he had spent only £25,100. That, on 21 April 1980, he had taken £110,300 in cash to a bank in the Isle of Man and on the following day (22 April) £44,000 to a bank in Jersey. The evidence mounted. Doddy belatedly opened his books and offered to pay whatever he owned the Tax Man. He argued that he was hopeless with money, and that money and flashy possessions meant nothing to him.

When the jury returned to give their verdict, he was found 'Not guilty.'

A great man. Let me finish with one of my favourite daft Doddy jokes.

'I was driving up the M6 at 70 miles an hour in the outside lane when I spotted a chicken in the rear view mirror coming up behind me. I pulled over to the middle lane and the chicken accelerated and overtook me. Then I noticed that the chicken had three legs. Yes Missus. Three legs. I put my foot down and the chicken, he put his three feet down. Clunk-clunk-clunk. Clunk-clunk-clunk. It reached 80...then 90...then the ton. I had difficulty keeping up with it. But then suddenly it swung over into the inside lane and took the Wrightington slip road. Remember this when you approach junction 27 on the M6. I followed it. It turned left. Then it took the first right at a good 70 miles an hour. And then it zoomed into a farmyard and vanished round the back of a barn.

I came to a screaming halt. The farmer was leaning against a gate.

'Have you seen a chicken with three legs?

'Aye!

'With three legs?

'Aye. I breeds 'em wi' three legs.

'Why do you breed chicken with three legs?

'Well, when we 'ave chicken, the son likes a leg, the wife likes a leg and I likes a leg.

'What do they taste like?

'Don't know. Can't catch the bloomin' things!'

BERNARD MANNING

Bernard Manning was a complete contrast to Ken Dodd. He was born to greengrocer John Manning and his wife Nellie on 13 August 1930 at 183 Great Ancoats Street and grew up in the Blackley area of Manchester. He left Mount Carmel RC Elementary School at the age of 14 to work for £1 per week at the Senior Service cigarette factory. When he was 17 he started performing as an amateur in pubs and then moved on to the working men's club circuit to earn a bit of cash to supplement his wages. From 1948–50 he did his National Service as a military policeman, a job that included guarding Nazis Hess, Doenitz and Speer in Spandau prison. In his two years' service he also performed as a singer with Manchester Regiment's dance band.

Back home, he was performing in Barnes Green Catholic Club in Manchester when the great comedian Jimmy James noticed him. The outcome was that he was given a booking to appear at the Oldham Empire. By this time he was already married to Vera (Veronica) Finnerann. Success at Oldham led to a booking, for the then princely sum of £100 per week, with the Oscar Rabin Orchestra in London. But soon he became homesick and returned to Lancashire. He now became compere at the Northern Sporting Club, and he began to intersperse his introductions to wrestling and boxing bouts and 'star' entertainers with his own jokes and wisecracks.

Manning's big decision was to purchase an old billiard hall on the same road as his father's shop. He then persuaded his father to give up his business and to join him and other family members in this new venture that he called the Embassy Club. Its doors first opened on 11 December 1959. Every evening he performed in the club, with guest artists, but the club closed early so that he could make extra money with late night performances at other Lancashire clubs.

On 12 June 1971 Manning made his first television appearance on Granada TV's show *The Comedians*. His first joke was simple: 'An Irishman come up before the court to have the maintenance fixed for his estranged wife. The judge announces, 'We have decided to award your wife £7 per week.' 'Thankyou,' says the Irishman. 'I'll send her a few bob myself!''

He then became compere on Granada TV's pseudo-working men's club, *the Wheeltappers' and Shunters' Social Club*, aided and abetted by another Lancashire pan-faced comic called Colin Crompton. The latter uttered some great lines as he rang his bell and called for order. 'First prize in tonight's raffle is a diving suit... No...Wait a minute...No. It's a divan suite! Order. Listen to mi. Pies 'ave cum!' By this time Manning was grossly overweight, giving Crompton the opportunity to point out, 'Manning gave some of his old clothes to Oxfam. They are still lookin' for a 24-stone starving African!'

By the mid-1970s Manning was an international star. In 1977 he appeared in the MGM Grand Theatre, Las Vegas, and was offered a further contract of £750,000 to appear nightly for six months. He refused and went home to his Embassy Club. And it was from then on that he became one of the most hated and despised comedians. As John Sweeney put it in *The Manchester*

Evening News, his act had become 'obscene, cruel, malicious, racist, sexist and degrading. And worst of all, he made people laugh.' It was and he did. Every night his club was crowded with people laughing at his foul language and foul jokes. But it need not have been so. One of the simplest and best jokes comes from Manning: 'One of the lads who rents out the rowing boats on Fairhaven Lake shouted through his megaphone, 'Come in boat 91, your time is up!' 'We've only got 90 boats,' said the other. 'Oh! Having trouble, number 16?'

LES DAWSON

People sometimes confused Les Dawson and Bernard Manning, and though both were short, stout men with broad Lancashire accents, their comedy and careers were quite different. Les was born in 1931 to Les and Julie Dawson of Thornton Street, Collyhurst on the east side of Manchester. The family was poor.... so poor that when they got behind with the rent and had no chance of paying it, they did 'moonlight flits'. He left Moston Lane Elementary School when he was fourteen and got a job in the drapery department of the local co-op. He then became an apprentice electrician before his two years of National Service in Germany.

When he returned he took up playing the piano in local pubs and became a very accomplished amateur pianist. He was so accomplished that he began to appear as Quasimodo (the hunchback of Notre Dame), playing the piano deliberately slightly off-key. Yet he failed to secure a real job in showbusiness, and to make ends meet he had spells as a Hoover salesman and very junior reporter with *The Bury Times*. Then, in the 1950s and early 1960s Les began to expand his act in the northern working men's club circuit. But having married Meg (Margaret) Plant, and with a family arriving, he needed a more secure income. Suddenly came his big break, when he appeared on Hughie Green's talent show *Opportunity Knocks*. For the first time British audiences saw the straight-faced, down-to-earth delivery that was quite different from the ebullient Ken Dodd or acrid Bernard Manning:

'The neighbours love it when I play the piano. They often break my windows to hear me better...My mother used to sit me on her knee and I'd whisper, "Mummy, sing me a lullaby, do." And she'd say, "Surely, my little bundle of happiness. Just hold my ale while I get the banjo."'

Les has been criticised for his famous mother-in-law jokes, but those who do criticise forget that mothers-in-law could be quite threatening to young sons-in-law in the confines of an extended family living near each other in rows of terraced streets. Hence their dragonlike reputations:

'My mother-in-law says I look effeminate. I suppose I do when I am standing next to her!'

'When the mice hear my mother-in-law approaching they fling themselves into the traps!'

Les never looked back and, in 1974, Yorkshire TV gave him his own first series, *SEZ LES*.

We must now go back to a much earlier Lancashire comedian, Norman Evans, 'Lancashire's Ambassador of Mirth'. Evans had a wide rubbery mouth and false teeth. As part of his very popular act he would appear, toothless, wearing curlers in a woman's wig and a pinny of the sort worn by most working class women in Lancashire up to the 1960s. And as Fanny Fairbottom he would come on stage (or screen, for he appeared on black-and-white TV in the 1950s), lift up his ample bosom and place it on the garden wall, and then chat to the audience about the weather, cost of living, women's problems, men, and so on.

When he came to a particularly risqué word he meemawed★ it so that the audience couldn't hear, but knew what he was at. For example: 'You know Julie Makinson? She's – meemawed up-the-club – again. Goodness only knows who the – meemawed father – is. It can't be her husband Billy's. He's been in –meemawed prison – this last nine months!' There were thousands of Fanny Fairbottoms in the Lancashire mill towns!

[* For the uninitiated: *Meemaw*. To mouth a word with exaggerated movements of the lips and tongue. Meemawing evolved in the cotton mills where the din of the machinery prevented normal conversation.]

Norman Evans was dead by the time that Les Dawson, joined by another great Lancastrian comic actor Roy Barrowclough revived the format of over-the-garden-wall in their sketches *Cissie and Ada*. Les' Cissie chatted to Roy's strait-laced Ada, Cissie bringing up local gossip and scandal of which Ada strongly disapproved. For his TV shows, Les also produced a suggestively perverted character of the Benny Hill school called Cosmo Smallpiece, in which he contorted his most contortable face and concluded with, 'Knickers, knackers, knockers!'

But other than in these little cameos Les Dawson remained a stand-up comic, wearing his trademark DJ and black bow tie. Typical of his dry humour was a few mad lines from the Royal Variety Show: 'In 1645 Prince Rupert's mercenaries smashed Cromwell's left flank at Naseby, and in 1871 the Franco–Prussian war took a serious turn at the siege of Rouen. And in 1952, from the Kyles of Bute, came the first report of a massive outbreak of sporran-rash!'

In the late 1970s and early 1980s Les was at the top of the BBC tree. 1977 saw a series of *The Les Dawson Show*, followed in 1978 by *The Dawson Watch*. And then he took over from the great Terry Wogan as compere and question master in Saturday evening's prime time show, *Blankety Blank*.

Success was tinged with sorrow. On 15 April 1986 Meg died of cancer. Then happiness. He married his second wife Tracey who bore him a daughter, Charlotte. Les died on 29 October

1993. Like Dodd and Manning, he never lived outside of his county, living his most successful years at Fairhaven.

ERIC MORECAMBE

Eric Morecambe was another completely different style of comedian to Dodd, Manning and Dawson. He was born on 15 May 1926 to George and Sadie Bartholomew in the holiday town of Morecambe. Neither of his parents was well educated, and his father worked as a labourer on the town's roads, his mother as a waitress. However Eric had innate talent. At the age of three he was performing song-and-dance acts, and when he was ten his mother, realising his potential, enrolled him for dancing classes. She paid for the latter by working extra hours as a charlady. By the time that he was twelve years old, Eric was performing a singing and dancing routine, broken up by impressions, throughout north Lancashire and winning talent contests in his home town. Indeed, he was too good.

This statue of one of Morecambe's favourite sons stands on the town's promenade, overlooking Morecambe Bay

When he was thirteen he was no longer allowed to enter contests in Morecambe because he always won and nobody else would take part. So Sadie took him by train to a talent contest at Hoylake, on the Cheshire coast, which he won. The prize was an audition in front of impresario and band leader Jack Hylton (a Lancastrian from Bolton). The audition was in Manchester, and sitting next to Hylton was another young performer called Ernie Wiseman, who had already turned professional.

Hylton booked Eric at £5 per week working variety theatres around the country, chaperoned by his mother. Each week they would arrive in a new town where he would perform in two shows every night for six nights. When they arrived in Swansea, Ernie Wiseman also arrived for the week. There they did their own acts, separately. But in 1941, at Liverpool's Empire Theatre, Eric and Ernie did their first ever double act. And with this came name changes. Eric became Morecambe and Ernie became Wise.

Success did not follow smoothly, for now the War was at its peak. They were given no new work so Eric moved back home to Morecambe where he took a job in a factory that made razorblades. Ernie returned home to Leeds, but then had second thoughts. He took the train to Morecambe (there was then a direct line) and persuaded Eric to go down with him to London. There they auditioned together at the Hippodrome and were given a job, at the then princely rate of £10 per week each, in a show called *Striking A New Note* at the Prince of Wales Theatre. By early 1943 they seemed a permanent part of the show scene, but in November Ernie reached the age of 18 and was called up into the merchant navy. In May 1944 Eric too turned 18 years old and was sent, as a Bevan Boy, to work down a coal mine in East Lancashire. He was invalided out because of the heart problem that would cause his demise.

Immediately after the war, Morecambe and Wise found it difficult to get bookings. So like many, they had a spell at the

Windmill Theatre, which had a stream of variety acts to break up its famed nude tableaux. Sad men, traditionally wearing gabardine raincoats and trilby hats, went solely to oggle at the nudes and when the other acts appeared, they heckled. But there they met Frank Pope, the agent for Moss Empire chain of theatres, who signed them up at £35 per week (with an extra £10 when they played the infamous lions' den of the Glasgow Empire). It was while they were playing the Edinburgh Empire that Eric met his future wife Joan, whom he married on 11 December 1952.

Now they were much in demand and very busy. In winter there was pantomime (their first, *Dick Whittington* in 1952 in Sheffield). Then there was the summer season booking, entertaining holiday-makers. Their first was in 1953 at Blackpool's Winter Gardens alongside another Lancashire comedian Ken Platt. Two years later their summer show was at Blackpool's Central Pier Theatre with the up and coming Ken Dodd (who apparently 'stole the show'). And between the Christmas panto and summer, their weeks were filled travelling on the Moss Empire circuit.

The early 1960s saw the death of variety and the blossoming of television. They had appeared on radio regularly since 1953, but their first TV broadcast was as late as 1966 in ATV's *Two Of A Kind*. In 1968 they joined the BBC to make *The Morecambe & Wise Show*, which attracted audiences of over 20 million. Their Christmas special shows are still (2010-11) being broadcast.

Beyond any doubt, Morecambe & Wise became the most loved family duo of the twentieth century, with their relatively light comedy based around straight man Wise and his foil, daft Eric. Their shows would have little plays written by Ernie ('This play wot I wrote!') that pretended to embarrass guest performers. There is, for instance, the classic, where conductor André Previn (called 'Andrew Preview' by Eric) conducts the London Symphony Orchestra with Eric playing the piano solo (badly).

Previn to Eric: You're playing all the wrong notes.
Eric to Previn: No. I'm playing all the right notes. But not necessarily in the right order!

Simple, but so funny that people laugh when they see it again for the umpteenth time.

Eric Morecambe suffered a series of heart attacks, the last, that killed him, in 1984.

And of other Lancashire comedians? There have been double acts, like Cannon and Ball (whom I personally have never found that funny). And there have been other stand-ups like Tom O'Connor and Jimmy Tarbuck. We must not forget comic actors like Leonard Rossiter, star of *Rising Damp* and *The Rise And Fall Of Reginald Iolanthe Perrin*. Or Ricky Tomlinson, who was born, not in Liverpool, but Blackpool. Or Caroline Aherne, who wrote and starred in *The Royle Family* and who, in her own show, *Mrs Merton*, coyly asked Debbie McGee (wife of the Yorkshire magician), 'What attracted you to the short, bald multi-millionaire Paul Daniels?'

Or the great comedy writer and performer Eric Sykes, who was born in Oldham and produced and appeared in some classics such as *The Plank*. Or the still young Bolton comedian Peter Kay, who should be making audiences laugh for years to come.

However, with the demise of Variety, comedy in the United Kingdom changed. Most young comedians have never learned how to entertain live family audiences as did Ken Dodd, Bernard Manning, Les Dawson and Morecambe & Wise. Most seem to have discarded discipline, hard work and practice, perseverance, and the ability to tell tall stories and funny stories in favour of a style of caustic chatter that simply knocks authority and the establishment. I cannot imagine the BBC broadcasting their performances a quarter of a century after their deaths.

Popular Music

After the Second World War, the USA dominated the world of popular music, with names like Frank Sinatra, Dean Martin and, from the mid 1950s, Elvis Presley. All this was to change as the 1950s gave way to the 1960s, and the change began in Lancashire. The epicentre was Liverpool, though there was a major input from Manchester and its surrounding mill towns.

Looking back, especially amusing were the names pop singers (now, highfalutingly called 'vocalists') gave to themselves and their groups (now, grandly called 'bands'). Ronald Wycherley (born 1940, died 1983) became Billy Fury, and his group *the Tornados*. Leigh's Clive Powell (born 1943) became Georgie Fame and his group the *Blue Flames*. In January 1965 their fourth single record *Yeh Yeh* became top in the UK charts, 21st in the US. Glynn Geoffrey Ellis (born 1945) and his group became *Wayne Fontana and the Mindbenders*; they achieved a UK Number 2 and a US Number 1 with the song *The Game of Love*. Bootle's William Howard (born 1943) became *Billie J Kramer*, who with the *Dakotas* (Dakotas? from Bootle!!) had his biggest hit in 1963 with *Do You Want To Know A Secret*. Other less well-known but madly named Lancashire performers included *Abraham and his Lot, Gerry Bach and his Beathovens*, and *Ray Satans and the Devils*! Most of the hundreds of pop groups founded in the county disappeared without trace. But one last will find an honourable mention later: Alan Caldwell appeared on stage as *Rory Storm with the Hurricanes*.

THE BEATLES

One group stood out in the '60s revolution: *The Beatles*. John Winston Lennon was born on 9 October 1940 to Freddie Lennon, who quickly fled the scene, and his rather flighty mother, Julia. By the time he was five years old, he had been taken in by his aunt, Mimi Smith, who lived at 251 Menlove Avenue, Liverpool.

James Paul McCartney was born on 18 June 1942 to Jim and Mary McCartney. Jim encouraged both Paul and his brother Mike to play musical instruments. They had piano lessons and, when Paul was 14, he was bought a trumpet which he swapped for a Zenith guitar. In 1955 the family moved into 20 Forthlin Road. Both 251 Menlove Avenue and 20 Forthlin Road are now owned by the National Trust.

In 1957 Lennon, together with Eric Griffiths and Pete Shotton, started to play in a group they called *The Quarrymen* after their school, Quarry Bank. That summer McCartney met Lennon at a fete in St Peter's church hall in Woolton, where *The Quarrymen* were appearing and within weeks he was a group member. The first public performance of Lennon and McCartney was on 18 October 1957 at New Clubmoor Hall, Norris Green. By 1958 Lennon and McCartney had started to write songs together, including early versions of *I Call Your Name, I'll Follow The Sun* and *Love Me Do.*

George Harold Harrison, born on 25 February 1943, was son of bus driver Harry Harrison and his wife Louise. He was 13 when he bought his first guitar and, with friend Arthur Kelly, started a group called the *Rebels*. He met McCartney on the school bus and, on 6 February 1958, went to see *The Quarrymen* performing at Wilson Hall, Garston.

By 1959 *The Quarrymen* had disbanded and Harrison was playing with the Les Stewart Quartet that had been booked for the opening of a new Liverpool club, the Casbah in West Derby. But the Quartet split up before the gig and Harrison went to Lennon and McCartney. They, with Ken Brown, reformed *The Quarrymen* and took the place of the Les Stewart Quartet at the Casbah. In December that year, Stuart Sutcliffe, a friend of Lennon, joined the group as bass guitarist. Soon Tommy Moore joined as drummer, and the group changed their name to the *Silver Beetles*. Lennon altered the spelling to Beatles, and later the 'Silver' was dropped.

In May 1960 *The Beatles* were booked for a tour of Scotland alongside *Cass and the Cassanovas* (!) and during the tour drummer Moore quit. His place was taken by Pete Best, whose mother ran the Casbah Club, and in August the group headed for Hamburg where for upwards of four hours every night they performed at the Kaiserkeller Club. Then there was another change: Stuart Sutcliffe was dropped as bass player, a role taken over by McCartney. Back home in Liverpool, early in 1961 *The Beatles* began to appear at the Cavern Club, a venue that took on iconic status as a centre for new pop music. That summer it was back to Hamburg, before returning to Liverpool and the Cavern in autumn.

And then the magic moment arrived. That October Brian Epstein heard them performing at the Cavern and on 3 October became their manager. As 1962 began, Epstein arranged auditions with EMI (they famously turned down *The Beatles*!) and Decca (ditto) before going to George Martin of the Parlophone label. Martin demanded an audition, but by now the group were back in Hamburg. When they returned that June, they auditioned for Martin who agreed to take them on, but he did not approve of their drummer, Pete Best. Despite his popularity with the fans, Best had to go and his place was taken by Ringo Starr.

Born Richard Starkie on 7 July 1940, as a boy Ringo spent a year in the Royal Liverpool Children's Hospital suffering from tuberculosis. There he found a drum kit and spent many long hours tapping and banging away. Back home and fully recovered, for Christmas 1957 he was given his own set of drums and by the end of 1958 he was drummer for the *Raging Texans* (from Liverpool!) who eventually metamorphosed into *Rory Storm and the Hurricanes*. In 1962 the Hurricanes went to perform for a summer season at Butlin's holiday camp at Pwllheli and from there, because of his great reputation as a drummer, Ringo was invited to join *The Beatles*. Now the four famous *Beatles* were together: John, Paul, George and Ringo. The 'Fab Four'.

Their first record *Love Me Do* was released in August 1962, followed by *Please, Please Me* (November 1962), and then the avalanche of *From Me To You* (it sold 220,000 in the first week), *She Loves You* (over a million), and *I Want To Hold Your Hand* (over 1 million advance sales).

In November 1963 their record *She Loves You* was Number 1 in the charts, with *I Want To Hold Your Hand* at Number 3. *The Beatles* rollercoaster accelerated. On 19 January 1963 they made their first TV appearance in *Thank Your Lucky Stars,* and on 13 October 1963 over 15 million viewers watched them perform in the Royal Command Variety Show. Early in 1964 they crossed the Atlantic, and the 74 million who tuned in to their act on the *Ed Sullivan Show* was the USA's largest ever TV audience. In February they had numbers 1, 2, 29, 35 and 54 in the US singles chart and their LP *Meet The Beatles* was Number 1 in the album chart.

The Beatles arriving at Kennedy Airport, New York on 7 February 1964

Now Beatlemania gripped the world. They produced two films (*Hard Day's Night* in 1964 and *Help!* in 1965) that had, in hindsight, rather juvenile story lines, but did promote them and their music. Lennon even had two short books of his writing published (*Spaniard In The Works*, and *In His Own Write*), the latter selling an incredible 40,000 copies in its first day in the bookshops! Their song *Can't Buy Me Love* had advanced sales of 1.7 million in the US alone, earning them a gold disk before the record was released. And when they returned to the USA they performed in New York's Shea Stadium before a record audience of 56,000.

Then, in the midst of this fame and increasing wealth came two key moments that resulted in change. On 10 November 1966 John Lennon met and became infatuated with Japanese artist Yoko Ono, and on 28 August 1967 the man who had managed them to fame and wealth, Brian Epstein, died. By then they had had twelve successive Number 1s. They continued to produce great hits: *Strawberry Fields, Penny Lane,* and *Sergeant Pepper's Lonely Hearts Club Band.* But cracks appeared and slowly *The Beatles* came apart. Their last public appearance was on 30 January 1969 on the rooftop of Apple records in London, and their last Number 1, *Abbey Road*, was released on 26 June 1969 (it was Number 1 before its release in both UK and USA). By April 1970, less than a decade after their first record was released, the world's greatest pop group was no more. At the time, John and Ringo were aged 30, Paul 29 and George Harrison 27.

John Lennon was shot dead in New York in 1980. George Harrison died from lung cancer in 2001. In 1997 Paul McCartney was given a knighthood by the Queen, and is still with us. And Ringo Starr, who ought to be given a knighthood, is also still with us.

CILLA BLACK

The late 1950s and 1960s produced many well-known pop groups, but relatively few soloists. Amongst the few great soloists was Liverpool's Cilla Black.

She was born Priscilla Maria Veronica White on 27 May 1943 in a council flat at 380 Scotland ('Scottie') Road. Her father John was a docker and her mother, also Priscilla, had a second-hand clothes stall on St Martin's Market. From a child she was a precocious performer, taking any opportunity of singing and showing-off in front of friends and family.

She left school when she was fifteen and, although she attended secretarial college for a year, put her music first. Eventually she homed in on the Cavern Club, where she acted as a dogsbody, washing up, acting as waitress and famously working in the cloakroom. Famously? Everyone who visited the Cavern in the late '50s and early '60s will tell you that they met Cilla Black when she was working in the Cavern's cloakroom! But she also took every opportunity of singing with the performers booked to appear there.

The Cavern was named after a Parisian club called *Le Caveau* and established by Alan Sytner in the basement of 10 Mathew Street in the heart of Liverpool. It opened in January 1957 and, through its heydays, over 350 groups performed there. Some groups made it their home base camp, including *The Beatles*, who appeared in the Cavern over 300 times. Anyone with talent, who became an integral part of the Cavern, would reach their potential. As did Priscilla White, who became *Cilla Black*.

She was signed up by Brian Epstein in 1963 and made her first professional appearance on the same bill as *The Beatles* at Southport Odeon on 30 August that year. Her first record, *Love Of The Loved*, reached only 35 in the charts, but after appearing in *The Beatles Christmas Show* in London, her next two songs *Anyone Who Had A*

Heart and *You're My World*, released in 1964, both reached Number 1. This made Cilla very special, for she was the first British female soloist to have successive Number 1s. That year she was booked to perform at the London Palladium for six months and toured the USA, appearing, as did *The Beatles*, on the important *Ed Sullivan Show*. *Step Inside Love* was her next big hit. Then, in 1968, the BBC gave her her own TV series *Cilla* in 1968.

We must now go back. When Cilla was 18 she met Bobby Willis in the Zodiac Club in Liverpool. Almost eight years later, on 25 June 1969, and after her string of hits and her own TV shows, they married. This was the time when her career changed. She became a mother, having three sons and a daughter (who sadly died soon after birth). Bobby became her mentor and encouraged her to put aside performing in favour of presenting TV programmes. The first was *Surprise, Surprise* (1983), and the second, and the long-running *Blind Date* (from 1985). Cilla was awarded the OBE in 1997 and died in August 2015.

Further Lancastrian pop successes included *The Hollies*: Salford's Allan Clarke (singer), Nelson's Tony Hicks, Burnley's Bobby Elliott, Blackpool's Graham Nash and Stockport's Eric Haydock and was founded in 1961. Their first single, *Just Like Me*, reached Number 25 in the charts in June 1963, *Searchin'* Number 12 and *Stay* Number 8.

Herman's Hermits were originally called the *Heartbeats* and consisted of four Lancastrians (Peter Noone, Keith Hopwood and Barry Whitwam from Manchester, and Karl Green from Salford) plus Derek (Lek) Leckenby from Leeds. They were the 'number two' group after *The Beatles*. Their first Number 1 was *I'm Into Something Good* (1964), which was followed by *Mrs Brown You've Got A Lovely Daughter* and *I'm Henry The Eighth I Am*; in 1965 they sold over 10 million records. Their album *There's A Kind Of Hush* was the most lucrative of their ten albums, being released in the same year as their two singles *A Must To Avoid* and *No*

Milk Today. And like *The Beatles*, they went into making films to back-up their music: *When The Boys Meet The Girls* was released in 1965, *Hold On!* in 1966.

Freddie and the Dreamers was a superficially daft act in which the lead singer, ex brush salesman Freddie Garrity, jumped up and down on stage like a demented flea as he performed. They had three top 3's in the UK charts in 1963. Even greater, and still well remembered, was *Gerry [Marsden] and the Pacemakers*. In 1963 they had three Number 1's: *How Do You Do It*, *I Like It*, and *You'll Never Walk Alone*. Few pop musicians manage two top-of-the-pops in one year; but three! Their other great hit, *Ferry Across The Mersey*, has become Liverpool's anthem, while *You'll Never Walk Alone* has been Anfield Kop's unofficial song for half a century.

Whilst the 1960s was a unique decade for popular music generated in Lancashire, produced by poor kids, who were born during the Second World War, and had talent, drive and the urge not to suffer drudgery as did their parents, the following four decades have produced some other notable performers. Soft Cell consisted of Southport's Marc Almond (singer) and David Ball (keyboard). Their record *Tainted Love* reached Number 1 in September 1981 and was that year's biggest selling single. Rick Astley, who was born in Newton-le-Willows, had 1987's biggest selling single with his song *Never Gonna Give You Up*; it was Number 1 in the charts for five weeks.

However the critics argue that the major UK band through the 1980s was *The Smiths*. They consisted of singer Stephen Patrick Morrissey from Davyhulme backed by Ardwick's Johnny Marr, Fallowfield's Mike Joyce and Manchester's Andy Rourke. In 1983 they signed a recording contract with Rough Trade Records and produced several singles that made it into the charts, the first *Hand In Glove* the same year. Their albums, including *The Queen Is Dead* (1986) and *Strangeways, Here We Come* (1987) were top sellers. When *The Smiths* broke up in 1987 Morrissey continued as a solo performer, his first single *Suedehead* (1988) reaching Number 5 in the UK singles chart, and his album *Viva Hate* (1988) Number 1.

Oasis was a Manchester group that dominated the pop scene in the 1990s. It consisted of Liam Gallagher (vocalist), and his brother Noel, Paul Bonehead Arthur, Paul McGuigan and Tony McCarroll. Their album *Definitely Maybe* reached No 1 in September 1994, and their single *Some Might Say* in May 1995. In October 1995 their second album *(What's The Story) Morning Glory* reached No 1 in the UK charts and the following February No 4 in the USA, selling a total of 7 million copies.

Chapter Four

FAMOUS LANCASHIRE SPORTSMEN

Making a selection from the vast number of Lancashire entertainers for this book was difficult, but when it comes to sportsmen (and women) it is well nigh impossible. Each of the two categories merits a large tome, not just a few pages. My choice has been based on two points: the players must have reached international class; they must have reached the very top in their sport (lots have represented England or Great Britain, but have won nothing); and I have ignored the media hype that is so dominant today.

Great Footballers

Lancashire clubs were amongst the founders of the Football League, the first organised League in the world. Accordingly they are the oldest clubs in the world: the oldest ten are Bolton Wanderers founded in 1874, Blackburn Rovers in 1875, Blackpool in 1887, Everton and Manchester United in 1878, Manchester City in 1880, Preston North End in 1881, Burnley in 1882, Bury in 1885, and Accrington Stanley in 1891. That other great club Liverpool was founded a year after Accrington, in 1892. Today the first division of the Football League is called the Premiership, and it has gained an immense worldwide audience through TV exposure. Its vast income has also, alas, tended to attract the best overseas players, so that home-grown talent has been somewhat neglected since the later years of the 20th century. Furthermore, the best players have been encouraged, through obscenely inflated salaries, to have little loyalty to their home team. I have borne this in mind when making my selection of great Lancashire footballers. My first two choices are classic examples of loyalty to their home team.

SIR TOM FINNEY

Tom Finney was born in Preston in 1922 and spent his entire football career at Preston North End from 1946 to 1960. This was in the era of the 'maximum footballers' wage', when super-rich could never have been used to describe our best footballers. So, at the insistence of his father, Tom went into the trade of plumbing and eventually had his own company, with headquarters on Lytham Road in north Preston.

Tales abound of him, in the early years, taking the corporation bus to Deepdale, and talking of the prospects of that afternoons's match with the other passengers who would be paying to watch him play. He played 507 games for Preston, scoring 217 goals, and he won 76 caps for his country, scoring 30 goals.

He was, primarily, a 'winger', who could beat opponent defenders by his speed down the right or left wing, and his sudden turns and swerves with the ball seemingly glued to his feet. His loyalty was demonstrated when he (encouraged by the clubs's manager) rejected a £100,000 transfer in 1952 to the Italian club Palermo. Preston was his home and there he remained.

Alas for him, the other members of the North End team were generally of a much poorer calibre. Consequently he never won a League Champion or FA Cup winner's medal. He was voted Footballer of the Year twice, was belatedly knighted in 1998, and died on 14 February 2014.

NAT LOFTHOUSE

Nat Lofthouse, born 1925 and died 2011, was of the same era as Finney. Born in Bolton, he signed as apprentice with Bolton Wanderers just before the outbreak of the Second World War. He was a centre forward who had great strength and an ability to score goals with both head and feet. Because of his strength, when playing for England against Austria in 1952 he became known as the Lion of Vienna. The Austrian players were determined to prevent Nat scoring by fouling him at every opportunity. With the score at 2-2 (Nat getting one of the England goals), the Austrians won a corner. Finney intercepted the ball and immediately passed it to Lofthouse who made a long solo run towards the Austrian goal, avoiding the attempts of the Austrian defence to stop him.

Tom Finney (left) and Nat Lofthouse at an England training session at Chelsea's Stamford Bridge ground in 1955

Then, as he came within striking distance and made the shot on goal, the goalkeeper deliberately collided with him. Knocked out, Lofthouse was stretchered from the pitch, but returned just before the final whistle. Nat Lofthouse played a total of 503 games for the Wanderers in the years 1946-60, scoring 285 goals (making him the seventh highest scorer in top flight football).

He played twice for Bolton in the FA Cup. The first time Bolton lost 3-4 to Blackpool in the famous Stanley Matthews final of 1953. But in 1958 Bolton beat Manchester United 2-0 at Wembley, Nat scoring both goals. He also played for England 33 times in the years 1950-58, scoring 30 goals. This still makes him England's most successful goal scorer, at 0.91 goals/game. The second in this list is Jimmy Greaves (0.77 goals/game), third Gary Lineker (0.6 goals/game) and Tom Finney is ninth (0.39 goals/ game; which is remarkable for a winger whose job was to pass the ball for others to score!). Wayne Rooney just makes the top ten, but players like the much-hyped David Beckham and Paul Gascoigne come much further down the list. In 1954 the Board of Bolton Wanderers received a very generous offer for Lofthouse from the Italian club Florentina, an offer that would have made Nat moderately wealthy. They did not consult Nat before turning the offer down. Such was professional football half a century ago, before agents, player power and TV cash.

In the 1950s and early 1960s the English FA had an antiquated and amateurish way of selecting their football team and a most pompous attitude to the World Cup; which was why Lofthouse played relatively few games for his country and why England never won the World Cup in those years. However, since the World Cup of 1962, England have attempted to do well in the competition but have succeeded only once, in 1966. Any player that does win a World Cup medal can be described as 'great', and the cynic can only smile each week when, in TV football programmes, even more effusive adjectives are applied to players who are palpably not 'great'! Eleven Englishmen won a World Cup winner's medal in 1966, four of whom were Lancastrians.

NOBBY STILES

Nobby (Norbert) Stiles was born on 18 May 1942 in Manchester. He played 311 games for his home team of Manchester United from 1960-71, scoring 17 goals (he was a fierce defender, famed for his toothless grin and short sight). Later he played for Middlesborough (57 games in 1971-2) and Preston North End (44 games in 1973-4). With Manchester United he won a European Cup winner's medal in 1968 and League Championship medals in 1965 and 1967, as well as his World Cup winner's medal for England, for whom he played 28 games.

ALAN BALL

Alan Ball was born in Farnworth on 12 May 1945. He played 116 games for Blackpool (in 1962-5) scoring 40 goals, 206 games for Everton (in 1966-71) scoring 66 goals, 177 games for Arsenal (in 1971-76) scoring 45 goals and 132 games for Southampton (in 1976-79) scoring nine goals. He played 72 times for England, scoring eight goals, and winning a World Cup winner's medal.

ROGER HUNT

Roger Hunt was born in Golborne on 20 July 1938 and besides football he had long involvement in the family's haulage firm. He played 401 games for Liverpool (in 1959-69) scoring 245 goals, and 72 games for Preston North End (in 1969-71), scoring 24 goals. In the 1966 World Cup he was very much a number two striker to the great Jimmy Greaves, but when it came to the crunch, manager Alf Ramsey chose the powerful Hunt instead. His decision was vindicated when England beat the Germans 4-2 in extra time at Wembley and Hunt deservedly took his winner's medal. He played 34 times for England, scoring 17 goals.

And the fourth Lancastrian World Cup winner? I unearthed this when gathering information for this book and found that none of my football-mad pals knew this. The answer is Sir Geoff Hurst who was born at Ashton-under-Lyne on 8 November 1943. Hurst never played football in the county other than with the opposition, spending most of his career (1959-71) with West Ham United. He played 49 times for England, scoring 24 goals, three of them in the World Cup final when they beat Germany 4-2.

Choosing two post-1966 Lancashire footballers who have made a great impact on the game was relatively easy.

EMLYN HUGHES

My first choice is Emlyn Hughes who was born at 94 Blake Street, Barrow-in-Furness (now officially in Cumbria) on 28 August 1947. His father, Fred, was a great rugby league player (he had represented Great Britain in the sport) who had a tarmac-laying business and, on the side, was a bookmaker at the Cartmel race course. But young Emlyn was football mad, playing for Barrow-in-Furness juniors. After school he became an apprentice motor mechanic in Barrow. But Barrow was not a soccer town, so his father contacted an old friend, Ron Stuart, who was then (early 1960s) manager of Blackpool. Ron Stuart took him down to Blackpool. At first Emlyn continued his apprenticeship as a motor mechanic, but then in 1964 he signed professionally for Blackpool at the mighty wage of £8 per week!

Hughes was noticed by Liverpool manager Bill Shankley, on 2 May 1966, when he was playing for Blackpool against Blackburn Rovers at Ewood Park. In 1966 and early 1967 Hughes played in 26 league games and six FA Cup games for Blackpool. But on 27 February 1967 Shankley signed him for a modest £65,000 and he moved to Anfield. His debut for Liverpool was on 4 March 1967 against Stoke City. A month later, Liverpool were playing Newcastle and Hughes was playing left back. Newcastle winger

Albert Bennett was running rings around Hughes and did it once too often. He took the ball past Emlyn who sprinted after him and rugby tackled him to the ground. Everyone (other than perhaps Bennett) thought that this was hilarious and the laughing referee, instead of sending Hughes off, merely rebuked him and awarded Newcastle a free kick. Liverpool won the game 3-1 and Hughes was given his nickname, 'Crazy Horse'!

Hughes was an integral part of a near-invincible late '60s and '70s Liverpool team that included the great goalkeeper Ray Clemence, the hard men Tommy Smith and Alan Hansen, and great goal scorers like Roger Hunt, Ian St. John, Kevin Keegan, John Toshack and Kenny Dalglish. And by 1969 he was part of the England squad although for the 1970 World Cup in Mexico, manager Alf Ramsey did not pick him for the side.

Altogether he played in 662 games for Liverpool (1967-79) and won four League Championship medals, an FA Cup winner's medal in 1974, UEFA Cup winner's medals in 1973 and 1976, two European Cup winner's medals in 1977 and 1978, and a European Super Cup winner's medal in 1977. He also played 62 games for England. In the 1972-3 season he made a record 74 appearances, which is a game every 4.8 days through the year! After his time at Liverpool he moved to Wolverhampton Wanderers, where he played 58 games and added a League Cup winner's medal to his collection. He transferred to Rotherham as player-manager (1981-83), Hull City (1982-3) and finally to Swansea City (1983-4).

Emlyn Hughes was a larger-than-life, ebullient and jovial character who was not cut out for the ruthlessness needed in football management. But he was perfect in front of a television camera. And so he appeared as a pundit on football programmes and, most famously, as team captain (opposite another Lancastrian, Bill Beaumont) in BBC's *A Question Of Sport*. Alas it was not to last. He died on 9 November 2003, aged only 57 years young.

PAUL SCHOLES

My last choice footballer played the beautiful game at the highest level before retiring in May 2013: Paul Scholes. His home town is Oldham and he was born on 16 November 1974 in Salford's Hope Hospital. After playing for both his primary and secondary schools and Boundary Park juniors (Oldham Athletic) he signed on as a trainee with Manchester United on 8 July 1991 and as a professional in 1993. He was then also playing for the England under-18 team.

Scoles's arrival at Manchester United coincided with the club's manager (Sir) Alec Ferguson's determination to produce as great a team as he could, by bringing in very young talent and honing it to world class. So Scholes arrived at roughly the same time as David Beckham, Ryan Giggs, Nicky Butt and Gary and Phil Neville. And Ferguson did turn them into a world class team.

Scholes's first appeared in United's first team on 21 September 1994 in a League Cup match against Port Vale; United won and Scholes scored a brace of goals. In the season that he became a permanent member of United's first team squad (1995-6) he scored 16 goals in the first 21 League games and won Premiership and FA Cup winner's medals. The following season he added another Premiership medal to the first. In 1998-9 Scholes was a member of the team that won the European Cup, the FA Cup and the Premiership again. And in the 1999-2000 season Manchester United won the Premiership yet again by an 18 point margin. Paul Scholes and the team, led by perhaps the greatest manager, continued to win competitions and gain trophies. Scholes has also won 66 England caps, scoring 14 goals, and had the other players selected to represent their country been of his calibre he would have had at least one World Cup winner's medal.

But why have I chosen Scholes? Why is he better than so many others of his vintage?

Firstly he has his feet firmly on the ground and lacks the *prima donna* lifestyle of so many others.

Secondly, he has never forgotten his roots. When Manchester United are not playing, he can be seen watching Oldham Athletic playing at Boundary Park, the team he supported as a boy.

Thirdly, he has shown great loyalty and turned down offers of big money from clubs on the European mainland. After all, does another few hundred thousand make that much difference to a Premiership footballer's lifestyle?

Fourth, he is a very great player. Sir Alec Ferguson was reported by *The Sunday Mirror* as stating, unequivocally, that 'Paul Scholes is the best player in England. He's got the best skills, the best brain. No one can match him.'

Great Rugby Players

Lancashire has long been a centre for rugby league, with places such as Barrow-in-Furness, Leigh, Salford, St Helens, Warrington, Widnes and Wigan being rugby and not soccer towns. The latter is now an exception, for its football team Wigan Athletic has grown from being a minor team to a Premiership one in recent years. Rugby is very much a team game and success relies on each team member, and a team with one or two outstanding players and eleven poor ones will never be successful. For that reason it has been difficult to pick very special players.

VINCENT KARALIUS

Vincent Karalius was born in Widnes on 15 October 1932. His surname is Lithuanian, from his grandparents who came to live in Britain at the end of the 19th century. As a boy he grew up playing football, but when he was 16 he was taken to watch a junior rugby match and, because one team was a man short, he finished off playing. He immediately changed his allegiance to the oval ball game and from the start showed great potential. So much so that in August 1951, St Helens gave him a six-match trial. The club then signed him up for the princely sum of £200. He played his first team game on 2 April 1952 and played a total of 252 games for St Helens.

At the end of the 1962-3 season he was transferred to Widnes, playing 132 games for them, before he retired in March 1966. He also represented Lancashire on ten occasions against other county teams (and against Australia in 1963, Lancashire winning 13-11), and Great Britain on 25 occasions, 12 of them Tests. In his five Tests against the might of Australia, Great Britain won three and lost two, it won the three Tests against New Zealand, and four against France. He was also a member of the Northern Rugby League XIII that defeated New Zealand 24-11 in 1955. And he won every trophy that it was possible to win in rugby league: the League Championship, the Challenge Cup and the Lancashire Cup (now alas defunct).

Karalius was a strong man, who besides rugby also had a scrap metal business. I recall him being interviewed on BBC television before some major match. There he was, chatting in the midst of a pile of heavy pieces of metal and throwing them, in the style of making a pass in rugby, into a huge skip. It is said that he could run over ten miles before official practice. And though a pleasant man off the field, was iron-hard on it. His place was in the forwards, but his speed and powerful crushing tackle made him the perfect loose forward who could attack the opposition scrum half and stand off should they get the ball, but protect his own side's scrum half when he received the ball.

If you leave Leigh by St Helens Road, your journey will take you over the Bridgewater Canal (Leigh branch) and at the bottom of the hill, on the right, is a pub, once called the Ellesmere. This is now Leigh's rugby league hostelry and called the Centurion.

There you will see, on the wall, a mural to perhaps the greatest of all players, Alex Murphy.

ALEX MURPHY

Alexander James Murphy was born on 22 April 1939 in Thatto Heath, St Helens, to boiler stoker James Murphy and his wife Sally. From being very young it was clear that Alex was destined to be a great player, and he proved this by representing his school, St Helens schools and Lancashire schools. Before he left school, he went to train with the St Helens squad and he signed professional papers (for a fee of £80) on his sixteenth birthday. Through his first season with St Helens he played for the 'A' team, but on 16 April 1956 he was chosen for the first team in the last game of the season. The opponents were Whitehaven, and St Helens won 22-7.

He played eleven seasons for St Helens, making 319 appearances and scoring 175 tries, 42 goals and a total of 609 points. He then moved to Leigh for four seasons (1967/8 to 1970/1), making 118 appearances and scoring 33 tries, 96 goals and a points total of 291. He ended his playing career at Warrington, appearing 67 times, and scoring 9 tries, 40 goals and a total of 107 points. He was also British Lions scrum-half in the 1958 and 1962 tours, Great Britain triumphing by two Tests to one in both. Altogether he represented Great Britain in 27 Tests, against Australia, New Zealand and France, England twice, and Lancashire 14 times. And like Karalius, Murphy won every trophy that it was possible to win. And like Karalius he was probably the best player in his position, scrum-half, ever.

Murphy was fast, with great acceleration. His side-stepping at speed made him difficult to tackle. His handling and passing ability was second-to-none. He was a great kicker of a rugby football. And he knew it. He had an air of debonair arrogance that drove opponents and their supporters to fury. Not surprisingly, when Murphy was contracted by the *Daily Mirror* to write a column about rugby, it was entitled, *Murphy the Mouth*. In his retirement he also became a BBC commentator with the great Ray French, and he was coach (1967-94)for St Helens, Huddersfield, Leigh and Salford, and for England in the 1975 World Championship. In 1999 he was awarded the OBE for services to rugby league and voted Player of the Millennium by the publication *Rugby Leaguer*.

But was he the greatest?

SHAUN EDWARDS

Shaun Edwards was born on 18 October 1966 in Wigan, son of Jack Edwards who played for Warrington in the late 1950s. From the start it was clear that Edwards was going to be a great rugby league player and it came as no surprise when he signed for his home team of Wigan on his seventeenth birthday for the large fee of £35,000. His first game was on 6 November 1983, when Wigan beat York 30-13. Altogether he played 467 games for Wigan, scoring a total of 1,140 points, including a record ten tries in one match (against Swinton, the score being 78-0). As stand-off or scrum-half, Edwards was the epicentre of perhaps the greatest-ever club rugby league side, for Wigan won eight League Championships and nine Challenge Cups (they lost in two other finals) in the fifteen years he was in the team. They also held two other records: they won eight successive Challenge Cups and won 43 consecutive cup ties. After leaving Wigan, Edwards played 1997 with London Broncos, 1998 with Bradford Bulls, and returned to the Broncos until he retired in 2000. He also represented Great Britain on 40 occasions, scoring 64 points.

Shaun Edwards was a strong player, whether running with the ball or in the tackle. But it was perhaps his ability to pass the ball to the player in the best position to gain ground or score that was his greatest asset. And that was the product of a great rugby brain, that could read the game and work out the best line of attack. It was therefore no surprise that, on retiring as a player, he should turn to coaching. What was surprising, however, was that he turned to coaching rugby union and not league. He became coach at London Wasps and part-time coach with the Welsh national team. The latter was England's loss. For his services to rugby, Shaun Edwards was awarded the OBE.

Lancashire has not produced many great players of Rugby Union, but two contemporaries stand out: Bill Beaumont and Fran Cotton.

BILL BEAUMONT & FRAN COTTON

Beaumont was born in Chorley in 1952 and played his club rugby for Fylde. He was capped 34 times for England, 21 of them as captain, and the highlight was when he led the team to a Grand Slam in 1980. He also captained Lancashire to the County Championship and the North of England to beating the might of New Zealand 21-9. A strong lock forward, Beaumont was a hard man on the field and a gentleman off it. He retired as player in 1982 and then became a household name as team captain in BBC's *Question of Sport*, opposite the great Emlyn Hughes (page 99). He was awarded a CBE for services to rugby. Away from sport, Bill Beaumont has run the family's factory at Chorley that produces top quality cloth.

Fran Cotton was born in Wigan in 1947 and, after returning north after leaving university, played his club rugby for Sale. He made 31 appearances for England, captaining the side in three of them. He was an important member of the famous 1980 Grand Slam team, led by Bill Beaumont. Cotton also played for the British Lions in South Africa (1974), New Zealand (1977), and again in South Africa (1980) where he suffered a heart condition that led to his retirement. He was an immensely powerful prop forward, with great stamina brought about in part at least by running over the coal-mining slag heaps of the Wigan-Leigh area. He did not turn his back on the game when he retired, remaining involved with Sale rugby club and, in 1997, being tour manager of the British Lions in South Africa. He did give up being a PE and sports lecturer and founded, in 2007, the successful clothing company Cotton Traders with fellow rugby player Steve Smith.

Great Cricketers

Lancashire has long been a centre of cricketing excellence, for it has the great county side based at Old Trafford and leagues where teams include professional players. But despite the large number of Lancastrians who have played cricket at the highest level – representing England in Test matches – I have had no difficulty choosing three outstanding players.

CYRIL WASHBROOK

Cyril Washbrook was born on 6 December 1914 in the tiny Ribble valley hamlet of Barrow. From a very young age it was clear that Washbrook would make a fine player and the plan was that, after leaving school, he would go Birmingham University and sign as an amateur player for Warwickshire. Happily for Lancashire, he failed to get a place at Birmingham on a technicality, and instead signed for Lancashire as a professional. He made his debut in 1933 at Old Trafford against Sussex.

One of the greatest opening batsmen, with great strength on the on-side, Washbrook played exactly 500 matches for his county scoring a total of 27,873 runs at an average of 42.15. He scored over 1000 runs in a season fifteen times and in 1946 scored a mighty 1,938 runs at an average of 71.77. He scored 58 centuries for Lancashire, seven of them double-centuries, and his highest score was an unbeaten 251 against Surrey at Old Trafford in 1947. He was county captain from 1954 to 1959; incidentally he was Lancashire's first professional captain.

He played as opening batsman in 37 Tests for England; this may seem a small number by today's measure, but one must remember that his career was interrupted by the Second World War (in which he served with the RAF), and that the number of Tests played was relatively small before travel by air became the norm. Twice, with Yorkshireman and England captain Len Hutton, he shared century opening partnerships in both innings of a Test against the Old Enemy, Australia: 137 and 100 at Adelaide (1946/7) and 168 and 129 ay Headingley (1948). And in the 1948/9 series against South Africa he and Hutton shared what was then a world record opening stand, and is still the England record, of 359 in 310 minutes, Washbrook scoring 195.

In 1956, Washbrook was appointed to the team of selectors that chose the England side. The first match was drawn and Australia won the second to go one-nil up. The selectors gathered to pick the team for the third Test and Washbrook was asked to leave the room. When he returned he discovered that he had been selected to open the batting for the England team in the third Test at the age of 41. He scored 98 and shared a third wicket stand of

Cyril Washbrook was one of Lancashire's great batsmen

187 with captain Peter May to bring England victory and to level the score. The fourth Test was at Old Trafford and will for ever be famous because Jim Laker took 19 of the Australian wickets to leave England one up with the last game to play at the Oval. There, Washbrook played his last Test, scoring a duck; but the match was drawn and so England won the Ashes. Washbrook continued to serve his county as committee member until 1988 when he was made president. He died on 27 April 1999.

BRIAN STATHAM

Brian Statham was born in Gorton, Manchester on 17 June 1930. As a boy Statham played football and tennis and it was not until doing his National Service with the RAF that he took up cricket, and especially fast bowling. The NCO who spotted Statham's innate talent contacted the Lancashire selectors, who invited him to go for a trial. The trial was a success and, after he was demobbed from the RAF he joined the ground staff at Old Trafford, making his debut against Kent just before his twentieth birthday.

Statham became one of the world's greatest ever fast bowlers. For Lancashire, he played 430 matches, and took 1,816 wickets for 27,470 runs, with a magnificent average of 15.12 runs per wicket.

His haul of wickets is still the record for the county. He took five wickets in a match on 109 occasions, ten wickets ten times, and took eight wickets in an innings four times, with a best of 8 for 34 runs against Warwickshire in 1957 (he took 15 wickets for 89 runs in the match). Statham took 100 wickets in a season nine times, in 1965 taking 130 wickets at an average of 12.8. He was no duffer with the bat, scoring 4,237 runs in 501 innings at an average of 10.52. Curiously, whilst he bowled right-hand, he batted left-hand. He was Lancashire captain from 1965 to 1967.

He appeared for England in 70 Tests, alongside two other 'greats' – Fred Trueman and Frank 'Typhoon' Tyson – taking 252

Brian Statham, the great Lancashire fast bowler who, with Fred Trueman, formed one of England's best opening attacks

wickets at an average of 24.84, and with a career best of 7 for 39 against South Africa at Lords in 1955.

On the winter tour in 1957/8 (abroad the England team was then known as the MCC) of South Africa, Statham performed the hat-trick of three wickets in three consecutive balls against the Transvaal team at Johannesburg. In 1972 I was lucky to be able to talk with Fred Trueman over a pint in a pub in Sedbergh. He reckoned that Statham was so accurate and had such a great ability to cut the ball both ways off the seam that he wore the batsmen down, so that when he came on to bowl they relaxed and he got their wickets. Trueman was the first to take 300 Test wickets. 'Some really were Brian's,' he graciously said.

Brian Statham died on 10 June 2000. He was made CBE for services to cricket.

MIKE ATHERTON

Michael Atherton was born in Failsworth, Manchester on 23 March 1968 and was educated at Manchester Grammar School and Cambridge University where he captained both cricket teams. There is no doubt that cricket was in the family blood, for his father played for Woodhouses in the Lancashire & Cheshire League.

However, his talent surfaced at a very young age. Atherton captained his school team at 15 and England's Under-19s when he was only 16. He was also captain of the Combined Universities team in 1989. By that time he had made his debut for Lancashire against Warwickshire at Southport in 1987. That summer, at the tender age of nineteen, he scored 1,193 runs for the county, and the following summer made his first century for the county, 152 not out against Sussex at Hove.

Michael Atherton was a great opening batsman. Greater, I think, than the statistics reveal, for he led by example in both Lancashire and England teams that had great weaknesses. He played in 151 first class matches for Lancashire, and in 252 innings scored 9,904 runs at an average of 44.41. His highest score was 268 not out against Glamorgan in 1998, and he scored 29 centuries. He appeared in 115 Tests for England, scoring 7,728 runs at an average of 37.69, and with a highest score of 185 not out against South Africa at Johannesburg in November 1995. In that game, England were getting thrashed, and a major defeat was expected. But Atherton's steely determination won through and because of him, the game was drawn. He captained England a record 53 times, but never Lancashire.

After retiring as a player Michael Atherton joined Sky TV as an erudite commentator. In 1990 he was *Young Cricketer of the Year* and one of Wisden's five *Cricketers of the Year*. He was made OBE in 1997.

JAMES ANDERSON

James Anderson was born on 30 July 1982 and from a young age desired to play cricket for a living. He played for Burnley Cricket Club in the Lancashire League before being propelled into international cricket for England at the age of twenty on the tour of Australia 2002/2003. This was before his county debut (for Lancashire obviously)!

Anderson's progression was hindered by injury and remodelling of his action, yet his determination and dedication to his personal fitness have led him to be the most successful fast bowler in the history of cricket. His total haul of 600 test wickets at an average of 26.9 to date places him as the fourth most successful bowler of all time. Anderson also holds the record for the most 'not outs' as a batsman in test cricket; admittedly his place in the lower order has helped this. However, occasionally he has produced some crowd-pleasing moments including a momentous innings of 81 against India in 2014, ably supported by Joe Root (Yorkshire).

James Anderson was awarded the Freedom of the Borough of Burnley in 2011 and an OBE in 2015.

A Great Horse Trainer

The greatest horse race in the world is, without doubt, the Grand National, for it is a test of horsemanship, of stamina, and the ability to jump big fences. Of course, the Grand National is run at one of Lancashire's race courses, at Aintree, and the greatest horse to win at Aintree was trained by a Lancastrian.

GINGER McCAIN

Ginger (Donald) McCain was born on 21 September 1930 in Southport, and his main business was as a car salesman in his home town. But horse racing was in his blood and behind his car showroom he established a small yard where he could train a string of horses.

Now we must cross the Irish Sea. In 1965 a foal was bred from the dam Mered, sired by Quorum. It was named Red Rum and was sold as a yearling for 400 guineas by Tim Moloney. In his first race at Aintree, a five-furlong sprint, he was in a dead heat with a filly Curlicue. Fom there he was sold for 1,400 guineas at Doncaster to Mrs Brotherton, and went into training with Bobby Renton at Ripon. He was ridden over jumps for the first time by Tommy Stack at Newcastle, and finished in third place. Two years later, in 1971, he won a three-mile chase at Catterick and was placed fifth in the Scottish Grand National run at Ayr. He was then put up at the Doncaster sales and purchased for 6,000 guineas by Ginger McCain on behalf of owner Mr Le Mare.

Back at Southport, Red Rum was famously trained on the beach with McCain's other charges. Then on 30 September 1972, with Tommy Stack in the saddle, Red Rum won a race at Carlisle by 20 lengths, and a total of five hard races in seven weeks. Clearly he was a great prospect for the big race. So in the 1973 National he started 9/1 joint favourite with another great horse, Crisp. He outran Crisp on the long run-in to take first place, with L'Escargot in third place. In the 1974 Grand National, Red Rum was first again at odds of 11/1, beating L'Escargot (17/2) into second place by seven lengths. The following year, L'Escargot (13/2) came out on top, with Red Rum second (at 7/2). By now, Red Rum was the nation's favourite. But in 1976 he was again only second (at 10/1) to Rag Trade (14/1). 'Would Red Rum ever win his third Grand National?' asked the housewives, who all put a flutter on him in 1977. And win he did. In 1977 he came first with odds of 9/1, with Churchtown Boy second at 20/1. In 1978 he was withdrawn from the race and given a well-earned retirement.

No other horse has come anywhere near Red Rum's Grand National record: ran five, won three, second twice. He died in 1995 and is buried just inside the gates of the race course at Aintree, where there is a bronze sculpture of him. As for Ginger McCain, he won his fourth Grand National with Amberleigh House in 2004.

Chapter Five

LANCASTRIANS WHO DID THINGS

Given the dynamism of Lancashire and its people throughout the Industrial Revolution, it is not surprising that the county has produced some major politicians, businessmen, inventors, artists and so on. And amongst them have been some great characters. Some of the Lancastrians who appear in this chapter have selected themselves; others I have selected and readers may disagree with my choices.

A Leash of Prime Ministers

SIR ROBERT PEEL

Robert Peel was born in 1788 into a wealthy family of cotton-mill owners in Ramsbottom. Educated at Harrow and Oxford, he became a Tory MP at the tender age of 21 and rose rapidly through the ranks to become Home Secretary aged 34. In the next eight years, before the Tories lost office in the 1830 election, Peel was involved in prison reform and, especially, the formation of the police force, initially in London and then the whole of the United Kingdom. Then the police had two nicknames with the public. One, 'peelers', is now largely forgotten, but the other, 'bobbies', still continues to be used. Both of these come from Robert (Bobby) Peel.

In 1834, amidst some political turmoil, he was summoned to the Palace by William IV and asked to form a government, which he did, but his first term as Prime Minister lasted only into 1835 and he was out of office again until 1841. He was then Prime Minister for five years, and once more drove major reforms. He introduced the *Mines Act*, which prohibited women and children working deep underground in coal mines, and the *Factory Act*, which drastically reduced the hours that children could be made to work in cotton mills and other factories. These reforms were major steps in employment legislation, but were strongly opposed by some mine and mill owners.

Peel's final reform was of the Corn Laws. These had been brought onto the statute books to protect the agriculture industry from cheap imports of cereals like oats and wheat. The consequence of this earlier legislation was that, when British production was low because of a cool wet summer and home-grown cereal very expensive (by the laws of supply and demand), the cost of imported cereal was also made artificially expensive. Poor people could not afford to buy grain to make staples like bread and oat-cake.

In 1845 the situation reached its nadir in Ireland, where the price of cereals had become so expensive that the millions of crofters had become dependant on the potato for sustenance. By late autumn of that year, potato blight had destroyed the bulk of stored potatoes, and so Peel hurriedly

Sir Robert Peel was a great reforming Prime Minister

arranged for £100,000-worth of maize and maize-meal to be shipped over from the USA. This arrived too late (in February 1846), and when it did arrive it was not very useful, for the yellow porridge produced from it was difficult to digest and resulted in abdominal pains. In 1846 Peel repealed the Corn Laws, keeping the price of edible cereals relatively low when home-grown crops failed and cereals had to be imported.

Alas for Peel, many Tory landowners disagreed with this policy, and he was forced out of office later that year. He died in 1850, and a monument to Sir Robert, the Peel Tower, was built on the moorland top at Holcombe, overlooking the Irwell Valley.

WILLIAM GLADSTONE

William Ewart Gladstone was born in Liverpool on 28 December 1809 into a family that owned a large commercial house in the city. Educated at Eton and Oxford, he was only 24 years old when he became Tory MP for Newark. The following year (1834) Sir Robert Peel made him Junior Lord of the Treasury and Undersecretary to the Colonies, and in 1841 he became Vice President of the Board of Trade. He then lost his seat at Newark, but was returned to parliament in the 1847 election as Member for Oxford University.

But then, in 1859, he fell out with the Tories and became a Liberal, quickly becoming leader of the party. In 1868 he became Prime Minister after his great rival Benjamin Disraeli. In 1874 Disraeli again became PM until 1880, when Gladstone returned to number 10 Downing Street. He lost power in the 1885 election, but retook power briefly in 1886. Then, he became Prime Minister for the last time in 1892 and gave up the post in March 1894. In all, Gladstone was a Member of Parliament for 62 years (one less than W.S. Churchill's 63-year record) and is the only man to serve as PM four times.

Gladstone continued the social development begun by Peel. He wanted social reform and an extension of electoral franchise, and he wanted the power of the House of Lords limited. He fought for home rule for Ireland. He served through Victoria's reign, which saw a vast expansion of the British Empire 'on which the sun never set', and which had large areas of the world atlas 'painted red'. His rival Disraeli, who flattered the Queen, had Parliament grant Victoria, in his second term as PM, the title 'Empress of India'. Victoria enjoyed the flattery and the Tories were opposed to Gladstone's anti-Imperialist reforms.

One of Gladstone's great plans which, alas, never came to pass was the abolition of Income Tax. He argued (rightly!) that if you lower taxes, then people have more money to spend and thus more money circulates through all strata of society. Of course, it was not long before the status of the Liberal party declined. The Grand Old Man of the Liberal Party died in 1898.

DAVID LLOYD GEORGE

But he was not the last Lancastrian to be Liberal Prime Minister. That accolade goes to one David Lloyd George who was born, not in Wales, but in Chorlton-upon-Medlock on 17 January 1863. He was the son of a poor schoolmaster William George, who died when David was only 18 months old, and he and his penniless mother Elizabeth were taken in by her brother, Richard Lloyd, a cobbler and Baptist pastor in the village of Llanystumdwy, just outside Criccieth in North Wales. So David George took his uncle's surname and became David Lloyd George.

Lloyd George has three claims to fame. Firstly, as Chancellor of the Exchequer in 1909 he founded the Old Age Pension at five shillings per week. Secondly, he was the last Liberal Prime Minister (1916-22). Thirdly, he was a great womaniser, nicknamed 'The Goat' on account of his penchant for tupping any woman who would let him! He died in 1945.

A Leash of Great Businessmen

ROBERT GILLOW

Robert Gillow was born in 1704 into a Catholic family living in the Fylde at Singleton. When he was 14 years old, he took up an apprenticeship in Lancaster as a cabinet maker, choosing to live and work in Lancaster, so it is thought, because his father was in the town's jail. The young Robert then travelled to the West Indies as ship's carpenter, and returned with one of the first quantities of mahogany brought into Britain. In 1728 he became business partner with George Haresnape and opened his first factory producing the finest of furniture. He imported the mahogany from the West Indies through the Port of Lancaster, sold much of his production to the gentry of England while reserving some to export back to West Indian plantation owners' houses. Visit the West Indies today, and you can still see 18th century Gillow's furniture in these houses which are now museums.

Robert Gillow died in 1772 and the business was then run by his sons Richard (1734-1811) and Robert (1745-1793). The family continued as Gillows of Lancaster into the 19th century, acquiring Leighton Hall, near Carnforth, as their home in 1827, now open to the public. But by 1897 the company needed financial help, which came from the Liverpool company of Warings, and in 1903 Gillows became Warings & Gillows.

In 1964 the company was taken over by Great Universal Stores and the main factory - on St Leonardgate close to Lancaster city centre - became the temporary home of the University of Lancaster (where I studied 1965-68!). Today Gillow fine furniture commands high prices at the major auction houses, and it is a pity that the quality fell, leading to a collapse of the company.

JAMES WILLIAMSON

James Williamson was born on 31 December 1842 to James (sr) and his wife Eleanor who had, in 1840, founded a company manufacturing coated (i.e. waterproof) fabrics.

After attending Lancaster Royal Grammar School, James went to work in the family business that produced vast quantities of oil-cloth (linoleum) floor coverings that were exported around the world. Until the 1960s most people had 'lino' on the floors of their rooms and, before the days of wall-to-wall carpets, lino covered the floor between rug and walls. Its great virtue was that it could be mopped without getting soggy or waterlogged. Williamson's factory by the Lune estuary below Castle Hill was vast, covering over 20 acres, and it made him one of the most powerful and wealthy people in the country. Not surprisingly he rose rapidly through the ranks of the high and mighty, as wealth flowed in.

He was a Lancaster town councillor (1871–80) and from 1881 a justice of the peace. In 1885 he was High Sheriff of Lancashire and from 1886-95 Liberal MP for Lancaster. In 1895 Lord Roseberry recommended four of his fellow Liberals to be created peer by Queen Victoria and one of these was Williamson, who took the title of Baron Ashton of Ashton (in 1884 he had purchased Ashton Hall, by the Lune estuary between Lancaster and Glasson, now home to Lancaster Golf Club) and had established Ashton Park, on the east side of Lancaster.

For some Lancastrians it rankled that he had taken the name Ashton instead of Williamson. But nationally there was something of an uproar. The Liberals had needed funds to fight the 1895 election and it was rumoured that Williamson had handed over £4,000 (then a great deal of money). Roseberry denied that he had sold a peerage to Williamson, and Williamson did not deny handing over the £4,000, but said that the money was not for

The Ashton Memorial dominates the Lancaster skyline

the purpose of helping fund the Liberal Party. Sleaze and politics is not, apparently, a 20th and 21st century phenomenon!

Williamson was a major employer in Lancaster and, with his rival in the manufacture of oil-cloth Storey Brothers, employed over a quarter of the male workforce of the town towards the end of the 19th century.

He funded many civic amenities and charitable causes, including the fine bronze statue of Queen Victoria in Lancaster's Dalton Square.

There are also Ashton Houses, either named after him or the place, in both Lancaster Royal Grammar School and Kirkham Grammar School. However Williamson's most visible legacy is the Ashton Memorial.

He married three times, his second wife being Jessie Hulme (married 1880). The family had already funded Williamson Park on a hill overlooking Lancaster from the east and it was there that he built a huge domed 'folly', the Ashton Memorial, in memory of wife Jessie. It was opened in 1909 and dominates the city skyline from the east (as from the M6) and from the west (the Lune estuary and the West Coast railway). Nicholas Pevsner, the expert of great British buildings, described the Ashton Memorial as the 'grandest monument in England'.

WILLIAM LEVER

William Lever was born at 6 Wood Street, Bolton on 19 September 1851. He left school (Bolton Church Institute) when he was fifteen years old to work in his father's (James) grocer's shop, and upon reaching the age of 21 he was made a partner in the business. In those days, soap was manufactured in large blocks and grocers cut off small pieces to sell to their customers. Lever came up with the idea of manufacturing soap in small, prepackaged bars that customers could buy, at a time when the Victorian adage 'Cleanliness is next to Godliness' prevailed. So with his brother James, who was more of a sleeping partner, he set up a company Lever Brothers and opened a factory in Warrington to manufacture a top quality soap, Sunlight Soap.

Warrington is by the Mersey and was ideally placed for barges bringing caustic soda from local chemical works. The soda was made from common salt (sodium chloride) produced by salt mines in nearby Cheshire. The other ingredient in soap manufacture is fat, or oil, and Lever went to west Africa for this. The Belgian Congo had, until its independence from Belgium in 1960, a policy of forced labour on the native population. So there Lever established large palm-oil plantations and had the cheap oil imported via the Liverpool and Birkenhead docks. This made Lever incredibly wealthy, incredibly quickly.

His Warrington factory was too small and there was no room for expansion, so Lever purchased land on the southern shore of the Mersey estuary, close to docks through which the ingredients for making soap could be brought. There he built a new factory and an idealised village for his workers, Port Sunlight. Of course Lever, a staunch Congregationalist, could not just build homes and let his employees/residents live their lives as they wished.

He was a philanthropist who expected something in return. So anyone who worked at Port Sunlight had excellent homes, sports facilities, jobs and wages that had the edge on other similar jobs, but the workers had to agree to a strict lifestyle. Nevertheless it worked, and Lever had his obedient workforce and an increase in his wealth and status. His nannying also saw him attempting to get other soap manufacturers to join him in making soap a big monopoly, arguing that this would benefit the people who bought soap. A curious argument, for all it would have guaranteed was a nice profit for all the manufacturers!

From 1906-9 Lever was Liberal MP for Wirral, his maiden speech arguing for an Old Age Pension, paid for by the state (Lloyd George's government brought this into being in 1909). He also fought hard for improving the rights and working conditions of workers (but not those in the Congo). In 1913 he became High Sheriff of Lancashire. In 1874 he had married Elizabeth Ellen Hulme. She died in 1913, so that when he was made a Baron in 1917 he took the title Baron Leverhulme of Bolton-le-Moors. In 1918 he served as mayor of Bolton, even though he had not served as a councillor. And then in 1922 he was made Viscount Leverhulme of the Western Isles (see below), the title being extinguished when the third viscount died without issue in 2000.

Rivington Barn is one of several old buildings in Lever's Rivington estate, now owned by the people of Bolton

Lever was a great philanthropist. He purchased a large estate at Rivington, west of Bolton, which he left to the townspeople as Lever Park. In 1902 Samuel Crompton's house Hall i'th Wood was financially precarious so he bought that and gave it to the town. He established the School of Tropical Medicine at Liverpool University and donated Lancaster House in London to the nation. Then he moved to the Western Isles, purchasing land and attempting to make changes that would benefit the local population. The folks of Lewis rejected his offers but those of Harris took to him and in the town of Leverburgh his name lives on. As it does also in the Leverhulme Trust, which continues his charitable work, and in Unilever (founded 1929), one of the world's major companies.

One Wanderer

Alfred Wainwright was born on 17 January 1907 into a poor working class family in Blackburn. He left school when he was thirteen and, instead of going 'in t'mill' like the rest of his classmates he got a job as an office boy in the Town Hall. Whilst there he spent long evenings studying until he became a qualified accountant. Through these early years he was a keen walker, and in 1930 had saved up enough cash to take a week's holiday in the Lake District. That was the turning point of his life. He had the means to escape from Blackburn (his qualifications) and the motivation (to walk the Lake District mountains). He took a job in 1941 in Kendal Borough Treasurer's Office and from 1948–67 was the town's Borough Treasurer.

Fourteen years after he had moved to Kendal and spent much of his free time walking the Lakeland peaks, he decided to produce his *Pictorial Guide to the Lakeland Fells*. At weekends he walked, using public transport or, occasionally, getting a lift from someone he knew to reach the mountain he wanted to climb that day; and through the weekday evenings he sketched and wrote, in his characteristic hand, every page of what turned out to be seven fabulous volumes that were published 1955-66. Having completed them, he turned his attention to the Pennine Way, his guide appearing in 1968. I used it in 1969 when I made the 270 mile trek, and it was clear that he hated much of the walk (especially the black oozy peat bogs of the southern Pennines), but the guide was perfect, especially when dense mist shrouded the higher peaks.

In 1972 he published his *Coast to Coast Walk*, St Bees to Robin Hood's Bay. But of his later works, the best are his Sketch-books, especially, for a Lancastrian, *A Lune Sketchbook* (1980), *A Ribble Sketchbook* (1980), *A Bowland Sketchbook* (1981) and *A Wyre Sketchbook* (1982). Out of print, these are now very expensive.

A.W., as many fell-walkers referred to him, was something of a grumpy old man, who hated the company of others when out walking, and would deny his identity when questioned. He was a single-minded, self-centred individual who would not have achieved so much had he been otherwise. Perhaps. In 1931 he entered a loveless marriage (on his part certainly) with mill worker Ruth Holden, with whom he had a son Peter. She left him in 1967 just before he retired. Then in 1970 he married Betty McNally (1922-2008) who, after A.W. had died on 20 January 1991, followed exactly what he specified in his will. He was cremated and she carried his ashes up Hay Stacks and scattered them in Innominate Tarn.

Three Great Painters

Lancashire has produced lots of good artists, and still does, as those who attend the summer exhibition of local artists in Leigh's Turnpike Gallery will agree. But there have been relatively few famous artists.

GEORGE STUBBS

George Stubbs was born the son of a leather dealer in Liverpool in 1724. After leaving school he worked for his father before becoming apprenticed in 1741 to a painter-engraver called Winstanley. He quickly gave that up as he hated copying other people's work, an integral part of any art apprenticeship. Instead he moved to York, where he studied human anatomy and illustrated a book on midwifery. He continued to study anatomy and made money by painting portraits up to 1754 when he moved to Italy, then famous as a mecca for young artists.

In 1756 he moved back to England and for two years lived in Lincolnshire where he studied the anatomy of the horse. He then moved to London where his talent was spotted by the Duke of Richmond who, in 1759, commissioned three paintings by him. He produced a classic book *Anatomy Of The Horse* in 1766.

From then on he made a considerable income painting large canvases for wealthy clients such as Lords Grosvenor and Rockingham (for whom he painted as wonderful a portrait of

George Stubbs' paintings of animals, especially thoroughbred horses, are perfection

125

a horse as any, Whistlejacket) and a large number of portraits of famous hunts and race horses and their jockeys. Certainly he was, and still is, the most celebrated artist in his field, with many classic masterpieces such as, The Grosvenor Hunt (1762) and Gimcrack on Newmarket Heath (1765), Stubbs died in 1806.

L. S. LOWRY

L.S. (Lawrence Stephen) Lowry was born at 1 Barrett Street, Stretford, Manchester on 1 November 1887 and later moved to Pendlebury, where he lived until he retired to The Elms, Mottram in 1948. After leaving school he trained at Manchester Municipal Art College and then went to Salford School of Art. Today people imagine that he was a full time artist, but he was not. For many years he was employed by the Pall Mall Property Company as a cashier and rent collector, but he kept this part of his life secret, and his employers seem to have been quite generous in giving him time off when his art conflicted with his work for them.

Lowry was a bachelor and led a rather shy, introverted quiet life. One problem that he had was his mother. His father died in 1932 and his mother, who seemed more or less bed-ridden, relied on him to look after her. So for many years he could paint for only a few hours when he was at home, when his mother had gone to sleep. She died when he was 51 years old in 1939 and this gave him the freedom to paint far more than he had done previously. Yet already his talent had been spotted. In 1943 he was made a professional war artist, and he was an official artist at the coronation of Queen Elizabeth in 1953.

Of course Lowry is best known for his industrial scenes from Lancashire, of cotton mills, cobbled streets, football grounds (he was a fan of Manchester City FC) and row upon row of terraced cottages. And of his 'matchstick men, cats and dogs'. At first critics were severe, calling these paintings naive and pointing out that the perspective in his paintings was often wrong. It was amateurish, said some, and smacked of a holiday and weekend artist rather than a serious painter. If only these critics were here today, to witness Lowry-esque paintings selling for umpteen million pounds! But Lowry was a far more versatile artist, and the Salford Quays art gallery, which houses the largest collection of Lowry's work, shows his surprising versatility. Artists like Lowry invariably get showered with honours as they grow old, but in this Lowry holds a record. He is the only person to turn down the offer of an OBE twice, a CBE and a knighthood! Which suggests a curious attitude to life, perhaps.

He was a bit of a recluse, yet he was helpful to all young artists who sought his advice; he even bought lots of their work to encourage them. As his fame grew, so people wanted to meet him and some even dared to knock on his front door. To avoid them, he pointed to a suitcase and said that he was going away in a moment so he couldn't spend time talking to them. Once, so the story goes, a great anonymous admirer called his bluff. He gave Lowry a lift to the railway station and watched him get on the train. Lowry got off at the next station and quietly returned home! Lowry enjoyed the paintings of other artists, especially Rossetti, and when his income grew as his paintings were ever more in demand, he spent much of his income on their work.

Lowry died of pneumonia on 23 February 1976 and is buried at Chorlton-cum-Hardy. A bronze statue of him was erected at Mottram. But go to Salford Quays to celebrate the man and his work.

JONATHAN LATIMER

Jonathan Latimer was born on 25 October 1976 at Billinge and is currently one of the world's leading wildlife artists. He trained at Blackpool & the Fylde College where he graduated with a First Class Honours degree in natural history illustration. He won the

Coppull artist and book illustrator Jonathan Latimer won Birdwatch Artist of the Year (2003) with a large painting of a female hen harrier flying across a Welsh hillside in superb lighting

Mary Elizabeth Barrow Award for excellence in art and design. After leaving college, Jonathan won the National Exhibition of Wildlife Art (2000). It is pleasing that the county still generates great people who are outstanding at 'doing things'!

Five Inventors

Imagine that you are going to weave some cloth. Stand at the end of the loom and fix in place the threads that run the length of the loom, away from you. They are the warp threads. As weaver, your job involves feeding the threads that go across, the weft, alternately from right to left, then from left to right, between the warps. Your job also includes moving every other warp thread up or down between every pass of the weft and then to tamp down the weft to create the tight mesh that is cloth. It sounds complicated, and so the creation of a loom that would do this quickly and economically was one of the greatest of all inventions.

However, before you can weave, you must have threads for the warp and weft. Originally, when wool was the main cloth-making material, the spinning wheel was used. Loose wool was spun, a handful at a time, to produce a single strand of woollen yarn (the sort used in knitting today). The problem, when the population of Britain started to grow rapidly from the middle of the 18th century, was that this method could not provide the huge quantities of yarn to satisfy the weavers' demands that would meet the growing need for cloth and clothing. Lancashire was the epicentre of the invention of machines that could produce the yarn and then weave the cloth.

JAMES HARGREAVES

James Hargreaves was born in 1720 at Stanhill, between Blackburn and Oswaldtwistle. In 1764 he invented a simple machine, called the jenny, that had eight spindles and could produce at least eight times as much thread as a spinning wheel. He then moved to Lower Ramsclough where he set up a workshop in a barn. There he improved his design but, with home-spinners feeling threatened by industrialisation and the building of big factories, he suffered from break-ins and the wrecking of his new machines. So he left Lancashire, moved to Nottingham and, in 1770, he patented a spinning jenny that could spin sixteen threads simultaneously. Hargreaves later moved back to Lancashire and died in Oswaldtwistle in 1778. His spinning jenny was soon overtaken by larger, even more efficient, spinning machines. By 1811 only about 3% of over five million spinning spindles in Lancashire were still jennies, all of them in small workshops and not factories. Besides efficiency, there was a problem with the thread produced by the jenny; it tended to be rough and weak, and suitable only for weft. This was no great problem, for by an Act of Parliament of 1721 it was illegal to make cloth from 100% cotton and other stronger threads (such as wool) would be used as warp.

SIR RICHARD ARKWRIGHT

Richard Arkwright was born in 1732 in Preston, and spent a short time in the 1750s living in Bolton, where he worked as a barber. There he invented a range of permanent dyes for the then-popular wigs and later for the dyeing of the cloth. He returned to Preston and then moved to Nottingham. There, in 1769, he patented his spinning-frame (though it is clear that the design was 'borrowed' from Thomas Highs of Leigh). Arkwright's spinning-frame spun with a better tension than the jenny, by using wooden and metal pegs instead of the hands and fingers of people. It thus produced thread that was excellent as warp.

However the 1721 Act was still in force, until Arkwright and other pioneers in the cotton cloth industry persuaded Parliament to repeal it in 1774. In 1771 Arkwright again moved, this time to Cromford, on the banks of the River Derwent in Derbyshire. There he built the first water-powered factory, and his spinning-frame became called the 'water-frame'.

Now that 100% cotton cloth could be made, more cotton was needed and that led to the slave plantations of the West Indies and southern United States. But when the raw cotton reached Lancashire (through the Ports of Lancaster and Liverpool) much had to be done before it was ready to be spun into thread. Seeds

Above: Samuel Crompton, the inventor of the Spinning Mule

Left: Hall i'th Wood, near Bolton, the birthplace of Samuel Crompton in 1753

and other trash had to be weeded out and the cotton fibres had to be aligned. Arkwright looked to the problem of dealing with the increasingly huge volumes of raw cotton and, in 1775, patented his cylinder carding machine that would produce quickly, fine, filmy lengths of clean cotton ready for spinning on his water-frame.

Whilst Arkwright continued to have his home in Derbyshire, he invested elsewhere, including his native county. He opened Birkacre Mill in the Yarrow valley near Chorley which, by 1774, employed over 600 workers. Though the mill is gone, some of the masonry used to power it can be seen in the river. Arkwright died on 3 August 1792. But even his water-frame was superseded by....

SAMUEL CROMPTON

Samuel Crompton was born in 1753 at Hall i'th Wood, off that part of Bolton's ring road named after him, Crompton Way. The demand for light, inexpensive cotton textiles was increasing rapidly and the water-frame was not producing threads fast enough. So in 1779 Crompton came up with his spinning-mule, with which a single spinner, hand-driving, could handle up to 144 spindles.

With the increase of water-powered mills in the 1790s and then the advent of steam-powered mills from the 1830s, much larger mules could be used, so that one worker could be responsible for up to 1,200 spindles. This great advance provided enough thread to provide cloth for the rapid growth of the human population of, not only Great Britain, but the world. Crompton's mule was never patented, and accordingly was adopted wherever cotton was spun into thread. Crompton died in Bolton in 1827.

JOHN KAY

John Kay was born in Ramsbottom, near Bury, in 1704 and it was he who revolutionised the weaving of the threads to make cloth by inventing his flying-shuttle. The weaver would fix the ends of the warps in place down the length of the loom. Then, instead of the weaver having to push the shuttle carrying the weft to and fro through the warps, Kay's machine did the work. Warps were separated, the shuttle quickly shot through (it flew through), the warps separated, and the shuttle shot through again..and so on. By having the shuttle flying through, especially when steam power became the normal way of driving cotton mills, broader cloth could be produced and, with the process becoming automatic, one weaver could attend to several looms. Kay died in France in 1780.

One more pioneer needs mention, the chemist John Mercer. He was born in 1791 at Great Harwood and died in 1886 at his home Mercer Park, Clayton-le-Moors. Pure cotton cloth is very soft and wears out easily and Mercer came up with a method of making it much more durable by treating newly-woven cloth with caustic soda. This seems to tighten up the fine cotton fibres. It is likely that, without Mercer's input, cotton would not have dominated clothing through the nineteenth and first half of the twentieth century before the advent of hard-wearing man-made textiles.

One Eccentric Steam Nutter

FRED DIBNAH

Fred Dibnah was the sort of person that has become rarer as the 20th century gave way to the 21st: an obsessed, eccentric nutter. And I am sure he would enjoy me describing him thus. He was born on 28 April 1938 in Bolton and grew up surrounded by mill chimneys, steam engines, canals and their barges, and rows of terraced streets. His parents both worked in bleach mills and he left school at 16 with some art training and the desire to 'do his own thing' rather than conform and be one of the thousands in t' mill. The result was that he made his money by climbing things, demolishing things, and appearing on TV, usually with a steam engine close at hand.

He had a head for heights, which most of us do not. So when he was 17 years old he had no qualms about climbing the 262 foot mill chimney at Barrow Bridge, just outside the town, for a ten shillings wager (in 1996 he repaired that chimney which now has a preservation order). Thus it was only natural that he should become a steeplejack. He once spent six months removing the top half of a 270 foot mill chimney, one brick at a time, because the mill was still in use. Then he was given the job of repairing and gilding the weather vane on Bolton's parish church. In 1978 it was noticed that sixteen stone pillars supporting the clock on top of Bolton's town hall were badly corroded through years of acid rain and soot. He made new pillars, put them in place and gilded the top of the clock. It was then that he came to the attention of the BBC and interviewed for *Look North-West*'s news programme.

He also felled the tall chimneys of abandoned cotton mills throughout north-west England, the last at Royton in 2004. His technique was simple and involved no explosives. He chipped away at the base of the chimney on the side that he wanted the thing to fall, removing brick after brick and propping the chimney up in the gap with wooden pit-props. When he calculated that, if all the props were to go, the chimney would fall, he built a fire in the bottom of the chimney around the props. The fire was lit, and Dibnah would crouch by its side, watching. Then, as the masonry he had not removed began to crack and the chimney began to fall, he would sound an old car horn in salute of its demise.

Once he was televised felling a chimney in Rochdale. As he emerged from the smoke and dust, horn in hand, he turned to the camera, 'Did yer like that?' he asked, with a broad grin. A TV star was born.

He loved ancient machinery, especially those driven by steam. In 1980 he bought, for £2,300, a 1912 Aveling & Porter traction engine and lovingly made it as new, making the parts that needed replacing himself. The traction engine, together with his trusty partners, became an integral part of his final TV programmes.

In 1979 the BBC docmentary *Fred Dibnah Steeplejack* won a BAFTA for best documentary. This led to him appearing on adverts for Kelloggs cereals and Greenall Whitley bitter. But then Dibnah appeared, wearing his oily overalls and hallmark flat cap, in a host of series from 1998 including *Fred Dibnah's Industrial Age*, his *Magnificent Monuments*, his *Buildings of Britain*, his *Victorian Heroes* (Brunel was his favourite), his *Age of Steam*, and his *Made in Britain*. The latter was made in 2003-4 (broadcast 2005)when he was suffering from the prostate cancer that killed him on 6 November 2004, and had him driving round Britain in the traction engine that had taken him over 20 years to restore. He also drove his traction engine to London in July 2004 to receive his MBE from the Queen.

Fred had a turbulent love-life, mainly because his obsession with steam came between him and two of his wives: Alison (to whom he was married 1967-85) and Susan (1987-96). He last wife Sheila (1998-2004) was with him to the end. So too were his sons Jack and Roger, who appeared with him on his traction engine in *Fred Dibnah's Made In Britain*. And he had similarly eccentric pals Donald Paiton and Alf Molyneaux who chatted away with him as though the TV camera was nowhere in sight. In this age, when TV and newspapers are full of shallow, air-head celebrities, Fred Dibnah was a down-to-earth man and I, for one, still enjoy putting on a DVD for an evening with Fred and his pals. 'Boys' toys on a grand scale!' was how Alf described steam engines. 'She's a bit on t' lively side!' was Fred's description of trying a steam engine he had never driven before, and he turned to the camera, *Rivets once held everything together, like.*

Following his death the BBC broadcast *A Tribute To Fred Dibnah* and his home town commissioned a bronze sculpture of him by artist Jane Robbins, which was unveiled on 29 April 2008, the day after what would have been his seventieth birthday.

Men Who Built Holiday Resorts

The Lancashire coast is famous for resorts like Southport, Lytham St. Annes, Blackpool, Fleetwood and Morecambe. Of these, Morecambe is the odd one out, for it was not founded as a resort, but it evolved into a resort when the railway was taken through to the coastal village that was then called Poulton-le-Sands.

Southport was not even a name on a map in the 18th century. There was a village at the north-east corner of what is now Southport called North Meols, also called Churchtown. From there, to the south and west, to the tiny hamlet of Birkdale, was one vast expanse of sand dunes. At one point, where a small stream flowed into the sea – a stream grandly called the River Nile – there were a few fishermens' shacks, that went under the name South Hawes.

In 1770 the Leeds and Liverpool canal reached the hamlet of Scarisbrick, about four miles inland of Churchtown. This coincided with the new craze of 'taking the water', or bathing in the sea. So people from the nearer towns of Lancashire, such as Wigan and St Helens, took a barge to Scarisbrick and then a carriage to the shore at Churchtown. The problem with that was the muddy shore at Churchtown. So they were then transported on a track through the dunes to South Hawes. In 1792 William Sutton, alias the Duke, decided that there was money to be made here. He built a shack of a hotel out of drift wood by the Nile and a year later built a proper hotel that he called South Port. That was the start of Southport as we know it, for throughout the 19th century the town was quickly built, with its characteristic straight, broad, sometimes tree-lined streets of mostly middle-class housing. As well as a place to visit, Southport became a major dormitory town, by train, in easy commuting distance of Liverpool and Manchester. The land on either side of the broad straight track through the dunes that led to the Nile and the Duke's Hotel was purchased in about 1830 by investors, who built grand houses and hotels there. And the track itself became the famous Lord Street, after the Lord of the Manor from whom it was purchased.

As for 'the Duke', he ended up bankrupt in Lancaster jail. He is still remembered as a street name, Duke Street.

BLACKPOOL

Blackpool is still one of the most visited seaside resorts in the world, and certainly the most visited in the United Kingdom. As early as 1750 the group of fishermen's cottages that stood just above the high water mark were attracting a few visitors. But then two men realised that there was money to be had and they laid the foundation of today's Blackpool. The first was Ethart a-Whiteside who, in 1735, built a cottage specially for the use of visitors. It was probably something of a boarding-house, and not very grand. Twenty years later, in 1755 Mr Forshaw built the first hotel at Blackpool, its position being on the corner of what is now the promenade and Talbot Square.

LYTHAM

Lytham is an ancient town, well over a thousand years old. In 1850, when Blackpool had already grown into a major holiday resort, there was almost nothing other than sand dunes between

*Blackpool Tower is a
landmark visible from a
large part of Lancashire.
Its design was based on the
Eiffel Tower in Paris*

the two towns. Lytham ended at the western end of the Green,
and Squire's Gate (the southern end of Blackpool) began four
miles away. This empty land was owned by the Clifton family
and, in 1870, Lady Clifton had a chapel of ease built midway
between Lytham and Blackpool that was dedicated to St Anne.
In 1873 the Lytham-Blackpool railway line was built along the
back of the dunes and in 1872 a road was built through the dunes
connecting the two towns. This became Clifton Drive.

In 1862 Thomas Fair replaced his father James as the land
agent for the Clifton family and it he who came up with the idea
of flattening the dunes and building a modern holiday resort on
the land. The Clifton family were unable to fund the work, but
a Rossendale mill owner, Elijah Hargreaves, and seven associates,
decided that an investment here would be very profitable. They
formed The St Annes-on-the-Sea Land & Building Company on
14 October 1874, with a 999 year lease from the Clifton family.
And in 1875 work commenced. Most of the buildings you can see

in St Annes town centre around Clifton Drive and the promenade date from this time.

But there was still a gap in the development between St Annes and Lytham, that included Granny's Bay, where local fishermen hauled up their boats. Here was constructed Fairhaven Lake (named after Thomas Fair), and some very grand houses. And to the north of Clifton Drive, further grand houses were built in an area called Ansdell, which took its name from the artist Richard Ansdell R.A., a friend of Thomas Fair.

FLEETWOOD

Rossall Hall, that is now a public school, was the northernmost building on the Fylde coast when Peter Hesketh was born there in 1801. When he was 23 years old he added another family name to his, becoming Peter Hesketh Fleetwood. At first he did very well for himself. In 1830 he became High Sheriff of Lancashire, and then from 1832 to 1847 was Member of Parliament for Preston. In 1835 he was influential in having a railway branch line put through to the mouth of the Wyre estuary, a couple of miles east of Rossall (it reached there in 1840), with the aim of building a new town there dedicated to holiday-makers and shipping.

To plan this, Hesketh Fleetwood turned to one of the leading architects of the day, Decimus Burton. Burton planned to have the highest sand dunes converted into a public park called The Mount, from which streets would radiate. These would be workers' cottages. Then there would be a rather grand Queen's Terrace and splendid North Euston Hotel overlooking the estuary. Finally, Burton planned two lighthouses, a small one and then a taller one called the Pharos, which were first lit in 1840, and a wharf for boats to tie up (opened in 1841).

But Hesketh Fleetwood did not have sufficient spare cash to fund the building of his town, Fleetwood. In 1841, to pay for the project, he began selling off his estates in the Fylde, and then in 1842 his estates around the new town of Southport. Finally in 1844 he sold Rossall Hall and moved out.

At first Fleetwood was a successful project, mainly because it had proved impossible to push the railway north through the fells between Lancaster and Penrith and so onto Scotland. People then took the train to Fleetwood, stayed in the North Euston Hotel and then took a ship to Ardrossan (Glasgow). In 1846 this was one of the journeys that travel agent Thomas Cook could arrange for you. And in 1847 Queen Victoria and Prince Albert arrived at Fleetwood from Scotland on their journey back to London. But then the railway was pushed through the Shap Fells, making the deviation via Fleetwood redundant. Later, of course, the town became a major fishing port as well as a sort of outlier of Blackpool, reached by tram.

How a Famous Word was Invented

Lancashire was the county and Preston the town where the temperance movement began in Britain. The instigator was Joseph Livesey who, in March 1832, encouraged people to come and 'sign the pledge of abstinence.' He held meetings to preach the virtue of total abstinence of the demon drink, he opened a temperance hotel in the town and he produced a magazine to further his drive.

That year, Richard 'Dicky' Turner, a fish salesman from Walton-le-Dale, had been drinking and was half sozzled. He saw a sign advertising one of Livesey's meetings and went in deliberately to have a laugh at Livesey's expense. But, like St Paul on the road to Damascus, he saw the light. He signed the pledge and gave up all alcohol. Now Dicky Turner suffered badly from stuttering, and it was at a temperance meeting where Dicky Turner told the audience: 'Tha mun be reet out and out abhat it. T..t..t..t..,' he stuttered, trying to get out the word 'total'. 'T..t..,' he forced it out, 't't'tee..tee..teetotal abstinence.'

And so a simple chap from Preston invented the word, 'teetotal'.

A Great Hero

Wallace Hartley was born on 2 June 1878 in Colne in east Lancashire. At school he learned how to play the violin and, after leaving school, played in small bands and eventually, in 1909, joined an eight-man band that entertained guests on the Cunard RMS *Mauretania*. At the begining of April 1912 he became engaged to his sweetheart, Maria Robinson, and was promoted to bandleader. And so when White Star Line RMS *Titanic* set sail on her maiden voyage, Hartley was on board, ticket number 250654 in Second Class (even staff had tickets, free of course).

As we all know, on 15 April 1912, the unsinkable *Titanic* hit an iceberg and sank. To calm the passengers making for the lifeboats, Hartley insisted that the band carry on playing, and it is said (no good evidence exists) that as a finale they played *Nearer My God To Thee*. Another version has it that the band stopped playing just before the ship went down and stood on deck as one by one they were washed away. It has even been reported (though by whom, we do not know) that Wallace Hartley's last words to his band were, 'Gentlemen, I bid you farewell!'

His body was found floating in the Atlantic two weeks after the sinking. Forty thousand lined the streets of Colne and one thousand attended his funeral. He was a great hero.

Wallace Hartley who is said to have kept his band playing as the Titanic sank

Chapter Six

THE SAD SIDE OF LANCASHIRE

Every family has skeletons in its cupboard and every county has its murderers, its disasters, its 'bloodshed for the sake of principles' (i.e. battles), and those who have died for a cause. Lancashire has more than its fair share. We will begin with some of the more famous murders, and start with one of the most heinous.

Murders and Murderers

BRADY AND HINDLEY

Ian Brady was born illegitimate in 1938 in Glasgow's Gorbals as Ian Stewart and, as his mother could not support him, he was sent to a foster home. However, by the time he had reached the age of 16 he had been charged three times for housebreaking and the court sent him to live with his natural mother, now living in Moss Side, Manchester, and married to a man called Brady. So Ian Stewart became Ian Brady. He continued to break the law and eventually served time in Strangeways jail. On his release he was given a job at Millward's soap factory.

Myra Hindley was born in 1942 in Gorton into a home where family violence was the norm. So when she was four years old she went to live with her grandmother, who brought her up a devout Roman Catholic. In 1961 she went to work in the office of Millward's soap factory and there she came under the influence of Brady.

Brady and Hindley became pornographic and perverted lovers. And a dreadful part of their perversion was the kidnapping, torturing and killing of young innocent lives. When their victims were dead they drove their bodies out into the wilds of Saddleworth Moors and there buried them in unmarked peaty graves. In October 1966 they were arrested and found guilty of the murders of Lesley Ann Downey (aged 10 years), John Kilbride (12 years) and Edward Evans (17 years). But police suspected that they were responsible also for the murder of other young people who had vanished without trace. Two of them, Pauline Read (16 years) and Keith Bennett (12 years), were definitely linked to what were infamously called the 'Moors Murderers', and in 1987 Hindley led police to the spot where Pauline Read's body had been buried. She also tried to pinpoint Keith Bennett's burial place, but his body was not, and never has been, found.

I cannot think of any other British murderers who have been so hated by their fellow citizens. There have been other child-murderers, but none, I think, have evoked such feelings of revulsion. Hindley died in 2002. At the time of writing, Brady resides in Ashworth high-security hospital at Maghull and has been declared criminally insane.

BUCK RUXTON

Dr Buck Ruxton (an apparently English name) was really Dr Bukhtyar Rustomji Ratanji Hakim, a Parsee and general practitioner, born in 1899. His home and surgery were at 2 Dalton Square, Lancaster, facing the statue of Queen Victoria and the Town Hall. He was married to Isabella (who was known as Belle), with whom he had three small children by 1935. The family had a maid, Mary Jane Rogerson whose responsibilities included looking after the children.

There was at least some friction between husband and wife for some time, for Ruxton had repeatedly accused her of having affairs with other men and, on one occasion, she ran across Dalton Square to the police station where she complained of her husband's threats of violence. On another occasion she went to Scotland for a few days with some friends, and was followed by her husband who accused her of having Robert Edmondson, who worked in the Town Hall, as her lover. But then on 14 September 1935 she drove in her husband's Austin 12 car to Blackpool where she saw her two sisters and enjoyed driving through the illuminations. She arrived back at home late and parked the car outside the house. The car was still there the following morning (the 15th) at breakfast time.

The Ruxtons' cleaning-lady, Agnes Oxley, was due to have called that day to do the cleaning, but Buck Ruxton went round to her house to say that his wife was away and that he was taking the children to Morecambe. Would she come and do the cleaning tomorrow? That lunchtime, Ruxton took his children to friends, the Andersons, in Morecambe, asking them to look after them as he had much to do and that his wife and maid were away. They noticed that he had a deep cut across three fingers of his right hand, the result, he told them, of a can-opener that had slipped. Later that afternoon he called on a patient he knew well, a Mrs Hampshire, asking her if she would come back to his house and help him clean up, as he couldn't because of his cut hand. She found the house in a complete mess. The bath was stained a brownish-yellow, and there was some filthy matted carpet which, when she tried to clean it, turned the water a dark reddish colour. Ruxton also asked her to destroy one of his suits that also was stained a brown-red.

Mrs Oxley, the cleaner, arrived on the 16th as arranged. She helped Ruxton to dress his injured right hand. And then Ruxton told her that his wife and maid had left for Edinburgh and that his wife was having an affair with another man. Again,

*Dr Buck Ruxton, the
Lancaster murderer*

that evening he took his children to stay with the Andersons in a hire car; he told them that his Austin was in the garage for servicing.

Shortly after lunchtime on 17 September Bernard Beattie was cycling on his bike in Kendal when a car hit his bike and knocked him off. The car continued south along the A6 without stopping, but Beattie noted its number and immediately contacted the police. A short while later a policeman in Milnthorpe noticed the car still heading south on the A6 and stopped it. Ruxton was the driver, and said that he might have had an accident but couldn't be sure. Having checked his identity the policeman allowed him to go, but told him that he had to present his driving documents at Lancaster police station as soon as he reached home. But first, when he did reach home, Ruxton had a fire lit in the surgery waiting room.

It was clear that Ruxton was in a highly disturbed state of mind. He told people that his maid had been pregnant and that his wife had arranged (illegally) an abortion for her. He said to all and sundry that his wife was having an affair. And he said that both had left him. But then, on 29 September, the whole thing came to a head.

Susan Haines, a tourist, stood by the side of the A701 to look down at Gardenholme Linn, a noted Scottish Borders beauty spot near Moffat. Below her, on the banks of the stream, she noticed bundles wrapped in white sheets, and, to her horror, saw that from one of these bundles stuck out a human arm. The police were called and they found four large bundles, which contained large lumps of human flesh, two heads and two arms. Some of the wrapping was sheets of a newspaper dated 15 September, and later it was shown that this newspaper, the *Sunday Graphic & Sunday News*, was from the Lancaster-Morecambe area. More gruesome remains were found the next day by the A74 Glasgow-Gretna Road, including one parcel containing a foot also wrapped up in newspaper. The remains were examined by scientists at Edinburgh University, who confirmed that the bodies were of Isabella Ruxton and her maid Mary Rogerson. When he learned this Ruxton immediately went to the police, protested his innocence and blamed the two murders on Robert Edmondson.

On 13 October Ruxton was arrested and his house examined. It appeared, from large blood-stains down the stairs and hidden by the carpet, that both his wife and maid had been stabbed to death on the landing, and it was then shown that Ruxton had expertly cut up their bodies in the bath. He had attempted to make both corpses unrecognisable by cutting away prominent features. For instance, the body that proved to be Isabella's had part of its left foot excised (where she had a bunion) and the front teeth pulled out (she had protruding teeth), and the head of Mary Rogerson had both eye sockets and eyes cut out (she suffered from a bad squint).

Ruxton was put on trial for both murders at Manchester on 2 March 1938 and, with overwhelming evidence, the jury found him guilty. He was hanged in Strangeways on 12 May 1936.

LOUISA MERRIFIELD

Louisa May Merrifield was born in 1907, and by the end of 1949 had been married twice. Now she married 67-year-old Alfred Merrifield. Mrs Merrifield had always been a spendthrift, seeking a 'good time' that always involved plenty of booze and the popular entertainment of the post-war era (in Blackpool where she lived, there were plenty of shows, dancing and pubs). So she was always hard up and seeking some easy cash. And along came the perfect source. She saw an advert in the *West Lancashire Evening Gazette.* Twice-widowed (both her husbands had committed suicide by putting their heads into the gas oven) and virtually bed-ridden, 79-year-old Sarah Ricketts sought a woman to live with her in her bungalow, 339 Devonshire Road, Blackpool, to care for her. Mrs Merrifield got the job and they both moved in. After a few weeks Mrs Ricketts was so happy with them, and so concerned that they might leave for a better position, that she had a will made up that meant, when she died, they would inherit all her property. The will was signed and dated 31 March 1953.

But then Mrs Ricketts realised that the Merrifields were spending a bit too much of her money on themselves, including lots of bottles of spirits. This brought tension, and Mrs Merrifield became worried that Mrs Ricketts' two daughters might hear of the will. The crunch came on 13 April when Mrs Ricketts asked Alfred to go and take some cash from the bank for her, and to call at her solicitor's and ask him to call round. That evening Mrs Merrifield asked their doctor to call, telling him that Mrs Ricketts was very ill and might not last the night. He called, found Mrs Ricketts no worse than was usual, and gave her a sedative. On the morning of the 14th Mrs Merrifield phoned the surgery again and this time the GP sent his junior partner who found that Mrs Ricketts was at death's door. Mrs Ricketts died almost immediately and Mrs Merrifield pleaded with the young doctor to sign the death certificate so that she could arrange to have the body cremated straight away. The senior doctor, Dr Yule, vetoed this and ordered a post mortem.

Pathologist G.B. Manning examined the corpse and found that her stomach contained a mixture of brandy and Rodine, a phosphorus-based rat poison. She had clearly been murdered. Scotland Yard were called in by the local police. They attempted to trace someone who had sold Rodine to Mrs Merrifield or her husband, and the garden was dug up, the bungalow thoroughly searched and the dustbin checked. To no avail. It was clear, on the strongest of circumstantial evidence, that one or both of the Merrifields were responsible, for no one else had come close enough to Mrs Ricketts to administer the poisoned brandy. On 30 April Mrs Merrifield was arrested, and on 14 May so was her husband.

The trial, held in Manchester, began on 20 July 1953 and ended on 31 July. It took the jury six hours to find Mrs Merrifield guilty of murder, but they were unsure about Albert. So he was acquitted, and she was hanged in Strangeways on 18 September, aged 46, by Albert Pierrepoint, the Preston executioner. As for Albert, he attempted to keep hold of the bungalow, but failed. He died in 1962 aged 80.

PETER GRIFFITHS

The conviction of Peter Griffiths was the result of some interesting detective work.

In May 1948, three-year-old June Anne Devaney was recovering from pneumonia in the children's ward of Queen's Park Hospital, on the south side of Blackburn. Late on the evening of 14 May the alarm was raised when she was found missing from her cot. The hospital was searched; there was no sign of June Anne. The police were called in and, at 3.17 on the morning of the 15th her body was found brutally murdered just outside the hospital grounds. Detectives went through the children's ward with a fine-tooth comb, but all they came up with was a set of fingerprints, that matched no one who had been on the ward during the previous 24 hours, on a large bottle by the cot.

The fingerprints matched with none held by the police, so it was decided to take the prints of all males over the age of sixteen years in Blackburn. This was a big task, for about 46,000 fell in this category and many objected that forceably taking prints was an infringement of their rights. The police did promise, however, that when the culprit was found and convicted, all the prints they collected would be destroyed. So day after day a band of police carefully went round, gathering the fingerprints of the 46,000 until on 12 August, the prints taken from Peter Griffiths, of 22 Birley Street, Blackburn, were found to match those found on the bottle.

At 9pm on Friday 13 August, Griffiths was arrested in the street. He was brought to trial on 15 October 1948 and found guilty of murder. He was taken to Walton Jail, Liverpool, and hanged. On 3 November all the thousands of prints collected in the investigation were destroyed.

GEORGE SMITH

Although he was not a Lancastrian, George Joseph Smith, the famous 'brides in the bath' murderer did commit one of his murders in Lancashire. Smith was a con man, who sought and then married women who had a modest amount of money, in the early years of the 20th century.

His first wife and brush with the law occurred in 1898 when, under the alias George Oliver Love, he courted and married Caroline Thornhill in Leicester. She was a housemaid and he got her to steal items made of solid silver from her employers, which he then sold. She was caught and given a 12-month prison sentence. When she was released her husband had vanished, but by chance she spotted him walking down Oxford Street, London. She confronted him with a policeman. He was arrested and given a two-year sentence for receiving stolen goods, and while he was inside, she emigrated to Canada.

In 1908 Smith met Edith Pegler in Bristol and set up home with her. On 29 October 1909 he married Sarah Fowler in Southampton under the alias of George Rose. She had £400 which he took and then skedaddled, returning to Edith in Bristol. Next to fall for his charm was Herne Bay's Bessie Mundy, from whom he took £135, a tidy sum in those days, before vamoosing into the ether.

His next victim was Alice Burnham who had the requisite small amount of cash. Against her parents' will, she took the cash and married Smith in Portsmouth on 3 November 1913 and afterwards they took the train to Blackpool for their honeymoon. They took bed-and-breakfast at 16 Regent Road on 4 November. On 12 November, Smith went downstairs to tell his landlady that his wife was dead in the bath. No questions were asked and he had her quickly buried in Blackpool.

The following September he married Margaret Elizabeth Lloyd and within days 'found' her dead in the bath. This time his luck was out. It was proved that he had drowned her and that the death of his previous 'wife' Alice (of course, he was still legally married to Caroline) was almost certainly also by his hand. He was found guilty of murder and hanged in Maidstone jail on 13 August 1915.

The Last Public Hanging

Mary Hamner, a single woman who worked in a cotton-mill in Droylsden, lodged near the mill in the home of Mary Broderick and her daughter Bridget. In June 1867 Timothy Faherty also lodged there, but moved out that October. He had taken a fancy to Mary, but she had rejected his advances.

On Christmas Day 1867 Faherty visited his old digs and told everyone that he was going to live in Ireland. Bridget went to her room for a short nap leaving Faherty and Mary Hamner together. As she fell asleep she heard Mary shout, 'Get off with you! Why have you come here?' She was awoken after a very brief sleep by Mary bursting into her room with blood pouring from head wounds and shouting, 'Bridget, I'm killed!' Faherty was behind her carrying the poker from the living room. He hit her on the head with the poker and at the same time yelled, 'I'll kill you!'

Bridget pushed her way past Mary's body and the irate Faherty and rushed down the stairs where she found neighbours, who had come to investigate the din. Two of them cautiously went up the stairs to find Faherty kneeling over Mary's body and moaning about how much he loved her and that he had killed her because she didn't love him.

Sentenced to death for the crime of murder, Faherty was executed in front of a huge gathering outside Manchester jail on Saturday 4 April 1868. Also hanged publicly that day was Miles Wetherhill, who had been found guilty of murdering the Rev Anthony Plow of Todmorden and Jane Smith, one of the Reverend gentleman's servants on 2 March 1868. They were the last public hangings in Lancashire. The last public hanging in England was on 26 May 1868 at Newgate, London.

The Last Hanging in England

John West, who lived near Cockermouth, Cumberland, had inherited a substantial sum of money from his mother and from his sister, who had committed suicide. On 7 April 1964 his neighbour heard lots of banging and prolonged screaming from John's house and went to investigate. He saw a car speeding away and then knocked on both back and front doors with no response. So he called the police, who broke the door down and, inside, found John's battered and stabbed body and a cosh with which he had been beaten. In his haste, the murderer or murderers had left behind a raincoat, in the pocket of which was a medallion engraved with the name G.O. Evans and a scrap of paper that had the name Norma O'Brien written on it. The police quickly located Norma O'Brien in Liverpool, and she told them that she had met Gwynne O. Evans in Preston and knew his address. They arrested Evans (real name John Robson Welby) who said that Peter Antony Allen had carried out West's murder. He said that they had both gone – in a stolen car – to borrow some money from West, with whom they had once worked, but he refused to lend them any. Allen was arrested and lay the blame on Evans.

At their trial in Manchester, on 7 July 1964 both of them were found guilty of capital murder, in their case murder during a robbery, and were sentenced to be hanged. Evans was hanged in Strangeways jail and Allen in Walton jail simultaneously on 13 August 1964. Following these executions, the death penalty was suspended for five years and finally abolished in December 1969.

Three Martyrs... and Three Others

Religious intolerance is as old as religion itself, and no period in English history typifies this more than the sixteenth and seventeenth centuries. During the reign of Henry VIII (1509-1547) the Anglican church split from Rome but, when Mary became queen in 1553, she attempted to turn England back into a Catholic state. Many churchmen who were unwilling to forsake Anglicanism were burnt at the stake, including Archbishop Cramner and one famous Lancastrian, George Marsh. Mary died in 1558 and her half-sister Elizabeth became queen and enjoyed a long reign (to 1603) in which Protestantism flourished, as it continued to do throughout the reign of James I. Then, being a Catholic was not something to boast about!

George Marsh was born in 1515 at Deane, Bolton and in 1547 he became a 'preaching minister' in the Protestant faith. That was the year Henry VIII died and six years later, with the accession of Mary, Marsh realised that his life was in danger. So he voluntarily went to see the local magistrate Sir Roger Barton, who lived at Smithills Hall a couple of miles northwest of the town, to discuss his predicament. After this first meeting Barton argued that he was guilty of preaching false doctrines and had him taken to the Upper Green Chamber of the Hall to face trial. There he pleaded guilty. As he was led away downstairs, members of his family and some friends attempted to persuade him to renounce his Protestant faith. But he vehemently refused, and to stress his refusal he stamped his bare foot heavily down on the gritstone slab floor.

George Marsh was taken from Bolton to Chester. Again he refused to deny his faith and accept Catholic teaching, and in April 1555 he was burnt at the stake.

Visitors to Smithills Hall today can still see the place where Marsh stamped his foot, for the flag floor has retained the bloody-brown footprint. And not far away from Deane, in the Daubhill

Smithills Hall, where George Marsh was tried before being sent to Chester where he was burned at the stake

area of Bolton, is the only Anglican church dedicated to St George the Martyr. Incidentally, how would you pronounce 'Daubhill'? 'Daub...hill?' Wrong. It is pronounced 'Dobble'!

EDMUND ARROWSMITH

Edmund Arrowsmith was born Brian Arrowsmith in 1585 at Haydock, the son of practising Roman Catholics, Robert and Margery. At the time Catholicism was illegal and, when Brian was eight years old, his parents were imprisoned in Lancaster Castle for their faith. We know little more of him until 1605, when he left England for the college at Douai in northeastern France, where Catholic Englishmen could train as priests safe from any persecution. There he changed his Christian name to Edmund. He was ordained priest on 9 December 1612, became a member of the Society of Jesus (i.e. a Jesuit) and returned as a missionary to his native Lancashire.

His work was of necessity an under-cover one, based in the Chorley-Walton-le-Dale–Samlesbury area and he used two aliases, Bradshaw and Rigby as he tried to avoid detection by the authorities. In 1622 he was captured and examined by the Bishop of Chester. This time, however, he was fortunate, for King James was attempting to secure friendly relations with Catholic Spain, and trying to get his son Charles married to the King of Spain's daughter. So, at the time, publicly prosecuting a Catholic priest would have been politically damaging. So Arrowsmith was released with a severe warning.

With the accession of Charles I in 1625, England was at war with Catholic Spain and France, and with an increasingly anti-Catholic, puritan Parliament, the persecution of Catholics increased. In the summer of 1628 a puritan 'priest-hunter' tipped off the authorities of Arrowsmith's whereabouts. He was arrested at Brindle and taken to be tried at Lancaster on 26 August.

Edmund Arrowsmith, a Jesuit Catholic, put to death for his faith

Found guilty, he was executed at Golgotha, east of Lancaster, by hanging, drawing and quartering. Golgotha? This was 'the place of a skull' where, according to St Matthew's Gospel, Chapter 27, verses 33-34, they crucified Jesus, and the awful name was given to the place of execution at Lancaster.

Some relics remain of Edmund Arrowsmith. At least one late 16th or early 17th century farmhouse has the remains of a priest-hole where Arrowsmith took refuge when danger threatened.

The farmer's wife told me that she, and her daughter, had seen a ghostly form in the house late at night. St Joseph's Church at Brindle has the altar used by him to celebrate the Mass and preserves his chasuble. St Oswald's Church, Ashton-in-Makerfield, which is very close to Arrowsmith's birthplace, has his preserved hand and is a site of pilgrimage.

St Edmund Arrowsmith was canonised on 25 October 1970.

JOHN SOUTHWORTH

John Southworth was a member of the staunchly Catholic Southworths of Samlesbury Hall. He was born in 1592 in the Samlesbury-Blackburn area of Lancashire. He went to train as a priest in the English College at Douai and, having been ordained, was sent back to England as a missionary on 13 October 1619. In 1627 he was arrested and condemned to death at Lancaster Castle, but he was reprieved and, in April 1630, he was put in the custody of the French ambassador and returned to Douai.

But by 1637 he was back in England, on mission in London, and in November he was again arrested and again released. On 24 June 1640 he was examined by the Commission for Causes Ecclesiastical, but again released.

Then, on 2 December of that year he was arrested and eventually put on trial in London. He pleaded guilty to being a priest and was sentenced to being hanged, drawn and quartered. After his death at Tyburn on 28 June 1654, his body was stitched back together and embalmed before being taken by the Duke of Norfolk back to France. During the French Revolution his body was hidden away, but in 1927 it was found and brought from Douai, and returned to London. There it was placed in the Chapel of St George & the English Martyrs in Westminster Cathedral. Like Arrowsmith, he was canonised in 1970.

HEATHER ARTON

The Rev John Arton, accompanied by his wife, was an Anglican missionary in the Congo in the late 1950s and early 1960s. They were supported by All Saints Church, Preston, a 'low' Anglican church that helped fund Christian missionaries throughout the world. In 1960 Congo gained its independence from Belgium and, as so often happened when African countries were freed from European rule, inter-tribal civil war broke out resulting in great bloodshed.

On 27 November 1964 the Artons, with their seventeen-year-old daughter Heather, were caught up in the warring. They were white and Christian, and symbolised the old colonial era. They were taken, stripped naked, beaten, shot and their bodies thrown in the river. The previous Christmas I had attended a party of 17- and 18-year-olds in Preston and there had met Heather Arton. I still find it numbing when I think that I knew a young Christian martyr in my lifetime.

Battles and Skirmishes

I once had a friend called Godfrey, alas long gone, who was a retired mining engineer and whose hobby was visiting the world's battlefields. He phoned and asked me to call round. 'I have a problem,' he began, as he showed me into a room that had maps on the wall and cabinets of war memorabilia. 'What is the difference between a battle and a skirmish?' 'Well,' I replied. 'A skirmish is usually between smaller warring groups who happen to come upon each other and nothing has really been planned. They fight and one group beats the other, or they both retreat.' 'So, what do you mean by smaller?' 'Well,' I said, 'Take the Battle of Preston. The main battle took place north of Preston and through into the town with huge numbers taking part, but probably no more than a hundred or so were involved in each of the skirmishes away from the main line of battle, at Penwortham and Chorley, perhaps.' 'That's done it!' exclaimed Godfrey. 'I will have to put Wigan on my map of English battles for every Friday night of the year, for the number taking part are much larger than that!'

Although Lancashire had a low population density until the late 1700s, it was, on several occasions, where major battles took place. The main reason for this is that the county is on a direct line between Scotland and the Midlands and, with its small human population, could be crossed easily compared with the more densely populated Yorkshire lowlands. So the once-Roman road-route, now known as the A6-A49 road, through Lancashire, from Lancaster, through Preston, Wigan, Ashton-in-Makerfield, Newton-le-Willows (once Newton-in-Makerfield), Winwick and on to Warrington features in many battles.

The earliest of these was in 642, when the Mersey was the boundary between the kingdoms of Mercia and Northumbria. The Venerable Bede tells us that, 'Oswald, the most Christian King of Northumbria, ruled for nine years...at the end of this period, Oswald was killed in a great battle by the same heathen people and the same heathen Mercian King [King Penda]...in a place called in the heathen tongue Maserfelth on 5 August in the thirty-eighth year of his reign.' It was once thought that Maserfelth was near Oswestry, though what a Northumbrian army would have been doing there, goodness only knows! Maserfelth is a variant of the more modern Makerfield, which included Ashton, Newton and Winwick, and it is no coincidence that the ancient church at Winwick is dedicated to St Oswald.

The most bloody battles that took place in the county were during the English Civil Wars. The route that I have just described is one reason for them taking place. A second is that the county had towns that were staunchly of one side or the other (i.e. Royalist or Parliamentarian). The sacking of Bolton is a good example.

SACKING OF BOLTON

The sacking of Bolton took place on 27 May 1644.

Early in 1644 the royalists' cause throughout much of Lancashire was at a low ebb, with towns like Liverpool and Bolton firmly for Parliament. In fact there were only two Royalist strongholds left in the county, Greenhalgh Castle at Garstang and Lathom House near Burscough, home of Lord Derby. On 24 February a Parliamentarian commission in Manchester decided that both of these should by taken and they were put under siege. At the time Lord Derby was on his estates in the Isle of Man, so his wife, the Countess of Derby, was left to withstand the siege. This she did successfully. She lasted out into May when, hearing that the King's nephew Prince Rupert was heading their way with an army, the Parliamentary force of about 5,000 men led by Colonel Alex Rigby left and headed to Bolton.

Prince Rupert, along with Derby who had returned from the Isle of Man, headed north from Cheshire towards Manchester with a force of 4,000 cavalry and 7,000 foot-soldiers. Hearing that the town was well defended by Sir John Meldrum and 5,000 foot-soldiers, they avoided Manchester and went instead to Bolton. Bolton was then a very small town, in today's measure no more than a village, and its defences, of hastily-made mud embankments, poor. Yet despite this the town drove back the first attack.

As the Royalist army re-gathered, Lord Derby asked Prince Rupert if he alone might lead the second attack, for he would certainly have learned that most of the defenders of the town were also those who had besieged Lathom House and he sought vengeance. So Derby and his army forced their way into every nook and cranny of Bolton, killing all they found, including women and children, and plundering as they went. Such brutality would be remembered. As for poor Bolton, the following year (1645) it was hit by a large outbreak of the plague and the tiny population remaining was made even smaller.

BATTLE OF PRESTON

The Battle of Preston took place on 17 August 1648, and was described by Stephen Bull (in his great book *The Civil Wars in Lancashire*) to be 'the most important battle, politically and militarily, of the civil wars.'

In 1646, the first English Civil War ended with the defeat of the King's forces and Charles' arrest and eventual holding on the Isle of Wight. However, the victorious Parliament was not widely popular, partly because it was very short of funds and couldn't pay its bills, and partly because it imposed a puritan life-style that rankled many (for instance, in 1647 it banned the celebration of Christmas and the playing of games on Sundays). But it was the Scots who sought to destroy the Parliamentarian regime and restore Charles I.

James Duke of Hamilton was the leader of the Scottish army that initially numbered 6,000 foot-soldiers and 1,200 on horse but had grown to a total of 18,000 or even 24,000 by the time that it left Scotland. The force heading south also included a force of Scots from Ulster, numbering about 3,000 men led by Major General George Munro, and a force from northern England, numbering about 5,000, and led by Yorkshire's Marmaduke, Lord Langdale, Westmorland's Sir Philip Musgrave, and Lancashire's Sir Thomas Tyldesley. The ultimate aim was to reach London, and to do so they decided to take the route through Lancashire and to cross the Ribble at Preston.

Not that the Scottish force was the only one to try to bring back Charles. When the first of the Scottish army crossed the border into England on 8 July 1648, Oliver Cromwell and his Parliamentary army were in Pembrokeshire, quelling an uprising there. Having sorted that out, Cromwell moved rapidly to confront the Scots. Quickly he marched across country to Leicester with just over 4,000 men, arriving there on 1 August. Now he was between the Scots and their target, London. He moved north into the West Riding of Yorkshire, reaching Otley on 13 August. No matter which route the enemy took, he was poised to attack them.

Hearing from spies that the Scots were heading for Preston, Cromwell moved west, reaching Skipton on the 14th, Gisburn on the 15th and Hodder Bridge (p13) on the 16th (he spent the night at Stonyhurst). By now the front of Hamilton's army was approaching Preston, with groups spread back along the road to Lancaster. Early on the morning of the 17th, Cromwell and his force headed westwards, and at Longridge the first party of Royalists were encountered. Cromwell now deployed his troops to face the enemy on a broad front, the enemy mostly being concentrated across what was then called Ribbleton Moor: from what is now Preston cemetery and Ribbleton Hall School,

The long, straight Watling Street Road at Preston is on the line of the Roman road. It was a track through the open country at the time of the Battle of Preston in 1648

westwards through Holme Slack to Moor Park. Cromwell's army was arranged to the north, on a line that is now Watling Street Road eastwards to where Longridge Road crosses over the M6 at Red Scar. Then this large tract of land, now heavily built-up, was what was then called moorland, open rough country.

The fighting was fierce and long, but despite the fact that Cromwell's men had endured long marches over previous days (it was said that most had worn out three pairs of shoes on the trek from Pembrokeshire) and that they were greatly outnumbered, the Parliamentarian force savaged the Royalists. The Royalists split up, some fleeing northwards and westwards, harried as they went. Others fled down the Ribble valley from Brockholes to Walton-le-dale. Many became trapped in and around the town of Preston (then quite a small place, consisting mainly of the four streets Friargate, Fishergate, Lancaster Road and Church Street, with around 2,000 inhabitants). There, many were killed or taken prisoner. Those that could escaped south, including Hamilton, who crossed the Ribble at Penwortham.

As the Scottish army moved south down what is now the A49 they were constantly harried by Cromwell's men. On 18 August, large numbers were killed at Standish, just north of Wigan, whilst those that could continued southwards. By the 19th they had passed through Wigan and Newton-le-Willows and as they approached

Winwick they came across a narrow, hemmed-in lane, now called Hermitage Green Lane. The remaining Scots, whose force was still several thousand strong, thought that they had a chance of getting back to the Parliamentarian army. It was impossible for Cromwell's men to proceed along Hermitage Green Lane on a broad front; they would have to advance two-abreast and perhaps even in single file and so could be picked off by musketeers hidden in the hedgerows. But it was not to be. Fighting continued there for many hours until slowly Cromwell's men gained the upper hand and what remained of the Scottish army retreated again southwards. Eventually the remnants of the invading army left Lancashire by crossing the Mersey at Warrington, a spent force, but not before a large number had surrendered and been taken prisoner.

After the Battle of Preston the Royalists left behind over 1,000 dead and 4,000 held prisoner. At Winwick, Cromwell estimated Royalist losses as 1,000 killed and 2,000 taken prisoner. At Warrington precisely 2,547 went into captivity. The total loss in Lancashire was probably close to 12,000. Those remaining were finally caught at Uttoxeter. And the final consequence of the Battle of Preston was the execution of Charles I on 30 January 1649, for waging war on his own people.

BATTLE OF WIGAN LANE

The Battle of Wigan Lane took place three years after the Battle of Preston. Following the execution of Charles I, royalists wanted his son Charles to be made king. Again the action was triggered by a Scottish army, this time with the potential King Charles II with them, heading south into England; and again royalist Lancastrians joined them, to be eventually led by James Stanley, 7th Earl of Derby who had been in exile in the Isle of Man. They reached Lancaster on 12 August 1651, there proclaiming Charles II as king.

The monument to Sir Thomas Tyldesley, killed in the Battle of Wigan Lane

By the 14th they had passed through Preston (where Charles rode on horseback as he rallied more men to join them) and reached Euxton. By now their force had risen to about 12,000 and they had met with no real opposition.

As they reached Warrington bridge they met the first Parliamentarian force and suffered 28 casualties as they headed on south. It was clear that the Parliamentarian force was growing and would soon match that of the Royalist force. So at Northwich Charles ordered Derby to go back to Lancashire and raise further troops, ideally, suggested Charles, 6,000 foot-soldier and 1,300 on horse.

When Derby reached Warrington on 19 August he called for a meeting of all royalist gentlemen who might be able to raise troops to join with Charles and his Scottish army. At the same time the parliamentary army officers heard what was happening in Lancashire and Colonel Robert Lilburne was given the job of preventing Derby and any force he commanded from getting away south to join up with the king. Derby, together with Sir Thomas Tyldesley, set off with a small army of about 1,400 men from Preston on 24 August, whilst Lilburne had fewer than 1,000, but they were better trained and equipped. Lilburne's troops pursued Derby's down what is now the A49 south of Standish. Instead of continuing into Wigan, where the town would have provided cover, Derby's army turned and faced the enemy. But Lilburne positioned musketeers in cover on either side of the road so that, as the Royalist cavalry advanced up the hill, it was met by a hail of lead. After an hour it was virtually over and the lane, down the hill where Wigan Infirmary now stands, was littered with royalist dead. And amongst the dead was Sir Thomas Tyldesley.

As for Lord Derby, he escaped with the survivors of his force and met up with Charles near Worcester. On 3 September 1651 the Royalist cause was lost in the Battle of Worcester. Charles survived, as did Derby. Charles escaped to France. Derby was later arrested in Nantwich, and put on trial on 29 September at Chester for treason. Because of his appalling behaviour in the Sack of Bolton (page 157), after being found guilty Derby was taken to Bolton where he was beheaded on 15 October.

The 1715 and 1745 Jacobite Uprisings

When Queen Anne died on 1 August 1714, George of Hanover was proclaimed King. However very many people, especially in the north of England and Scotland wanted James II's son, also called James, as king. Supporters of James were called Jacobites, and at the proclamation of George, rioting occurred in towns such as Manchester. In the autumn of 1715 the Jacobites had raised forces in southern Scotland and Northumberland and they headed south. On 7 November the growing army reached Lancaster, and there James III was proclaimed king.

They then moved on to Preston, arriving there on 9 November, but although several of the county's leading Catholics joined the Jacobite cause with their own recruits, the gloomy news reached them that a Hanovarian army led by General Wills was heading north from Wigan and another led by General Carpenter was heading west down the Ribble valley. So the Jacobites erected defensive barriers at the ends of Preston's four main streets (see page 160). Wills arrived on 12 November and began the attack, Carpenter joining in the fray the next morning. By 7pm on the 13th the Jacobites had had enough and they surrendered their arms in the market place. Forty-three of the leading Jacobites were executed, most of them in Preston, but others at Garstang, Lancaster, Manchester, Liverpool and Wigan, to warn the Catholic population of Lancashire never to take sides against the Hanovarian king.

And it worked. When a second Scottish Jacobite army, with the 'young pretender' Bonnie Prince Charlie, reached Lancaster on 25 November and Preston on the 27th, only one Lancastrian Catholic gentleman joined them with some men he had raised. That was Francis Towneley, brother of Sir John Towneley. They reached Derby unscathed, but then, when they heard of the strength of the opposition, had to retreat quickly. They arrived back in Lancaster on 13 December and then left the county for Scotland.

Eventually the Jacobite cause was lost at the Battle of Culloden on 16 April 1746, when their 7,000-strong army, consisting then of Scots, Irish, a force from Manchester and from France, led by Charles Edward Stuart, faced an 8,000-strong Hanovarian army led by the Duke of Cumberland. Charles escaped back to France, but 2,000 of his men were killed in contrast to only about 50 of his opponents. Fearing for his life, Sir John Towneley also made his way to France, but his brother Francis was less fortunate. He was captured attempting to hold Carlisle for the Jacobites. He was taken to London and executed.

The Blitz of 1940–41

Although the Second World War began in 1939, so little happened through the first few months that people began to speak of a 'phoney war'. Then, towards the middle of 1940 Germany's aggression to Britain reached Lancashire. The first air-raid

In the Liverpool blitz, 70% of homes were destroyed and the number of casualties neared 3,000

warning siren sounded in Manchester at precisely 3.14am on 20 June; it appeared to be a false alarm. Then on 8 August a wave of German bombers attacked Salford, aiming for the docks that are now known as Salford Quays. Amongst the bombs dropped was a large parcel of propaganda leaflets calling on the British people to avoid unnecessary bloodshed by getting their politicians to negotiate for peace. The parcel failed to burst open and scatter its leaflets; instead it hit a policeman on the head!

Small raids occurred through the late summer and autumn, including one in August that hit the Manchester city centre Palace Theatre, but it was not until December that the blitz really hit. The choice by the Germans of the pre-Christmas period for the biggest hits on the two cities of Liverpool and Manchester was probably on two grounds. The first was simply to do as much structural damage to the cities as possible, to hinder our war effort. The second was that, by causing maximum damage to the ordinary people – their families and homes – just before the Christmas festival, the Germans hoped that our morale would be shattered and we would be more likely to capitulate. They were, of course, wrong.

On 20-21 December 1940 German bombers attacked towns on both sides of the mouth of the Mersey in great numbers and, though they concentrated on the docks of Liverpool, Bootle, Birkenhead and Wallasey, 3,875 people were killed (including 166 who died when an air raid shelter on Durning Road was hit) and 7,144 seriously injured. The docks were one of the main life-lines for the beleaguered island of Britain, with ships bringing in food and equipment from abroad, especially from the USA.

River front of Liverpool includes the 'Three Graces': the Liver building (1), the Cunard building (2) and Mersey Docks and Harbour Board building (3). The modern buildings around them replaced those lost in the Blitz

One estimate is that about 90% of essential imports to Britain passed through the Liverpool docks. By wiping the Liverpool docks (and the docks of London, Bristol and Southampton) from the face of the earth, the Germans would have argued, they would be cutting a vital lifeline. Much damage was done to the docks for the blitz rendered about half of Liverpool's docks out of action, but the fire-fighters, that included 200 firemen and their fire engines sent to Liverpool along the East Lancashire Road from Manchester, eventually quelled the blazes caused by hundreds of incendiary bombs and the port remained open to traffic.

On the 22-23 December it was Manchester's turn to feel the full might of the German bombing. Sirens were sounded at 6.38pm on the 22nd. At 6.40 the first bombs fell on the Albert Square area and by 8pm the Victoria Buildings, Royal Exchange Theatre and shops, offices and warehouses had been flattened or were ablaze. Over 450 people were trapped in one air raid shelter close to Oxford Road and the railway viaduct on the Altrincham line was severely damaged.

The following evening the sirens sounded the alarm at 7.15pm and bombing continued to 1am on the 24th. That evening the area of the city centre was clearly the primary target and the problem of the huge number of incendiary bombs was increased by an increasingly strong wind, that blew the flames from bomb-hit buildings to others that had not been hit. To stop such fires spreading, undamaged buildings were pulled down to create fire-breaks. The last fires were finally extinguished on Christmas Day.

Altogether, the December 1940 blitz on Manchester destroyed or seriously damaged over 200 businesses, 160 warehouses, 150 offices, many schools, and 30,000 homes, killed 380, and injured around 2,400, 455 of them seriously, and made thousands homeless. The Free Trade Hall and Victoria Buildings were demolished, as was the headquarters of the prestigious

Manchester Literary & Philosophical Society whose vast collections of rare specimens and papers were destroyed. Several other important buildings, including St Anne's Church, Chetham's Hospital and the Cathedral were badly damaged. A further 70 were killed in Stretford and 215 in Salford.

That was the worst Manchester had to bear, though bombing of that city continued on and off until August 1942 (for instance, in June 1941 Salford Royal hospital was hit and 14 nurses killed, and Manchester United's ground at Old Trafford was badly damaged). And on Christmas Eve 1944 the German sent a V1 'buzz-bomb' in the direction of the city. It overflew its target and instead hit Oldham, killing 27.

Liverpool, however, suffered badly through May and the first part of June 1941, and especially 1-7 May when 681 bombers dropped 2,315 bombs packed with high-explosive on the city. In all there were 79 separate raids on the city in 1941. Large areas of dock warehouses were destroyed, including the great Huskisson Dock. There the ship *SS Malakand* had been loaded with 1,000 tons of bombs when one of the barrage balloons, which were meant to interfere with the bombers, broke its mooring. It became tangled with the ship and then was set alight by one of the fires. This set off the bombs in the ship's hold, which devastated the dock. But perhaps the impact on the human population of the city and their homes was greater. The total number of casualties reached 2,895 and of approximately 280,000 houses in the city, over 6,000 were completely flattened and about 185,000 suffered some sort of damage.

The last German bombs fell on Liverpool on 10 January 1942. One of the houses hit was number 102 Stanhope Street where, remarkably, one Alois Hitler lived. He was Adolph Hitler's half-brother!

Chapter Seven

WITCHES, GHOSTS AND THE INEXPLICABLE

Are there really witches? Witches who can cast spells that make people's hair fall out, give them aches and pains, and even kill? Do ghosts really exist, or are they really in the imagination? If you doubt, then explain this...

Since the early 1960s I have spent countless hours on the Lancashire coast observing the large flocks of wildfowl and wading birds that spend the autumn and winter there. I reached the shore at Fluke Hall near Pilling at dawn, climbed the sea wall and gazed through my binoculars across the flat expanse of mud and sand. Then a movement caught the corner of my left eye. About thirty yards away, a man on a bike reached the crest of the sea wall where a concrete ramp had been constructed to let shrimpers' carts pass easily. He then cycled down the ramp, onto the hard sandy-mud and headed off in the direction of Heysham nuclear power station in the distance. I noticed that he wore wellington boots, a long brown raincoat and a trilby hat. He must have set a night-line for flounders, I reasoned.

But then, when the man and his bike were about two hundred yards away, they simply vanished, and for a few seconds I heard the strains of some eerie, almost electronic music coming from across Morecambe Bay. I looked at my watch. 7.15am. I rubbed my eyes and looked carefully. Perhaps the man was hidden in a hollow out on the shore. But he wasn't. I strode across to the concrete ramp, walked to the bottom of it and looked for tyre tracks. There were none.

I am sure that, that morning, I saw a ghost. I have one other experience of a ghostly apparition, but you must wait for that.

Lancashire Witches

People who boast of being witches, or are said to be witches by others, go back to the dawn of civilization, but came to the fore in England during the 16th and 17th centuries when religious fervour and persecution reared its ugly head. One of the first recorded in Lancashire was Edmund Hartley of Tyldesley who, in 1597, was hanged for bewitching seven members of the Starkie family. However the preoccupation of those in authority with witches and their witchcraft peaked in the early 1600s with the publication of King James I's small book *Daemonologie*, which encouraged people to root out and destroy witches. And not surprisingly, when such a subject is almost hysterically raised with a gullible public, the 'problem' is found to be far worse than anyone could have imagined.

On 18 March 1612 a poor, young girl called Alizon Device went begging on the road that went from Newchurch-in-Pendle to Colne. When packman John Law of Halifax approached she asked him to give her some pins, but he refused to stop and open his pack. She cursed him loudly for his refusal. He immediately had a stroke and a vision of a black dog with red glowing eyes. Fortunately there were others on the road, who carried poor John to a nearby inn and then sent for his son Abraham to come and help him. John was able to describe what had happened and it was clear (!?) that Alizon had cast a witch's spell on him.

On 30 March she was taken, accompanied by her mother Elizabeth and brother James, to Roger Nowell, the magistrate at Read Hall. There she confessed to being a witch, told Nowell that her grandmother had initiated her into witchcraft, that another family in the area, the Chattox family, were also witches, and that the black dog, 'with very fearfull fierie eyes, great teeth, and a terrible countenance' was her 'familar'. She had met this dog two years earlier and admitted that it did 'suck at her breast'.

Alizon told how her father, John Device, had been paying Old Chattox not to harm his family. When he stopped paying, he died. She then described how her friend Anne Nutter had laughed in the presence of Old Chattox, that Chattox had considered this an insult, and that Anne had died three weeks later. She told of John Moore, who accused Old Chattox of turning his ale into vinegar; Chattox had made a clay model of him and he had died soon after. She said that her grandmother had killed someone by her witchcraft, and that Old Chattox had killed at least four innocent people.

Alizon's grandmother was Elizabeth Southern who had adopted the alias Old Mother Demdike. In 1612 she was eighty years old, more or less blind and lived in squalor at Malkin Tower near Newchurch. With age she had grown spiteful, cursing people for little reason and had thus gained the reputation of being a witch who could cure or injure folk by casting spells. Her daughter and Alizon's mother, Elizabeth Device, was a widow, and she also lived at Malkin Tower with Alizon, another daughter called Jennet and a dimwitted son called James.

Chattox was not the real name of the other family Alizon had told Nowell were witches. The matriarch of the family was Anne Whittle ('Old Chattox'), like Old Mother Demdike, a repulsive old woman who was nearly blind and lived at Greenhead near the village of Fence. With her lived her two daughters Bessie Whittle and Anne Redfern, and Anne's husband Thomas.

The Whittles and the Southerns had fallen out a decade earlier, when Bessie Whittle had stolen food and clothing from Malkin Tower.

On 2 April 1612 Roger Nowell examined Old Mother Demdike. The poor old lady must have been completely bewildered, and so confused that Nowell got her to admit that she had first met the Devil at Newchurch. He had been in the form of a boy, her familiar, called Tibb, who had then metamorphosed into a brown dog that had then fed on her blood. Tibb could also appear as a black cat and as a hare. She then confessed that she had brought about the death of the son of one Richard Baldwin by casting a spell on him.

Nowell then interviewed Old Chattox, who told him that she had been initiated into witchcraft in 1598 by Old Demdike and that she had a familiar called Fancie, which could appear as a man, as a brown dog and even as a bear. The consequence of these rantings by two old crones was that Nowell had them, together with Alizon Device and Anne Redfern, sent to Lancaster Castle, under James I's Witchcraft Act.

Nowell later heard that on 12 April (Good Friday) a 'witches' sabbath' had been held at Malkin Tower, with the aim of rescuing the imprisoned witches. It was also said that at the witches sabbath, a cat was christened as a familiar, that spells were cast and that the witches flew high into the night sky, presumably on their broomsticks. He had the site of the rituals examined, and human teeth and clay charms were found. On 27 April, Nowell and another magistrate Nicholas Bannister, examined Elizabeth, James and Jennet Device.

All three admitted to being involved in witchcraft and, most surprisingly, they also told the magistrates that Alice Nutter of Roughlee Hall was also a witch. According to James Device, Alice Nutter had joined with his mother Elizabeth in the killing by witchcraft of Henry Mitton, because he had refused to give Old Demdike a penny. This was surprising because Alice Nutter was a well-known wealthy lady; it is clear that they implicated her through jealousy of her property and social standing. As magistrates Nowell and Bannister delved deeper into the case, so others became implicated. And as a result Elizabeth and James Device, Alice Nutter, John and Jane Bulcock, Katherine Hewitt (also spelled Hewet) and Alice Grey were bundled off to Lancaster Castle dungeons to join Old Demdike, Old Chattox and Alizon and Anne Redfern. Later Margaret Pearon of Padiham was taken to the Lancaster dungeon, together with seven witches from Salmesbury and Isobel Robey from Windle, near St Helens.

One other 'witch', Jennet Preston, lived at Gisburn, then over the Yorkshire border, so she was sent to trial at York. She was tried with bewitching Thomas Lister of Westby Hall, Gisburn in 1608, the damning two pieces of evidence being that Lister had cried out her name in his death throes and that, when she touched his corpse, where she touched bled fresh blood. The latter was the sure sign of a witch for, as the King's book *Daemonologie*, pointed out, 'in a secret muther, if the deade carcase be at any time therafter handled by the murtherer, it wil gush out of blood.' At the first trial Jennet was found 'not guilty', but she was convicted at a second. Immediately after that trial, Thomas Potts wrote that he wanted to 'satisfie the world how dangerous and malicious a witch this Jennet Preston was. How unfit to live.'

The trial of the Lancashire witches took place at Lancaster Castle on 17-18 August 1612, with Sir James Altham and Sir Edward Bromley presiding. Roger Nowell was the prosecuting council and the lawyer from London, Thomas Potts, clerk of court. Old Demdike had passed away before the trial. Notice that there were no defending lawyers. Accordingly, Nowell and Potts raised all the evidence that they had already extracted from the prisoners, and had them give evidence against each other. Nine-years-old Jennet Device, for example, stood on a table so that she could be seen easily, and announced that her mother was a witch who, with her familiar brown dog, had killed Henry Mitton and James Robinson from Barley-in-Pendle. Old

Chattox, in court, described how she and Old Demdike had been to a banquet where light was brought by spirits and their familiars Tibb and Fancie had put in an appearance. And so it went on. And so on.

The outcome was that nine Pendle witches (Old Chattox, Elizabeth, Alizon and James Device, Anne Redfern, Alice Nutter, Katherine Hewitt, John and Jane Bulcock) together with Isobel Robey, were sentenced to death. They were executed at Golgotha (see page 154) on 20 August. Margaret Pearson was also found guilty, but sentenced to being pilloried on market days in Clitheroe, Whalley and Lancaster and to a year in Lancaster Castle jail. Remarkably, all the rest, including the seven from Salmesbury, were acquitted.

[The original account of these witches was produced by Thomas Potts, James I's chief witch-finder, in a book first printed in 1612, and called The Wunderfull Discoverie of Witches in the Countie of Lancaster. It was reprinted by the Chetham Society in 1845.]

The Most Haunted House in England

CHINGLE HALL

Chingle Hall lies up a track off the Broughton-Longridge road close to Whittingham hospital and the village of Goosnargh. It was built in 1260 as a moated manor house by Adam de Singleton. You must remember that Preston and the villages around were, from early times, Catholic strongholds. The name of Preston itself, for example, is a contraction of Priests' Town, and one of its four main old streets is Friargate, or the street leading to the friary.

Thus, when Henry VIII fell out with Rome, and through the Elizabethan and Stuart reigns, the area had many places where illicit Masses took place (see also Edmund Arrowsmith, page153).

One of these was Chingle Hall, where its thick walls had hidden priest-holes constructed by Jesuit Nicholas Owen.

In 1600 the Hall was purchased by the Wall family, who had a son John born in 1620. He was baptised a Catholic by Edmund Arrowsmith. He travelled to Douai in northern France and then Rome, where he trained as a priest and was ordained in 1645. He then returned to England as a missionary in Warwickshire. In 1678 he was captured, found guilty of being a papist and martyred at Worcester on 22 August 1679. His head was obtained by some of his followers, who secreted it abroad, to Douai. Later he was canonised and his head brought back to Chingle Hall where it was hidden somewhere in the masonry. It is thought that most of the mysterious events that have been recorded at the Hall began with the return of St John Wall's head.

Several visitors have reported seeing a robed figure, sometimes described as wearing Franciscan garb in the house. One report was of two monks together. And there have been many reports of groanings, crashes, doors suddenly opening and then closing, pictures on the wall shifting slightly, furniture being moved and sometimes barricading doors, the clanking of chains, heavy footsteps and an aroma of incense.

On Christmas Day 1980 *BBC Radio Lancashire* sent a team to investigate and record ghostly happenings in the Hall. They noted a sudden drop in air temperature (this has often been reported when other ghostly events occur) and recorded knocking coming from inside the Hall's thick walls. They also took a 'spectre detector' with them and, when the air temperature dropped, it suddenly changed its pitch, indicating a ghostly presence.

A very similar ghost has been reported from Mowbreck Hall, a mile north of Kirkham. During the reign of Elizabeth I it was owned by the Catholic Westby family. In 1583, on the Feast of All Hallows (now better known as All Saints' Day, 1 November) the family was gathered in the chapel where their priest, Vivian

Haydock, was preparing to celebrate Mass. Apparently Vivian Haydock had a son called George, who was also a priest. This sounds rather odd, for as we all know, Catholic priests are meant to be celibate; but perhaps things were different in the 16th century. Suddenly Haydock had a vision of his son's head all battered and bleeding. Vivian Haydock appears immediately to have suffered from a heart attack, from which he eventually died. Later it transpired that George Haydock had been captured on that very day and taken to the Tower of London. In 1584 he was executed by being hanged, drawn and quartered. There have been reports of the battered priest's head floating in the air at Mowbreck Hall, and of heavy footsteps, groans and the clanking of chains.

The Most Haunted Town in England

Westhoughton is not only a very ancient town, it is reputed to be Lancashire's most haunted town. The Ex-servicemen's Club is haunted by a woman dressed in bright red. In the Labour Club, loud footsteps can sometimes be heard, ringing throughout the place, but the footsteps cannot be linked with anybody walking about. A ghostly apparition comes and goes in the *Wheatsheaf Inn*, and a woman wearing a long flowing dress haunts a house in Tempest Road.

But the events of 1993 in Westhoughton were the most mysterious. Water started to drip from the ceiling of a child's bedroom, but plumbers could find no leak. Soon water was dipping from all the ceilings in the house, and again plumbers could not find its source. That the problem in this house was down to the supernatural was confirmed when ornaments, crockery and cutlery started to fly across the rooms.

The vicar came and conducted a service of exorcism, but to no avail. So the services of a medium were sought. She divined that the problem had been caused by the son of the family playing with a ouija board; this had, apparently, invoked the spirits. The medium went to work and, having exorcised three ghosts, the problem vanished.

White-Robed Ladies... and another Priestly Ghost

Samlesbury Hall, a Tudor building and the first in the county to be built of brick, lies close to the Blackburn-Preston road and was home to the Southworth family. In the second half of the 16th century, Dorothy, daughter of Sir John Southworth, made the mistake of falling in love with a son of the de Houghton family of Houghton Tower.

But there was a major obstacle to her happiness. The Southworths were Roman Catholics, the de Houghton's Protestant. Dorothy planned to elope with her lover, but her family heard of this and her brothers killed the lover and two of his friends and buried their corpses in the Hall grounds. Sir John then exiled Dorothy to a convent abroad. When she died, her ghost returned to Samlesbury and, wearing white robes, has been seen wandering through the garden and the hall, seeking her lover.

According to some authorities, there is no evidence that Sir John had a daughter called Dorothy, but that he did have a sister of that name. As for Sir John himself, he was heavily fined by the authorities during his life for his Catholicism, and it seems that his life ended violently on 3 November 1595. Apparently he was murdered in Samlesbury Hall by being stabbed, with his death-blood staining the wooden floor. His ghost is also said to haunt the Hall.

During the Civil Wars, when Lancashire was the focus for several important battles, a band of Cromwell's soldiers searched Heskin Hall, near Eccleston, for Papists and Royalist sympathisers. The Hall had long been held by Catholic families (the Molyneaux through most of the 16th century, then the Mawdesleys in the

17th), and it had a priest-hole where the family could hide their priest when danger threatened. This time the Parliamentary force were successful and found a priest in hiding. To placate them the priest denounced his Catholic faith. Then, with the soldiers' encouragement, to prove that he really hated Catholics, he took the family's young daughter and hanged her. The ghost of the young girl, clad in a white robe, has haunted Heskin Hall ever since, and there have also been reports of loud bangs and knocking and objects being moved that could not be explained other than by the supernatural.

Park Hall to the west of Chorley and home to the theme park Camelot has a lake, and there have been reports of a white lady emerging from that lake. The lake is a flooded medieval quarry, and it is thought that the white lady is from that period and is the ghost of a young women who, having failed to marry her lover, committed suicide by throwing herself in the lake.

Dunkenhalgh Hall, close to Hyndburn Brook at Clayton-le-Moors, is the family home of the Petre family. Early in the 18th century the family employed a French governess called Lucette to care for and to educate their children. Sadly for Lucette, she became pregnant by one of the Petre family and, as such families did in those days, they refused to allow her to marry the child's father and disowned her. Whereupon she threw herself into the Hyndburn, which in places is a very deep stream. Her white-shrouded ghost has been seen in and around the Hall and stream.

Castle Hill, near the lake at Newton-le-Willows, is an old Norman motte and bailey castle (i.e. a mound of earth). Since the 1950s – there are no earlier accounts – there have been sightings of a 'white lady' on and close to the mound, by the lake and on the nearby Newton Lane. Others have also experienced an unexplained 'happening'. In 2005-8 I went once every week by train from Newton-le-Willows to Manchester Museum where I studied the Museum's collection of water insects. On my way home, after leaving the station I walked by the lake to where I had parked my car. One November evening, at dusk, I was walking along the lake dam where I heard someone behind me – light footsteps and heavy, short breaths. I turned, but there was no one there and both steps and breaths immediately ceased. Others have had a similar experience.....

Meols Hall, at Churchtown on the northeast end of Southport, is an ancient manor house. Today it is over a mile from the sea, but 250 years ago the tide came within a quarter of a mile of the Hall's gates. The story goes that a ship was wrecked close to Churchtown and a young lady rescued. She was taken to the Hall and several of the estate workers found out that she was from a wealthy family. They tried to extract money from her, but when she refused to cooperate, they murdered her. Since that day her white-robed ghost has been reported gliding through the estate grounds, although my informant – a Churchtown man – suggests that the tale was put about to discourage poachers from visiting the Hall!

There have also been female ghosts clad in raiment other than white. At **Turton Tower** there is a lady dressed in black who may be seen, if you are lucky, gliding up the staircase.

In contrast at **Worsley Old Hall**, the home of the canal-building Duke of Bridgewater, the ghost of Dorothy Legh glides down the stairs wearing green attire.

And if you visit **Gubberford Bridge**, which carries traffic across the River Wyre to the village of Scorton, you might see the grey ghost of a servant girl gazing down into the water. It is said that she was murdered by a jealous lover.

The Rabbit of Crank

Sometime in the 19th century, an old lady lived in a cottage at Crank, a mile or so west of Billinge, with her daughter Jenny. She was a noted healer, who sought herbs in the field with which to practice her craft. Not far away lived a man called Pullen, who developed some sort of wasting disease. He asked the old woman for help and then, when her herbal medicine failed to cure him, he went to local poacher, Dick Piers, to seek revenge. He told Piers that the old woman was a witch and that she had poisoned his body. He then asked Piers to go to the cottage with him, and to help him kill the woman by slashing her wrists so that she would bleed slowly to death.

Piers did as his friend asked, but the old lady began to scream out, loudly, as they severed her arteries. In rushed Jenny, carrying her pet white rabbit. Pullen and Piers now turned to Jenny, who was a witness to the murder they were is the midst of committing. Jenny dropped the rabbit and fled out into the dark night. The two murderers killed the rabbit, kicking it to death and then fled. The next day Jenny's body was found on Billinge Hill. She had died from fright, exhaustion and hypothermia.

Shortly after, Jenny's rabbit – or the ghost of the white rabbit – confronted Piers. He fled in terror and committed suicide by hanging himself in a quarry on Billinge Hill. The rabbit then confronted Pullen, who turned mad and died of a heart attack. It was said that the rabbit of Crank appeared to others in the Billinge-Crank area, and that whoever saw it, died soon afterwards. Happily, it seems, there have been no recent reports.

The Phantom Horseman of Wycoller

Wycoller is a 'hamlet frozen in time' in East Lancashire, close to the village of Trawden. Also close to the Yorkshire border, it is part of Brontë country, and Wycoller Hall was the model for Ferndean Manor, in Charlotte Brontë's *Jane Eyre*. The Hall was built by the Hartley family in the 16th century and later owned by the Cunliffes, but it was abandoned and much of its masonry

All that remains of Wycoller Hall, Jane Eyre's Ferndean Manor and home of the Phantom Horseman

robbed for other buildings. Now the centre of a Country Park, Wycoller is well worth a visit.

Once every year, the story goes, a phantom horseman, dressed as a Charles I cavalier, would gallop up the drive to the Hall, rein in his horse, dismount and go rushing in and up the stairs. From the upstairs, witnesses would hear loud screams, and then they would see the phantom horseman rush out of the Hall, regain his mount and gallop off into the night. Since the Hall has been left in ruins, and much of the stone taken away, the phantom horseman still visits, but now he simply clambers amongst the ruins before leaving.

It is thought that the phantom horseman was a member of the Cunliffe family who, during the Civil War when the family was in financially dire straits because of his support for Charles I, murdered his wife upstairs in the Hall after a violent argument. And the screams heard by witnesses are from his wife's ghost.

This is perhaps the most fascinating road name in Lancashire

The Lost Fisherman and his Wife

Today the village of Banks is separated from the tides of the Ribble estuary by over a mile of land reclaimed from the sea in the late 19th and 20th centuries. Before the reclamation it was a small fishing village, with boats moored in a creek called the Crossens River.

One winter's evening a fisherman called Ralph failed to return home and his wife went out to look for him. As she walked along the cart track that led from the village to the creek, people heard her crying out, 'Ralph! Ralph! Where are you, Ralph?' But alas, he never replied. His small boat had been wrecked and he was drowned. Ralph's wife died soon afterwards from her grief.

Today the cart track is the road leading into Banks village from Southport, and on wild and windy winter evenings a ghostly form can be seen wandering along, crying 'Ralph! Ralph! Where are you, Ralph?' And the road is called Ralph's Wife's Lane.

Haunted Pubs

The ghost of a Cavalier soldier killed by a party of Parliamentary soldiers during the Civil War glides silently through the very old *New Inn* at Foulridge.

Lizzie Dean worked at *The Sun Inn*, Chipping. She was betrothed to be married, but in 1835 she saw her beloved leaving Chipping Church having married another woman. In her grief she hanged herself in the Inn and her ghost still haunts the place.

During the 18th century the *George Hotel* on Church Street, Preston was a coaching inn. About this time the landlord, Robert Clay, is reputed to have murdered two young girls and buried them beneath the cellar floor. Much later, workmen were renovating the place and they removed a slab of stone from the cellar floor and by so doing, released Clay's ghost that occasionally puts in an appearance in the bar and cellar.

A landlord of the *Coach & Horses* in Everton hanged himself and his ghost haunts the old inn.

The Railway Inn at Waterfoot is haunted by a ghost called Jane, who can pass through the walls from one room to another.

During the English Civil War (again!) the son of Lord Stannycliffe was in the *Ring O'Bells* in Manchester when a band of Parliamentarian soldiers walked in. He tried to hide in the cellar and then escape to the sanctuary of a nearby church, but he was hacked down in the churchyard. His Cavalier ghost still haunts the *Ring O'Bells*.

And if you walk down the lane in the hamlet Greenhalgh, northwest of Kirkham and Wesham, at midnight, beware. A coffin floats along in the air at head-height!

Chapter Eight

DISASTERS AND TRAGEDIES

The county of Lancashire has seen perhaps more major disasters than most. For a start it has a treacherous coastline of wide estuaries, and a tidal range that is greater then almost anywhere else in the world, other than the Bristol Channel and Newfoundland. The tidal range of spring★ tides are in excess of thirty feet, and far more when a south-westerly gale backs the tide. Also the county has a very large population, so when a disaster occurs, more people are more likely to be involved. And then two important jobs in Lancashire were, and let me stress *were*, the most dangerous of jobs: deep-sea trawlerman and coal-miner. Some of the events described here could have been put elsewhere in this book, but the nature of the events make them more aptly described sudden disasters or tragedies.

    ★ Spring tides have nothing to do with the season of spring, but the action of springing up. They coincide with New and Full Moons, and in Lancashire tend to occur around midday and midnight, whereas the lowest neap tides tend to occur early morning and late afternoon. Note too that in Lancashire estuaries the ebb (the tide going out) takes roughly nine hours, whereas the flood (the tide going in) takes just over a third of that. Thus the flood is far more rapid and potentially dangerous.

Drownings in Morecambe Bay

Until the railway was completed around Morecambe Bay in 1857, from Lancaster, via Hest Bank, Carnforth, and Arnside, and over the River Kent viaduct to Grange-over-the-Sands, then through Kents Bank and Cark & Cartmel, across the River Leven viaduct and finally into Ulverston, getting from Lancaster to Cartmel Priory and from there to Ulverston was a nightmare. The inland route was a tortuous track, up and down steep hills for about 35 miles, now smoothed out to some extent by A6 and A580 trunk roads.

The alternative was simple: you walked, or rode your horse, or took the coach from Lancaster to Hest Bank and, when the tide was out, crossed the Bay to Kents Bank, a distance of between six and seven miles. And to get from Cartmel to Ulverston, you went from Cark and did the three mile crossing of the Leven estuary to either Conishead Priory (via Chapel Island, where you could

The High Sheriff of Lancaster and his entourage crossing Morecambe Sands – a detail from a painting by Thomas Sunderland (1744-1823)

186

stop and pray) or directly to Ulverston. It is this link across the Bay with Lancaster that gave Furness the title, 'Lancashire-over-the-Sands' and why the railway station sign is of Grange-over-the-Sands and not just 'Grange'. That link continues even today, though this part of the county is administratively in Cumbria, for post codes begin with LA, Lancaster.

There were only three problems on such journeys. First, river channels had to be crossed, and these channels change their routes fairly often. Second, the Bay has areas of dangerous quicksand (known as 'syrte', while the sign that an area you were approaching was quicksand – a smooth, flat shining area of sand without ripple-marks – was known as a 'poo'). Third, the tide floods very quickly so that, unless you know the precise time of high water, you can get stranded and drown. And many folk have been drowned.

One crude statistic: the register of Cartmel Priory records 141 souls lost in the years 1559 and 1880. And this is certainly not all by a long way. Here are some instances:

In 1687 draper Christopher Harrys from Cartmel was taking goods to the market in Lancaster on two pack-horses. As they reached the middle of the Bay one horse shed its load, and it took him so long to repack and secure the load that the tide overtook him and he and his horses drowned.

In 1846, nine young people went across the Sands from Cartmel to the Whitsuntide fair in Ulverston. On their way home, the cart they were riding in suddenly disappeared into a syrte and they were all drowned. Several other travellers making the same journey at the same time heard and saw nothing.

In an undated tragedy, a fisherman, his wife and two daughters set out to cross the Sands, but suddenly a fog came down and they became disorientated. The fisherman went on to check the best route, leaving the women in the cart. The daughters became frightened, so they left the cart and followed

187

their tracks back to dry land, though they had to swim part of the way, presumably across the channel of the River Kent. Husband and wife both drowned. This recalls a much more recent disaster in the Bay.

In January 2002, a 50-year old man from Ulverston took his nine-year old son fishing for flounders in the channel of the River Leven off the village of Bardsea. Suddenly a fog came down and they could see nothing. Lost, and with the tide making, the man phoned his wife on his mobile phone and she got in touch with the rescue services. They too could see nothing from the shore, nor pinpoint cries for help.

As the tide swept in, the man put his son on his shoulders, and the son used his father's phone to plead with the rescue team to find them. But they could do nothing. Suddenly, the phone call stopped and man and boy were tragically overcome and drowned. Never go into the mountains or far out onto the shore without a compass.

Sometimes people have just survived. A boy had joined the regular stage coach across the Bay from Kents Bank to Lancaster one cold and wet January evening. The Kent channel was very deep and the sand very soft, so he and the other passengers had to get out and walk the last four miles.

One man set off on his horse to make the same crossing, but he was overtaken by the tide. He survived by keeping hold of the mane of his horse, which quickly drowned. But he held onto the tail and was swept up the Bay, clinging on to the floating corpse, with the flood tide and back out on the ebb. Then, he and his dead horse landed on a sand bank and he was able to walk back to dry land. There are several records of horses and carts, or coaches becoming mired in quicksand and the occupants escaping and completing their journey on foot. I suppose the thousands who did make the journey nearly all set out with the heart beating a little more quickly than normal.

The old signpost at Cartmel assumed that travellers would all go 'over sands'

As long ago as 1326, the abbot of Furness Abbey petitioned the king, Edward II, to provide an official guide. A guide was provided, whose job was to go out on horseback with a bundle of branches and with them mark the safe route that the travellers should take. There still is a guide, paid for by the Queen, currently Cedric Robinson. Each summer Cedric leads parties on foot across the Bay in safety, raising money for local charities. It is a great experience. But no guide could have prevented the disaster of 5 February 2004.

That evening a party of 38 illegal immigrants from the Fujian Province of China went out from Hest Bank onto the Bay to gather cockles, urged on by a gang-master and two accomplices. Their reward for this hard work, in cold conditions and with inadequate clothing, would be £5 for every 25kg bag of cockles that they brought off the Bay. It seems that no one had

Many have died trying to cross Morecambe Bay. This is the striking, open view from Ulverston, with the refuge of Chapel Island in the distance.

checked the time of high water and, by the time that most of them were aware of the danger, the Keer channel behind them was filling quickly, and the tide flowing and rising speedily over the surrounding Warton Bank. So, in the dark and with the sea water temperature at barely 5C, they attempted to get back to the safety of Hest Bank.

Only fifteen survived. Twenty-three were drowned, two of them women, in the age range 18-45 years. After the disaster, 21 bodies were recovered. The remains of another were found in the Bay six years later, in 2010. One has never been recovered.

On 28 March 2006, gang-master Lin Liangren was convicted of manslaughter and sentenced to 14 years in prison. Lin Muyong was sentenced to 4 years and 9 months, Zhao Xiaoquing to 2 years and 9 months. But perhaps also responsible was the local authority's licensing body which, having been warned by *bona fide* local fishermen that parties of ill-prepared Chinese from Liverpool were coming into the Bay and collecting cockles, did nothing...until it was too late.

The Mexico Disaster

The *Mexico* was a 484-ton, cargo-laden barque – a three-masted sailing ship – that left Liverpool on 5 December 1886 bound for the port of Guayaquil, Ecuador. The weather had not been good for some days, but the ship's master, Capt Gustave Burmester, was very experienced, and thought that there would be no problem tacking out into the Irish Sea against the strong West-North-West wind and then, having cleared the North Wales coast, running south and out into the Atlantic. But as the wind became stronger, Capt Burmester decided to take on a pilot, who knew the waters of Liverpool Bay better. The pilot left the ship on 7 December, with the *Mexico* having reached the northern tip of Anglesey, Point Lynas.

It was hoped that the ship would now run easily round the rest of the North Wales coast, but this was not to be. The wind strengthened to severe gale and, though the lighthouse on Douglas Head (Isle of Man) was noted in the ship's log, it was impossible to make further headway.

The next day the wind reached storm force and the ship's sails and rigging were beginning to come apart. By 3am on the 9th the *Mexico* had been pushed back to the Great Orme, Llandudno, and as darkness fell on the afternoon of the 9th it had drifted back across Liverpool Bay and was approaching the shallow waters of the Ribble estuary. To stop the ship drifting further into the treacherous estuary, Capt Burmester had anchors out but, with the combined effects of the storm and the flooding tide, they failed. Shortly after midnight, on the morning of the 10th, the *Mexico* hit bottom and was bounced for a short distance, by the tremendous waves and wind, until it came to rest on Trunk Hill Brow, a sand bank off Birkdale, south-west of Southport. The ship had been seen out in the mouth of the estuary on the afternoon of the 9th, so when the first distress flares were spotted that evening it was assumed that it was the same ship that was in trouble. It was also noticed that the *Mexico* had foundered in almost exactly the same position as the 1,068-ton barque *Nereus* had on 27 December 1884.

The Southport lifeboat was named the *Eliza Fernley*. It had been launched twelve years earlier and had already saved 48 lives, including the crew of the *Nereus*. The full crew of the lifeboat (Coxwain Charles Hodge and twelve men) plus three volunteers who wanted to join the rescue, made a crew of sixteen instead of the usual thirteen. She was towed by horses and launched at 11pm on 9 December at Ainsdale, so that the now near-gale's direction would assist the men rowing out to the stricken vessel.

The *Mexico*'s distress lights were spotted from St Annes, about eight miles away across the estuary, sometime between 8.30pm and 9.15pm and at about 9.45pm two cannon were fired to inform the crew to come to the St Annes lifeboat station. As the men arrived, helpers were preparing the lifeboat *Laura Janet* for launching down the slipway. Some of the regular crew didn't hear the cannon (the last to arrive was Coxwain William Johnson) but there were plenty of bystanders who volunteered to take their places and at 10.45pm the St Annes lifeboat headed out into the rough but moonlit seas of the estuary crossing.

Just after 9pm on 9 December 1886 distress lights were noticed just to the west of the end of the pier at Southport from the promenade at Lytham, and it was also noticed that the lights came from the position that the *Nereus* had come aground. Then the warning cannon were heard from St Annes.

Immediately volunteers were sent out to summon the crew of the Lytham lifeboat, the *Charles Biggs*, and at 10.05pm she was launched, 40 minutes before the St Annes boat and almost an hour before the Southport boat, with Coxwain Thomas Clarkson in command, making three lifeboats on the mission to rescue the crew of the *Mexico*.

By 11pm, Cox Clarkson had taken the *Charles Biggs* west in the lee of the north side of the Ribble mouth, and then sailed her in foul conditions through a maze of sandbanks and channels close to the *Mexico*. He flashed a light that was answered by Capt Burmester. Now Cox Clarkson moved the *Charles Biggs* alongside the ship, breaking three oars and almost filling the small lifeboat with icy sea water as he did so.

Then, one by one, the eleven men and finally Capt Burmester were taken on board before the *Charles Biggs* was allowed to drift away from the stranded ship. Then the sail was raised. At first Cox Clarkson thought of taking his boat to the shore at Birkdale, for that did not involve crossing the very dangerous estuary where the tide was in full ebb.

He then suggested heading to Southport pier and dropping the *Mexico* crew off there, but Capt Burmester preferred to go on in the lifeboat. At just before 3.15am on 10 December the *Charles Biggs* reached its base at Lytham, having rescued all the crew of the *Mexico*. But what of the *Eliza Fernley* and *Laura Janet*?

The *Eliza Fernley* had made progress against the violent seas but there was a big swell and foam-capped waves were breaking powerfully in the relatively shallow water. They were within easy reach of the *Mexico* and just about to put out an anchor when a huge wave hit and immediately the lifeboat overturned.

Two men were tangled in the lifeboat's rigging and drowned there, while the others were thrown into the sea which, with a temperature of probably about 6C, would readily kill by hypothermia. Lifeboat and men were washed to the shore and, of the sixteen who set sail, only two (Harry Robinson and Jack Jackson) survived.

There had been no sign of the *Laura Janet* since her launch and in the early light of the 10th, crowds gathered at the St Annes lifeboat station, waiting for what was clearly going to be bad news. The Blackpool lifeboat, the *Samuel Fletcher*, was launched in an attempt to find her, but she was nearly wrecked herself. At 10.30am the *Charles Biggs* was launched to look for her and her crew. To no avail.

Early in the afternoon, three bodies were found on the beach at Ainsdale, wearing St Annes gear. Shortly after, the overturned *Laura Janet* was found with the bodies of Cox Johnson and two other men trapped in rigging. Then, over the next two days the bodies of all but one of the missing St Annes lifeboatmen were recovered from the sea and taken to their home town for burial. The last body, the badly decomposed corpse of Thomas Bonney, was washed up on the beach at Southport three months later, on 4 March 1887. Twenty-seven brave men lost their lives in the *Mexico* tragedy, and it is still the Royal National Lifeboat Institute's greatest single loss of life.

Trawler Disasters

From the 1880s, after the town was built (see page 138), and up to the end of the cod-war with Iceland in 1976, Fleetwood was a major deep-sea fishing port.

As a boy I can remember strings of vessels, lying low in the water and with black smoke billowing from their funnels, heading out for the far-off fishing grounds, and similar queues of trawlers returning, lying even lower in the water with their holds full of cod, haddock, halibut and other fish. Then the dock at Fleetwood was a hive of activity, as the boats were unloaded and their catches auctioned. And every day a 'fish train' left the port carrying a large proportion of the catch quickly away to the English midlands and south.

The memorial to the St Anne's lifeboat crew who lost their lives in the Mexico disaster

Alongside coal-mining, being a hand on a trawler was the most dangerous of jobs. The places that the trawlers went to were dangerous. Often they were rocky, with dangerous reefs, islands and promontories. They were amongst the windiest places on earth, where gales were the norm, making the seas violently rough so that the boat pitched and tossed and rolled with waves breaking on deck.

In winter they were bitterly cold; so cold around Iceland that the weight of ice on the rigging put the ship in danger of capsizing unless the ice was hacked off with axes. And the work was long and hard, with only snatches of sleep in-between long bouts of cleaning fish, repairing damaged tackle, and taking in essential nourishment.

The first disaster recorded in which men's lives were lost was in 1882, when the smack *Mary Ellen* sank with the loss of five crew. But it wasn't just the geology, sea and weather that resulted in the loss of ships and men, there was also enemy action in the two World Wars. It must have taken extraordinary courage to set out for the Rockall Bank or the east of Iceland, knowing that if the seas didn't get you, a U-boat might instead.

In the First World War, twenty Fleetwood fishing boats were sunk by U-boats, and in the Second World War, 44. It wasn't just that going down with a trawler, or getting swept off the deck by a tremendous wave, were not peaceful ways to die. Many of those lives lost left dependent loved ones back at home. Thus, when a ship went down with all hands, the entire town of Fleetwood would have been in mourning.

Early in the 20th century ship-to-shore and ship-to-ship communication was not as good as it became, so that trawlers just 'disappeared'. One such was the *Doris* (registered FD141) that set sail, with ten crew, on 21 January 1914, for fishing grounds off the west coast of Scotland. On the 22 or 23 January, conditions west of the Isle of Skye were appalling and it was presumed that she simply foundered with all lives lost. In February wreckage from the *Doris* was recovered from the sea together with one body. The bodies of the other nine trawlermen were never found. In such disasters it must be especially hard for families, who cannot say goodbye to lost loved ones.

The loss of the *Merisia* (FD153) was especially tragic. She had set sail for the Icelandic fishing grounds on 26 January 1940 when a severe blizzard, dreadful visibility and gale force winds forced her onto rocks close inshore in the Isle of Man's Bulgham Bay, about five miles south of Ramsey. Having hit a sharp rock she was holed and began to sink. As her hull sank, so her crew of twelve climbed to the relative safety of the rigging and awaited rescue. But the Douglas lifeboat was out of action and the coxwain of the Ramsey boat said it was too dangerous for them to proceed (c.f. the *Mexico*!). The lifeboat from Port St Mary at the south end of the island did set sail, but her lights failed and in the darkness she was useless.

The last resort was the Ramsey Rocket and Lifeboat Brigade, who made their way to Bulgham Bay, clambered down to the beach below the cliffs, and attempted to get a line aboard the *Merisia*. But they failed and had to retreat as the tide pushed them from the beach. Consequently, as hypothermia set in, the twelve men were washed, one by one, from their precarious positions, and drowned.

The disappearance of the *Goth* (FD52)was something of a mystery for 48 years. She had set sail for Iceland's fishing grounds on 4 December 1948 and was last heard of through a radio message on the 16 December, saying that Skipper Wilfred Elliott was taking her to shelter in the cove of Adalvik, near Isafjordur Bay, in the far north-west of Iceland. And that was that. *Goth* and her crew of 21 were expected back on or just before Christmas Eve, but neither she nor they turned up, and Christmas 1948 was a time of mourning for their families and sadness for the entire town.

The weather conditions when the *Goth* was last heard of were as bad as they get, with 100mph winds creating mountainous seas, and everyone presumed that the waves had overwhelmed her. Remarkably, in 2006, the net of an Icelandic trawler pulled from the seabed the funnel of the lost ship, which was sent home to Fleetwood. So at least the people of Fleetwood now know what happened to the *Goth*, and have the funnel as a memorial to the lost men.

A Fleetwood trawler sets sail for Icelandic waters. But not today

Early on the morning of 30 January 1953 the trawler *Michael Griffith* (FD249) set sail from Fleetwood. That evening, as she steamed past Barra Head, the southernmost tip of the Outer Hebrides, she was hit by a tremendous storm. Skipper Charles Singleton put out a radio message saying that he had lost steam and that the ship was drifting helplessly. The message was picked up by two other trawlers, *Wyre General* and *Velia*, which attempted to reach the stricken ship, but to no avail. The *Michael Griffith* had gone down with a crew of thirteen.

Nothing was found of her, other than some lifebuoys that were washed up on the Antrim coast. Eleven women were left widowed and twenty children lost their fathers.

Mining Disasters

For trawlermen, danger comes from primarily the sea and the weather; for coal-miners working deep underground, danger comes from the rock strata through which the mining passages run. The most obvious danger is from falling rocks or, even worse, the collapse of the roof that blocks retreat to the relative safety of the shaft and the cage that takes men back to the surface.

Less obvious, for it cannot be seen, is methane, known to miners as fire-damp, and also as marsh-gas. Methane is commonly produced in the partial decomposition of vegetation in oxygen-lacking bogs (which is how coal has been produced over millions of years). It is still produced by peat-bogs and years ago before the Lancashire mosslands were reclaimed, leaking marsh-gas would burst into flame. At night these eerie little flickering flames, out there on the dangerous bogs, were called 'Will o'the wisp'.

In a mine, the build-up of fire-damp led, not to little flickering flames, but to great and catastrophic explosions. The flame produced by the explosion of methane also set alight the fine coal dust particles suspended in vast quantities in the air, and this would result in a ball of flame, with an incredibly high temperature of up to 1,200°C, shooting down the tunnel or passage burning those in its path.

WESTHOUGHTON PIT DISASTER

The Pretoria Pit was named after the British had taken Pretoria in the Boer War in June 1900 and was part of the Hulton collieries, on the border between Westhoughton and Atherton. Shafts were sunk over 1,300 feet, vertically down, and in 1910 coal was being

hewn from three of the five seams: Trencherbone at 438 feet, Plodder at 822 feet, Yard at 912 feet, Three-Quarters at 1,083 feet, and Arley at 1,320 feet beneath the surface. These seams were fairly thin, Trencherbone the thickest at 3' 6", and Three-Quarters the thinnest at 18".

However, the pit was very productive, averaging exactly one ton of coal per worker per day. It was also, like most Lancashire pits, a very 'gassy' mine, Yard seam especially producing much methane that had to be voided to prevent explosion.

The monument in Westhoughton cemetery commemorating the 344 miners who tragically died in the Pretoria Pit in 1910

But there was an explosion. At 6.45am on 21 December 1910, four days before Christmas, the first cage of the morning shift descended and by 7.45am, 890 men and boys were working underground. Suddenly, at 7.50am, there was a tremendous explosion as a build-up of methane was ignited by a faulty miner's-lamp. That explosion carried shock-waves throughout the mine and a ball of fire raced through the workings of Yard seam. So strong was the explosion that one man working 60-feet from the shaft in Yard seam was hurled out into the shaft and he then fell over 400-feet to the bottom of the shaft.

The explosion was heard on the surface at Westhoughton and Atherton, bringing anxious relatives of those who worked at the mine to see what had happened. The explosion killed 344 men and boys. The 545 surviving miners were in great danger after the explosion was over. Only one cage was left working. Down at the bottom of the shaft, from where men went to take coal from the Arley seam, there was a rapid build-up of methane. The danger was that the methane would make the men sleepy: and to lie down and go to sleep would be fatal. So the older, experienced men kept others awake and certainly saved lives that would otherwise have been lost. Eventually one cage operated to take the survivors to the surface and safety.

The loss of the 344 hit Westhoughton, Atherton and the nearer parts of Bolton hard, and especially the small town of Westhoughton, where 239 of those killed had lived. First there was the retrieval of the bodies, many badly burned, others almost too mutilated to be identified. One, unidentified for some time, was finally named when his mother identified a morsel of his sock. But conditions were so bad that retrieving the bodies took weeks, and the funerals likewise, which kept grief in the forefront of everyone's minds. Then there was the problem of looking after the dependents of those lost. There was a huge fund-raising event and compensation claims were heard in the court in Bolton.

This was Lancashire's biggest mining disaster and the third biggest in Britain; but there were many others:

On 9 October 1850, 16 men and boys were killed at Bent Grange colliery at Oldham.

On 20 May 1852, 36 men and boys died at Coppull colliery near Standish (Wigan).

On 24 March 1853, 58 men and boys, and on 18 February 1854, 89 men and boys were killed at Ince Hall colliery at Wigan.

On 2 February 1858, 53 men and boys were killed by an explosion in Bardsley colliery, Oldham.

On 23 January 1866, 30 men died at High Brooks colliery, Ashton-in-Makerfield.

On 20 August 1867, 14 lost their lives at Garswood Park colliery, Ashton-in-Makerfield.

On 25 November 1868, 62 died in an explosion at Hindley Green, Leigh.

On 26 December 1868 (working on Boxing Day!) 26 men and boys lost their lives in an explosion at Queen Pit, Haydock; 59 died there in an explosion on 21 July 1869.

On 1 April 1869, 37 lost their lives following an explosion at High Brooks colliery, Ashton-in-Makerfield.

On 7 June 1878, 189 men and boys died in an explosion at Wood Pit, Haydock.

On 7 November 1883, 68 men and boys lost their lives in an explosion at Moorfield colliery, Oldham.

And so the list of men and boys lost in mining disasters during the 1800s goes on. In total, up to the end of 1899, there were at least 83 such disasters, totalling a minimum of 1,828 dead.

During the early years of the 20th century safety became increasingly important and the frequency of mining disasters fell, especially after the industry was nationalised in the 1940s. Of course, coal mines were such dangerous places that catastrophes, like the one at Pretoria Pit, were bound to occur sooner or later. Methane, plus spark, equals disaster. It was that spark. When I took parties of students down mines in the Leigh-Parkside area, all pockets had to be checked and not even a piece of foil wrapper could be taken down, just in case.

On 18 August 1908, 75 men and boys were killed in an explosion at the Maypole Colliery (Abram, Wigan); that was the worst 20th century disaster apart from Pretoria. But up to the closure of the Lancashire coalfield in the 1980s, from 1900 there was a total of 25 mining disasters in Lancashire (roughly one every three years), and 595 lost their lives. The last two major disasters, both caused by explosions caused by methane + spark, were at Hapton colliery at Burnley on 22 March 1962 (19 men died) and at Golborne colliery on 18 March 1979.

There is now no deep coal mining in Lancashire. When the Bickershaw/Parsonage mine complex was still producing lots of coal in the 1970s, I asked some of the coal-face workers why they were prepared to suffer from ill-health (a large proportion eventually suffered badly from the lung disease emphysema) and risk their lives deep in the dark bowels of the earth. The money helped, they admitted. It was true that coal miners were paid far more than most working class men. But all agreed that it was the camaraderie of those 'workin' down t' pit'. Somehow, it seemed, the fact that they relied on each other for their lives made going down there worthwhile, and even enjoyable.

Poor Samboo

Slavery was one of the most hideous features of Britain's Imperial past, when ships from the ports of Liverpool and Lancaster traded in human life.

Early in the 18th century Lancaster was a major port, but the wharf in the city centre could not be reached by larger ocean-going ships. Instead the ships landed their cargoes at the mouth of the Lune at Sunderland Point, and the major cargo was cotton. The cotton could then be taken onto Lancaster by smaller boats or carried by wagon.

One Lancaster trader, Robert Lawson, built a warehouse at Sunderland Point; they are now three-storey cottages, but in the 1730s they stored cotton, rum and tobacco from the West Indies.

The captain of one of the ships that brought goods to Sunderland Point kept a young slave as his cabin boy, to fetch and carry. That slave cabin boy was called Samboo and, in 1736, he died whilst the ship was there unloading its cargo. We do not know what he died from. Romantics say from home-sickness; but it was much more likely to have been some disease like measles or influenza.

Samboo's gravestone at Sunderland Point

He was buried at the end of the Point (unconsecrated ground), and there you can see his simple grave, usually with a few flowers put there by visitors, and a poem carved on a big stone:

> **Full sixty years the angry Winter's wave,**
> **Has thundering dashed this bleak and barren Shore**
> **Since SAMBOO'S Head laid in this lonely GRAVE,**
> **Lies still and ne'er will hear their tumult more.'**

And the last verse:

> **'But still he sleeps – till the awakening Sounds**
> **Of the Archangel's Trump new life impart,**
> **Then the GREAT JUDGE his Approbation founds**
> **Not on Man's COLOR, but his WORTH OF**
> **HEART.'**

There were thousands such tragedies in the 18th and 19th centuries.

The Munich Disaster

When UEFA launched the European Cup in 1955, a trophy competed for by teams which had won their national leagues the previous season, the English Football League refused to let champions Chelsea take part, on the grounds that it would interfere with the 1955-6 domestic season. That season Manchester United won the league and again the Football League said that they could not play; but play they did, for manager Matt Busby and the club's board defied the League. So in the 1956-7 season United took part and reached the semifinals, losing out to Real Madrid. They were also League champions and were qualified to take part in the 1957-8 European Cup.

The team that Busby had put together was known as the 'Busby Babes': it was young and included some of the world's best and improving players, like Bobby Charlton, Bill Foulkes, goalkeeper Harry Gregg, Roger Byrne, the outstanding centre forward Tommy Taylor, and the legendary Duncan Edwards. When New Year 1958 arrived, the young United team were on course for winning every competition, including the European Cup, which would make them European champions. The first leg of the quarter final was against Red Star Belgrade at Old Trafford on 21 January 1958, and United won that 2-1. In the return match at Belgrade on 5 February, United were three up by half time, with two goals by Charlton and one by Denis Viollet. But in the second half Red Star came back at them, the game ended in a 3-3 draw, but United went through by the extra goal scored at Old Trafford.

The team, together with some well-known sports journalists and Manchester United staff, set off back home on flight BEA 609, in an Elizabethan class propeller plane, an AS-57 Ambassador named *Lord Burghley*. The pilot Captain James Thain had been at the controls on the outward flight, so co-pilot Ken Rayment took the controls on the return journey which involved a refuelling stop at Munich. The plane landed safely at Munich at 1.15pm GMT and all the passengers embarked and went to the terminal lounge. By 2.19pm all were back on board and at 2.31pm the plane was cleared for take-off. The first attempt at take-off was aborted because the engines were over-accelerating. Apparently this was a known problem with this type of plane, and the solution was to open the throttle more slowly, which co-pilot Rayment did on the second attempt; but again the engines over-accelerated and the take-off was aborted.

The Munich authorities suggested to Thain that it might be best to remain there overnight, but Thain was advised that an even slower opening of the throttle, which would lengthen the take-off down the runway, should succeed and, not wanting to waste time, just before 3pm everyone returned to the plane for a third attempt at take-off. Wet snow was falling heavily and settling on the runway.

At 3.03pm the plane began to accelerate. When it reached a speed of 85 knots there seemed to be a slight problem, so Thain eased back a little on the throttle, before accelerating once more. At 117 knots Thain reported V1, the speed at which the take-off could not be aborted. But then, instead of accelerating further, the speed decreased to 105 knots. It was impossible to stop the plane, and take-off was impossible. The plane shot off the end of the runway, smashed through a fence and its port (left) wing hit the side of a house, which caught fire. Then the tail was torn off the plane and the starboard (right) side of the fuselage collided with a shed containing a wagon, rubber tyres and fuel, which burst into flame.

All in all, 23 people were killed in the crash or later in Munich's Rechts de Isar Hospital: two crew, Capt Ken Rayment and cabin steward Tom Cable; eight players, Geoff Bent, Roger Byrne, Eddie Colman, Duncan Edwards, Mark Jones, David Pegg, Tommy Taylor and Billy Whelan; three Manchester United staff, Walter Crickmer (Club Secretary), Tom Curry (Trainer) and Bert Whalley (Chief Coach); eight journalists, Alf Clarke (*Manchester Evening Chronicle*), Danny Davies (*Manchester Guardian*), George Follows (*Daily Herald*), Tom Jackson (*Manchester Evening News*), Archie Ledbrooke (*Daily Mirror*), Henry Rose (*Daily Express*), Frank Swift (*News of the World*) and Eric Thompson (*Daily Mail*); and two others, Bela Miklos (travel agent) and Willie Satinoff (a friend of Matt Busby).

Nine players survived, but two of them, John Berry and Jackie Blanchflower were too badly injured to play football ever again. Matt Busby was critically injured and was so close to passing away that twice a priest gave the last rites. But he eventually recovered and led another great team, which included survivors of Munich (Bobby Charlton, Bill Foulkes and Harry Gregg), together with the great, though flawed, George Best. And on 29 May 1968 Sir Matt Busby's team did win the European Cup!

The Peterloo Massacre

In the first half of the 19th century an economic crisis and a political crisis dominated English politics. And politics itself, or rather politicians, were the root cause. The government was in the hands of a wealthy few, whose sole interest was the acquiring of more wealth and in the keeping down of the masses of workers. Most power was concentrated in the southeast of England: in 1819, for instance, Lancashire had only two Members of Parliament, and the growing urban centres of places like Manchester, Bolton, Rochdale and Preston were not represented at all.

When the harvests failed in 1815, Parliament passed Corn Laws that protected the prices for English grain by adding a big import duty on foreign grown grain. This meant that the landowners who grew the grain kept their income, but the poor who needed bread had to pay more for it. And with high unemployment, poor workers in the cotton industry saw their wages decline. So in 1803 a weaver would have earned fifteen shilling per week, but by 1818 he received only five shillings per week. At the same time, the price of the two staples had grown: wheat to four pence per pound; and potatoes to a penny per pound.

The Peterloo Massacre was one of the most disgraceful events in Lancashire history, where the authorities killed peaceful protestors

Furthermore, the government was autocratic and undemocratic and would brook no dissent. There was no right to protest, no free press, and the law of *Habeas Corpus* (by which people cannot be held without trial) had been repealed. The Home Office could open any letter that was considered potentially seditious, and employed spies who infiltrated societies and organisations that they thought suspect. The Home Secretary made things even worse. He was Henry Addington, 1st Viscount Sidmouth, who was aided as Under Secretary by his younger brother, Hiley Addington. They were against any change to the status quo, and hated the poor of northern England as much as the poor despised them in return. And they encouraged their well-paid spies to such an extent that the spies told them what they wanted to hear, that northwest England was on the verge of revolution.

Of course, the people tried to rebel. In April 1812 a riot in Manchester had to be broken up by the army. The Manchester Patriotic Union was set up to promote the rights of poor workers. During 1816 meetings were held throughout south Lancashire and were infiltrated by two Home Office spies called Campbell and Fleming. They reported back that an illegal militia had been formed and that arms were being cached somewhere in Manchester. This was not true, of course, but it made the authorities more determined to stamp on the slightest unrest.

A member of the Union found an old law that permitted a party of no more than ten to travel to London and petition the King. So ten men were chosen to petition the King, George III, then a sad blind old man, suffering from some degree of insanity. They planned to walk the 180 miles, carrying a blanket each so that they could sleep under hedgerows or in supporters' barns on their journey. For this reason they became called the 'Blanketeers' and one of them actually reached the capital. It was decided to send them on their way with a big rally in the centre of Manchester at St Peter's Field on 1 March 1817. About 30,000 turned up and, as John Bagguley was addressing them and they were cheering in support, a magistrate arrived with the army and read the Riot Act. Bagguley and the other organisers of the meeting were then arrested and the crowd dispersed by the army, who killed one and injured many with their swords.

But the situation steadily worsened amongst the workers of south and east Lancashire. Prices rose further; their incomes fell. Workers went on strike; there were outbreaks of violence. It was time, the Patriotic Union decided, to have a big demonstration, to get Parliament to do something to alleviate the suffering. With their chief spokesman John Bagguley languishing in jail having been found guilty of sedition, Joseph Johnson, the secretary, wrote to Henry 'Orator' Hunt, a Wiltshire man who had developed a reputation for eloquence. He was a great rabble-rouser. The letter was opened and copied by spies for the Home Secretary to read, before being sent on its way.

The meeting was originally planned for 9 August 1819, but having heard of the meeting the local magistrates had signs put out warning people not to attend. Instead the meeting was rearranged for the 16th, at St Peter's Field, and those who would attend were told, by Hunt and the Union officers to be clean, dressed in their Sunday-best, sober and peaceable, and they had on no account to carry a weapon of any kind. Of course the Home Office prepared for the worst, having read the letter to Hunt and heard of bands of men drilling in and around Manchester. They sent 600 men of the 15th Hussars to Manchester.

Estimates of the number who gathered in St Peter's Field have varied from 30,000 to 150,000, but was probably about 60,000 (equivalent to six per cent of the population of Lancashire in 1819).

Lt. Col. Guy L'Estrange had the job of organising the 'peace-keeping' force. The 15th Hussars were placed in Byrom Street, and the Manchester & Salford Militia in Portland Street, with other forces if needed. And if things really got desperate, L'Estrange also had two six-pound cannon with a troop of the Royal Horse Artillery on hand in Lower Mosley Street.

Hunt arrived flamboyantly in an open-topped carriage and the crowd cheered, wildly. The magistrates took this cheering to be the beginning of an uprising and they tried to read the Riot Act, but failed. The Chief Constable suggested that military action would be necessary for the arrest of Hunt and the other organisers of the meeting. So L'Estrange was sent a hurriedly written letter, telling him that 'the Civil Powers [are] wholly inadequate to preserve the peace'. The same message was sent to Major Trafford of the Manchester & Salford Yeomanry, a volunteer cavalry unit, whereupon Trafford immediately sent his men into the crowd with the aim of making the necessary arrests.

However, as the horses galloped into their midst, the crowd panicked, which led to the cavalry horses panicking, and the Yeomanry attempted to get the crowd moving away using the flat of their sabres. Moments later, in rode the 15th Hussars, led by L'Estrange, who pointed to the tumult and bellowed, 'Good God....Don't you see they are attacking the Yeomanry. Disperse the meeting!' By now the sharp edges of the sabres were being used on a crowd that wanted to escape. They tried Peter Street, but that was blocked by the 88th Regiment of Foot with their bayonets drawn. Slowly the huge tumult of bodies subsided as people escaped, but it was well into the 17th that outbreaks of violence ceased.

The number of recorded casualties was 654 at the lowest estimate, of which 168 were women (almost exactly 25%). The true figure was certainly much higher, for those slightly or moderately injured would not risk further physical injury or imprisonment by going to seek medical aid. Fifteen people lost their lives, mostly by sabre cuts or being trampled under horses' hooves. Four of the dead were women (again, about a quarter of the dead). But estimates suggested that women were only 10-12% of the total number at the meeting, so the number of female deaths and casualties is twice what would have been statistically expected. Perhaps the Yeomanry and Hussars were especially hard on the fairer sex. Or it may have been that women were more vulnerable than men.

Whatever. The tragedy became known as the Peterloo Massacre. The name was a touch of sarcasm by the people and press of Lancashire, for it was only four years after the Battle of Waterloo, which was greatly celebrated by the authorities in London. It was brought on by authorities who feared change and true democracy. Have not we, in the last few years, witnessed similar repression of their peoples by dictators and small unelected elite governments in countries around the world? And have we not seen how those unelected governments try to put down dissent and peaceful demonstration.

In fact, the effect of the Peterloo Massacre was to harden the government, who brought in more stringent laws controlling the mass of the working classes. It was much later in the 19th century that true reform began, and it was not until the 20th century, over a hundred years after Peterloo, that all adult men and women had the right to vote for the government that they wanted.

The Freckleton Air Crash

During the Second World War an expanse of low-lying ground just to the north of the Ribble estuary at Warton was turned into an aerodrome. Today the place is used for the manufacture and testing of war-planes,but then it was a base for the Unites States of America's Air Force.

On 23 August 1944 a B24 Liberator, piloted by 1st Lt John Bloemendal took off on a test flight, but as the plane returned to its base the weather had turned atrocious, with heavy rain and gale-force winds. The first landing was aborted and Bloemendal tried to circle round over the nearby village of Freckleton before making a second attempt. He failed. The plane hit the village, demolished three houses, the Sad Sack Snack Bar, and Holy Trinity's junior school.

A total of 61 people were killed.

The three crew were killed in the plane.

Fourteen died in the Sad Sack Snack Bar and three houses: seven American airmen, four members of the RAF, and three civilians.

Forty-two died in the school, thirty-eight of them children.

There is a Memorial Garden (opened 1945) and Memorial Hall (1977) in Freckleton, a village that will never forget its great disaster.

The memorial garden at Freckleton to those lost on 23 August, 1944

Accrington Pals

During the First World War, Lord Kitchener famously called men from around the United Kingdom to enlist in the army because, 'Your Country Needs You!'

The mayor of Accrington encouraged men to join up so effectively that, in ten days, a full battalion was signed up, the 11th East Lancashire, consisting of four companies each 250 strong. Not all came from the town of Accrington itself, for men joined from other nearby towns such as Blackburn and Burnley. The battalion was also known as the Accrington Pals, and it joined the 94th Brigade of the 31st Division of the British army.

After serving in Egypt, the Accrington Pals were sent to north-east France, to the Somme valley where they were to attack the Germans who had dug in there. They were part of eleven Divisions of the British army that would attack the German defences on 1 July 1916. But first of all the plan involved softening up the Germans by bombarding their trenches with shells fired from 220 howitzers. The shelling was not only aimed at the German soldiers, but also at the barbed wire that had been positioned in No-Man's Land to hinder any troops advancing, and specially made wire-cutting shells were to be used.

General Sir Henry Rawlinson suggested that the bombardment should last 30-60 hours, in stages, but General Sir Douglas Haig (Commander-in-Chief) thought that was too long. In any case, the effects of the bombardment, which would go on over several days before the troops left their trenches to engage the enemy, would be seen by observers from the Royal Flying Corps. Unfortunately, bad, wet weather on 26-28 June prevented the Corps flying on those days, so the full effects of the bombardment could not be ascertained properly.

Just before the advance on 1 July, Brigadier General H.C. Rees ordered the Pals, 'You are about to attack the enemy in far greater numbers than he can oppose you, supported by a huge number of guns. You are about to fight in one of the greatest battles in the world, and the most just cause. Remember that the British Empire will anxiously watch your every move, and that the honour of the North Country rests in your hands. Keep your heads, do your duty, and you will utterly defeat the enemy.'

The Pals left their trenches at 7.20am on the 1 July and lay, waiting for the order to advance. That came at precisely 7.30. As they walked forward, to their horror they found that the barbed wire had not all been destroyed.

Unbeknown, the Ministry of Munitions, under Lloyd George, had abandoned quality control and many shells had either failed to explode or, in the case of the special wire-cutting ones, had not cut through the wire. So the wire was largely intact and the German trenches had not received the battering that had been planned. So as the Pals made their way forward, slowed down by wire, Germans in the front trenches opened fire with machine guns.

Seven hundred Accrington Pals advanced at 7.30am and by eight o'clock only 115 were still standing. 235 had been killed and 350 wounded. Few families in east Lancashire were not hit by that awful half hour.

The disaster was not only with the Accrington Pals. Seven battalions of Manchester Pals went into action and of 10,000 who enlisted, 477 were killed. And of 24 officers and 650 men of the Salford Pals who strode forward from their trenches at 7.30am on 1 July 1916, 21 officers and 449 men were killed or wounded.

The Pals battalions from many towns and cities of the industrial north suffered similarly, from incompetent leaders and German bullets. Lions led by donkeys is quite an apt simile, when it comes to the disaster of the Somme.

IRA bombings

When one mentions Lancashire and IRA bombings, most people immediately think of the 3,500-pound bomb that went off in the Arndale Centre, Manchester on 15 June 1996, for it was the largest bombing of Britain since the Second World War. It affected 670 businesses and caused £700 million worth of damage. Of course, the damage was repaired. That included moving two pubs, the *Old Wellington Inn* (built pre-1550) and *Sinclair's Bar* (1738), that had been in The Shambles, to a new site near the Cathedral. They were side-by-side in The Shambles, but are now positioned at right-angles. Interestingly, this was not the first time that they were moved. In the early 1970s they had both been raised by 4'9" to accommodate new development in The Shambles. They are thus unique in the entire world.

However, far worse was the bombing of Warrington, for no one was killed at the Arndale Centre.

On 26 February 1993, at four o'clock in the morning, three explosions occurred at a gas storage depot. A policeman, PC Mark Toker was shot and injured when he tried to stop a hijacked white get-away van.

At 11.58am on 20 March 1993 the Samaritans received a call warning of a bomb in Boots chemist in Liverpool. Fourteen minutes later, at 12.12pm, two bombs exploded in Warrington, one outside Boots and one outside the Argos store. Both had been placed in cast iron litter bins which, when they shattered, scattered as shrapnel, thus increasing the chance of killing and maiming. Three-year-old Johnathan Ball died immediately. Twelve-year-old Tim Parry died of his injuries five days later. The bombs injured 54, four seriously.

Man's inhumanity to Man. When will we ever learn?

PLACES OF INTEREST
IN LANCASHIRE

The following are only a selection of many places that are worth making a special effort to visit. I have left out sports venues, as these will be visited anyway by enthusiasts (e.g. Haydock Park by race-goers and football grounds by the soccer-mad). To fit in as many entries as possible, I have given minimal details apart from telephone numbers. Check using that or by using the internet for more details. Note that some of these places are now in the administrative regions of Cumbria and other 'Heath-en' inventions. So Earby, West Riding of Yorkshire is now administered by Lancashire, but it houses the Yorkshire Dales Mining Museum!

National Football Museum, Manchester
0161 605 8200

See the statue of Lily Parr (1905-77) the six-foot winger from St Helens who played for the most successful women's soccer team of all time, the Dick Kerr Ladies, based in Preston. Her factory team played 828 matches and lost only 24, with Parr scoring around 1,000 goals for them. In 1920 she represented England v France in front of a crowd of 25,000 but the FA banned women from playing on their member grounds in 1921. In June 2019 Lily Parr became the first female footballer to be commemorated with a statue.

Museums and Art Galleries

Air and Space Museum, and **Museum of Science and Industry**, Castlefield, Manchester. 0161 832 2244

Albert Dock UNESCO World Heritage Site at Liverpool includes several museums:

> **International Slavery Museum** 0151 478 4499
> **Liverpool Maritime Museum** 0151 478 4499
> **Piermaster's House** 0151 478 4499
> **Tate Liverpool** 0151 702 7400
> **The Beatles Story** 0151 709 1963
> **Yellow Duckmarine** 0151 708 7799

Astley Green Colliery Museum, Astley Green, Tyldesley. No telephone number – use internet

Beatrix Potter Gallery, Hawkshead 01539 436355

Blackburn Museum and Art Gallery on Museum Street also includes the **Lewis Textile Museum** on Exchange Street, Blackburn 01254 667130

Bolton Museum and Art Gallery, Le Mans Cresent, Bolton 01204 332226

British Commercial Vehicle Museum, Leyland on the site of the now-gone **Leyland Motors/British Leyland** factory 01772 451011

British in India Museum, Hallam Road, Nelson 01282 613129

Clitheroe Castle and Museum 01200 425111

Crosby Beach: Antony Gormley's sculpture 'Another Place'

Dock Museum, Barrow-in-Furness 01229 876400

Fleetwood Museum, including the trawler *Jacinta*, Queens Terrace, Fleetwood 01253 876621

Harris Museum and Art Gallery, Market Square, Preston 01772 258248

Helmshore Mills Textile Museum, Holcombe Road, Helmshore, Rossendale 01706 226459

Imperial War Museum North is at Salford Quays 0161 836 4000

Lancaster City Museum and Art Gallery, Market Street, Lancaster 01524 64637

Lancaster Maritime Museum, St George's Quay, Lancaster 01524 382264

Laurel and Hardy Museum, Brogden Street, Ulverston (where Stan Laurel was born) 01229 582292

Lifeboat Museum, Promenade, Lytham (close to Lytham windmill) 01253 730155

Liverpool's Cultural Quarter is based on and around William Brown Street and includes:
St George's Hall 0151 225 6909
Walker Art Gallery 0151 478 4199
World Museum 0151 478 4393

Manchester Art Gallery, Mosley Street, Manchester 0161 235 8888

Manchester Museum, Oxford Road, is part of the University of Manchester 0161 275 2634

Pendle Heritage Centre, Barrowford 01282 661702

Museum of the Queen's Lancaster Regiment, Fulwood Barracks, Preston 01772 716543

Ribchester Roman Museum, Riverside, Ribchester 01254 878261

Ribble Steam Museum, Preston 01772 728800

Ruskin Museum, Yewdale Road, Coniston 015394 41164

The Lowry (named after artist L.S. Lowry) is at Salford Quays and, as well as the art gallery dedicated to Lowry, includes theatres and restaurants 0843 208 6000

Towneley Hall Art Gallery and Museum, is at Towneley, Burnley 01282 424213

Whitworth Art Gallery, Oxford Road, is part of the University of Manchester 0161 275 7456

Wigan Pier and Trencherfield Cotton Mill, is at Wigan Pier 01942 828020

Some Great Buildings everyone ought to visit

(NT = National Trust)

Abbeys and Priories:

Cartmel Priory of St Mary and St Michael is still a place of
worship 01229 467432

Cockersand Abbey (ruins) at Cockersand on the Lune
Estuary southwest of Glasson Dock

Furness Abbey (ruins), Dalton-in-Furness

Sawley Abbey (ruins) is really in the West Riding of Yorkshire

Whalley Abbey (ruins), Whalley

All Hallow's Church, Mitton (includes the Shireburn Chapel)

Ashton Memorial (01524 33318) in Williamson Park, Lancaster

Carnforth Station Visitors' Centre, Carnforth Station (setting
for *Brief Encounter*) 01524 735165

Dalton Castle (NT), Market Square, Dalton-in-Furness
01524 701178

Downham village on the slopes of Pendle Hill is regarded as
Lancashire's most beautiful village

Gawthorpe Hall (NT), Padiham, Burnley 01282 771004

Greenhalgh Castle (ruins), Castle Lane, Garstang

Hall i' th' Wood, Green Way, Bolton 01204 332370

Lancaster Castle (01524 64998), with which the Priory Church
of St Mary (01524 64637), the Judges' Lodging (01524 32808)
and the Cottage Museum (01524 64637) share the Castle Hill
vantage point overlooking Lune and city

Leighton Hall, Warton, Carnforth 01524 734474

The Three Graces (Liver Building, Cunard Building and Port
of Liverpool Building), River Front, Liverpool

Liverpool's Roman Catholic Cathedral of Christ the King
(0151 709 9222) and (right next to it) the Anglican Cathedral
Church of Christ (0151 709 6271)

Manchester Wheel, Exchange Square, Manchester 0161 831 9918

Rufford Old Hall (NT), Liverpool Road, Rufford 01704
821254
Speke Hall (NT), Speke 01257 541400
St Patrick's and St Peter's, 9th century chapels at Heysham Head
Salmesbury Hall, Preston Road, Salmesbury, near Blackburn
01254 812010
Wycoller Country Park has several buildings including the
ruins of Wycoller Hall and some ancient bridges

Markets Well Worth Visiting

Ashton-under-Lyne Market. Open daily except Tuesday and Sunday
Bolton Market. Open Tuesday, Thursday, Friday and Saturday
Bury Market has been voted the best in Britain! Open Wednesday,
Friday and Saturday
Lancaster Market. Open daily Monday to Saturday
Preston Market vies with Bury as the best and includes an indoor
market, covered outdoor market and the uncovered Flag
market and is open daily, Monday to Saturday

Lancashire's Great Nature Reserves and Wild Places

Ainsdale Dunes National Nature Reserve, Ainsdale,
Southport (Natural England)
Brockholes, Samlesbury, Preston (Lancashire Naturalists' Trust)
Forest of Bowland Area of Outstanding Natural Beauty (most
is really in the West Riding of Yorkshire), Clitheroe-Whalley-
Abbeystead
Formby Point Nature Reserve (National Trust)
Leighton Moss and the Eric Morecambe Pool, Silverdale (RSPB)
Morecambe Bay, Hest Bank (RSPB)

Marshside, Southport (RSPB)
Martin Mere, Burscough (Wildfowl and Wetlands Trust)
Mere Sands Wood, Rufford (Lancashire Naturalists' Trust)
Pennington Flash, Leigh (Local Authority reserve)
Ribble Estuary National Nature Reserve, Southport-Banks (Natural England)
Rivington and the West Pennine Moors, Horwich-Chorley and, The County Palatine also includes South Lakeland!
South Walney, Barrow-in-Furness (Cumbria Wildlife Trust)
Yarrow Valley Park, Chorley (Local Authority reserve)

And a Few Miscellaneous Places

Blackpool Pleasure Beach and the Golden Mile, Europe's Number One tourist attraction!
Cowman's Sausage Shop, Castle Street, Clitheroe, where up to 80 different sorts of sausage may be bought!
Glasson Dock which includes a working harbour and the Port of Knowsley Safari Park, Prescot (0151 430 9009) where lions may eat your car!
Lancaster Smokehouse (open daily), a gourmet's delight (01524 751493)!
Lord Street, Southport, the Arndale Centre and Trafford Centre Manchester, and Bent's Garden Centre at Glazebury near Leigh (voted Number One in the UK every year) which are shopaholic havens!

Plus a Couple of Great Flower Shows!

Holker Garden Festival, Holker Hall, Cark is a three-day event in June (015395 58838)
Southport Flower Show is one of the oldest flower shows in the world and is a three-day event in August (01704 547147)

INDEX